DIARIES

AND

CORRESPONDENCE

OF

THE EARL OF MALMESBURY.

———

VOL. IV.

DIARIES AND CORRESPONDENCE

OF

JAMES HARRIS,

FIRST EARL OF MALMESBURY;

CONTAINING AN ACCOUNT OF

HIS MISSIONS AT THE COURT OF MADRID, TO
FREDERICK THE GREAT, CATHERINE THE SECOND,
AND AT THE HAGUE;

AND OF HIS SPECIAL MISSIONS TO

BERLIN, BRUNSWICK, AND THE FRENCH REPUBLIC.

EDITED BY HIS GRANDSON,

THE THIRD EARL.

SECOND EDITION.

VOL. IV.

AMS PRESS, INC.
NEW YORK

ERRATA, VOL. IV.

PAGE

31, lines 33 and 36. *After* Amyand *dele* and.

65, line 5. *Amend the punctuation thus:*—on common subjects. On public and grave ones I at all times, &c.

70, line 18. *For* the sense of this *read* this sense of the.

143, line 7 from bottom. *For* Heley *read* Hiley.

157, line 7. *For* 17th of December *read* 27th.

191, line 23. *For* peculiar *read* public.

236, line 9 from bottom. *For* cared *read* could.

285, line 13. *For* he should *read* we should.

Reprinted from the edition of 1845, London

First AMS EDITION published 1970

Manufactured in the United States of America

International Standard Book Number:

Complete Set . . . 0-404-04170-1

Volume 4 0-404-04174-4

Library of Congress Catalog Card Number: 73-121023

AMS PRESS, INC.

NEW YORK, N.Y. 10003

DIARIES AND CORRESPONDENCE.

ENGLAND.

[IT was in 1800 that Mr. Pitt, for the *third* time, contemplated renewing his attempts to make Peace with France, and he offered the Mission again to Lord Malmesbury. Lord Grenville wished to appoint his brother, Mr. Thomas Grenville; and Lord Malmesbury, whose deafness and infirmity had much increased, readily consented. This Mission, however, never took place; and it was left to Mr. Addington, who superseded Pitt, with a new set of men, to make the Peace of Amiens, and to bear the odium of that hollow (and to the English) unsatisfactory treaty.

After a long *hiatus* I find Lord Malmesbury's Diary resumed in 1801, as follows.]

FEB. 1, 1801.—It had long been in contemplation, as a necessary measure in the minds of many of those who brought about the Union with Ireland, to establish a new Test law here, and to do away many of the restrictions now imposed on the Catholics there. The idea was to substitute an Oath, binding those who took it to an allegiance to the King and Constitution, instead of a Sacramental Test ; and this would, in effect, (as it was to extend to Great Britain,) enable Catholics to sit in Parliament, hold offices, &c. &c.

Mr. Pitt, either from indolence, or from perhaps not paying always a sufficient and due attention to the

B

King's pleasure, neglected to mention *ministerially* to His Majesty, that such a measure was in agitation, till he came at once with it for his approbation.* But the opposers of the measure, at the head of whom are the two Chancellors of England† and Ireland, and Lord Auckland, took care that it should reach him in a way the most likely to displease him; and the King, at the Levée on Wednesday, the 28th January, the day after the measure was communicated to him by Pitt, intimated to Windham (Secretary at War), that " he should consider any person who voted for it as personally indisposed towards him." This being immediately spread about, gave rise to the rumour of Pitt going out; and from what I can collect, even now (Feb. 2nd), he has not yet come to a fair explanation with His Majesty, or seen the King on the subject.

In the Cabinet Lord Westmoreland and the Chancellor are decidedly against it—and perhaps Lord Liverpool, but he does not attend. The Duke of Portland hesitates, but will ultimately vote against it. Lords Grenville, Spencer, Dundas, Camden, are strongly for it —all the Bishops are against it.

FEB. 5.—Dissension still very great—King will not give way, and Pitt maintains his opinion. If this continue, a change *must* take place. The idea seems to be, not to call in Opposition, but to form an Administration of such of Pitt's friends who do not think as he does on this particular point. The Speaker‡ is mentioned— Lord Auckland *mentions himself.*

FEB. 6.—Same steadiness prevails on both sides— Ministers determined to go out if King does not give

---

* See Correspondence between George III. and Mr. Pitt on this subject, published in 1827, by Philpotts, Bishop of Exeter.

† Lord Loughborough, who resigned the Great Seal on the 14th of April, and was succeeded by Lord Eldon.

‡ Mr. Addington, afterwards Lord Sidmouth.

way; that is to say, Pitt, Lords Spencer, Grenville, Dundas, and Windham—others doubtful. They declare they will support any new Government, and propose one made up of Pitt's friends, *not* thinking like him with respect to the Catholic question.

The Speaker to be First Lord of the Treasury—Duke of Portland to remain, also Lord Chancellor.

Pitt has not, even to this day, written to his brother, Lord Chatham, on the subject. Lord St. Vincent talked of for the Admiralty. This measure, so likely to be attended with the most ruinous effects to the country, is to be attributed in part to Pitt's carelessness, and in part to his want of *real* respect for the King; for had he been provident enough to prepare the King's mind gradually, and to prove to him that the Test proposed (supposing the measure to reach to Great Britain) was, as far as went to Allegiance and Supremacy, as binding as the present Oath, no difficulty *could* have arisen. Instead of this, he reckons on his own power, never mentions the idea at St. James's, and gives time for Lord Loughborough directly, and for Lord Auckland indirectly, through the Archbishop of Canterbury and Bishop of London, to raise an alarm in the King's mind, and to indispose and exasperate him against the framers of this measure—this very blamable in Pitt.

SATURDAY, FEB. 7, 11 A.M.—Ministers determined to resign—profess doing it in perfect good-humour, and declare that the Government shall have their full and unqualified support on every other measure but this, which necessitates their resignation, and on which they can come to *no compromise.* It does not appear that Pitt has ever had to this day an audience with the King, or that any attempt whatever has been made to conciliate their opinions. All has passed through the Speaker (Addington).* The new Ministry is not yet made up—Addington to be First Lord of the Treasury and Chancellor of Exchequer; Lord Hawkesbury, Secre-

* Afterwards Viscount Sidmouth.

tary for Foreign Affairs;* Duke of Portland to remain;
Mitford,† Speaker; such, at least, is the present idea:
Canning goes out.

It looks at times to me as if Pitt was playing a very
selfish, and, in the present state of affairs, a very criminal part; that he goes out to shew his own strength,
and under the certain expectation of being soon called
upon again to govern the country, with uncontrolled
power. But, besides the culpability of this conduct,
(which it is perhaps unfair to attribute to a man of his
established character,) it may be a very erroneous calculation. His followers will leave him in shoals; and
it remains to be seen whether they will range themselves
under the banner of the new Administration, formed out
of the shreds and parings of his; or whether it is not
more likely that they will form Opposition; and the
next change (and that a very near one) may be, Fox
and Opposition taking possession of the Government.

TWELVE O'CLOCK, FEB. 7.—The resignation no longer
a secret; bruited about; talked of in the streets.

Lord Macartney‡ said to be destined for the Board of
Controul, in the room of Dundas; but this I heard denied in the evening.

SUNDAY, FEB. 8, 2 P.M.—Canning, after having kept
away for several days, came to tell me of the resignation, and of the Speaker's being appointed First Lord of
the Treasury.

He said he himself had not hesitated about going out;
that Pitt had pressed him to remain in; but that his
mind was made up. He confessed he had been one of

---

* Lord Hawkesbury afterwards succeeded to his father's title as Earl of
Liverpool, and became Prime Minister after Mr. Perceval's assassination.

† Sir John Mitford, afterwards Chancellor of Ireland, and created Lord
Redesdale   He died in 1830.

‡ Lord Macartney held Governments in the East and West Indies, and
was Envoy to Russia. His last and most interesting service was his
embassy to China.

those who had strongly advised Pitt *not* to yield, on this occasion, in the closet.* That for several years (three years back) so many concessions (as he called them) had been made, and so many important measures overruled, from the King's opposition to them, that Government had been weakened exceedingly; and if on this particular occasion a stand was not made, Pitt would retain only a nominal power, while the real one would pass into the hands of those who influenced the King's mind and opinion out of sight.

Canning sneered at the Speaker's being Pitt's successor, and intimated as if *he* considered it as an unfriendly conduct in the Speaker towards Pitt. Mitford succeeds him; and Grant, Mitford. Further information either Canning had not, or would not communicate it. He said, Pitt's wish was, that all his friends should remain in their present offices, or get higher ones; and he believed this they would *all* do, and that a tolerably strong Administration might be composed.

He said he suspected those who had tainted the King's mind, but would not name them. He glanced at Lord Westmoreland as being one.

TUESDAY, FEB. 10.—The resignation now publicly known, and canvassed, as well as the merits of those who are coming in. Addington resigned the chair. The new Administration treated with great derision, and even slight, in both Houses. Lord Carlisle took the lead on it in the House of Lords with more wit than wisdom. Blamable conduct in those who have resigned, particularly in those who were more immediately connected with Pitt, to declare *openly* that he and his friends intend to give their full unqualified support to the new Government, and *privately* to sneer at and deprecate it. Canning told me Pitt had made him promise *not to laugh* at the Speaker's appointment to the Treasury ; and this was *all* he could possibly undertake.

---

* Canning remained firm to his opinion in favour of Catholic Emancipation, and eventually was sacrificed to his consistency upon it.

Lord Gower* resigns the Post-office; Lord G. Leveson the Treasury; G. Rose and Ch. Long† go out; Steele‡ remains; so does Ryder.§

Lords Loughborough and Auckland appear to have *over cunning'd* the business, and not to have resolution or firmness of character to act openly on what they have combined (I apprehend) secretly. The consequence is, that the Chancellor will resign (against his will), and the other remain just where he is (against his expectation); and both under the dread, particularly Lord Auckland, of Pitt's return to power; and that they shall incur, as they well deserve, his displeasure. Lord Hobart is to have the Board of Controul. This a little comforts Lord Auckland, who, however, affects to say he is a bold man who consents to make a part in this new Administration.

WEDNESDAY, FEB. 11.—New Speaker (Sir J. Mitford) elected; proposed by Lord Hawkesbury, seconded by H. Browne. No new light thrown on the real cause of this change. Pitt's adherents now openly cry down the new Government; still declaring their intention to support a weak, flimsy Government, as they call it. On the other side, the courtiers canvass separately for the King, and shew their loyalty, (injudiciously, in my opinion,) by endeavouring to make this a personal case for the King ; this may breed a most dangerous faction, if not stopped in time.

The Prince of Wales appears to side against the Crown and Pitt, and takes up and cherishes the avowed partisans of Jacobinical opposition. He gives a dinner to-morrow to the new Proselyte lords, Darnley and Cowper; and his language in the streets is such as would

---

* Afterwards Marquis of Stafford, and grandfather to the present Duke of Sutherland. He rendered important aid to Mr. Pitt, when he came into power, on the defeat of Mr. Fox's India Bill.

† Afterwards Lord Farnborough.

‡ Thomas Steele, Esq. a gentleman of Sussex, who was joint Secretary of the Treasury with Mr. Rose under Mr. Pitt's first Administration, and afterwards Paymaster-General.

§ Afterwards Lord Harrowby.

better become a member of Opposition than the heir to
these kingdoms.*

The Duke of York remains firm to the King, and is as
discreet in his language as proper in his conduct.

THURSDAY, FEB. 12. — Pelham † called on me at
twelve; he said he had since refused office, and now occupied it in consequence of the King's *almost* commands,
conveyed to him through the Duke of York; that he had
told Mr. Addington this fairly, and that, although he
would support him freely and sincerely, yet it was but
right he should know on what grounds this support was
given. He told me in confidence that he was to have
the conduct of the war, and lead in the House of Lords,
up to which he was to be called; that on his first declining it, this had been mentioned to Lord Hobart,‡
but now, on his accepting, the King said this proposal
should be considered as not having been made to Lord
Hobart, and the office given to Pelham. He goes to-
morrow to Stanmore, to settle about the county election;
and returns on Tuesday, when Fitzharris (now at Durn-
ford) is to come to town to meet him. Pelham told me
the King had mentioned me for the Foreign Department, and regretted my being too unwell to accept it.

Lady Sutherland called on me this evening. Her
leanings with those gone out, and with an evident expectation that they will come in again. This a little
explains Lord Carlisle's conduct, and accounts for Lord
Gower's persisting in his determination to resign. Windham came later; he is in spirits; said it was all a sad
story; told me Colonel Yorke (Lord Hardwicke's brother) was to succeed to this office as Secretary at War;
agreed and admitted that it was highly blamable not to
have settled the measure with the King before the
Union was brought forward; that this was inexcusable;

---

* He became more decent soon after this.—Orig. Note.
† Afterwards Lord Chichester.
‡ Afterwards Earl of Buckinghamshire.

he had no share in it; was never consulted, &c., &c., and, on the whole, seems glad to get out of office.

SATURDAY, FEB. 14.—General Bude.*—Said the King had declared this was the first time he had ever had any difference of opinion with Mr. Pitt; that he (the General) thinks Mr. Pitt was wrought upon by bad advisers; that Dundas wanted to extricate himself from the difficulties in which the country was involved, and thought it creditable to cover his retreat by Pitt's going out at the same time.

Lord Grenville he also supposes as not having acted straightforward; he wished also to go out, and is very obstinate and "*tétu*" in his opinions; he has already dismissed his servants, and let his house to Lord Temple, his nephew.

Lord Glenbervie to be Paymaster; Dundas furious with this arrangement ; said the Irish peerage was given on the express condition of his going to the Cape. It is said Lord Hardwicke is intended for Ireland.

General Sir Charles Stuart to be Commander-in-Chief there.

Lord St. Vincent accepts the Admiralty, and retains the command of the Channel Fleet. East India Company give Dundas 2000*l.* a-year; to be made up 4500*l.*

Difficulties respecting Pelham's having the War Department; Lord Hobart tenacious of it, and Dundas against his being at the head of the Board of Controul, on account of a difference of opinion respecting East India politics; this I heard from W. Elliot and Windham: Pelham in this case to be at the head of Board of Controul; Lord Glenbervie to be Paymaster, (not Postmaster,) *vice* Canning; Lord Charles Spencer Postmaster, and Lord Francis to come in for Oxfordshire.

Addington told Lord G. Leveson this day, when he called on him to give in his resignation, that he was sorry that he did not remain his colleague as long as he

---

* General Bude had a place about Court. He had been preceptor to the Duke of York.

held his present office, which he did only "as a sort of *locum tenens* for Pitt," to whom he should be most happy to return it whenever that could be brought about (rather a weak speech to make to a person just resigning from his connexion with Pitt).

Canning much out of sorts; it seemed the tone to-day for Pitt's friends to blame his conduct, as if they began to feel the loss of place.

General Bude, who talks the language of St. James's, censures Pitt much; said the King declared this was the first and only difference of opinion between them, and that the measure took him quite by surprise, and hurt him very much.

If Lord Cornwallis gives up the Ordnance, Bude said he hoped the Duke of York will have it.

Lord Hardwicke still talked of for Ireland. Dundas declines the pension from the East India Company. (N.B., but afterwards accepts it for a term equal to the duration of their Charter.)

While all these arrangements are making at home, and during this scramble for office, all public business is at a stand; we forget the host of enemies close upon us, and everybody's mind thinks on one object only, *unmindful that all they are contending about may vanish and disappear if we are subdued by France.*

SUNDAY, FEB. 15.—Lord Hobart persists in being Secretary of State, with direction of the war.

Tom Grenville.—Full of alarm—particularly about Ireland; blames Pelham for accepting office; ridicules Addington—says he might now sing, "My hat, my cane, and wig, I have hung upon a peg."

Sad accounts of Berlin; King literally obliged to be governed by the voice of the people; and Emperor of Russia ordered *his cruisers* to take all ships of all nations going to England. Strange *neutral* law this! Said Dundas had refused the pension because it was *only* 2,000*l.* T. Grenville observed, Ireland would be *well* governed with a Stuart Primate, a Stuart Commander-in-Chief, and perhaps Lord Bute Viceroy. He disapproved Lord Hardwicke's nomination.

Lord Uxbridge.*—From him I find the tone of Court is, to lay the whole blame on the Grenvilles; that it was their doing—particularly the Marchioness of Buckingham; her insolence extreme—said she would not answer the King when he spoke to her on Thursday at the Drawing-room.

Windham.—Pelham certainly *not* to have the direction of the war; Windham is for his accepting. T. Grenville and Lord Spencer against it; the latter influenced by his wife, who leaves the Admiralty with much regret.

Wm. Elliot.†—Just come from Dundas, who pressed him to take the government of the Cape; he persists in his refusal on principle. Lord Glenbervie had solicited it—got a peerage, under the idea of supporting it with dignity—and, the moment Pitt went out, he went to Addington and asked for office.

Feb. 16.—Pitt's conduct generally disapproved—at least, so I collect from the people who visit me—and all sort of idle conjectures as to the *real* cause of his going, and every fanciful one credited, in preference to the plain and simple one.

Horne Tooke chosen for Old Sarum.‡   Lord Camelford§ should be confined for this act of madness and wickedness.

Almeida‖ with me; he to have the Foreign department at home.   Told me he could not get a sight of

---

* Father of the present Marquis of Anglesea.   He was much at the Court at Windsor, where his regiment of Staffordshire Militia was long quartered.

† Secretary in Ireland, and an intimate friend of Mr. Windham.   His ghostly appearance won him, from *Monk* Lewis' tragedy, the name of " The Castle Spectre."

‡ The Rev. John Horne Tooke (a clever demagogue) was tried for high treason in 1794, and acquitted.   He took his seat for Old Sarum in 1801, and the same year Government brought in a bill, which passed, making clergymen ineligible for the House of Commons.

§ Lord Camelford was a Post-Captain in the Navy.   He was a man of great courage, which he proved, by remaining in his ship after the crew had left her, as they supposed, foundering.   He fell in a duel.   His sister married the late Lord Grenville.

‖ Portuguese Minister at London.

Lord Grenville, and that Lord Hawkesbury's appointment was not regularly notified; he also said Portugal had sent to Paris, to treat for a separate peace on *any* terms. Aranjo in London.

TUESDAY, FEB. 17.— King got a bad cold; takes James's powder. God forbid he should be ill!

French fleet, under Gantheaume, of eight sail of the line and four frigates, escaped out of Brest—one dismasted, and others injured by storms. A squadron of ours after them, under Sir Robert Calder.

WEDNESDAY, FEB. 18.—Fitzharris with Mr. Addington; received him kindly; said he had him in his thoughts the moment he took office; offered him a seat the moment those who were coming into office were in Parliament.

Tom Pelham, not having the War Department, refuses the Board of Controul and the Peerage, but offers to assist Government in the House of Commons, and hold a seat without office in the Cabinet. He has, in my mind, acted with great temper and forbearance, as well as public spirit, as there can be no question but he has been tricked by Lord Auckland, and had the fullest claim to be War Minister; nothing else could be meant or implied when he was repeatedly pressed to accept office.

Lord Glenbervie (Silvester Douglas) talked of for the Board of Controul.

King better; Lady Radnor saw him yesterday evening, and he clearly had *only* a bad cold. Peace signed between France and Austria—a most inglorious one for Austria—the Emperor treats in the name and for the German Empire without any authority, and gives away one-fifth of its soil. Insolent, vapouring declaration from the Consuls to the nation on this occasion.

THURSDAY, FEB. 19.   Tom Pelham.—He told me the whole of his story. When he left London on Friday, it was given him to understand in a way he could not doubt, that he was to be Secretary of State, with the conduct of the war, and Minister of the House of Lords. The King himself said nearly as much, and the Speaker (Addington) confirmed it. The Duke of Portland considered it as so far settled, that he consulted him in the choice of a proper officer to succeed General Knox in the West Indies. Pelham went, therefore, to Stanmore on Friday, under the full persuasion that this, and no other office, was intended for him. He proposed to his father to be raised to an earldom, or that he should himself be made a baron. The first was what Pelham wished for, and was agreed to by his father. On Sunday morning he receives a letter from the Duke of Portland, who says that he fears it will be impossible for him to have the War Department *at present*, and as impossible for him *not* to accept the Board of Controul. Pelham expresses great surprise in his answer; declines the Board of Controul, but offers his support to Government with a peerage. On his return to town (Monday evening) he sees the Duke of Portland, who repeats what he had written; explains the whole, in his way, and intimates that the thing might *still* be done, and new arrangements made; but no cause alleged for Lord Hobart's being named, but his not being liked by the India Company, and of course not a fit person to be at the head of that Board.

On Tuesday Pelham dines with Addington; a large Ministerial dinner. Lord Hobart artfully tried to draw Pelham into an avowal that he *will* at all events come up to the House of Peers, and holds the language of the Minister in that House to him. Pelham avoids the question; waits till all the Company is gone, and then sees Addington. An unsatisfactory conversation follows. Addington can give no reason but that it was impossible to do otherwise, and, after an hour's discourse (it was very late), Pelham goes away, leaving the matter unexplained, and with having made a sort of promise to support Government in the *House of Lords*, and in the Cabinet *out of office*. But, on Wednesday morning, on thinking the point over, he conceives this unadvisable; for, if he once appeared in the House of Lords, Lord Hobart having the lead there, *he* never could assume it; and he, therefore, writes to Addington to say he had decided to remain in the Lower House and support the Government.

The Board of Controul quite out of the question. An office he knew nothing about; of no consequence but for its patronage; and, while Mr. Dundas remained, it would still be influenced by Dundas, and all the merit and praise be considered as his. He said, the Duke of York was greatly vexed, and that Colonel Calvert (Adjutant-General) had written to him to say so. After having talked the matter *quite over*, I advised Pelham to go directly to the King to explain *himself* the whole to him. That, although at the Queen's House, the King would certainly see him, and it was what was due both to the King and to himself. I told him not to mind etiquette, but to drive up to the Queen's House, and send in his name. This he promised me to do (an hour ago, three P.M., Thursday).

The whole he says is a trick of Lord Auckland and his abettors; perhaps a little helped by Pitt, who does not like Pelham; but still more to be attributed to Addington's weakness, who, desirous of pleasing everybody, will, if he begins in this way, soon please nobody.
—— Adams and Garthshire to be Lords of the Admiralty.

THURSDAY, FEB. 19, HALF-PAST FIVE.—Pelham came back to me from Court; he had seen and consulted the Duke of Portland, who approved his seeing the King, but said it could not be *to-day*, as the King was unwell, and that on such occasions it was not usual to disturb him but on great public business (N.B. This the first symptom of the King's serious illness); that he would write to the King, and prepare His Majesty to receive Pelham to-morrow. To this Pelham assented. I am sorry for

it.   I believe the Duke of Portland friendly and sincere,
and anxious Pelham should have the office first offered
him; yet he is so indolent, so torpid, and so easy,
that there is no reliance to be had in him when anything
requires the least exertion or argumentative explanation.

Pitt told Addington he was sure Pelham would accept
the Board of Controul.   This confirms me in the idea
that *he wishes* Pelham to be there, rather than Secretary
of State, strange as it is, after Lord Auckland's behaviour to him.

The King certainly was not informed yesterday of the
office being to be given to Lord Hobart, for he asked
the Duke of Portland what title Pelham's father would
take, and that it must not be *Earl of Sussex*, which he
intended for one of his sons.

Hatton, a lawyer, to be Under Secretary of State in
room of Wickham, who wants to be Governor of Malta.
Hatton is brother to Finch Hatton, who married Lord
Stormont's daughter by his first wife (a Pole or Saxon).

FEB. 20.—Horne Tooke spoke in yesterday's debate
without any effect—no notice at all taken of him.*

Wm. Elliot.—Nothing settled as to Ireland.   Lord
Cornwallis approves the resignations, and maintains the
expediency of the measure that gave rise to them, but
desirous not to distress Government by coming away
precipitately.   No successor named.   Duke of Montrose
has refused it.   Lord Hardwicke offered it.   Abbot,
they say, to be Secretary to the new Lord-Lieutenant.

Heard from understrappers that it was Lord Auckland
who advised Lord Hobart to get possession of office.

Nothing yet settled as to Ireland.   Lord Cornwallis,
as Elliot assures me, approves the resignations here ;
persists in the expediency of the measure of Catholic
Emancipation ; and has expressed his intention of
coming home, but will not leave Ireland in a way that

* He spoke on February 19th in support of Mr. Sturt's motion for an
inquiry into the failure of the expedition against Ferrol.

may be injurious to the public service. Council held
to-day at St. James's to swear in more Privy Councillors.
King very far from well.

SATURDAY, FEB. 21, 11 A.M.—Lord Glenbervie.—Said
he was not to go to the Cape, but to be Paymaster; not
in the Cabinet; was quite in the dark, &c. ; sure the
ostensible and *real* reasons of all that had passed were
different; for it was supposing wise men to become fools
to act as Pitt, Lord Grenville, &c., had done, on such
motives alone as they *avowed.* It was Lord Grenville
wanted to drive a nail through the King's head ; he
looked yesterday very much down. The King, he said,
seemed quite well, and evidently only a cold. So said
Lord Glenbervie ; but the *fact* is otherwise. King very
bilious.

FIVE O'CLOCK. William Elliot.—Arrangements still
may be made which may bring Pelham into high office.
Duke of Portland may go to another post. Lord
Hawkesbury kissed hands for the Seals. Lord Grenville
in great haste to return to Dropmore.

In the midst of all this a loan of twenty-eight millions
is raised without difficulty, and on easy terms ; the interest (1,700,000*l.*) equal to nearly the united revenues
of Sweden and Denmark !

Bad accounts from Queen's House ; the answer at the
door is, the King is better ; but it is not so — he took a
strong emetic on Thursday, and was requested to take
another to-day, which he resisted.

SUNDAY, FEB. 22, 12 O'CLOCK.—His Majesty still bilious ; not better ; apprehensions of his getting worse.
Fatal consequence of Pitt's hasty resignation. Princess
Amelia unwell. Queen not well. At Carlton House
they dance and sing.

SIX, P.M.—Lord Hardwicke, it is said, takes Ireland.
Lord Hobart to be War Secretary of State, with 2000*l.*
a-year appointment. (N.B. He has already 4000*l.* in

other employments under Government.)   Lord Lewes-
ham to have the Board of Controul.

ELEVEN, P.M.—King much worse ; Dr. J. Willis attended him all last night, and says he was in the height of a
phrenzy fever—as bad as at the worse period (when *he*
saw him in 1788).

If this should increase, and a Regency Bill become
once more in agitation at such a period as this ; or if it
should terminate in His Majesty's death; there are two
descriptions of persons to whose conduct all the misfortunes that inevitably must arise from either of these
great calamities must be attributed—those who secretly,
and unknown to the Ministry, *practised* on the King's
religion, and disposed him to resist the intended measure
of Catholic Emancipation; and those Ministers themselves, who, after having *neglected to prepare* His Majesty
for it, considered themselves as ill treated, and resigned.
Both have a very great responsible charge against them.
Amongst each there is little doubt that many acted
from principle, and conscientiously ; but it is also, I fear,
not without some degree of truth that others are to be
found who had their own private interests in view, or
who acted in order to gratify their private resentments,
or promote their ambitious views ; and these men, let
them be who they will, may be considered as the most
consummate political villains that ever existed.   They
ought to be held in execration by the country, and their
names handed down to posterity with infamy; for they
will have been the first cause of the destruction of the
intellects or life of a Sovereign, to whose kingly virtues,
and to whose manly and uniform steady exertion of them
during a reign of forty years, this country, and every
subject in it, òwes the preservation of its liberties and
everything that is valuable to him.   These liberties are
now most fearfully put in hazard, whether we look at
the active, persevering, and implacable enemy we have
from without, or to the weakness, wickedness, and
schisms existing in our own bosom.

Dundas accepts the 2000*l.* per annum pension from
East India Company.

MONDAY, FEB. 23.—The three Willises now called in. His Majesty's pulse at ninety only, but delirium very strong; very difficult to persuade him to go to bed. Prince of Wales sees Lord Moira,* who is chief, and, they say, sole adviser; he was shut up this morning with the Duke of Clarence.

Lord Hardwicke has actually accepted Ireland.

TUESDAY, FEB. 24, 10 P.M. Lord Uxbridge. — Said, from the Duke of York, that the King was better; inveighed against Pitt; talked of Arthur Paget; said Lord Hawkesbury had given room to hope he should have Berlin. It is supposed, and from good grounds, that about three months ago Lord Auckland wrote to his brother-in-law, the Archbishop of Canterbury, a letter, stating that he held it his duty to inform him, as head of the Church, that a measure was in contemplation, which, if carried into effect, would put the Church in danger; that it was one resolved on by the leading members of the Cabinet; and that he submitted it to the Archbishop's judgment whether it would not become him, as Metropolitan, &c., to state this danger to the King. Lord Auckland recommended secrecy as to himself. The Archbishop consulted, they say (though of this he was certain), the Bishop of London and Primate of Ireland, and they both agreed that it was his duty to speak to the King.

If this be fact, Lord Auckland made a mockery of religion, and rendered it subservient to the most selfish political ends.

WEDNESDAY, FEB. 25.—His Majesty not better; yet signed, about four P.M., the repeal of the Brown Bread Bill;† declaring very distinctly his opinion on it, and saying it was a very good bill.

---

* Afterwards Marquis of Hastings.

† In accordance with the report of a committee on the high price of provisions, a resolution passed the House of Commons, December 18, 1800, prohibiting the use of bread finer or dearer than a certain standard. This act was repealed in the following year.

Addington two hours with the Queen yesterday.

10 P.M.—Pitt's friends wish and advise him to draw towards the Prince of Wales, and endeavour to form a Regency, if necessary, under his sanction. Pitt, I hear, actually saw the Prince on Monday ; but they did not meet or part like persons likely to think the same. The Chancellor (Lord Loughborough), I also hear, saw the Prince this morning, but rather did harm than good.

Amongst the advisers of Pitt, to a reconciliation with the Prince, are Lord Spencer, T. Grenville, and Pelham. I doubt Canning and that description of his friends to be of this way of thinking.

THURSDAY, FEB. 26.—Confirmed that Pitt had seen the Prince on Monday, but no good came from it; Pitt very unwell—much shaken—gouty and nervous. Chancellor says, (incautiously enough,) that when he carried the King the Brown Bread Act to pass by commission on Tuesday evening, at 4 P.M., His Majesty was in the perfect possession of his understanding.

King's pulse at 130 Tuesday night; this makes in favour of his mental derangement, and proves it to be only the effect of delirium in consequence of fever, but it puts his life in very great danger.

Opposition very active. Lord Fitzwilliam at the head of it. Prince of Wales sent Francis to him, to say he should want his advice.

TEN, P.M.—Tom Pelham said, if a Regency becomes necessary, which is much to be feared, that the two contending parties at the last Regency Bill should each to a degree give way: that those who opposed the then Regency Bill, and maintained the opinion that the Heir Apparent had a right to assume the Regency in case of King's incapability to act, should no longer insist on this point; and that Pitt, and those who maintained then contrary opinions, should now not bring them into discussion, but that both should concede something ; in order that the formation of the measure might take place without putting the country, at a moment

like this, into a state of fermentation. Such was Lord
Spencer, Duke of Portland, and Tom Grenville's opinion; but although Pitt admitted it *apparently*, yet
there was reason to believe he did not thoroughly acquiesce in it. He (Pitt) had been *sent for* by the
Prince on Monday; and Pelham apprehended, from what
he heard, was more stiff, and less accommodating than he
should have been. Pitt was to see the Prince again to-
day; and in the meanwhile Lord Egremont, who was
very eager and anxious at this moment, had been at
Carlton House, and strongly advised the Prince to continue Pitt at the head of the Government, and not to
wrangle for an unlimited Regency, but to take such a
one as the two leading parties might agree on.

In discoursing of this, Pelham said it was necessary
and becoming that nothing should be done which might
be in contradiction to the King's known intentions and
probable wishes; that, therefore, though Pitt was certainly at this moment Minister of the country, and ought
to remain so, yet Addington was the man who possessed
the King's confidence; that Addington, therefore, should
be put into high office, Pitt remaining Minister, in order
that His Majesty, on his recovery, might find nothing
done contrary to his wishes, or materially altered during
his illness; that he (Pelham) was in hopes this might
be effected, though they were well aware of the uncertain
fickle disposition and character of the Prince, and how
little any reliance could be placed in him.

I mentioned to him, as a proof of this, his having sent
Francis to Lord Fitzwilliam (I believe, on Sunday) to
beg he would stay in town, as he *should soon want his
advice;* and that Lord Fitzwilliam had directly sent a
message to Fox, who came to town on Monday, and
lived in Lord Fitzwilliam's house. Pelham did not
know the first of these facts. I strongly pressed him to
go to Pitt, to urge him to be supple and accommodating,
and to try to persuade him to desist from any idea of a
Regency Bill like the last; that the case was different—
it was now well understood what the King's complaint
was; that there was no room to fear a *lasting* derange-

ment of intellects; that he would either recover, or sink
under the illness; and that the physicians actually said,
that, at his time of life (sixty-three), the probability of
one of these events happening much sooner than in 1788,
was very great; that, therefore, all that was required
was a representation of the Executive power, for the
purpose of carrying on the necessary acts of Government
while the King's faculties were suspended; and that the
giving greater or less power to the Regency, either in
the person of the Heir Apparent, or to any Minister ad-
joined to him, would be useless to him and to them, and
manifestly an injurious measure to the public.   Pelham
undertook to see Pitt to-morrow.

With respect to arrangements, at this moment everything is hung up; but he thinks it will end in his
having the Seals for the Home Department, and the
Duke of Portland going to another Cabinet office.   The
Duke of Portland had offered to take Ireland, and consulted Pelham on it; Pelham much embarrassed how to
advise.   The Duke goes and offers himself to Addington, who foolishly enough says, that *Abbott* must be
Secretary.   The Duke replies, that when he (a Cabinet
Minister) makes an offer of this sort, it cannot be supposed that he would take any Secretary but one of his
own choice; and thus *this* matter rests.

I persuaded Darnley to put off his motion.*   He is
evidently ashamed of what he is doing, but too vain,
and too much hampered with his new connexions to be
a free agent.   The King on Monday, after having remained many hours without speaking, at last towards
the evening came to himself, and said, " I am better
now, *but I will remain true to the Church.*"   This leaves
little doubt as to the idea uppermost in his mind; and
the physicians do not scruple to say, that although His
Majesty certainly had a bad cold, and would, under all
circumstances, have been ill, yet that the hurry and
vexation of all that has passed was the cause of his
mental illness; which, if it had shewn itself at all, would

---

* For an Inquiry into the State of the Nation.

certainly not have declared itself so violently, or been
of a nature to cause any alarm, had not these events
taken place.　Just as the King was taken ill, in 1788,
he said, after the last levée he held, in the closet, to
Lord Thurlow and the Duke of Leeds, on the first advising him to take care of himself, and return to Windsor,—" You then, too, my Lord Thurlow, forsake me,
and suppose me ill beyond recovery; but whatever you
and Mr. Pitt may think or feel, I *that am born a Gentleman* shall never lay my head on my last pillow in
peace and quiet, as long as I remember the loss of *my
American Colonies.*"　I had this fact from the Duke of
Leeds, who was present; and it describes precisely the
state of the King's mind at that moment, as does what
he said on Monday, — " I will remain true to the
Church,"—shew beyond a question the object uppermost in it now, and the goad in each case of his delirium.

Lord Spencer very much hurt at what has passed, and
feeling a great deal for the share he has had in it; and
Pitt, though too haughty to confess it, feels also a great
deal.　Duke of York's behaviour incomparable; he is
their great and only comfort and support at the Queen's
House, and without his manly mind and advice, neither
the Queen nor Princesses would be able to bear up
under their present distress.

Prince of Wales, on Sunday, the 22nd, the second day
of the King's illness, and when he was at his worst,
went in the evening to a concert at *Lady Hamilton's,*
and there told *Calonne,* (the rascally French ex-minis-
ter,)—" Savez vous, Monsieur de Calonne, que mon
Père est aussi fou que jamais?"　Lord Hobart still
maintains possession of his office, without a shadow of
right.　It is now in contemplation to give the Ordnance
to Lord Chatham; Duke of Portland to be President,
and T. Pelham Secretary of State.

Nobody admitted at the Queen's House, not even General Bude.

THURSDAY, FEB. 26, 12 o'CLOCK.—King supposed and hoped to be rather better.

Two, P.M. J. Stuart Wortley.—Said, that as long ago as Sept. 3, Lord Loughborough (on his return from Weymouth) called on the Duke of Portland, to ask him what he thought of the measure *at that time* in discussion in the Cabinet, with respect to the Catholic Emancipation. The Duke replied, he believed it a necessary measure. " Have you thought;" said the Chancellor, " of all the consequences to which it may lead? I have put my thoughts on paper relative to it, and wish you would let me leave them on your table." A few days afterwards, the Duke told Lord Loughborough that his paper had convinced him of the danger of the measure, and that he now wished to know how it could be prevented. They agreed to state it to the Archbishop of Canterbury. Lord Auckland, in consequence of a secret intelligence with Lord Loughborough, wrote his letter about the same time. (See Tuesday 24th.) This was done. The Archbishop wrote to the King, then at Weymouth; and the King wrote a long letter to Pitt, expressing his knowledge, and his disapprobation of such a measure. Yet did Pitt take no pains to prepare him afterwards for it, but brought it on, *ex abrupto*.

King at Windsor about the 6th or 7th instant—read his Coronation Oath to his family—asked them whether they understood it—and added, " If I violate it, I am no longer legal Sovereign of this country, but it falls to the House of Savoy."

Lord Bute has been in town, but seen none of his own family—it is thought he will accept nothing. Sir Charles Stuart not able on the score of health to go to Ireland.*

THREE, P.M. Lord Darnley.—Had seen the Prince last night; in great agitation of mind and spirits, as at the last Regency. Complained of being treated with no attention at the Queen's House; never informed how the King was; held Opposition language, and encouraged

---

* He died on the 25th of March following.—Orig. Note.

Darnley in Opposition principles. He shewed me a coaxing, undignified letter from the Prince to him.

TEN, P.M. Pelham.—Good arrangements in his mind respecting the Regency. Prince promises to be passive; and, unless Pitt *stiffens*, no difficulties likely to occur.

Lady Salisbury said the King was well enough to have the Queen and Princesses at dinner—"*qui prouve trop ne prouve rien.*" Any degree of fever would render this improper in anybody; and, if you take away the fever, you leave the intellectual derangement without a cause or hopes of recovery. I fear there is so much fever, that his life is in imminent peril. Duke of York deeply affected, and worn out with his assiduous attentions at the Queen's House.

Lord Egremont so anxious that the Prince should be passive, that he wrote a letter to Admiral Payne (Jack) from Godalming, urging what he had said in conversation at Carlton House; and this had effect on the Prince, who also pledged himself to Pelham not to oppose what might be proposed; but he is so fluctuating, and so little to be depended on, that it is impossible to be safe under these assurances.

FRIDAY, FEB. 27, 3 P.M. Lord Radnor.—Lord Thurlow told him a very short time after the King's recovery, in 1789, that the first thing the King said to him on getting well was, " What has happened may happen again : for God's sake make some permanent and immediate provision for such a Regency as may prevent the country from being involved in disputes and difficulties similar to those just over. Lord Thurlow (then Chancellor) reported this to Pitt: they both agreed as to the infinite expediency of such a measure, but differed as to the mode in which it should be framed. Lord Thurlow, not long after, went out in ill-humour, and Pitt thought no more about it. Moreton Pitt dined with me; he for the Catholic Emancipation; offered to state his reasons, which I declined hearing.

Ten, p.m.—I was told this evening by Pelham, that His Majesty had for a long time since been dissatisfied with Pitt's, and particularly with Lord Grenville's " authoritative manners" towards him, and that an alteration in his Ministry had been often in his mind; that it was with this view he had sent for Windham and myself in August last to Weymouth; that he meant Windham should be his First Minister, and I have the Seals for the Foreign Department; and although he never came to a direct explanation, either with me, who stayed only three days at Weymouth, or with Windham, who stayed longer, yet my informant says he is sure of the fact. I do not recollect anything which passed while I was at Weymouth, in several very long conversations His Majesty honoured me with, that goes to ascertain it positively. He communicated with me most confidentially, and without reserve, on every matter of public business, and treated me in such a way as to prove his full confidence in me. He also more than once said, and in a very expressive way, " I believe you, and I always did and always shall think the same *on all great points*, as well such as relate to home as to foreign politics." To this I may add, what was quite new *to me*, the pains the Queen took to shew there were no remains of old animosity,* and the care that every evening I should be put to the *first* party with the Princesses. This did not strike me at the time as having any other meaning than a general demonstration of good-will towards me and Catherine;† but on connecting it with what I now have heard, and heard from so good authority, I suppose it had. The ill-success of the Austrians, the proposals brought forward for peace by Pitt through Otto, perplexed the King, and diverted his attention from his purpose; and Windham also, by his odd, absent, and unacquiescent manner, did not encourage His Majesty in his views. I have now no doubt that it transpired

---

* On account of Lord Malmesbury's vote against Ministers on the Regency bill in 1788. The Queen took a strong part against the Prince of Wales on that occasion, and against those who advocated his claim.

† Lord Malmesbury's eldest daughter, who afterwards married General Bell.

somehow or other through the Chancellor, who has been acting various parts lately.

This also explains to me why the King, to the surprise (real or assumed) of Pitt, was so uncommonly ready to make me an earl, and why he said to me aloud, at the levée, " I can assure you I never did anything with more pleasure;" and the same day, Wednesday, the 20th October, after the levée, he said, in the closet, to the Duke of Portland, who told it me afterwards at dinner, " I believe Lord Malmesbury to be the best Foreign Minister I have; he is too good for Lord Grenville." Neither the Duke nor I quite knew what this meant, but we considered it as a singular speech. The repeated particular inquiries His Majesty has since made about my health, and in the last instance his declaring his concern (through Pelham) that I was too unwell to take the Seals, leave me little doubt of the truth of what I this day heard of his dislike of Lord Grenville, and of his object in summoning Windham and me to Weymouth in August. Lord Darnley, in consequence of my advice and earnest solicitation, put off to-day, in the House of Lords, his foolish motion for an inquiry into the state of the nation *till further notice*.

The Prince of Wales sent for Addington; asked him if *he* was Minister. " No, sir," replied he, " not I, but Mr. Pitt." " In that case, pray send Mr. Pitt to me." Addington, I am told, hesitated, and said, most awkwardly, he would consult the Duke of York.

" No advice can be wanted on such occasions, Mr. Addington," said the Prince; " and if you decline acceding to my *request*, be so good as to obey my *commands*."

SATURDAY, FEB. 28, 3 P.M. Tom Grenville.—Said Fox, whom he had met and walked with, was violently against our war with the Northern nations—not only as a measure, but in its principle, and contended their claims were just. T. Grenville surprised at this. I recollect Fox saying, in 1783 (he then being Secretary of State), that the principles of the Armed Neutrality being now universally admitted, it was needless to attempt to resist them; and he even was ready to give way to them as the price of an alliance with Russia.*

He told Grenville he was come to London on his private concerns. Grenville *believes* he has *not* seen the Prince. *I* believe he *has*. Grenville apprehends, the appearance of a weak Government here may encourage the Court of Berlin to take Hanover. Lord St. Vincent, it is said, assisted a day or two ago at a sort of Cabinet; finding nothing like business going on, he got up, and said, if he was not wanted, he must go away, as really he had *no time to throw away*, and so left the Cabinet.

Dundas has taken back the boxes, &c. from Lord Hobart, who is re-become nothing. T. Grenville supposes Fox's eagerness to declare his opinion on the principles of the rights of neutrals arises from his wish to make peace at any price and rate, and that he holds this language with a view to be able to give up the point more easily, should the making of peace fall to their lot; and this looks as if he thought it possible; and though he says he has not seen the Prince, and the Prince confirms it, yet I strongly suspect the contrary, and that at Carlton House they are caballing at the same time with Pitt, Lord Fitzwilliam, Fox, and Lord Moira.

Sunday, March 1.—Better accounts of the King, both in the Physicians' report and from private information in the morning; in the evening, however, a slight increase of fever.

William Elliot said he hoped he had secured a seat in Parliament for himself; one in Ireland, not Roxburghshire, as I hoped.

Monday, March 2nd, 10 p. m.—Lord St. Vincent a most active First Lord of the Admiralty.

----

* Vide the Russian Correspondence in vol. i. of this work.

The King was really better, and, at his worst, he said, never so ill as when Warren reported him, in his last illness, *convalescent.* Public business, he also said, could go on very well a week longer without any Regency measure, and in a week he hoped the King would be well enough to do all the common acts required of him.

ELEVEN, P. M.—Bulletin not good; "The King's fever increased last night, and has not since abated." I fear more now for his life than for any thing else.

TUESDAY, MARCH 3.—King so much worse last night, that his life was despaired of; about ten he fell into a profound sleep, and awoke in about six hours quite refreshed, and *quite himself.* His Majesty said he was thirsty, and, on being asked what he wished to drink, said, *if allowed,* a glass of cold water; this was given him; it put him into a perspiration; he fell asleep again, and awoke in the morning with the fever abated, and better in every respect.

The crisis of his disorder; crowd of people round Queen's House, and their expressions of joy very great.

Prussia holds hostile language; threatens to seize Hanover. It occurs to me that the money (a million) belonging to the King should be put *à couvert.* Pitt's declaration to Ireland, (if true,) like Cardinal Wolsey's *Ego et Rex meus.*

Otto, French agent for prisoners in London, recalled by Buonaparte, under the pretext of our conduct towards their fishing-boats;—insolent, impudent, and lying excuse.

Letters from Vienna of the 12th; all *balls and fêtes;* shame and disgrace on them.*

TEN, P. M. Lord Glenbervie.—Said Lord Wellesley had concluded a very advantageous treaty with the Nizam, by which we gained a great share of the Mysore country, and a vast extent of riches and population, security and power.

---

* The treaty of Luneville between Austria and France had been signed, forced upon the former by Moreau's victories over the Archduke Charles.

WEDNESDAY, MARCH 4. Lord Tichfield.—Dr. Reynolds told the Duke of Portland to-day, at one o'clock,
that the King's fever abated, and that all the symptoms
were favourable, but that much time would be necessary
to complete the cure; that the King's mind, whenever
he came to himself, reverted at once to the cause of his
disquietude: that it was highly advisable he should see
no one, none of his own family; that this retarded his
recovery the last time, and that he, seeing then two of
the Princesses too soon, and talking to them out of the
window, produced a disagreeable relapse.

THREE, P.M. Canning.—Cool, temperate, and uncommunicative; holding new and moderate language;
smoothing the way for Pitt's return to power; regretted
he had so much of the milk of human kindness, that he
never would punish those who had now, or at other
times, betrayed him. Thought he was embarrassed to
come in without Lord Spencer and Grenville, but this
he (Canning) did not consider as a difficulty; they were
neither of them eager for office. Very clear, from all
Canning said, that Pitt inclines, and expects to return
to power.

MARCH 4. Lord Pembroke.—Fred. St. John, in the
Kent East-Indiaman, taken by a French privateer, not
far from the Bengal coast; sent ashore in a boat; Lord
Wellesley uncommonly kind to him.

I received an account of the beginning of the King's
illness from Fitzharris, who had it from Addington.

On Friday, Feb. 13, (the fast-day,) the King remained
so long in church, and the weather was so snowy and
cold, that His Majesty became excessively chilled on
returning home—to that degree, as to have cramps all
over him. Mr. Addington called the next day, and advised him to go out of town for a few days. On Sunday
morning His Majesty wrote to him to say he should not
go out of town, but not assigning illness as his reason.
Mr. Addington called, and found him with a severe cold
on him, and almost a total loss of voice. Mr. Addington did not see His Majesty again till the following

Tuesday, when he found him in his chair, wrapped up in
a black velvet cloak; he had taken frequent doses of
James's powder, and he remarked that his manner was
more hurried, and his countenance more heated than
usual.

On Thursday Mr. Addington called, and found His
Majesty so much better as to congratulate him on his
apparent recovery. The next day he met His Majesty
at the Council, where he behaved with great dignity and
calmness. He did not see him after this, but on the
following Sunday, Feb. 22nd, the Duke of Cumberland
called on Mr. Addington, and informed him of the unpleasant turn His Majesty's disorder had taken.

William Elliot.—Said the measure respecting our
conduct towards the French fishermen, and which had
produced the recall of Otto, and an impudent note from
Buonaparte, never known to Cabinet, but settled by
Pitt and Dundas; likely now to be disavowed, and Otto
to remain. The First Consul overbearing, and assuming to a degree. This foolish; as there can be no doubt
that the French fishing-vessels do *more* than fish, and
that Otto is a very dangerous man to be allowed to remain here.

Addington's mind is full of peace—no great proof of
strength of character, wisdom, or statesman-like knowledge, in such times as these.

MARCH 4, 9 P.M. Tom Pelham.—Addington was
likely to contest power with Pitt, if Pitt really should
desire to resume it.

Lord Hobart now ready to be Secretary of State for
Home Department, and give Pelham the War; this Pelham declines, and determines to take the Home Seals, in
case he comes in at all.

I advised with him respecting the money in the stocks
in the name of the Regency of Hanover. I am very
anxious the King should not lose it; and, from what I
know of *some* of the Hanoverian Regents, they would be
ready to pay their court to the King of Prussia, *at any*

rate. Pelham thinks I had better see the Duke of York; I desired him to mention it to him—he said he would.

Irish Catholics suspicious and displeased with Pitt. The moderate part of them expected nothing—the violent require much more; say the having a seat in the Irish Parliament, now it is melted into the English, is of no value. The Protestant part of the country say it was positively understood by them, that no farther enfranchisement should be granted to the Catholics; and all sides seem to agree, that no solemn pledge was made to them.

The declaration made by Lord Cornwallis, on the resignation of Ministers, never intended to be published—doubtful how he communicated it, whether by giving it to the leading persons among the Catholics, such as O'Brien, McDonald, &c., to read, or whether he allowed them to take copies. The part attributed to Lord Cornwallis, was an extract from Lord Castlereagh's letter; and that supposed to be Pitt's, was drawn up by Dundas and him—its style is calculated to raise a commotion in the country. The whole of it a very injudicious and incomprehensible conduct.

Lord Hobart.—In the evening said nothing on public affairs—rather out of sorts.

Lord Glenbervie.—Being anxious to get office and power, offers Dundas to leave to his entire disposal all the Scotch patronage, if he will let him have the Board of Controul, and be the *nominal* Scotch Minister—very uneasy lest Pitt should recover his power, and revenge himself on those who are now accepting office. *Il mendie des suffrages en sa faveur.*

THURSDAY, MARCH 5.—King's fever continues to abate.

TWO, P.M. Lord St. Helens.—Said he had seen His Majesty for four or five days previous to his illness—that he was agitated and hurried—and often thought aloud—said evidently what was on his mind, but not intended to be part of the conversation.

FOUR, P.M. William Elliot.—Thinks Addington means Peace at any rate.

HALF-PAST FIVE, P.M. Duke of York.—Most comfortable assurances respecting the King. Talked over the money in the stocks belonging to Regency of Hanover—desired me to get more accurate information. On my saying Addington meditated Peace, he said it would produce the worst of effects, if the King on his recovery found any such measure had been agitated ; blamed gently, but feelingly, those who had *deserted* the King; was himself, as usual, all kindness, right-headedness, and uprightness; and on my saying how much the conduct he observed on the present occasion must endear him to everybody, and in particular to those who were truly and sincerely attached to him, His Royal Highness was affected to the greatest degree, and could scarce restrain his tears. He said Pelham *must* be employed, that it was the King's particular wish; and he added, speaking to me, " You were the first person in the King's mind on Lord Grenville's resignation; but His Majesty knew your state of health, and would not embarrass you with a proposal that you could not undertake to accept, and which he was well aware it would hurt you to refuse when coming from him." The Duke said he would call again in a day or two. He looked thin and fatigued, but in high spirits on the state of the King's health.

TEN, A.M. Lord Carrington.—Batavia taken—news come through an American ship from America: quære as to the truth.

Lord Whitworth.—Said *Paul* was sulky, melancholy, and black—going on with sequestration of English property.

Wrote to Amyand, and one of the Directors of the Bank, desiring him to come to me.

FRIDAY, MARCH 6, 12 O'CLOCK.—*King much better.*

Mr. Thomas Amyand, and one of the Bank Directors, at my request called on me. I desired him to procure me exact information as to the sum vested in the Three

per Cent. Consolidated I had mentioned to the Duke of
York and Pelham. In whose name it stood?—what was
its amount?—and who paid the dividends? This he undertook. He said that he believed, in 1785, the house
of Frieter and Co., at Leipsic, remitted 300,000*l.* from
the Elector of Saxony, in part of payment of a debt due
to the Elector of Hanover; that about half the sum,
150 million francs, had passed through their hands, and
the remainder through those of another correspondent of
Frieter and Co. in London.

On my asking him, whether the menaces of the
Northern powers alarmed him and others who dealt in
the Hambro' trade, he said, By no means—trade could
not be stopt.

He said, on the first rumours of this event, a flock of
Frenchmen (about six weeks ago) had come over—were
so eager to buy or contract for English goods, and particularly cottons and calicos, at the sale at the India House,
that they raised the price ten per cent. That they said
and spoke as from authority, that we need be under no
uneasiness, for, if all the ports in Germany and the Baltic
were shut against us, Dantzic and Boulogne would remain open, and be made free ports. This remarkable.
Buonaparte will do himself exactly what he prevents the
North from doing, and, by this means, increase his trade
and views at their expense.

FIVE, P.M. William Elliot.—Lord Minto has leave
to return—Lord Hawkesbury only wishes him to stay
till a successor is appointed, which cannot be till the
King is well.

Sir W. Farquhar.—Dr. Gisborne (one of the physicians attendant on the King) says, his pulse is at 72,
and everything quite in a promising way.

The Prince of Wales told Lord Darnley on the 4th instant, after complaining of the ignorance in which he
was kept of what was passing at the Queen's House, that
the King's mind was completely deranged, whatever his
bodily health might be. This is most unfeeling language; if true, it little became him to say so—but it is
not. He knew as much of what was going on at the

Queen's House as he chose to know—nothing was concealed from him. Darnley, the dupe of it, and of his affected confidence in him.

SATURDAY, MARCH 7.—Received from T. Amyand an account of the King's money in the Bank—1,100,000*l.* Three per Cent. Consols—in the name of the Lords of the Electoral Regency of Hanover; dividends received, and additional transfers accepted by Messrs. C. Humber, George Best, &c.

TEN, P.M. Tom Pelham.—His Majesty recovered *in mind*, as well as body. Duke of York with him for the first time this morning. The King received him most affectionately. The Duke found him looking pale and ill, but perfectly collected. He inquired what had passed—if any resignation had taken place? Duke of York said none could, without His Majesty's leave. "Has the Chancellor resigned?" "No, sir," said the Duke, " he never will give the Seals into any hands but yours." This pleased the King, who himself had ordered Willis yesterday to go to Pitt, Addington, Lord Loughborough, and Lord Eldon, to say he was recovered. Willis (I believe the clergyman) *wrote* to Pitt; and Pitt in his answer by him (which was most *dutiful*, humble, and *contrite*), said he would give up the Catholic Question. This the King told the Duke of York, and was disposed to expatiate on it. The Duke most judiciously stopped him, by saying, " Sir, since this point, which has given your Majesty so much uneasiness, is settled, it is better now to forget all that has passed." "You are right, quite right, Frederic," said the King; then went on with common inquiries about what had been done and said during his illness. The Duke of York, with that excellence of head and character belonging to him, said, " All parties have behaved equally well—all party spirit has ceased, and one common universal anxiety about your Majesty pervades them all. But, Sir," said he, "it will take us too much time to tell you all this now." On this the King said, " Frederic, you are more nervous than

I am; I really feel quite well, and *I know full well how ill I have been*; and then repeated his questions.

The King, in directing Willis to speak *or write* to Pitt, said, " Tell him I am now *quite* well, QUITE recovered from my illness; but what has *he* not to answer for, who is the cause of my having been ill at all?" This, on being repeated, affected Pitt so deeply, that it immediately produced the letter mentioned above, and brought from him the declaration of his readiness to give way on the Catholic Question.

King inquired of the Duke of York how he found the Queen, and thanked him for the care and affection he had shewn her and his sisters. " I saw them and the Dukes of Kent and Cumberland yesterday," said the King, " because I could send *them* away at any time; but I wished to see you *alone*, and for a long time, and therefore put it off till to-day."

Idea of a Council at Buckingham House on Tuesday; but it is hoped not, and that the Chancellor *by himself* will carry the King the Loan Bill to sign.

In inquiring about the Queen's health of the Duke of York, the King expressed great solicitude lest she and the Princesses should have suffered a great deal of uneasiness on his account. " They certainly did, Sir," replied the Duke; " but the only uneasiness now remaining on their minds, and on all our minds, is, lest your Majesty should, as you get well, not take sufficient care of yourself." The King, much moved by this, said, " I will, you may depend on it. I have, I fear, neglected this too much, and presumed a great deal more than I ought on the strength of my constitution. Be assured I will be more careful for the future."

TEN, P.M.—Prince of Wales yesterday evening and this morning with the King; his behaviour there right and proper. How unfortunate that it is not sincere; or rather that he has so effeminate a mind as to counteract all his own good qualities, by having no controul over his weaknesses!

On Monday His Majesty will sign warrants and money bills, and public business be resumed. Addington very unwell. From Pitt's letter, and from other circumstances and rumours, I now am confirmed in my ideas that Pitt wishes to remain at the head of Administration; and that, if he does, he will remain with less power, but with better and more sane judgment; and the acquiring the last will, in my mind, amply balance the decrease of the first. He has discovered himself, from what has passed, to have an overweening ambition, great and opiniative presumption, and, perhaps, not quite correct constitutional ideas with regard to the respect and attention due to the Crown. Possibly this is neither in his real character, nor are his real sentiments, but caused by listening to bad and silly advisers, and, above all, to an uninterrupted course of *political* prosperity (as far as related to his personal administration), without *a single check of adversity*, for nineteen years. But, whatever may be the cause, he has lost much of his popularity and of the public good opinion, from his conduct at this period; and if he retains office, he will find his followers much diminished, and by no means so inclined to vote implicitly with him as before. His *absolute* power (if I may use the word) will therefore be broke in upon; and, from the well-timed check of adversity he has now received, two very great and good changes may be operated in his character: he may learn moderation, becoming pliancy, and a right respect to the Crown. It will stand him in good stead also, if he apply these conciliatory qualities in his intercourse with individuals of weight and consequence, whom hitherto he has treated, not *uncivilly*, but with slight and great inattention; and it will do what is still better, it will force him to give exertion to his abilities, and not to suppose that everything must bow down to them, and he not be responsible for any sinister incidents which arise from his want of forethought, or from not condescending to consult with others on subjects he himself cannot be master of. In short, it may stand him in lieu of that *apprenticeship* which he never served in his profession, and be an efficacious though violent means of giving him experience, prudence, diffidence, and several very essential qualities he most wanted in a statesman. If so, it is impossible not to rejoice at his still holding office; *his abilities are superior to those of all others.*

Addington unwell—a bilious fever. Fleet not sailed from Yarmouth; ice said to be in the Sound. Nineteen sail of the line ready. No troops to go.

MARCH 8, SUNDAY, 12 O'CLOCK.—King continues to recover. From report I hear Lord Auckland aims at the Seals for the Home Department, on hearing of Duke of Portland's intended resignation.

Canning.—Begins by saying things are very bad, yet rejoices in King's recovery. Why then, I asked him, are things bad? Pitt, he says, will not make a forward movement towards the King; nor Addington a tender of giving up his claim to be First Minister. I reply, Pitt is in the wrong, supposing, as I hear *he* does not, persist in the Catholic motion.

C.—He does *not* persist; it is *asleep;* will be forgotten; yet Pitt will not stir unless Addington begins.

M.—Does Addington know that?

C.—He cannot *but* know it.

M.—But suppose he should not: is it not idle to let the public welfare, now inseparably and immediately connected with that of each individual in the kingdom, go to ruin from the want of two individuals coming to a right understanding?

C.—Pitt is to blame, highly to blame, I confess; but he thinks it unbecoming him to take the first step.

M.—Surely this is a very erroneous idea: can there be one more calculated to gratify the proudest man, than the feeling his own consequence so great, that not only the hope of his Sovereign, but the welfare of the public, depend on what he is to do?

C.—You are right; yet I fear Pitt does not see it in this light.

M.—Do you, who are in the habit of seeing him, and to whom he listens, make it manifest to him.

1801.] ENGLAND. **37**

C.—He may mistake my motives.

M.—*He* cannot: he well knows that your rapid advance in public life is an act of his own private friendship, as well as of your political merits and conduct, not of solicitation on your part: he knows you also *now* to be *independent.* It is therefore to his private friendship you are obliged, and you ought towards him to behave as a *private friend,* unbiassed by any other considerations, either of opinion, temper, or possible misconstruction.

C.—I had resolved to say nothing. I was displeased with Pitt, and am out of humour; but I will think it over.

M.—Think it over, but consult no one: Pitt owes it to the King and to his country to recant to a certain degree: it is not an act of humiliation; it cannot be, under any circumstances, from a subject to his Sovereign; and, in the present case, it is one of dignity as well as duty. If the Government of the country loses Pitt's abilities, and Opposition (which must be the case) acquire them *through any fault of yours,* how much will you have to answer for!

C.—You almost drive me from my purpose. I believe you are right. I will think it over, and see you to-morrow.

M.—Consult only your pillow, and none of your friends and companions: they are all in a state of fermentation—incapable of giving you sound, dispassionate advice. I that am tied to my chair, and never expect to move ten yards from it, see without prejudice. *It is your duty.* It is your duty to persuade Pitt, if you can, to *humble* himself before the King: it will be the most dignified humility ever heard of.

C.—I will consider it over, and see you to-morrow.

N.B. I gave this advice with great warmth and eagerness, being fully persuaded that if Pitt does what I recommend, he will return to office with great and good effect; with less power, but *power enough;* and that his behaviour will be infinitely more becoming a subject and Minister in a country like this than before, as he will have received the lesson of adversity I wish him to receive.

In the course of our conversation, I defended Mr. Addington, on whom Canning was disposed to press rather hard, by ever reverting to the idea that he would not *voluntarily* give up office, or go *voluntarily* to the King to say, " Now the *Catholic Question* is asleep and forgotten, I am ready to resign my office to Mr. Pitt." I argued, supposing that to be true, which, however, was only assumed, it was folly not to come to an explanation with Mr. Addington on the point; that the King had chosen *him* because Pitt *would* resign, and Addington avowedly accepted the place on the same grounds; that now, therefore, that Pitt was disposed to concede on the only subject which had produced all this fracas, *he* was bound, *not Addington*, to make the first move, and to use his endeavours that all which had passed should be considered as a bad dream, and as such forgotten; and I again and again urged the extreme folly of suffering the country to be involved in endless calamities, because two men were either too proud or too weak to come to a right understanding; that if they would, all might be recovered; that Pitt held the magic wand like Prospero, and, if he did not employ it, deserved the highest censure.

Canning said, Addington was influenced by selfish friends, Bragge, Adams, his brother, &c. I said, it would be very strange if such very nothingy men were to stand in the way of so great a measure, and one of such public utility : that I hoped if, *on closer investigation*, it appeared that there had been any persons who, while they were externally acting with Pitt, secretly inflamed the King's mind against him on account of this Catholic Question, and alarmed His Majesty's conscience, *merely* to serve their own purposes, that *such men* would not be suffered to remain in office with impunity; and that Pitt would not forget that, to preserve power and make it respected, it is necessary to know how to chastise as well as how to reward; how to reprimand as well as to praise; and to that sort of apathy which had been observed towards bad or insufficient public men *in every line* during his ministry, were owing the worst traits in it.

MONDAY, MARCH 9. Lord Darnley.—Endeavours to prove the propriety of his conduct; he is not going into headlong Opposition—he knows the Prince of Wales does not depend on him; but that it is better *he*, and men who think like him, should be about him, than those who think differently, and wish to make the Prince subservient to their private purposes. I told him he was not of a size for this purpose: that he would be drawn into the vortex without being heeded, or having done the smallest good. Darnley's fault is vanity; he means well, but acts badly.

FIVE O'CLOCK. William Elliot.—He thinks now Ministry mean to try for Peace: it is his decided opinion. Addington still ill of a rheumatic fever.

HALF-PAST NINE, P.M. Tom Pelham.—Dundas with the Duke of York yesterday, to say that, as the great obstacle of the Catholic question was suspended, he thought Pitt might retain office and still be at the head of affairs, and he proposed to the Duke to forward this idea in the King's mind. The Duke said he was sincerely and truly desirous of seeing Pitt return to office, and would willingly do what he could with propriety; but, before he pledged himself to any positive measure, he wished to consult Pelham—to this Dundas most readily assented. This morning, at 9, the Duke of York sent for Pelham, and informed him of what had passed; Pelham agreed with him as to the eligibility of Pitt's remaining at the head of Administration, but rather disapproved the idea of the Duke taking any step whatever with the King. It might not please the King—it might lead him to suppose the Duke was setting himself up for a maker of Administrations, and if it did not produce this effect on the King's mind, it most assuredly would on that of the Prince of Wales, and create a great deal of unpleasant feeling in that quarter. The Duke acquiesced most perfectly in all this, and desired Pelham to lose no time in repeating it to Pitt and Dundas, who he knew were together at Wimbledon. Pelham immediately rode there; he met Pitt on the Common, returning, and rode back with him. Pitt, without hesitation, agreed as to all that he said in regard to the Duke of York—that *he* was sure of the Duke's good-will towards him, but that he thought His Royal Highness should, on no account, mix himself up in political arrangements of this sort, but consider himself as belonging to the King, and independent of all Ministers; Pitt then went into the question deeply—stated the pros and cons—mentioned several difficulties; the principal one was, how Addington would feel it, even suppose the King was inclined to his retiring, of which he was not *yet* sure—that, besides, he had friends to consult, and he was apprehensive of the effect it would have on the Irish Catholics. He talked a great deal on all these points, and the result seemed to me, that he inclined greatly to return to office, but wished that the *King should move towards him, and Addington spontaneously offer him his place.* Pelham combated all this in the way it naturally was to be combated; and as he already saw the drift of Pitt's conversation, he took less pains to argue the collateral points, than to shew the importance of his remaining Minister, and to prove that if he, Pitt, really wished the public good, and had the public good at heart, he should not stand out in any point of etiquette with the King, or expect that Addington, till he was told the King's wishes, could or would spontaneously come forward. This led him into detailed arrangements, and the different offices which were vacant, or could be vacated; and it was evident that Pitt had thought the whole over and over again; that his mind was full of it, and that he was anxious to come in, but that his *pride* led him to wish that it should be by *entreaty*, not by any voluntary forward movement of his. Pelham, when he left Pitt, returned to Dundas, who, having much less pride and fewer scruples than Pitt, spoke much more decidedly on the subject. He did not

hesitate as to what Pitt should do in respect to the
King; and as for Mr. Addington, he said, if he was so
tenacious of office, he should be gratified by a Cabinet
place, and if not satisfied with that, be overlooked entirely in an arrangement so essential for the public
good; and, after all, said Dundas, very unadvisedly,
probably unintentionally, if *these new Ministers stay in
and make Peace*, it will *only smooth matters the more for
us afterwards*. This betrayed a *great deal*, and struck
Pelham's mind, as it did mine when he told it me, that
from the beginning there has been ever some second and
back view in all this; and that really what appears in
the French papers and in ours, has some degree of truth,
viz., that Pitt went out because he felt himself incapable either of carrying on the war, or of making peace.
On his return to London, the Duke of York, who was
quite satisfied with all Pelham had done, told him the
King had expressed a wish to see Pitt—Pelham meeting
Pitt accidentally on his way to the House, told him this;
and Pitt said he had received such an intimation from
Willis, and that he was really embarrassed how to act;
if he saw the King *before* anything was determined on,
it would give rise to the most awkward reports, and he
would consider of it till the next morning. Pelham
very handsomely desired not to stand in anybody's way;
but this Pitt would not hear of, and in their ride from
Putney said he thought there should be three Secretaries of State—one for the Colonies (Lord Hobart), one
for the Foreign Affairs (Lord Hawkesbury), and one
for the Home and War department (Pelham). That
Lord Cornwallis should either remain in Ireland, or be
at the head of the Board of Controul; Lord Chatham
have the Ordnance, and the Duke of Portland the Pre-
sidency. But all this was under the idea of his, Pitt's
staying out; and I have no doubt a very different Cabinet would be formed if he comes in again.

The impression the whole of this taken together leaves
at this moment on my mind is, either that Pitt is inclined to let this Ministry remain in office long enough
to make peace, and then to turn them out; or that he,

&c., mean and wish to keep the government of the country in their hands.   That, if they can, they will try to be *entreated* by the King to do so; and if this does not succeed, they will gratify their pride another way, by vapouring on the sacrifices they are ready to make for the good of the public.   The whole is a very sad story —the work of mean and bad passions; a trial of strength which a great subject presumes to institute with his King, and a King to whom he owes all his greatness.   It began in this, continues in this, and will end in it, and ruin follow to the common weal.

MARCH 10, ELEVEN, A.M.   William Elliot.—Says Lord Cornwallis writes him word all is quiet in Ireland, but that he laments the Catholic question having been given up.   Says ninety-five out of a hundred Irish members would have voted for it.   Quære?

HALF-PAST ONE, P.M.—Charles Fox was announced. As an old friend and acquaintance he said he came to see me, and at the same time confessed his chief reason was, that, having never kept copies of what he wrote when Secretary of State, he wished I would shew or give him a copy of an official letter he wrote me when I was at Petersburg in or about May 1782, on the subject of the Armed Neutrality.   He said it was written in consequence of a Cabinet held at the Duke of Grafton's in Clarges-street; and that, as far as he could recollect, his private sentiments, which he believes he wrote me in a private letter, were for my going *farther* than he could instruct me to do in his official despatch, if he made it conformable to the Minute of Cabinet.   That he had this Minute somewhere, but could not find it.   I told him I remembered little more than that his general sentiments on the Armed Neutrality were, that it was a point not worth contesting, since all Europe have subscribed to it; and if we could get any great advantage by acquiescing in its principles, it would be well so to do.   That *I* differed from him at the time, and that it was the subject of several conversations we held together on my

return home in 1783. He desired me to let him see a
copy of what he wrote, which I promised I would as
soon as I could get it from Park Place.* We of course
did not talk much of the present times. He said the
King was quite recovered; he knew it from unquestionable authority. On my saying it was a fortunate event,
he said he certainly was glad of it; but that " things
were come to such a pass, nothing could do either harm
or good."

THREE, P.M. Mrs. Harcourt.—Held *the language of
the Court;* outrageous with Pitt, &c. ; said the Prince's
behaviour was very bad ; always went at a time he was
sure he could not see the King, and then complained of
being slighted. Yesterday went at an hour he was certain he should be refused, His Majesty having taken
physic; and, on being refused, sent word to Lord Uxbridge, with whom he was to dine, by Jack Payne, that,
as the King would not see him, he really felt too much
to think of dining in company. Sad grimace. They all
knew him full well at the Queen's House, yet all loved
him. The Princess of Wales had behaved very well.

TEN, P.M. Tom Pelham.—Confirmed all said before
about the Prince. Complains of not being received by
the King, and goes at hours he knows the King cannot
see him. Dundas tells him that Addington will probably not make a voluntary offer to Pitt to give up to
him; yet Pitt seems to expect he should. Duke of
Portland undertakes to see Addington, and to persuade
him to go to the King to inform His Majesty of Pitt's
having dropped the Catholic Question, and that he, Addington, now submits it to His Majesty whether it
would not be proper to continue Pitt in office. This the
Duke said he could do with perfect consistency, as it is
conformable to the language he has held all along. He
and Pelham both agree that Addington should see the
King before he sees Pitt, and that the arrangement,

* I find no letter from Fox bearing exactly upon this point (probably because Lord M. returned it to him), but his letters published in the first
volume of this work express (like those of his predecessors in office) a sense
of the importance of the Empress's friendship, and his readiness to purchase
it by great concessions and unbounded flattery.

whatever it is, should appear to originate with the King, and come from the King to Pitt, and not *vice versâ*. Pelham rather injudiciously tells Dundas of this, and Dundas rather unfairly tells it to Pitt, who immediately goes to the Duke of Portland and insists on his not using any influence with Addington to induce him to give way; and that if he will not do it *proprio motu*, it will not satisfy him.

WEDNESDAY, MARCH 11.—King quite well; saw Addington and Chancellor. No bulletins to be given out after to-day, nor any inquiries expected to be made any longer. Prince of Wales saw His Majesty for the first time to-day. Sir W. Farquhar told me Pitt also was in high health.

NINE, P.M. W. Elliot.—Fox quite paramount in the House of Commons yesterday—brow-beat the Speaker— held very odd language — hinted at Parliamentary Reform.*

FOUR, P.M. Tom Pelham. — Pitt's visit to the Duke of Portland defeated that part of the plan, and Pitt seems to stiffen in his determination not to allow that any means shall be taken to direct Addington's conduct.

In the mean while, to the great surprise and satisfaction of almost everybody, Lord Cornwallis writes to Lord Castlereagh a letter in his own hand, stating that as the Catholic Question is given up, and very wisely so in his opinion, considering the repugnance the King had to it, he considers those who have resigned as bound to continue their services. That, in ordinary times, perhaps a contrary conduct might be permitted; but in these, it would be "*highly criminal*" if they acted otherwise. Dundas much pleased at this letter — Lord Spencer still more so; but Pitt, probably in secret com-

* The debate of the 10th of March rested on the eligibility of Mr. Horne Tooke to a seat in Parliament (he being in Priest's orders). Lord Temple moved for evidence to prove his being so before he moved for a new writ for Old Sarum. Fox opposed the motion, and took the opportunity of alluding to the nature of that Borough, which in fact consisted of an old encampment and two or three cottages.

munication with Lord Grenville, does not seem to be influenced much by it. Lord Castlereagh, eager for his remaining in power, told him, if he declined office now, he never could expect to resume it with credit or authority.

It is really difficult to account for Pitt's obstinacy; whether it is the consequence of an excess of pride and haughtiness, which, after he has treated his Sovereign with indignity, make him expect that, instead of expressing a concern for what he has done, he should be courted and entreated to remain in power; or, whether there is really some second and back view, and that he and others wish to let the new Ministry try to patch up a Peace, and then that they should reap the advantages of it, by a return to power, is a point impossible to resolve.

It is, however, not difficult to pronounce, that both motives are mean; and that, while Pitt is acting upon them, Fox will gain so much ground in the House of Commons, as to become a most powerful and dangerous rival.

THURSDAY, MARCH 12. —Chancellor and Addington had seen the King yesterday, and also the Prince of Wales.

FIVE, P.M. Duke of Portland.—Felt deeply and sincerely the difficulty of the times. King's getting so well a most fortunate event. The Duke then stated to me nearly everything I had heard from Pelham (except what immediately related to himself, and his going out); looks upon Pitt being at the head of Government as of the last consequence; and he is so earnest for it, that, considering his agreement with Pitt as at an end, he determines to see Addington to-morrow ; Pitt's hesitation unaccountable; he yields entirely on the Catholic Question, and goes so far as to declare " *he never will stir it.*" On talking of this question, the Duke said it was to have gone much farther than appeared at first— was to substitute a new Test Oath, and ultimately to make several alterations in the Church establishment. Duke of Portland blames Pitt much — agreed with me that it is the most culpable pride possible, if it *was* pride; but that *that* alone, strong as it was in his character, did not appear sufficient to prevent him doing what his ambition certainly prompted him to do, and which he confessed to be right. Pitt's argument, that he will support Government *out of office*, idle. Pitt and Office cannot be separated. Sorry Addington not quite so ready to give way as he ought — it would be the most honourable thing possible to give up to Pitt; and the Duke of Portland said he would try to prevail on him to make this tender to the King, who, the Duke says, would certainly be very glad to see Pitt again in full possession of his power. In speaking of the King, the Duke said, on the Wednesday, 18th of February, before he was taken ill, His Majesty was quite himself, and talked to him most sensibly and judiciously on all subjects. Said, " he was an old Whig; that he considered those statesmen who made barrier treaties, and conducted the ten last years of the succession war, the most able ones we ever had." He spoke in a loud tone of voice. On Friday the 20th, the Duke saw him again, and then was most excessively alarmed. On Saturday the illness declared itself. One material difference between this and the first long illness. Then, sleep never relieved the King; he woke sometimes, after ten hours' sound sleep, to use Warren's phrase, *like a giant refreshed by wine* — more turbulent than before; now sleep always recovered him, and he woke quiet and composed.

In speaking several weeks ago to the Duke of Portland on the Catholic Emancipation, he said, " Were he to agree to it, he should betray his trust, and forfeit his Crown; that it might bring the framers of it to the gibbet"—very strong words for him to use; and the Duke said, he was sure " the King had rather suffer martyrdom, than submit to this measure."

King now quite well—wishes to do *some* business, and have *some* occupation, but not to be overcharged with it. On speaking of Lord Grenville, we both agreed that he was the most close character possible — never relieved his mind by trusting *any one;* that now he was alone at Dropmore, and probably very uncomfortable, but he kept it all to himself.

The result of what the Duke said left still a chance of Pitt's retaining office. No final arrangements to be made till next week.

SATURDAY, MARCH 14.—Pitt saw the King at three, and actually resigned; Addington at four to-day. King aired to Kew. I do not hear what passed with respect to Mr. Addington. I examined to-day carefully a sea-chart of the Baltic, and took notes of it.

SUNDAY, MARCH 15.—Wryford, my old butler, gets an office of 100*l.* a year, and my old valet Howden the same, through George Rose and Windham. This gives me great pleasure.

TEN, P. M.—Lord Castlereagh.—Much talk about the Neutral Powers; he very right—very clever and steady.

MONDAY, MARCH 16.—Addington stiffens against any share of power with Pitt; replies very coldly and formally to a letter from Lord Camden (his intimate friend), in which Lord Camden intimates a wish that Government should be assisted with the abilities of their friend Pitt in office.

Pitt has taken a house in Park Place, and it is said his income is about 1000*l.* a year. Sir Robert Calder, it is feared, is gone on, and not followed De Gantheaume into the Mediterranean;* great expectation of success against the Danes.

TUESDAY, MARCH 17.—Report that the government in Holland is to be changed by proclamation, and that the same form of government which exists in France is to be declared. Hereditary Prince of Orange to be First Consul; the Stadtholder having, says the report, declined

* Sir R. Calder had been blown off from his blockade of Brest, and Gantheaume had got out, and gained Toulon with his fleet.

it. This is just possible, from the close connexion between France and Prussia, and from the strong leanings
I know the Hereditary Prince of Orange had to put his
family and self under the protection of France.

Two, P. M.—Bishop of Oxford.—Censures Pitt—
croaks as to the times.—N. B. He belongs to the
Grenvilles.

Three, P. M.—Canning.—He had written, not spoken,
to Pitt in the way he said he would; he preferred this,
that his sentiments might remain on record. His letter,
which he repeated, was in substance what I so strongly
urged. Pitt left it unnoticed for several days, and on
Thursday the 12th answered him shortly, but very
kindly; saying he was grieved to differ from him in
opinion, but *his mind was quite made up* on the subject.

Saturday the 14th, Pitt resigned, and in the evening
Canning went to him, and held a long conversation,
which ended by Canning putting two very material
questions to Pitt, and which, according to his own account, he put in the most solemn way possible, declaring
that he would regulate his conduct by the answers he
received, *if* Pitt could and would give him the true and
real ones. The first was, whether Pitt and Addington
had from the beginning to this day *acted in concert;*
and whether Addington had in no instance withheld
anything from him, or betrayed a strong wish to preserve office rather than restore it to Pitt. To this
question Pitt, without hesitation, and in the most unqualified manner, replied, that it was impossible to have
behaved with more confidence, more openness, more sincerity, than Addington had done, from the first moment
to this; and that the manner in which he had conducted
himself, added to his long friendship for him, had raised
him higher than ever in his good opinion.

Canning's second question was, (and he again appealed to Pitt's sincerity,) whether Pitt was *more satisfied* with him for *resigning* office, than with others who
retained their places. Pitt answered, that he certainly
could not but be pleased with Canning's having resigned
office, *taking him in the light of an individual and private*

friend, but as a public man, he very truly and sincerely said, *he was more pleased and more obliged to such of his friends who had kept their places.* After saying this, Canning told me that he recanted all he *suspected,* all he really might have said, and all that was attributed to him as having said, with respect to Mr. Addington. In sending him in his resignation to-day, that he had written to him in terms of the highest respect, with assurances of such support as he could give him.

If all Canning says is true, and I confess appearances look as if it was, the whole transaction is enveloped in a thicker cloud than ever; for why, after avowedly and publicly saying, he would not touch on the question of the Irish Catholics, but give it up; why Pitt, having done this, and hearing from Addington the King's wishes, and Addington's readiness to make over his Ministry to him, why he rejects this, and yet promises a constant and unvaried support to Government, is quite incomprehensible. I cannot but suspect that more is meant than meets the ear; that Pitt advises Addington to make peace, will assist him in it, and that peace once made, he will then no longer object to take office.*

This is my own private opinion; and I think many small facts, which taken together prove a good deal, go to make it a reasonable conjecture.

Canning keeps the place of Receiver-General of the Alienation Office. He said the Duke of Portland was to go out, or rather to be made President of the Council, and T. Pelham, Secretary of State.

WEDNESDAY, MARCH 11.—Rumour as if the King was not so well; had talked too much when Lord Hardwicke, &c., kissed hands for the Privy Council.

* The whole story may be told with a quotation from the " Arabian Nights." According to Eastern custom, when a man divorces his wife, another man must marry her, and divorce her again, before the first can take her back again ; and this happens more than once in the stories related in that book. The second husband is called a Hullah. Mr. Addington is *Britannia's Hullah,* and is too safe a man to play Pitt the trick one of them did, viz., refuse to divorce the wife again.—Original Note.

Lord Glenbervie dined yesterday with Trotter, where he met Otto. Little doubt but that the first act of the new Administration will be a trial for Peace; and as little doubt that Buonaparte will listen to their overtures. The generals who command the French armies in Germany and Italy, see in themselves as good a right to be First Consul, as he has. They are not disposed to obey him, and he certainly fears to bring the armies back into France. Yet if we consider a moment at what a period we make peace—that it must be by concessions disproportionate to our successes, and of course inglorious; and that we cannot possibly reduce the war establishment so as to ease the burthen now laid on the public, without making it insecure and unsafe, the measure is surely an unwise and weak one.

The *Invincible*, a 74, commanded by Admiral Totty, wrecked off Yarmouth yesterday morning,—only the admiral, three lieutenants, the purser, and one hundred and ninety-five seamen saved,—had the best pilots and best master possible. She was going at the rate of twelve knots an hour, when she struck on the sand, carried off a large piece of her keel, and soon after went down. The admiral, and those who were saved, jumped overboard at the last moment, and were picked up by fishermen.

MARCH 19.—Lord Whitworth.—Letters from Riga to Mr. Bonar say that an Ukase was just arrived there to prevent the exportation of any of the productions of Russia to the Prussian dominions; difficult to understand this, unless we are to suppose Paul thought the Prussian merchantmen connived at executing the commissions sent from hence.

EIGHT, P. M.—Tom Pelham.—Long conversation with him on the new arrangements; settled that he is to have the Seals for the Home Department.

It gave me great concern to hear that, on the day of the Council, (I believe Monday,) the King, in conversing with the Duke of Portland, was so extremely nervous as to alarm the Duke exceedingly. His Majesty took him

by the hand, and pressed it against his bosom; talked of
the great obligation he had to him for making way for
Pelham—" for *Lord* Pelham," said the King, " for I
will not hear any more of *Mr.* Pelham;" and then,
moving towards the window-seat, sat down, and wanted
the Duke to sit by him.   This betrays very weak nerves,
but not, I think, any mental derangement.   It was unfortunate that His Majesty, in the Council subsequent
to this audience, also talked *too feelingly* of the satisfaction the new Administration caused him.   Several indiscreet *counsellors* were present, and the report of the
King's being again unwell got abroad, and I indeed had
heard from Lord Morpeth that it was so this morning.

It is to be feared that he may fall into a state of *en-
fance*, and this makes the necessity of an immediate Regency Bill indispensable.

FRIDAY, MARCH 20.—Uncomfortable accounts from
the Queen's House; the Queen unwell; the King extremely nervous and low-spirited ; and the physicians
seem less to dread any mental derangement, than that
the intellectual faculties should be impaired so much as
never to recover their former tone.   Medical persons observe this to happen frequently after such an acute illness as the King has just had, particularly at his period
of life (sixty-three), and when one of the causes of it
was vexation of mind.

Lord Darnley's motion to come on; he confident in himself, and sadly vain.

SATURDAY, MARCH 21.—Twenty-five Peers and three
proxies voted with Lord Darnley; debate long, and not
amusing; a most remarkable speech of Lord Auckland,
who, getting up for the apparent purpose of noticing
something that had been said respecting a point of
finance, took the opportunity of animadverting on the
late resignations; " lamented the loss of Pitt's abilities,
&c.," and went on by saying, that " there was something *behind* in all this he could not comprehend; some

mysterious motives, (*honourable* motives, he did not
doubt,) that were the cause of it, since, without some
such explanation, their throwing up office was like a
general getting into a post-chaise, and leaving his army
in the middle of a battle." What could induce him to
be thus imprudent, it is difficult to say. Lord Auckland has received from Pitt obligations that no minister
but one possessing the power of Pitt could bestow, or
any one less eager for office than Lord Auckland ask;
yet scarce has he left office than Lord Auckland insinu-
ates that he did it from some concealed motive, and
that the ostensible one is insincere. Lord Spencer answered him with spirit, but treated him too gently;
Lord Grenville, having spoken twice, was silent. The
King, it is hoped, is better; but why not pass a Regency
Bill?

SUNDAY, MARCH 22.—Lord Auckland's speech the
topic of conversation at the Opera, and he much abused
for it. King slept well, but still low and depressed; apprehensions I described still great; unequal to business.

MARCH 23.—Lord Hawkesbury has seen and conversed with Otto; peace certainly in the minds and intentions of new Ministers, and, I fear, peace without reflection or consideration.

FOUR, P.M.—Canning.—Confirms my notions respecting the Ministers' intentions to make peace. I inquire
of him if Pitt does not disapprove; Canning says, *No*, he
always was too pacific, but he is now quite *enfeebled* and
won over, and this is the *real* reason of his declining resuming power and business. Laments it, and the consequences of it; says he will retire into the country;
violent against Lord Auckland's speech.

Conversation on Armed neutrality.

MARCH 24.—Canning.—I related and explained to
him what passed with regard to the Armed neutrality

from 1780 to 1783; compared Fox's declaration now with his instructions then. Fox appears never to have positively affirmed " we were justified in asserting our claims of visiting ships at sea as a legal right;" but he always maintained it " to be a measure of the greatest consequence to England, and which could not be given up but as a great sacrifice, and for which great and real advantages should be obtained." Lord Carlisle, Lord Lansdowne, Lord Fitzwilliam, and Fox have coalesced. It is said they informed the Prince of Wales, through Lord Moira, of this step; tendered him an offer of their services, and that they should hold their conferences at Carlton House. The Prince, it is said, replied, that he was under too much anxiety for the King's health to think of politics; that he thanked them for their communication, but not only declined their proposal, but observed that, out of respect to the King, he considered it as his duty to acquaint Mr. Addington with it; and this he immediately did.

THREE, P.M. General Grenville.—King much better; a Drawing-room on Thursday. Lord Auckland sent me a printed copy of his speech. If *any one* but he had spoken it, there would have been much to approve in it, and little to censure; but from him it must appear, not as the feelings of an honest, independent mind, but as the action of an *ungrateful* man.

WEDNESDAY, MARCH 25.—Strong symptoms of new Ministers' intention to open their administration by an attempt to end the war. Vansittart, who is Secretary to the Treasury, in the place of Rose, sent to Copenhagen. Conciliatory, softening language, to be held at Berlin. Lord Hawkesbury sees Otto, and it seems no longer to be doubted as having for object to try the ground.

THURSDAY, MARCH 26.—Strong division yesterday in the House of Commons on Grey's motion for a Committee to inquire into the state of the nation—minority,

105; majority, 293.   Fox spoke well; so did Grey; Pitt very well—defended and supported new Administration very powerfully.   Addington spoke late—not with much effect; but he seems not well in health, and very weak.

EIGHT, P.M.—Tom Pelham.—Said that it would be a fortnight before he could take office.   He intended Fitzharris for his private and confidential Secretary.

I received letters from Lord Minto, in answer to those I wrote to him to inform him of what had passed and was passing here.   He says he stands pledged to vote and act for the Catholic Question; that he has pressed for his recall, and written his sentiments to Lord Grenville and Windham.   I am sorry he has committed himself to the first of these; the last is his sincere friend.

Drawing-room to-day very crowded.   Queen looking pale; Princesses as if they had been weeping.   They insinuate that the King is too ill for the Queen to appear in public, and to censure her for it.   Dukes of York and Cumberland there.

The Prince of Wales *was* at the Drawing-room, but behaved very rudely to the Queen.

FRIDAY, MARCH 27.—Lord Whitworth.—Came to tell me that a negotiation for peace was likely to be opened, and that, if it took place, he was to be the person employed.   He had just seen Lord Hawkesbury and Mr. Addington, and they both told him to come to me, and acquaint me with his nomination; that it was a secret as yet, not to be told any one else.

TEN, P.M.—Strong language from Staremberg, the Austrian Minister, who abuses and depreciates his own Court most indecently.

SATURDAY, MARCH 28.—Lady Spencer, whom Mrs. Robinson* saw this morning, says great concessions are

---

* Lord Malmesbury's sister.

to be made, in order to obtain peace—the Cape, *Gibraltar*, and Minorca—(Gibraltar, Lord St. Vincent says, is of no value)—this Lord Lansdowne's language, who wanted to give it away in 1783, *but for an equivalent.*

I fear Ministers have shewn too much eagerness for negotiation. Buonaparte will avail himself of it—either to be insolent (if he feels strong in his seat), or to betray them into a bad peace by an affected complaisance, if he is insecure in it. There is reason to suppose the distant French armies are not disposed to be very obedient, and that those who command them consider themselves as possessing as good claims to govern France as the First Consul. He dares, not, therefore, bring them back into France, and is by no means sure that they will keep the countries they now are in possession of, for him or *his* purposes.

I dread a naval armistice; if we accede to it, it will be like the foremost jockey giving time for the others to come up with him while the race is running. But this, and concessions as to the claims of the neutral nations, and probably some boon or act of complaisance to *Paul*, will, I apprehend, be proposed to us; and my best hope is, that Buonaparte, giddy with success and vanity, and reckoning too much on our too easy compliance, will convey these proposals in such overbearing and insolent language, as even the present pacific enduring Ministers will be offended at, and the nation reject with disdain and contempt. If Buonaparte is *supple* and cunning, the evil will be very great indeed.

Sunday, March 29.—Pitt, I am told from authority, encourages Addington in his pacific plans—states the finances of the country to be such as require peace. I always perceived these to supersede in Pitt's mind every other consideration; and that even when he declaimed the loudest, and with the greatest emphasis, for a continuation of *war*, his real and genuine opinion went for *peace.*

No news from the Baltic. Unfavourable reports from

Egypt.   The French appear to have got two ships, with reinforcements and stores, into Alexandria; and the Turks by no means hearty and zealous in giving us their support.

TEN, P.M.—No answer from Paris.

MONDAY, MARCH 30TH.—I went to Richmond.   William Elliot told me, when I set out, that T. Pelham had seen the Duke of Portland, who had said nothing as to his change of office in the Cabinet, and that, till Lord Cornwallis comes, it must remain as it is.   Lord Hardwicke (who *is* recovered) to go on the 17th to Ireland.

Early in April I went with my family to Brighton. Pelham, who was with us part of the time, received a proposal from Lord Hawkesbury to go to Russia.—The news of Paul's assassination reached us in April; and it was in consequence of the change of system in favour of this country, which was expected, that the proposal was made to Pelham.   As, however, it was considered by him, that his being made Secretary of State, and his father to be raised to an Earldom, was a settled point, this proposal appeared to him a very singular one.   He advised with me as to his answer.   I admitted the immense importance of having an able man at Petersburg at the outset of a new reign, and the vast advantage the country and himself might derive from his going.   But that I would insist, in the first instance, on being placed in the Cabinet, and my father being created an Earl, since they were points determined on previous to this proposal, and ought not to be delayed by it.   Pelham wrote to this effect, declining the offer, but on the terms I have just mentioned; and, receiving no answer, the business dropt, and Lord St. Helens was appointed   Nothing could be so slovenly written as Lord Hawkesbury's letter; and it is difficult to say what his object was in pressing this Mission on Pelham, at a moment when he was to come into the Cabinet and high Office.

[The following is an extract of a letter from Mr. Ross to Lord Malmesbury, from Petersburg, where he was attached to the Embassy.]

I have been over the Palace where the scene was acted, accompanied by a Scotch surgeon, Dr. Grieve, who was much in the confidence of the late Emperor, and who gave him a draught on the very night he was murdered, about an hour before it took place. For a long time before his death, but particularly for the last ten days, his mind was in a constant state of irritation. His naturally suspicious temper preyed upon himself, and conjured up to his fancy an enemy in every person he saw. He suspected that some plot was going on, but could not fix on the authors of it. It is more than probable, that, had he lived forty-eight hours longer, his sons would have been shut up in the fortress. He taxed *Pahlen* with being concerned in it, who adroitly turned it off by remarking, that, supposing such to exist, it was essential to *his* security that he should be acquainted with it, and that he would answer for this with his head. The last evening of his life he even had some suspicions of Dr. Grieve; and whilst he was shaking the draught, he went to the end of the room, and turning quickly round, and fixing him, he said, "Mais apropos, mon cher, ne vous faites vous pas une affaire de conscience de guérir l'ennemi de vos compatriots?" Dr. Grieve's answer was, "Que tout homme de son état ne devrait avoir d'autre but que de bien remplir les devoirs de l'humanité." With this he was satisfied, and embracing him he said, "Je n'en doute pas, et ne m'en suis jamais douté." About an hour after, the conspirators entered.

Those who were to be the immediate actors, (about ten in number,—at the head of them were Platon Zubow, and General Benningsen, an Hanoverian by birth, esteemed an excellent officer, and a very resolute man, since made Governor of Lithuania, together with the Adjutant on duty, who had always a free entry to the Emperor,) had supped together, and drank freely. On coming to the outer folding-door, his valet-de-chambre, who always stood as a sentinel, (dressed en

Hussar,) between this door and the inner one, seeing the
Adjutant on duty, opened the door of the chamber where
the Emperor was in bed; but suspecting something
wrong, immediately after, from the number of people at
that hour, he shut it again and called to the Emperor.
The man was immediately struck, but not killed, (he is
now in the service of the Empress Dowager,) and the
party proceeded into the room.   Paul, alarmed by the
noise, had jumped out of bed.   It is thought he had attempted to find the door to the Empress's apartment,
but failed ; and was found by General Benningsen
behind a screen, in his shirt.   He immediately threw
himself into one of his attitudes, and began to expostu-
late with them; but almost immediately he received from
one of the party a blow on the temple, supposed to have
been given by the butt-end of a pistol, and, after some
struggling, was strangled with a sash.   The business
took up nearly three quarters of an hour.   It is not the
least singular part of it, that an Hanoverian should have
assisted in despatching him, and that his body should
have been given afterwards to *three Scotch surgeons to
cut up*—Drs. Green, Whaley, and Guthrie.

The persons concerned in this transaction could not
trust the Emperor's own battalion of Guards.   The
officers of the other were gained over, and their men
were marched up to the Palace, with Pahlen and another
of the Zubows at their head, whilst the affair was carrying on.   The next morning all was quiet.   The people
were seen embracing, and giving each other joy in
the streets; and, from that time to the present, everybody
has his own story.   This account (from the quarter
from whence I got it) comes, I think, nearer the truth
than most others which have been circulated.   The Empress Dowager openly expresses her detestation of the
persons concerned in it.   It was through her influence
that *Pahlen* has been banished.   She has taken into her
service the persons who were the principal sufferers by
her husband's death.   The Emperor pays her every attention.

During my stay at Brighton, Nelson forced the passage of the Sound, and fought the battle of Copenhagen. The landing of our troops also took place in Egypt, and in a way to promise success.

[Sir Ralph Abercrombie had landed his army in Egypt on the 8th of March. On the 21st, he totally defeated the French, but was mortally wounded, and died on the 28th. I found this event so well alluded to in a familiar letter from Mrs. Parkhurst to Lord Malmesbury, that I could not resist giving the extract.]

"Over Sir R. Abercrombie I do not much lament—full of years, and full of honours, he seems with his own hands to have made a monument of glory, and then calmly entered it. When death *must* come, it never comes better than disguised as Glory. Such ashes should rather be revered than deplored."

On my return to London in May, and till I left it in June, I had little or no intercourse with public men. Pelham's marriage with Lady Mary Osborne took place; but his nomination to the Secretary of Stateship (partly from no very cordial good-will towards him, I believe, in Addington, &c., and partly from the rooted habits of procrastination which belong to the Duke of Portland, who was to make way for him,) was postponed till August, when the King was at Weymouth. It then was settled in the manner agreed on; but some very important branches of business were lopped off from his department and given to Lord Hobart.

Negotiations for peace going on very secretly, but very earnestly, during the months of August and September, between Lord Hawkesbury and Otto; and, from the little which I could collect, it seemed as if the latter was the much more able Negotiator; the event since has proved it.

In July, the Princess of Orange, the Hereditary Prince of Orange, General Larrey, the Greffier Fagel, and his brother, passed three days at Park Place, to take leave on her going to the Continent. I avoided all politics at so disagreeable a moment, and under such a fluctuating state as Germany, and even we ourselves were in; and contented myself with strong, but sincere, assurances of my zealous attachment to the interests and well-being of the House of Orange. Nothing could be more kind and friendly than the Princess; and on getting into her coach, after embracing Lady Malmesbury and my daughters, she could not refrain from tears.*

When I came to London, on the 14th July, I found, from Lord Pelham, that it was in contemplation to enable the King to give a large sum of money to the House of Orange,—220,000*l*. This, Addington said, was the value of the ships seized at the breaking out of the war, and surrendered to us in behalf of the Stadtholder; and, as such, Addington wished it should be employed to his advantage.

The indelicacy, as well as the something like injustice of this idea, struck me at once, and I found it had also struck more forcibly the Princess, who wrote to the Greffier a most excellent *ostensible* letter, to be shewn Addington. Lord Pelham, Lord Auckland, and myself were to be the three trustees for the Princess in her interest in 60,000*l*.; and it will appear by the letters, that the remaining 120,000*l*., instead of being paid at once, was to be converted into an annuity of 20,000*l*. a-year to the Prince of Orange. The letter of the Princess to Mr. Fagel was intended as an answer to one written to her by Mr. Addington. His letter dwelt on the value of the ships, and rated the money to be given to the House of Orange according to their value.

It was a well-meant, but most ill executed intention. First, the letter and style were ill suited, either to the high situation of the writer or rank of the person to whom it was addressed, and, in fact, Addington was made so ashamed of it by what I remarked on it (which

---

* The Princess probably thought of the adverse days of 1786, when Lord Malmesbury was struggling with her to restore the Stadtholderate to its power, of the triumphant result of those efforts in 1787 ; but even with this experience of the caprice of Fortune, she could not have imagined, at this hopeless moment, that her House would regain, in 1814, more than all it had lost.

I did without scruple), that he begged to have it back again and suppress it.

The idea of an annuity also, instead of a lump of money given at once, was mine, and from the principle that it should be considered as a retaining fee, *un subside d'attente*, to the House of Orange; a connexion with which we should never lose sight of, and whose conse-quence and high name it was our interest, independent of what was due to the present representatives of it, to maintain and uphold.

The Princess of Orange and her suite left London for the Continent on the 16th of July, and sailed next day from Dover.

TUESDAY, SEPT. 29.—After an absence of three months, I came for a few days to London. On getting out of my carriage in St. James's Park, I met Mr. Addington (the Minister); he was in uncommon high spirits, from which I readily inferred that the peace negotiation was likely to terminate successfully. At my own house I found Fitzharris and William Elliot; they also said, from all they had observed during the course of a day, that Lord Hawkesbury and Otto were on the point of signing the preliminaries;* yet it was known that, about ten days ago, there was a hitch in the negotiation on the part of Buonaparte, which seemed to look as if he wished to break it off. Windham came in the evening, full of apprehensions: he said, he considered the peace, made at the time and in the way it was, would be as the most mistaken of measures—as the death-blow to the country.

* The Preliminaries of the Peace of Amiens between His Majesty and the French Republic were signed October 1st, 1801, in London, by Lord Hawkesbury, Secretary for Foreign Affairs, and Monsieur Otto, at that time residing in London as an agent for the exchange of prisoners. Great Britain acquired Ceylon in the East, and Trinidad in the West Indies. Egypt was to be réstored to the Porte, whose possessions and territories, as well as those of Naples and Portugal, were to be preserved entire. France retained her other conquests and recovered her colonies.

On the 3rd November an address of thanks for the Peace was moved in both Houses: in the Lords, opposed by Lords Grenville, Spencer, Fitz-william, &c., but carried in a division of 94 to 10. In the Commons, after a long debate, in which the treaty was approved by Pitt, Fox, Sheridan, and censured by Windham, T. Grenville, &c., the address was carried without a division.

WEDNESDAY, SEPT. 30.—Great secrecy in the Cabinet as to peace. Lord Pelham (now Secretary of State for the Home Department) called on me. We went over all the politics of Europe, both foreign and domestic; but, by his avoiding the slightest reference to the negotiation, he convinced me of what we suspected, and that peace was really agreed to. Lord G. Leveson averse to peace, but ignorant of the state of the negotiation.

LONDON, THURSDAY, OCT. 3.—Windham in morning and evening—quite in despair. The preliminaries were, I believe, settled this evening conclusively. Pitt counselled, and, of course, directed the whole. The other members of the Cabinet do not appear to have been recalled with *full* confidence on this occasion. What had passed was communicated to them; but they do not *all* appear to have been advised with (as their office implies) on what was to be done. The Chancellor (Lord Eldon) rather against peace — so the Duke of Portland, so Pelham; but they were either lukewarm about it, or overruled. Lord Westmoreland angry at not being of more consequence.

FRIDAY, OCT. 1. — Colonel Drinkwater early told me of the signature of the preliminaries. It was kept a secret to all London but the Lord Mayor; but Addington wrote a circular letter to half England—to Cirencester, Reading, and George Rose, &c. Childish exultation and joy at an event of which the issue at best *must* be doubtful. I returned to Park Place in the evening. During the month of October, I observed that the people's joy, which was immoderate at first, abated, and that the more thinking and wiser part of the community began to demur as to *all* the *certain* advantages that *must* follow peace. Lord Bathurst,* Lord Pembroke, Lord Camden,† and Lord Radnor, all disapprove

* Earl Bathurst was subsequently for many years a Cabinet Minister under Lord Liverpool's administration.

† The Marquis of Camden was Lord-Lieutenant of Ireland in the Rebellion of 1795.

of it. Lord Grenville and all his family are violent against it—more like party violence than public wishes; Lord Spencer induced by them to be the same. On the 2nd of October Lord Pelham came to Park Place; I had a very long conversation with him, and gave him every information in my power respecting my two Negotiations at Paris and at Lisle. I told him I disapproved of peace as a measure, and could I have prevented it I would; but, the measure being concluded, I thought it my duty to make the best of it, and not to add to the evil by contributing to raise a violent and factious opposition to it; that, however, not being able to attend, it was of little consequence what my opinion was, or indeed would be.

Oct. 29.—Lord G. Leveson came to consult with me as to what he should do in Parliament, and what he should say if my Negotiations were referred to. I desired him to state, should that happen, just what I had said to Pelham, that if it should be found that the terms were the same I proposed at Lisle, not to contend that point, but to point out the much higher ground *we* stood on now respecting France than at that period, though France perhaps *now* stood somewhat higher respecting Europe; but that the great difference was in the state and strength of the French Government; that, had we made peace at Lisle, France would have been under what was then termed a *moderate* Government—moderate in every sense of the word—composed of a motley set of men, half royalists and half *modérés*, and all thinking sincerely and in earnest that the wisest of all measures for France was, by peace to consolidate the power she had attained, and not to risk that by attempting to gain more. It is not so now. The Government of France, while Buonaparte remains as First Consul, is like that of Persia under Kauli-Khan: it knows no bounds, either moral or civil—is ruled by no principles; and to pretend to say that Buonaparte's ambition is circumscribed, or that, with the means of doing everything, he will do nothing, is talking criminal nonsense; that *this* is the great difference between September 1797 and October 1801; and on this alone I wished him to make a stand, if the subject was mooted.—Secret article in favour of the Electorate of Hanover. On this the King said, " If Ministers think they can *win* me over to their opinion as to a peace with these fellows by stipulations about Hanover, they are mistaken."   Lord Rosslyn (late Loughborough) gives his proxy to the Chancellor (Lord Eldon), his successor; he is dying, they say. On the 12th, a Frenchman, called Lauriston, occasional aide-de-camp to Buonaparte, brought over the ratification. A Jacobin saddler in Oxford-road saw him pass in his way to Otto's, who lived in Hereford Street; he assembled the mob, persuaded them he was Buonaparte's brother, and Lauriston was drawn about by them in a hackney-coach to all his visits. Government did not know it in time, and John King, (Under-Secretary of State,) when I met him, treated it very lightly; yet it was a most disgraceful circumstance, and a sad precedent.   Opposition, that is to say, Fox, &c., I am told, are preparing themselves to coalesce with Addington's ministry, and think that they can come into office under his shelter.   They all support the Peace, by saying any peace must be good after such a war—but a bad compliment to their new intended ally.

Part of the 26th, the 27th, and 28th of November, I was at Windsor.   I went there to present to the King and Queen copies of the new edition of my father's works.   I saw them both alone on the morning of the 26th, and was with them that and the next evening at their card party at the Lodge.   I likewise saw Princess Mary on the 27th, in the morning; each evening the Queen named me of her party, and played at cribbage with me.   I was with the King alone near two hours. I had not seen His Majesty since the end of October, 1800, of course not since his last illness; he appeared rather more of an old man, but not older than men at his age commonly appear; he stooped rather more, and was apparently less firm on his legs; but he did not look thinner, nor were there any marks of sickness or decline in his countenance or manner; these last were much as usual; somewhat less hurried, and more conversable, that is to say, allowing the person to whom he addressed himself more time to answer and talk, than he used to do when discussing on common subjects, on public and grave ones. I at all times for thirty years have found him very attentive, and full as ready to hear as to give an opinion, though perhaps not always disposed to adopt it and forsake his own. He was gracious even to kindness, and spoke of my father in a way which quite affected me. He expressed great satisfaction at seeing me less ill than he expected; asked how I continued to keep well; and, on my saying, amongst other reasons, that I endeavoured to keep my *mind quiet*, and dismiss all unpleasant subjects from intruding themselves on it, the King said, " 'Tis a very wise maxim, and one I am determined to follow; but how, at this particular moment, can you avoid it?" And without waiting he went on by saying, " Do you know what I call the Peace?—an *experimental Peace*, for it is nothing else. I am sure *you* think so, and perhaps do not give it so *gentle* a name; but it was *unavoidable*. I was abandoned by everybody, Allies and *all*. I have done, I conscientiously believe, for the best, because I could not do otherwise; but, had I found more opinions like mine, better might have been done."

I thought the subject might agitate the King, and therefore tried to lead him from it; he perceived my drift, and said, " Lord Malmesbury, you and I have lived on the active theatre of this world these thirty years; if we are not become wise enough to consider every event which happens quietly, and with acquiescence, we must have lived very negligently. What would the good man who wrote these excellent books (pointing to the copy I had just presented to him, and which lay on the table, of my father's work) say, if we were such bad philosophers, having had such means of becoming good ones?" and then His Majesty reverted again to the peace, spoke of the state of Europe, of France and this country; and by the turn of conversation it happened, that the King and myself, almost in the same moment, agreed that it was a most erroneous and dangerous maxim which prevailed, that Jacobinism was at an end or diminished; that it was only quieter because it had carried *one* point, but we should soon see. it blaze out again, when it had another in view; and from that the King passed to the Court of Berlin, which he spoke of with great displeasure, even acrimony: "This is the young man," said he, "of whom the great Frederic said, ' On ne lui arrachera jamais la couronne,' and we shall live, possibly, to see him without even his Electoral dominions." His Majesty expressed resentment against Lord Grenville, spoke friendly of Pitt, and slightingly of Lord Hawkesbury—"He has no head for business, no method, no punctuality," said the King. Of the Prince of Orange he said, he was at the bottom a good man, but with some sad defects; that he had left the country very rapidly, and asked me if I knew why. (Now I did know why, but thought it wiser not to say so.) Of the Princess he spoke in terms of the highest commendation; also of Fagel, the present Greffier. Of Nagel he said, he was a very good courtier, but not a man of business. (His Majesty here is mistaken.) He asked me a great deal about Russia; mentioned Lord Auckland with no great praise. Of Lord Pelham he said, he was likely to be a good man of business, and was glad Fitzharris was under him; inquired about Alfred—if I still meant him for the Church, and if it *still* was his own free choice; of Lord Minto, that he was grown more conversable, and had done vastly well at Vienna. Of the Emperor he expressed but a mean opinion.

The Queen kept me only a quarter of an hour; she said she should see me again in the evening, as I must be tired with standing so long with the King: spoke kindly of my father, and of my dear children. Princess Mary was all good-humour and pleasantness; her manners are perfect, and I never saw or conversed with any princess so exactly what she ought to be. While I was at Windsor, I lodged with Colonel Sneyd, who com-

manded the Staffordshire militia. On my return I
called at St. Leonard's (General Harcourt's).

———

APRIL 8.—Rode with Mr. Pitt in Hyde Park—he
joined me, and began immediately on the peace: he
owned that he had, when the preliminaries were signed,
thought that Buonaparte had satisfied his insatiable ambition, and would rest contented with the power and
reputation he had acquired—that for a moment, therefore, he was disposed to believe he was become more
moderate, more reasonable; and that, having so completely attained every object of his wishes, that he would
remain quiet, and consider a restoration of peace and
tranquillity as a wise and salutary measure, not only
for France, but for the maintenance of his own high
situation, and preservation of his popularity—that, however, all that had passed since went to convince him he
had been in error, and that the electing himself President of the Italian republic, the attainment of Louisiana,
the two Floridas, and the island of Elba, left no doubt
on his mind that he was, and ever would remain, the
same rapacious, insatiable plunderer, with as little good
faith and as little to be relied on as he formerly found
him to be; and that, in consequence, he (Mr. Pitt) was
obliged to return to his former opinions, and to declare
that no compact, no covenant, made with him, coúld be
secure; that still he did not regret having spoken in
favour of the Peace—it was become a *necessary* measure; and rest for England, however short, was desirable; that the duration of it would depend on ourselves
and on the conduct we adopted; that except the positive
and real situation of the country, which was one of
peace, everything should bear the aspect of war; that
we should appear warlike in our provincial measures,
warlike in our diplomatic ones, and, above all, warlike
in our military and naval establishments, so that it
might be made *evident to Buonaparte that England
will submit to no insult, nor suffer any injury.* I asked
him to define *insults* and *injuries.* " Acts," said he,

F 2

" which may affect, either immediately or in their consequences, the *dignity, honour, safety,* or *real greatness of
the country.*" He explained farther by saying, ' the
torpid and disgraceful state of public spirit in all the
great European Courts puts it, I fear, out of our means
to prevent Buonaparte's attempts to encroach, or ag-
grandise himself on the Continent; for, unassisted as we
probably shall be by the Courts he is trampling on, it will
not, from the nature of our force and insular position,
be practicable for us to hinder him; but any attempt on
his part to contest, attack, or molest our commercial or
colonial interests, made directly on our rights and possessions, or through the rights and possessions of others,'
(and he illustrated this position by supposing a usurpation of Holland as of the Cisalpine republic, and an
attack on Spanish America,) would, in his mind, call
upon us for *immediate resistance,* and not only be a
justifiable, but an indispensable, cause for war; that the
being prepared for this would prevent it, and we should
take care to make Buonaparte see we were prepared by
every act of our Government; that if Government did
this, as he trusted, and was indeed assured they must,
there was only a shade of difference between his opinion
and the opinions of those who had formerly been his
colleagues in office, and whom he ever should consider
as his friends. They still had the same end in view—
to watch and contract the overweening ambition of Buonaparte; they differed, and the question was, which was
the best way of doing so: whether by carrying on a war
which would weary out the patience of the country, and
dwindle away its resources without its being able to
make any important impression on our enemy; or, by
relieving it from the state of warfare it had been in
for so many years, recruit its resources of every kind
under the quiet of peace, and by being in such a state
of defence and preparation as could in the shortest
period enable us to come forward with a force equal to
repel any insult, and resist any act of aggression or hostility. Pitt then enlarged on the pecuniary resources of
the country, and said with confidence, ' that a very few

years of peace would be fully sufficient to enable England to go on (if provoked to it) with many years of war; and that, during this period, it was, he thought, not indulging an unlikely hope that some one of the great Continental powers might awake to a due sense of its honour and interests; and that in a future contest we might derive from some part of Europe, at least, that aid and co-operation it was out of the question to look for or expect at this moment.'*

This was by far the best, indeed, the only good apology, I have as yet heard for the peace, if it can so be called, for it breathed war as much as any of Windham's speeches. Of him Pitt said, that 'nothing could be so well-meaning or so eloquent as he was; his speeches were the finest productions possible—of warm imagination and fancy; yet still he must condemn such parts of them as hold out the French nation as the first in point of military and political abilities, and, therefore, *deservedly* the first in Europe. This part of it was a language he strongly reprobated as not correct, and as unbecoming the mouth of any Englishman.'

After giving his general principles on the peace as a measure, we fell into a discourse on the conditions of the Treaty itself, to several parts of which I made objections, and also animadverted on others which were omitted. He agreed that it had been rather hastily drawn up, but that he did not conceive any thing very likely to occasion disputes; or that justifiable disputes would arise, either from the wording of the articles inserted, or from any points that were omitted; and this led us to that particular omission of all former treaties, and the loose state in which the rights and possessions of both countries would be placed. As to the Continental treaties, Pitt observed (meaning those from the peace of Munster to the peace of 1783), they had been so completely done away by that of Campo Formio and Luneville,† that it was idle to consider them as in force.

---

* The events that took place from 1807 to 1815 proved how right Pitt was in his opinions, though he did not live to see them realised.

† In 1797 and 1801.

The commercial ones, he owned, were of more importance, and he confessed he saw, in their not being renewed, room for regret, and a difficulty of explanation:
that the most material ones were our convention in
1786 with Spain, respecting the right of cutting log-
wood in the Bay of Honduras; and that of 1787, called
the East India Convention, made by Lord Auckland at
Paris: that they both gave us valuable and important
privileges, and the last particularly was an avowal, on
the part of France, of the supremacy of our territorial
jurisdiction in Bengal. That he saw but one way of defending the omission of this last, which was to maintain
that this jurisdiction was so universally admitted, and
had been so long established, that it was become a pre-
scriptive right, which required no stipulation with any
European power to continue, and the exercise of which
nothing but force could deprive us of; that, therefore,
if the French refused to admit the sense of this Convention, we had nothing to do but to declare the *territorial
jurisdiction* as indisputably belonging to us, and that
they would, by annulling it, lose the usual privilege it
gave them, viz. the importing of a certain quantity of
salt, and the receiving of a certain quantity of saltpetre
and opium. That this mode of reasoning, however,
could not apply to the Lord Carmarthen's Convention
with Del Campo in 1786, as the sovereignty of Spain
was a Power we never disputed in those parts, and all
the privileges we obtained from this Convention arose
out of this circumstance; that, therefore, he at that
moment saw no opening for us to obtain these privileges, unless the Convention was renewed; and he regretted that that, and our other commercial Conven-
tions with Spain, had not been renumerated. Our conversation was long and interesting. He said, he was glad
to have had an opportunity of explaining himself fully
to me on a subject on which I had been always well acquainted with his opinions, and on which I naturally
must a good deal employ my own thoughts.

I frequently saw the Russian Ambassador (Count
Simon Woronzow) in the course of March and April;

his professions towards the country are very friendly, but those respecting the present Ministry very hostile. He admitted their meaning and principles to be good, but charged them with extreme weakness, extreme ignorance, and a total want of statesmanlike habits. Lord Hawkesbury he seemed particularly angered with, and communicated to me several papers which had passed between them, about Mr. Buxter, the Russian Consul, that he said were unparalleled in their tone and style, when coming from a Secretary of State to the Ambassador of a friendly and a great Court. On the face of the affair, and according to Woronzow's statement, Lord Hawkesbury appears to have been in error; but Woronzow takes it up too warmly, and his reply to Lord Hawkesbury was conceived in such terms as never were employed in a correspondence of such a nature. Woronzow mentioned a more legitimate cause of complaint against the inattention of the Foreign Office, by saying, that an offer he had made officially in the Emperor's name, and by the Emperor's order, on the 27th of March, to the guarantee of the Treaty of Peace between Turkey and France, and which offer he conveyed by sending Lord Hawkesbury a copy of the Emperor's letter, had been left without any answer, and that it was *impossible* for him not to take official notice of this. I mentioned this part to Pitt, and he, rather unwarily, said, "It was very wrong; *I will tell Lord Hawkesbury of it; it shall be set right;*" avowing thus his direction over Lord Hawkesbury and the present Government.

On the 7th April Woronzow dined with me. He was more exasperated than ever against Lord Hawkesbury; talked of him in the most injurious manner; and as I was fearful this might, on his return to Russia, influence his general political respect, and give it an unfavourable turn respecting this country, I thought the best mode was to make it a *personal affair* between the *two men*, on which matter neither the interests nor the measures of the *two empires* were involved. It appeared very indifferent what he said of Lord Hawkesbury in

Russia, but very material that he should represent the country in a friendly and favourable light.   I told Pitt what I had done, and he quite agreed with me.   At the same time, acquainted as I am with the general character of the Russians, and the sort of *use* peculiar to Woronzow, I am not without my misgivings that Russia is drawing herself from us, and towards France;* and that he expresses this anger and dislike to the conduct of our ministers *now,* in order to lay to their charge the alteration which *may* take place in the sentiments and behaviour of his own Court.

APRIL 11.—Monday, March 26th, I met the Duke of York in the streets; he asked me for news; I said, without any great reflection, " *Peace, Sir, in a week, and war in a month.*"   At the next Drawing-room, (this day,) the King said to me, " You are a great prophet; I believe your prediction will be true."   I had forgot what I had said to the Duke of York.   The King brought it to my mind, and added, " I should prophesy the same; I am persuaded you are right; the first half of it is already fulfilled," (the Definitive Treaty was signed March 27th,) " and I expect the other will not fail." His Majesty then repeated what he had said to me before, that he was never more embarrassed than to know how to make up his mind on this measure of peace; he was told one day, it was necessary—we had no supplies —and the next, he observed, we overflowed with wealth; that he hoped he had done right, but he was sure it was a fearful experiment.   All this, and a great deal more to the same effect, was said *almost* loud enough for the persons round us to hear, and certainly so to those who were good listeners.   He ended by saying, " I can always talk to you as I think, because, for thirty years and more, I believe our opinions in foreign concerns have never differed."

Lord Grenville sat with me, reading over parts of my

* I was but too right in my conjectures; the German indemnities proved it.—Orig. Note.

Correspondence at Lisle and Paris, for several hours. He is greatly against the peace itself, and, besides condemning the measure in itself as weak, dangerous, and ill-timed, he considers the way in which the Treaty is drawn up as highly blamable, full of diplomatic errors, and with many important omissions, none of which were left out of the Lisle project; that of not renumerating treaties the most dangerous one; and amongst those treaties the East India Convention of 1787, and the Honduras one of 1786, the most fatal omissions in their effects. He went over all we should lose in India and in South America, and the endless quarrels and disputes we were exposing ourselves to. All he said was like the reflections of a man who had thought much and seriously on the subject, and who was preparing himself to debate the matter in Parliament.

APRIL 12.—In a short conversation I had this day with Mr. Addington, I found his exultation on the prosperous state of the country in point of finance very great, but that with respect to the advantages of peace less than before; and the whole bent of his language went to the necessity of a strong and powerful peace establishment. This corresponds with what Pitt said to me Sept. 25th.

APRIL 27, and MAY 2.—Mr. Jackson, who was sent as Minister to Paris during Lord Cornwallis's Negotiation at Amiens, was with me; he said, " That impressed as he was on going to Paris with the ideas of the character of the present French nation, yet their attempts to deceive, their duplicity, their bad faith, insolence, and vanity, surpassed his utmost belief." That the way in which they treated everybody of every description dependent on them, was insupportable; that Buonaparte's manners were sarcastic, vulgar, and impertinent, but certainly with a degree of cleverness and *esprit;* that Talleyrand (the Minister of Foreign Affairs) was the most barefaced teller of untruths he ever met with; and that no one but Barbé Marbois had even a desire of passing for an honest man. Jackson illustrated what he advanced by many things which had happened to others, and some few to himself, during his four months' stay at Paris. That, in addition to these qualities, they joined a weak and puerile degree of jealousy and suspicion ; that they watched everybody, foreigners and natives, and always interpreted their behaviour in the way little and illiterate minds conceive; that through their duplicity *their rooted hatred to this country* was evident, and it was to him perfectly clear, that they were only lying by to wait for what they might think a safe and favourable opportunity to crush us; as a proof of this, he instanced Lucien Buonaparte's speech at the opening of the Concordat, in which he excites Ireland to rebel, and says, " *le sort de ce Pays a dépendu d'une nuit propice.*" That the society of Paris is void of amusement, because void of security; that no one trusts his neighbour, and that Buonaparte's great end is to diffuse suspicion everywhere—considering it as his best hold.

In speaking of the Negotiation, he was compelled to say, its having terminated so disadvantageously to us was greatly to be attributed to Lord Cornwallis, " his *drowsiness*," and his total want of practice and experience in matters of *that kind ;* that Merry wrote all the despatches; and that although he, Merry, thought very well, and was a strong-headed man, yet he was far from being an equal to cope with those opposed to him at Amiens.

Jackson said, that at the time Buonaparte went to Lyons, and had been himself elected President of the Italian Republic, it was the general and unconcealed opinion at Paris that the Negotiation for Peace must break off; that it was quite impossible for England not to consider this event as one which cancelled the Preliminaries; and that *even* Buonaparte and his adherents expected that we should at least *raise* our claims, and were prepared to give way in case we persisted in them. They felt the hazard of the step, saw the danger of their fleet in the West Indies, and would actually have given

up Malta, rather than have renewed hostilities at that
moment. That the *French* ratifications were executed
and exchanged in a great hurry the very morning of the
procession of the Concordat to the Church of Notre
Dame, because Buonaparte felt it would be absurd to
talk of a general Peace being restored before this exchange had taken place.

That Merry, who had come from Amiens on purpose,
was sent by Lucien Buonaparte at nine in the morning,
and that he found the French instruments ready, but
neither the Dutch nor Spanish; and that, on his rather
demurring on this, he was pressed to conclude, being
told it was of no consequence; and, in fact, Buonaparte
himself, the same day, talked to Azara, (the Spanish
Ambassador,) and to Schimmelpenninck, (the Dutch
one,) on this step in a way and style he would have
treated his lowest dependents, and they bore it *as sub-
missively*.

Jackson observed, how wrong we were in allowing an
Ambassador to come from them, or be sent to them;
that we had with blamable complaisance left the choice
to them, and that they of course had chosen a representative of the first rank, while we were ignorant that
they, in their new code of etiquette, had broke through
all the old forms and ceremonials, and that an English
Ambassador, now at Paris, would be obliged either to be
in one perpetual state of dispute, or to submit to *avanies*
no Ambassador ever suffered before; that now all the chief
ministers in France took precedence of our Ambassador,
under the absurd notion that they made integral parts of
the Constitution, and that in no public ceremony any
fixed rank was allowed to Ambassadors, who formerly
disputed the *pas* with princes of the blood;* that the timidity and *radotage* of Philip Cobenzel, the Imperial

* Until late years, foreign Ministers resident in London had no precedence ; but not liking to be nondescripts, and having shewn susceptibility on
the subject, the "Fountain of all honours" decided upon giving them the
pas after the English Marquisses, and *before* the Earls ; an arrangement
which appeared absurd and offensive to such as studied and valued the like
privileges, for they argued that it was inconsistent with the fiction of our
"Peerage," which is an integral equality, and that we might now expect the
foreign Consuls to walk between the Bishops and the Barons.

Ambassador, and the Jacobinical principles of Azara (the Spaniard), had allowed them to establish this principle; that the other Ambassador (Gallo), from Naples, was disposed to assert his right and rank, but the weak and dependent state of his Court rendered his attempts fruitless.   That he himself, Jackson, was unpopular at Paris, merely from not being servile and subservient; and that the general base and humiliating conduct of the Foreign Ministers was disgraceful to a degree.   He told me that he had made Lord Hawkesbury the same report he had made me; that he saw *it did not please*, that it did not agree with his system and conduct; and that for this reason, more than from discrediting Jackson's penetration or urbanity, he was disposed to call the truth of it in question.

TUESDAY, MAY 11.—A long confidential conversation with Lord Pelham this morning; he feels and laments the system his colleagues pursue, and the inability with which they pursue it; he read me the protest he made in the Cabinet at the beginning of March, against signing the Definitive Treaty of Peace in the same terms as Preliminaries, and stated for reason the same motives brought forward by the opposers to Peace, viz., Elliot, Lord Grenville, &c.   Yet his brother Ministers have put the burthen on him of answering all the attacks made in the House of Lords; and, although acquainted with his sentiments, expect him to take the lead there.

Lord Pelham hesitated when he gave this reason for his dissentient voice, whether it would not have been right to resign his office; but he felt the sort of confusion such a step would produce in the Cabinet; and, as on all other points he agreed with his colleagues, he considered it better to remain in.   He told me he had carried the petition of right to the King from the Prince of Wales, in order to place the decision of his claims on the amount of the revenues of the Duchy of Cornwall, during his minority, in the courts of Law.   The King was very placid and good-humoured about it, and well-pleased that it should not be again discussed in Parliament.

Much discourse about the Continent, on which we generally agreed. Addington and Lord Hawkesbury dread alliances; think commercial treaties useless, and seem to have filled their minds on foreign connexions with the silliest and most dangerous ideas.

Lord Carysfort* does not go to Russia.

From May till October, 1802, I was in the country. I was not in the way of hearing anything from sufficient degree of authority to make it worth while to notice it. I was in Gloucestershire, Herefordshire, Hampshire, and Wiltshire; and I could, from general conversation, and from the temper of the people, perceive, that their satisfaction at the Peace began very much to decrease; and that the encroachments France made on every side, both on the Continent of all Europe, and in that of America, and her intolerable insolence, the oppressive and infamous derision of Germany, under the mock title of a plan of Indemnities—her arrogance in insisting on our controlling the press, and giving up the French emigrants ; all these circumstances, which were very early to be foreseen, but which the childish fondness for Peace had made many overlook, now appeared to begin to operate, and the country at last to apprehend that neither credit, satisfaction, nor even security had been attained by the Treaty of Amiens. The New Government people I conversed with during the summer, and the Duke of Portland and Lord Glenbervie, held a language that went to reprobate rather than defend the conduct of the Administration of which they make a part; and strong symptoms of its weakness, and of its want of the confidence of the country, began to shew themselves.

OCTOBER 20th. — I received a letter from Canning, dated Walmer, 18th, expressing a strong and urgent wish to see me. I told him I should be in London the

---

* Brother-in-law to Lord Grenville.

29th or 30th; and on the last of these days he came to see me at eleven o'clock in the evening.

He said that Mr. Pitt told him that he went out, not on the Catholic Question simply as a measure in which he was opposed, but from the manner in which he had been opposed, and to which, if he had assented, he would, as a Minister, have been on a footing totally different from what he had ever before been in the Cabinet. This obliged him to resign; but as his sincere wish was, that his going out should neither distress the King nor the country, he had required no one to follow him. Those who did, did it voluntarily, and against his desire. That he quitted office, leaving behind him means and preparations so likely to ensure success, both in the expedition to Egypt* then pending, and in the proposed attack on the Northern Powers,† as to free him, in his own breast, completely from any deserved reproach of deserting his post at an hour of distress, and abandoning war measures when they were in an unprovided or inauspicious situation: and it had been his anxious hope and endeavour to leave behind him such a Ministry as would be most agreeable to His Majesty, and who, on all great national points, would act on the same principles as he had acted. It was to forward this his favourite purpose that he had pledged himself, but *himself singly,* to advise and support the present Ministry. This pledge he considered as solemnly binding, not redeemable by any lapse of time, nor ever to be cancelled without the *express consent* of Mr. Addington. He perhaps had, in the first instance, gone too far, and pledged himself too deeply; and his Parliamentary conduct during the last session was to be explained by the strict and solemn engagement into which he had entered. He owned he was often very sorry to feel it incumbent on him to support measures he could not wholly approve; sorry, not for peace, but for a peace made in

* Under Sir R. Abercromby, who landed at Alexandria on the 7th March, 1801, and was completely successful.

† The result was Nelson's victory at Copenhagen, which, with the death of the Emperor Paul, broke up the Northern Coalition.

such an unskilful, hasty, and conceding way. That, had
he remained in power, he felt it would have been necessary, at all events, to recur to a pacific negotiation
(and his facility respecting the Naval Armistice * proved
this), but he also felt that it either would have failed
entirely, or terminated in a Treaty very different from
that signed at Amiens. That defective, however, as this
Treaty was, and inadequate to the high situation in
which the country then stood, he at the time thought
he saw means of turning it to advantage, and confessed
he had entertained the idea, that if we, whilst observing
faithfully and honourably the stipulations of the Treaty,
had not been in such haste to disarm, but continued to
have worn a war aspect as long as any doubtful points
remained, and indicated plainly to Buonaparte that we
had the means and determination to resist France, if
France did not with equal good faith abide by her re-
gulations, Buonaparte would have confined his ambition
to Continental encroachments : probably he would have
exercised it in a very unjustifiable and oppressive manner, yet that he would not have done it in so very outrageous a one as necessarily to call forth the interposition of Great Britain ; with whom he (Pitt) was also
then induced to suppose Buonaparte would be glad to
preserve peace, and, by forming commercial connexions,
and establishing a commercial intercourse, share with
her the trade of the world. In short, that Buonaparte
would have been wise and moderate enough to be satisfied with the great advantages he had obtained by the
peace, and, by availing himself of them judiciously,
have gained popularity and secured his authority. It
was under this notion that he had defended the forbearance of Ministers.

Canning asked him, after hearing this, whether he did
not now acknowledge that he was grossly mistaken with
respect both to Buonaparte's wisdom and his modera-

---

* Negotiations for a naval armistice were entered into between the British
Government and the First Consul in Sept. 1800. They lasted a month, and
fell to the ground, Buonaparte wishing to introduce a clause which would
enable him to throw supplies into Egypt.

tion; and again, whether his having countenanced forbearance in the present Ministers had not been mistaken by them; and if they had not construed it into an
opinion that, on one side, the Continent should be
wholly abandoned, and, on the other, have induced them
to act towards France with the most unbecoming and
degrading complaisance, by making a system of what he
intended only as an expedient, or at most as an experiment, and thus exposed the country to insults, and to all
the dangerous consequences of bearing insults from an
arbitrary, daring, hostile power. Pitt admitted they
had. Canning further urged, whether their dangerous
consequences were not, even at this present moment,
pressing very hard on us; and whether the mandatory
representations of France respecting the Press * and the
Emigrants, (demands which bore directly on the independence and honour of this country,) without adverting to the formation of the Italian Republic, the partition of the German Empire, the annexion of Piedmont
to France, and the dictating a government to Switzerland, did not place us in the fearful dilemma either of
resuming a state of war, or of bearing insult after insult,
practised on ourselves and on Europe, till such time as
France should feel herself quite ripe and able to crush
us. To this Pitt also assented.

The conclusion then, Canning observed, to be drawn
was, that if measures perfectly different from those now
promised were not adopted, the country would be placed
in a most perilous situation. *"Yes."* "But is it within
the compass of the abilities of the present Cabinet, even
supposing the principle to be in them to effect this, to
assume a character of resolution and vigour sufficient to
awe Buonaparte, and induce him to alter his plans?"
"No." "But if we suppose in him, which from every
thing we observe and hear is proved almost to a certainty, a decided *malus animus,* a rooted determination

---

* August 17th, 1802, Monsieur Otto sent in to Lord Hawkesbury a note
of haughty remonstrance, requesting that the attacks of the Press on the
French Government should be put a stop to; and that the members of the
French Royal Family, and other distinguished emigrants, should be sent out
of His Majesty's dominions.

to fall on this country the moment he is ready, are the present Ministers then of sufficient powers to meet the event—to become *war Ministers* and directors of such a war—still less to serve, possibly to save, the country?" —then should there not be a change of Ministers?" "*Yes.*" "Is not then the time arrived when you, Pitt, are called upon, by the strongest and most paramount of all duties, to come forward and resume your position?" "I do not deny it; I will not affect a childish modesty; but recollect what I have just said—I stand pledged; I make no scruple of owning that I am ambitious—but my ambition is *character*, not office. I may have engaged myself inconsiderately, but I am irrecoverably engaged." "You nevertheless admit, that at this moment it is a duty for you to resume office?" "*I do.*" "And that you are withheld from performing it, solely from the solemn engagements you say you have contracted?" "*Yes.*" "But you said these engagements could be dissolved, if Mr. Addington chose it?" "*Most certainly.*" "Does it not then follow, that it is also a duty in you to apply to Mr. Addington to release you from them? He has all along declared he looked upon himself as your *locum tenens*, and ready to resign his office back to you, whenever the country or you require it at his hands." "Not *distinctly* this, in any conversation with me; but something, I own, very *similar* to it." "I repeat, therefore, is it not your duty, after the sentiments you have avowed, and the dangers you admit the country to be in, to require this release from him?" "I cannot bring myself to do it. It is impossible to prevent its wearing the aspect of caballing and intriguing for power. I may be overfeeling about *character*." "It remains then to ask you, whether, if Addington were voluntarily to offer you his place; or the King, from his proper movement, were to propose it to you; or if Parliament were to call for a change of Ministers; whether in any of these cases you would look upon yourself as freed from your engagements, and accept of office?" "Yes; in either of them, or in any other shape than by my direct and personal application to Mr. Ad-

dington for leave to retract my promise, if any such can
be devised, and I find the country and my friends ready
to range round me." "Of this you can have no doubt."
" It will, however, be absolutely essential for me to be
assured of it. I am well aware, for example, of Lord
Grenville's personal friendship for me; but I am apprehensive we differed so widely in the sentiments we delivered last year in Parliament,* that our public and
political connexion may be loosened." Canning told him
then that Lord Grenville intended very soon visiting
him at Walmer, and that then he would hear from Lord
Grenville himself how much he was under an error.

This is the substance of what passed between Mr.
Pitt and Canning (one of his most confidential friends)
during an intercourse of six weeks, in September and
October last. He continued to state, that Lord Grenville
went to Walmer soon after. He and Pitt had a free
and unreserved exchange of their ideas and opinions on
the present position of public affairs; and finding that
they now agreed most perfectly on all of them, Lord
Grenville (informed of what had passed) declared, in the
most express terms, that, whenever Pitt would resume
the lead in the King's councils, he (Lord Grenville) was
ready to support him most strenuously and invariably;
that he would do it with the same zeal and assiduity,
whether in or out of Office, as might best suit Pitt's
arrangements; and he entreated Pitt to consider what
he now said as the truest and most genuine description
of his wishes and feelings. After saying this much of
himself, he ventured to promise the same for his brother
Thomas; and Lord Spencer undertook to pledge himself,
that, if Pitt would again take office, *all* his friends would
support his Government with the whole of their weight
and influence, without fettering him in the first instance
with any engagements for them, and without any expectation of being brought with him into Office on his first
return to power. Their sole object was to see him in

---

* In the debates on the Peace of Amiens, Mr. Pitt defended it on general
grounds ; but Lord Grenville severely censured the terms, and voted against
the Address in the House of Lords.

power, and to maintain him in it to the full extent of their means.

This naturally led to a conversation similar to that which is already related, and which ended in the same assurances and expressions on the part of Pitt—of his disapprobation of what is going on, his readiness to take Office, but coupled with the same invincible objection to make the *first move* towards it himself. It was suggested to him, that he might at least abstain from giving his advice to the present Ministers when asked; that this would be an intimation of his general sentiments. To this he replied, it would not be an intimation, but a distinct and clear declaration that he meant to withhold his support, and amount precisely in its effect to his saying what he never would say, either directly or by implication, "the time was come when Addington should retire, and he take his place;" that he certainly should keep out of the way of being advised with on *every* measure of Cabinet, but he could not refuse his advice on any abstract question, when asked. All he could say was, that if, after having asked his opinion, it was not followed, he certainly should not consider himself bound to support any other than his own, and would maintain that as well in as out of Parliament. After obtaining this knowledge of the state of Pitt's mind upon the situation of public affairs, and his present disposition as to the acceptance of Office, it became a matter of deliberation how to remove the great obstacle which impeded the accomplishment of so desirable an event, and also how to obviate those which in the course of the business might arise on the part of the King.

In regard to the first, the only three modes which could be devised have already been pointed out. First, either by making Mr. Addington's resignation a voluntary act. Secondly, the producing it through the King's authority. Thirdly, by forcing him to it through the intervention of Parliament.

The first was in my opinion the most desirable, but also the most difficult, since no one but Pitt himself had a right to touch on the subject to Addington. It could scarcely be expected that any members of this Ministry, however different their opinions might be from his, would address themselves to him on a point which must, either immediately or eventually, lead to *their* loss of Office. No private or intimate friend of his could be found likely to undertake so unpleasant a commission, and it could not be undertaken by a common acquaintance. It was, indeed, once in contemplation to draw up a paper, to be signed by several independent members of all descriptions of each House, calculated to impress Mr. Addington with the necessity that now existed for his removing from Office, and making room for Mr. Pitt; and that this should be sent to him, not as from any particular person, but from several who thought and felt alikè: but, on consideration, this was found liable to many objections. In the first instance, as it would tend to premature publicity, and that in its shape and manner it would bear rather the form of a conspiracy and cabal than of a grave and patriotic representation.

On the second (namely, the doing it by the King's authority,) the difficulties were as great, since this could only be attained by representing to the King, in the closet, the necessity of removing Mr. Addington, and reinstating Mr. Pitt; and such an audience, it is well known, would produce (let who will ask it) a very different effect on His Majesty's mind from that intended.

The third and last mode, therefore, was the only one deemed practicable; and it was determined, after much discussion amongst Pitt's friends (unknown to Pitt, at least uncommunicated to him,) that, on the first day of the Session, notice should be given of a motion to be made on that day fortnight, that if, before that period, no additional strength should have been given to His Majesty's Councils, the state of public affairs was become such as to make it necessary to move an Address to the Crown on the subject. Movers and seconders were thought of in both Houses; and this part of the business, if nothing happens before the meeting of Parliament to render it unnecessary, is a measure determined on.

The remaining difficulty, and that not a small one, was the making easy and palatable to the King a step that, however consonant it might be to His Majesty's concealed but real sentiments, yet was evidently hostile to the Government he had chosen, and apparently protected. It was still more important that it should be done in a way not to irritate his mind, or affect his health; and it was on this point that it was thought proper to apply to me partly for advice, and partly because it was supposed I might be usefully employed in it.

To smooth the way, (it would, indeed, have been an insurmountable stumblingblock,) Canning said that the Catholic Question was to be completely abandoned, and that both Pitt and Lord Grenville were ready to declare they considered it as gone by and dead; that the strongest assurances of this might be given to the King.

That the idea was not the displacing one set of men for the purpose of bringing in another, but to blend the two Administrations as far as was possible, and to do every thing that was fair and honourable towards Mr. Addington and those who came in with him, by giving them titles, places of emolument, or by letting them remain in the offices they now held. That the end was, to *stop*, while it was yet time, the *mischiefs* that had ensued, and must ensue, from pursuing measures of concession to France, and to give the country its right tone, and restore it to its right level and rank, both at home and abroad. That this did not mean war, but only the wearing an aspect of preparation and defence, and holding such a language of firmness, spirit, and dignity as became a great nation, and which, when it was held judiciously and decently, ever prevented, and never produced, hostilities, particularly from such a character as Buonaparte, who, if he found we bore his insults and arrogance, would attack us much sooner than if we made it appear to him that we knew the nature of an insult, and would not be insulted with impunity.

This being promised, it was proposed to get at the King through the Duke of York, as the person who could approach His Majesty with the greatest facility, and the Prince, with whom the King was most in the habit of discoursing on political economy. It was therefore asked me through Canning, if I had any objection to wait on the Duke of York, and explain to His Royal Highness so much of what I had heard as would enable him to lay the substance of it before His Majesty; thus, to get at the King's feelings on the subject, and to prepare him for the measure which it was in agitation to take in Parliament. I was too well acquainted with the Duke of York's opinions and sentiments, too much in the habit of discoursing freely and confidentially with His Royal Highness, to have any difficulty in seeing him on this occasion. I was also deeply impressed with the importance of the subject, and fully convinced of the indispensable necessity of the measure itself, or of one similar to it. I had not also to learn that the King was infinitely hurt at what was going on ; that he lamented most feelingly the tame and submissive tone we held to France; and that, both on the peace itself, and what had arisen out of it, his feelings were as strong as possible. But I had my doubts, and I expressed them, as to the King's being ever again cordially disposed to take Pitt, and, above all, Lord Grenville, into Office. I was told, (and an authority was quoted, though not named, but of the veracity of which Pitt himself was satisfied when he heard it,) that the King lately had often been heard to express his regret that Pitt was not now in Office, and his fears that his ill state of health would disable him from ever resuming it. That, as for Lord Grenville, he is himself persuaded, but from reasons known to himself, and which he did not explain, that his peace is now made at Windsor, and that the moment it is known he has abandoned the Catholic Question, every objection to him will cease.

When I had heard all I have now put on paper (and I had listened to it with the utmost attention), I asked Canning whether it was from himself alone, or in the name of others as well as himself that he had spoken.

He said, he spoke the sentiments of *all* those who were

anxious to restore Mr. Pitt to power, but in the name
only of some few (he named them) to whom the choice
of means, the best calculated to effect it, had been confided. " My coming to you is at their desire, and it is
on their behalf that I request that you would see the Duke
of York ; and I am also commissioned to desire you to
assist at such meetings as may be hereafter held by them
on this and other public subjects." I replied, that I was
so convinced of the absolute necessity of Mr. Pitt's resuming office, that I was very ready to see the Duke of
York, if it was supposed my doing so could at all contribute to so desirable an end ; but that I would not go to
him as deputed by any man or set of men, or as for any
special purpose, but simply as one whom he admitted to
his confidence. That this would only change the mode
of doing what they wished, as far as related to myself,
but that the end proposed by them would be precisely the
same; for I would communicate to the Duke of York
historically, and as from certain authority, every thing
which was suggested to me by them, or which suggested
itself to me as the most likely to prevail on him to mention the matter to the King. That I doubted of success
on this point, as I knew how very cautious the Duke of
York was in speaking to His Majesty on any point relative to his Ministers; and that, unless the King began, I
was nearly sure he would not bring the subject on.
That, in regard to assisting at their conferences, I had
no scruple to say, my opinion and my sentiments went
heartily with them, as well as my fears and anxieties;
that I saw the evil, and the only chance of checking it,
exactly as they did; and, perhaps, from having lived a
great deal on the Continent, and knowing it more, I saw
it still more strongly ; and that, as my wishes most warmly
coincided with theirs, so long as they acted on the same
principles, and pursued the same ends they now professed,
—but that I declined attending any conferences, from the
same reasons I declined attending Parliament,—I should
ever be found ready to advise, or act, in *my individual
capacity*, as far as I was able, when called upon. That
beyond this I would not undertake to go; since such a

line of conduct was the only one I was disposed for, and, indeed, equal to adopt.

MONDAY, NOVEMBER 1.—I waited on the Duke of York at the Horse-Guards. The conversation of itself very soon took a turn on his part which gave me an opportunity of introducing, unaffectedly, what I had to say. His Royal Highness spoke with great anxiety and alarm on the situation of affairs, and deplored the deficiency of ability and want of vigour in the present Administration to oppose and resent the insolence of France. After agreeing with him fully on both of these points, I said, I, however, was happy to hear and to be able to tell His Royal Highness, from unquestionable authority, that Mr. Pitt felt and thought precisely the same, and that he was now become fully convinced that it was his duty to accept Office. I then mentioned what I knew to be the state of Pitt's mind upon the present situation of public affairs, and of his present disposition as to the acceptance of Office, if it should be proposed to him. The Duke expressed great satisfaction at it; declared Mr. Pitt must come in, that it was impossible he should not; that the public called for him, and would force Mr. Addington to give way. He then mentioned some proofs that this was the public wish, from what passed at a dinner given on the opening of the West-India Docks, and from several things he had heard Brook Watson and others say. In reply, I observed, that this might ultimately be the case, and the public *might force* Mr. Pitt in, and Mr. Addington out; but that must be a slow mode of producing what was wanted immediately; that delay might realize the danger so highly apprehended; besides, the doing this through the public must necessarily be a matter of publicity, and if any opposition was attempted (as it was but natural to suppose there would be) on the part of Mr. Addington and his friends, it would give a handle for the disaffected and seditious to come forward. It therefore, in my mind, though a sure and necessary

step, should be reserved for the last resort. In this the
Duke acquiesced. It would, I observed, be infinitely
more desirable if it could be intimated to Mr. Addington that such a step was in contemplation, and would
be taken ; and, as Mr. Pitt was known to be disposed to resume Office, to represent to Mr. Addington
how much honour he would acquire by so disinterested
a measure as a voluntary resignation, and how much
satisfaction to his mind from the confusion and disputes
he would be the cause of preventing by it. The Duke
agreed in this, but said he feared Mr. Addington was
too vain to appreciate justly either the limits of his own
abilities, or the extent of the danger; that, however, it
was manifest that some of Mr. Addington's friends were
more awake to both, and that he had reason to believe
Lord Auckland and Lord Hobart were prepared to withdraw from him ; that if he (Addington) saw this, he
would, perhaps, be frightened into resignation.

I said his resignation would be certainly a very desirable event, but I, in my individual and particular feelings, should consider it as an unfortunate one, if it should
tend to distress and hurt the King ; that the country
would be but *half* saved, if this was to happen. The
Duke said, " You well know we never talk to His Majesty on public affairs ; but, from the few things I have
heard him say, I cannot but suppose His Majesty considers the state of them to be very humiliating to this
country." " Perhaps then," I said, " if His Majesty
also knew that Mr. Pitt had *entirely given up the Catholic Question*, his return to Office would be even an agreeable circumstance to him ; " and I then stated to the
Duke of York the certainty I was under that this was
the case. " It is a great point, certainly," replied the
Duke, " but I rather think His Majesty bears no great
ill-will towards those who were the original promoters
of it ; if he did, he would have opposed Lord Castlereagh's having a place in the Cabinet : but although,"
continued the Duke of York, " Mr. Pitt abandons the
Catholic Question, what will those who supported it, in
common with him, do ? The Duke of Cumberland said

the other day, that Pitt and Lord Grenville were on the coldest terms, and seldom saw each other." This gave me an opportunity of saying what I knew of Lord Grenville's sentiments, and of his late visit at Walmer, and I related it to the Duke of York nearly as it was to me by Canning. The Duke expressed much satisfaction at this, and again asserted, with vehemence, the indispensable necessity of Mr. Pitt's coming in. I again repeated that the first wish in my mind certainly was, that this event should happen; but it would cease to be my wish, and become my fear, if I was not quite sure it could be brought about in a way which not only would not displease His Majesty, but which would clearly and distinctly prove that those who promoted it had it at heart as their governing principle, to do what they thought was agreeable to His Majesty, and most consonant to his feelings. The Duke, as he always does when the King's name is mentioned, avoided any explicit answer, and, on my urging the point still further, he said, with a good deal of reserve and embarrassment, that he wished as much as I appeared to do, that His Majesty should be informed early of what was going forward, and be informed of it fairly and impartially; that it was not in his power to do this; all he could undertake was, that if any occasion offered, either in the common course of conversation, or when he was doing official business with His Majesty, that if I would authorize him to mention it, he most certainly would. With this I was satisfied, and pressed the point no further on him. Before I ended my visit, the Duke expressed a desire I would see him again if I obtained any more information on this very important subject.

The day after this conversation passed, it was thought right to draw up a paper, to be signed, if approved, by persons of eminence in different public avocations in each House of Parliament, to be presented by them to Mr. Addington; its object, as will appear from the paper itself, was to prevail on him to remove spontaneously, and prevent the matter being brought before the public.

[As this paper was altered, and appears afterwards in its amended shape, I have omitted the first copy here, the sense of it being given by Lord M.]

When this paper was shewn to me, I observed on the propriety of my reading it to the Duke of York, not only because such a confidence, after what had passed, was due to him, but from its containing in substance the whole marrow of the business ; and, by putting him in possession at once of the great end to be obtained, would enable him, better than anything I could say or suggest, to explain it to His Majesty, and prepare his mind for the step, in case the Duke of York should ever have an opportunity or an inclination so to do ; and I carried it to His Royal Highness, at the Horse-Guards, on Wednesday, November 3rd.

I found the subject had made considerable impression on him. In my last interview with him, he had heard me, indeed, with great attention; but he was then rather cautious and reserved in his answers, carefully avoiding remarks, or giving advice, and every thing looking like participation. Now, he was eager to renew the subject, anxious to know what I had to say, strong in the expression of his opinions as to the absolute necessity of a change, and in his wishes that means could be devised to produce one, without creating great dissensions and dangerous resistance. He heard the paper attentively ; and, when I had finished, said it was ably written, but that he was apprehensive that, however respectably signed, it would not have any effect on Mr. Addington ; and that he could not help imagining that, though very cautiously and carefully drawn up, it might be so represented as to appear to the country an unconstitutional measure, and to His Majesty as trenching on his prerogative.

After dwelling on this, the Duke went on by stating, that, in his opinion, the mode the best calculated for the purpose, and at the same time one which he thought neither the King nor the country could misconceive, would be, that some person or persons high in rank, independent in character and fortune, should see Mr.

Addington, and distinctly and clearly state to him the contents of this paper; adding, that they did it with the most friendly views towards him, and to prevent the subject being brought forward in Parliament. He named the Dukes of Bridgewater, Marlborough, and Beaufort, and Lord Stafford, as persons of the description he meant ; at the same time that he scarce could suppose either of them would undertake so difficult and disagreeable a task. That it would perhaps be easier to find among Mr. Addington's friends one who might be prevailed upon to break the matter to him; or that it might be imparted to him by some one of his colleagues in Office, who saw the situation of the country in its true light, and who was wise and disinterested enough to urge such wholesome advice. The Duke, after insisting on this, as by far the best way to proceed, and having during the whole time nearly taken the conversation on himself, begged me to recollect that he was talking to me quite as a private and as a confidential friend. He entreated me never to commit him, and ended by giving me the strongest assurances that he would do every thing in his power to smooth the business, though it was of the last consequence to him that it never should be supposed he was in any shape concerned in it. For this I readily engaged myself, and, when I had to relate what had passed, I contented myself with saying that His Royal Highness had heard me with great attention, and approved the language of the paper ; but I added, as an inference I had drawn from his manner, that he did not quite approve the mode of bringing it forward. And this, by a very natural question which was put to me, gave me an opportunity of mentioning, as from myself, the advice and opinion he had given ; and I urged it strongly as a more eligible and less exceptionable method.

It was agreed that it would be judicious at least to try it first; and, after some deliberation, Lord Eldon, the Chancellor, was pitched on as the only person at all fit to be trusted with so delicate and important a commission. It was settled, that the communication to him should be confined simply to a faithful picture of the dangers which threatened the country, the necessity of Pitt's resuming Office, and the certainty that it would be called for early in the session. This communication was made on Saturday the 6th Noveember, and was received by the Chancellor with the utmost interest and satisfaction. And, though he evidently saw something behind, and guessed what it was, he did not press for anything beyond what was agreed to be said to him; nor was any answer or acknowledgment of an intention to act pressed for from him.

It was left to operate in his mind, and there were strong symptoms of its working very kindly.

NOVEMBER 11.—The two letters which follow will state the further progress of this transaction, or rather, an unexpected impediment that has arisen in it—not at all unexpected indeed by me; neither did it take the others *quite* by surprise, as on the morning I left London (Nov. 4th), Canning informed me that he had received some accounts which gave him uneasiness as to the steadiness of Lord Grenville, and alarmed him lest he should depart in the end from what he had said at Walmer, and return to his old family politics.

" He cannot be persuaded," added Canning, " but that Lord Buckingham would be a good and popular Prime Minister ; and, whenever his family come upon him with this idea, it bears down before it every other consideration."

I said this was nothing new to me; that I had been convinced of it for many years; and that although I believed Lord Grenville and his party had rather see Pitt First Minister, than either Addington or Fox, or any indifferent person, yet that they had much rather see Lord Buckingham First Minister than Pitt. This is necessary to explain a part of the letters which follow.

LETTER FROM MR. CANNING TO LORD MALMESBURY.

Dogmersfield, Tuesday, 9th Nov. 1802.

MY DEAR LORD MALMESBURY,—I reached the place of my first destination (Dropmore) from town on Sunday, and found the master of the house just returned from a family and party conclave, held at his eldest brother's house (Stowe), consisting of the three brothers* and Lord Spencer; the result of which has completely justified the apprehensions which I told you I had begun to entertain, from my correspondent's last letters, that his counsellors would induce him to depart from the resolution which he had avowed, and either to insist on a more thorough change, or to decline having any part for himself, or those belonging to him, in the arrangement.

It turns out just so. He stated to me, with the utmost frankness, that though his own opinion remained nearly the same, and though for himself he would willingly have sacrificed any feelings of reluctance to a compromise, yet he owed the utmost deference to the opinions of those who had acted with him for the last eighteen months; that *they* thought he could not, without disgracing himself, consent to have anything to do with Addington and his coadjutors, or to sit in any council of which *they* should form a part; and that (he would fairly own) he found the question, which *he on his part had agreed to consider as given up, was by no means so readily to be put aside by others*, though there was, on the other hand, no sort of desire to push it to extremity now, or at any other time. And that upon all these grounds he had nothing left for him to do, but to desire that he and his might be considered as nothing in any arrangement which might be made; and he proposed to write to this effect to Bath, by yesterday's post.

He assured me, however, at the same time, that though all personal *interest* on his part, and that of his friends, in the success of the projects which we had

* Lords Buckingham, Grenville, and T. Grenville.

talked over together, was thus entirely done away, he nor they were not at all the less anxious for the success of those projects, nor would less readily lend what assistance they could to their accomplishment. The return of the *one person** they still unanimously considered as essential, and would promote it as far as lay in their power, though they could not bring themselves to think of returning with him *into such company.* I am sorry, but not much surprised, at this determination, and still less inclined to blame it, for (whatever else it be) it is at least manly and consistent. At first, it struck me as throwing insuperable obstacles in the way of our progress; but upon mature reflection, and after discussing the matter fully with Leveson and Morpeth here, our joint opinion is, that it affords *greater feasibility* for the return of the *one person* (supposing him not to start at the *imputable* shabbiness of returning alone), inasmuch as it takes away most of the difficulties of jarring alarms, and must make the concession on the part of those who must give way much less mortifying.† I write in this sense to Bath to-day. At the same time, we are not without hopes that the imperfections of such an arrangement might be only temporary; that, supposing the *most formidable* crisis to arise some months hence, it would then be possible for the *one person* to complete it much more civilly, and with much better public effect, than if the whole were done at once at this moment.

All this is for your private information. How much of it need transpire to the quarter‡ where you are pledged to any such further communication as you might think worth making, you must judge. If you do not think such a communication necessary, the best way of making it is, (as it strikes me,) not as anything new, but as a further and more satisfactory confirmation of the truth of what you had hinted before, that those persons would not put themselves *in the way;* that their

---

* Mr. Pitt.

† To Addington, for whom it would be less mortifying to give way to Pitt alone, than to Pitt and Lord Grenville.

‡ The Duke of York.

sole object was to see the *one person* in his place; and,
so far from desiring to be considered with him, they
were determined not to be included in any arrangement,
knowing well the difficulties that must attend it, and
desirous that an object so salutary should meet with no
impediment, or even delay, from any consideration
personal to them. This sounds (as in truth it is) magnanimous; and if there be anywhere any lurking dislike, or distrust of any of them, which would create a
hesitation about a change in which they were to be
brought forward, this declaration, which you may now
state positively and confidently, must effectually remove
it.

What I am more doubtful about is, whether it is
necessary for you to say anything about *the question,**
which we thought at an end, but which (as I have said)
still exists in sufficient force to form a part of the disinclination which these persons feel to taking such a
part as was first intended. You best know how far you
gave it to be understood that they were quite prepared
to abandon it. You certainly were authorized by me,
and I by them, so to understand them. It would not
be fair that this impression should be left to work, if it
is a false one; yet it is not worth while to excite
unpleasant feelings, by making any *unnecessary* communication upon it. Of this you must judge. But if the
communication is made necessary by any stress laid,
either in the manner of mentioning or of receiving the
former statement, then I am desired to say, that the
following is the form of words in which the actual state
of these persons' minds upon that question would be
truly expressed.

Supposing an arrangement made, in other respects
such as that they could hope to be of use by taking a
share in, they would feel as to *that question a sincere
desire to find, if possible, such a solution of it as might
be satisfactory to the King, and at the same time not inconsistent with the maintenance of their public characters.*

This you see leads to nothing, and is necessary there-

* The Catholic Question.

fore only, if a contrary impression has been taken which might lead to offers, and those offers to a discussion wholly unexpected, and such as would justify the offerer in considering himself as having been deceived ; otherwise it need only be stated (if at all) as one of the ingredients which go to making up their minds not to put themselves forward on the present occasion.

Let me know what you think of all this, and how much of it you communicate.　　　GEORGE CANNING.

Bath, Friday, Nov. 12th, 1802.

MY DEAR CANNING,—I was much more surprised when I heard what you related to me as having passed between Pitt and Lord Grenville at Walmer, than at what you now tell me was said to you on Sunday last at Dropmore; but as you spoke to me in Spring Gardens from authority, and in Lord Grenville's name, I did not at that time feel at liberty to admit a doubt or express an opinion. I agree with you, that what he now says is perfectly consistent with every part of his past public conduct and known principles, except (and it is a most important exception) with *what he declared at Walmer*, and remember *this was his last profession of faith ;* that it was clearly and distinctly explained ; and that, considering the firmness of his character and strength of his understanding, it is difficult to find a reason which can justify any qualification of its tenets, much less a deviation from them. The avowal of them (if I understand you right) was not drawn from him by any tricks, either diplomatical or sentimental, but a free and unbiassed act of his own choice. With a provident thinking mind like his, he *must* have foreseen what would inevitably be said to him by the persons he was to meet at Stowe; and, foreseeing it, should he not have been prepared (and he certainly possesses the powers) rather to convert them to *his* doctrines, and *his* purpose, than suffer himself to be *re*converted to theirs? And this, be assured, my dear Canning, is widely different from the wise, prudent, and public-spirited plan you have traced out. I am truly sorry for it, as I cannot but apprehend the non-concurrence, even the neutrality of this party will not only impede the measure itself in its progress, but be felt very forcibly by *the person* on whom the whole rests. Pitt is not now here, but he returns on Sunday; and I am not sure he could receive your letter before he went, though he certainly did that from Dropmore.

I sincerely wish I may be mistaken in my fears, and that you and my two young friends* may be right; for every day, and every hour of the day, convinces me more and more of the immense importance of replacing the Government of this country in the hands it. was in two years ago.

It seems to me quite necessary to communicate something to the Duke of York, and, in this communication, that it is impossible to sink *the question* entirely. The Duke of York expects to hear from me; and what you now write to me relative to it differs so completely from what I was authorized to say in my first interview, that, although I did not then commit my authority, I spoke so very plain, that, both as a matter of policy and as one of fair and honourable dealing, it is indispensable that I should not let him remain with the impression I then gave him, much less that he should state it as a *point agreed on* elsewhere. But I will not write at all till I hear again from you, and then do it in the way and in the words you recommend. The delay in writing will be of no consequence, as he never visits the King in the country, and the King will not be in town till Wednesday next.

The account you sent me by Ross of the result of your conference on Saturday last, was much more satisfactory than what passed at Dropmore. It will, I do not doubt, operate, and be productive of very good effects. I am anxious to hear more from you, though perhaps you will have little more to say before the meeting. At all events, pray lose no time in answering this letter, or rather that part of it which relates to what I am to send to the Duke.

* Lords G. Leveson and Morpeth.

It has occurred to me, just as I am finishing my letter, that as the Duke told me in the course of our last conference, that his father, he thought, had no great remaining ill-will towards the favourers of *the question*, (quoting Lord Castlereagh's coming into the Cabinet as a proof,) that I may introduce what I have to state of the change in Lord Grenville's sentiments by reminding him of this, and by deducing from it, that this change cannot be very material, although it is my duty to inform him of it, and then employ the words in your letter. It is quite unnecessary to take any other notice of anything that passed at the conclave, or even that it has taken place, as, although it does, in my mind, very deeply affect our main object, yet it has nothing to do with that part in it which we wish to distribute to the Duke, and with the King it would, I fancy, rather facilitate than impede.

Don't be apprehensive, from anything I have said, that I shall speak with acrimony of Grenville, or in a way as if I blamed him, and wished others to do the same. It is only in writing to *you* that I do not hold it necessary to suppress this feeling, or conceal my opinion.

Yours, &c.   MALMESBURY.

Before this letter reached Canning, I received another from him, as follows:—

Dogmersfield, Friday, Nov. 12th, 1802.

MY DEAR LORD MALMESBURY,—I return to town to-morrow, and shall be there till the day (Thursday or Friday next) on which I am to meet Pitt at Dropmore, on his return to town.

From town, I shall probably be able to tell you in a day or two what is the prospect of success in obtaining signatures, or what (supposing that desperate) is the substitution for that part of the plan. In the mean time, I send you a corrected copy of the paper, which, you will observe, is so framed, as that, in the case of

signatures not being to be had, it could be given in as a
sort of notice to Addington of the intention to make
him quit, in order to obviate the objection of taking him
by surprise. Tell me what you think of this, in case
the other should not prove feasible; not imagining,
however, that we have any thought of giving it up, if
it can be managed. Is not such a notice, taking it for
nothing better, better than nothing to precede the Parliamentary measure? Give me, and *get* me an opinion.

I commit the paper to your discretion. If signable
people should fall in your way, or if unsignable, but
such as would be likely to be swayed by understanding
the whole measure as thoroughly as this explains it,
use it.

If you write early in the week (which pray do) direct
to me at Lothian's Hotel.   Ever, &c.   G. C.

To this I wrote the following answer:—

Bath, Sunday, Nov. 14th, 1802.

MY DEAR CANNING,—I will not lose a moment in answering yours of the 12th. According to your desire, I
direct to Lothian's Hotel.

The correct copy you inclosed appears to me to be
perfect, and well calculated for either of the purposes
you state. I fear you will never obtain a sufficient
number of such names as alone can command effect, and
that ultimately you must have recourse to the common
legal practice of giving notice to quit, before you proceed
to move for a writ of ejectment.

The signatures certainly would be the preferable mode;
but it seems very difficult to collect them in time, or,
indeed, at all, without the risk of a publicity which might
mar the whole.

Lords Camden, Carrington, and G. Rose are here;
also the Earls of Essex and Buckinghamshire. The first
three would, I conceive, be *certain* followers; but would
not assist in the present stage of the business, either by
advice, or use influence. Lord Essex is, I have little

doubt, eager for the event; and Lord Buckinghamshire, of course, quite the contrary. Besides these, I have not seen or met any one of sufficient consequence, to ask whether they can write their names or not.

I have not had any opportunity yet of talking with Pitt, who returned from a distant part of the country yesterday. I shall see him on Tuesday or Wednesday at dinner, and wish, by return of post, you would tell me how far you think it expedient for me to go;—if beyond what we agreed on in London, and how far beyond it. If you mean that, by *getting* you an opinion, I should endeavour to learn *his*, I must necessarily enter much deeper into the subject than, at the time, we thought advisable.

Remember that on this point, and on what made the subject of your last letter, I await your answer.

Ever yours, &c. (Signed) MALMESBURY.

On Monday I received, by the coach, the following letter and inclosure:—

Lothian's Hotel, Sunday, Nov. 14th, 1802.

MY DEAR LORD M.,—I found your letter on my arrival in town last night. I have not time to say anything in answer to it; but I am anxious to transmit to you a newly-corrected copy of the paper, in the hope of its reaching you before you have made use of that which I sent you on Friday. By comparing the two copies, you will see that the new alterations are made almost wholly with the view of softening passages and expressions, so as to fit them for the inspection of the father,* to whom they will very probably be submitted in the first instance; and the mention of *the question* is introduced in a way which I think you will approve; at once quieting, without committing, one party, and dutiful and flattering to the other; while, at the same time, it makes the transmission of the duplicate of the paper to Pitt perfectly natural and necessary, which before looked, perhaps,

* The King.

too much like the threat which it is, *in fact,* intended to be.

Return me the other copy.

Yours, &c. G. C.

(Copy.)

AT a moment of unprecedented embarrassment and public anxiety, it is hoped that the Chancellor of the Exchequer will not consider the communication contained in this paper as being, either in intention or in substance, in the smallest degree personally disrespectful to him.

Nothing but motives of a very different nature could have induced the persons who transmit it to him to take this mode of expressing to him their sentiments on the present state and prospects of public affairs; sentiments which, as they feel them very deeply, and in common (as they sincerely believe) with a very large proportion of the public, they think themselves bound to communicate to him without reserve, previous to the opening of the session.

It appears to them unnecessary to dwell on the actual situation of affairs.

It is but too evident, that instead of having derived from the conclusion of the late war those blessings of tranquillity, economy, and confidence, which have usually attended the restoration of peace, the country finds itself in a state which necessarily calls for expensive preparation, a state of increasing insecurity and of continual alarm.

Without wishing to seek for any other cause for this state of things, beside that which is to be found in the unexampled situation and conduct of France with regard to other nations, it is the entire persuasion of all those who are parties to this statement, that the only method of tranquillizing the apprehensions and anxiety which generally prevail, and of enabling this country to meet with advantage the dangers which threaten it, would be by the administration of the Government being replaced in the hands of Mr. Pitt.

This would, as they think, afford the best chance of averting war.

And they are confident that it would offer almost the only hope of carrying it on, if unavoidable, with that vigour and success which can arise only from unanimity at home, and of reconciling the great mass of the people to those burdens and difficulties with which it must necessarily be attended.

In stating this proposition to Mr. Addington, they know and appreciate all the advantage which it derives from its conformity with those opinions and wishes which he is understood to have acknowledged, without reserve, in the first moments of his appointment, and which the increase of the public dangers must still more strongly have impressed upon his mind.

It is with the view of offering to him an honourable opportunity of declaring and acting upon those opinions and wishes, that they have taken the liberty to make to him this communication.

They have been the rather induced to do so in this way, and at this moment, because in addition to what they themselves feel, and believe Mr. Addington to feel, of the benefit which would be derived to the country, under the exigency of times like the present, from the restoration of the invaluable services of his predecessor; and in addition to what they know of the prevalence of the same feeling in their respective neighbourhoods, and (in so far as individuals can collect or estimate a national sentiment) throughout the nation at large; there is every reason to apprehend, from the present state of parties and opinions in Parliament, that this particular subject must, in all probability (as things now stand), be brought forward *there* as matter of distinct and very early discussion.

And they are unfeignedly anxious that Mr. Addington, instead of being called upon to meet the public wish, should have it in his power to anticipate it.

They hope and believe that Mr. Addington, in his earnest and sincere endeavours to render to his country the greatest service which it is at the present moment capable of receiving, would not encounter the smallest difficulty from any recurrence to a question, the discussion of which is now laid at rest.

And it is for the purpose of conveying, in the most respectful manner, to Mr. Pitt, this expression of the reliance which is placed upon his dignified sense of duty to his Sovereign and to the public, that they think it right to transmit to him a duplicate of this paper, not feeling themselves at liberty to withhold from him the opinions which they have communicated to Mr. Addington upon a subject in which, as they think, Mr. Pitt's own character (as well as the safety of the country) is deeply involved.

This I answered immediately as follows:—

Bath, Monday, Nov. 15, 1802.

MY DEAR CANNING,—I received your parcel by the coach about an hour ago. The paper, as now amended, certainly meets the great object, as you state, much better than the other. It ought not only to satisfy His Majesty, but the manner of introducing and declaring the intentions respecting the Catholic Question will prevent those who may communicate it to him officially from attempting to renew and awaken his alarms on this sore point, and thus indispose him against any change.

As to the second improvement, that of softening down the threat, it is perhaps a wiser, but it may not be so *sure* a mode of proceeding; but, if you think enough left in it to preserve that character, I am satisfied.

I am eager to hear from you to-morrow; you will, I trust, in the mean while, not disapprove my joining with the three* persons I mentioned yesterday, in endeavouring to persuade Pitt to remain on here, and not attend the opening of Parliament.†

I am, &c.   MALMESBURY.

* Lords Camden and Carrington, and Mr. Rose.
† Parliament was called together on the 16th, and the King's speech delivered on the 23rd November.

On Tuesday, the 16th November, I received the following letter from Canning :—

Lothian's Hotel, Monday, Nov. 15th, 1802.

MY DEAR LORD MALMESBURY,—I trust you will have received the packet in due time, which I took all possible pains to convey to you safely by the mail-coach of yesterday, containing the latest amendments of the paper; which, in that state, the sooner you can communicate to the young person,* and get his opinion (it is *his*, not Pitt's, I intended) upon it, the better. I know it may not be easy to get this, and I state it rather as what I wish than what I expect.

I do not despair quite so much about signatures as you do, and as I did; but to-morrow and Wednesday will probably decide.

We have several names that would do to follow a leader, and, by the time I mention, we shall have made *three* attempts, the success of all of which would set us up; of any two, would help us materially; and the failure of *all* would let us down to the next stage—the presentation—which, however, I am afraid, would be more difficult than the signature. It is not that there are not plenty of wellwishers; but such as would give sufficient weight are not easily to be *found*, and cannot be *sent for*. The first three of the names you mention could be of no use till at a later stage of the business ; but why not Lord Essex ? You know better than I what opportunities you may be able to find of talking with him, and whether he can be talked to safely ; but I think he might do. At all events, I hope he will be up for the meeting; and I think an intimation, to the effect that there would be use in his coming, would do no harm. If, after all, neither imposing signatures nor spokesmen can be had, the last resort is to send the paper unsigned, with something like the enclosed præscript. This, however, is only in case of a last extremity; but as that extremity (if at all) may arrive soon, certainly before there is more than room for one

* The Duke of York.

interchange of letters between Bath and London, perhaps it would be as well to communicate this, as *provided against the worst*, at the same time with the amended paper.

Oh that Pitt could be kept where he is till after Tuesday! This would be worth every thing to us. And there are rumours in town that he means to stay, but I dare not believe any thing so good. If you could find out this, you would do an essential service. Perhaps he may not mention it to me, though I am expecting to hear from him.

With regard to the communication upon *the question*, I really think with you, that it may very well be deferred till you have an opportunity of personal communication. As the persons are out of contemplation for the present, their tenets may be explained at leisure. At present, I am afraid the explanation might create alarm, and be construed to mean more than it does. On this ground, I consented the more readily (for the suggestion was not mine) to reinstate the mention of the question in the papers.

I think this is all that I have to say to you. I will write again on Wednesday.

Ever, dear Lord Malmesbury, &c.　　　G. C.

P.S.—Parma* comes in good time, since it was to come at all ; but, to be sure, it opens a long list of apprehensions and alarms beyond those of which one was already warned.

Is Lord Pembroke returned? and where to be found?

I hope Lady Malmesbury is going on as well as I hear Pitt is.

PROPOSED PRÆSCRIPT (ENCLOSED).

It is thought to be most respectful to Mr. Addington and Mr. Pitt, that the enclosed paper should be trans-

* The infant Duke of Parma dying on the 9th October, the First Consul issued a decree on the 23rd, annexing the province to the French Republic.

mitted to them without the signatures, which are ready to be affixed to it.

The suggestions which it contains are offered, not on behalf of those who would subscribe them, but of the public.

And the consideration which, it is trusted, both Mr. Addington and Mr. Pitt will give to them, must be independent of any weight which they could be supposed to derive from the names of individuals.

To this I replied the same day in the following terms : —

Bath, 16th Nov.

MY DEAR CANNING,—I must answer in a hurry yours of yesterday; the post came in late, and leaves but little time to answer you, and to write (as I must) to the Duke of York. ·

I was puzzled about whose opinion you wished me to get, because, on the particular point you wanted one, the Duke of York had very distinctly given his—viz. " that notice at all events should be given, and much better through a spokesman than in any other way." If I omitted this in my narrative to you, I made you a very imperfect report.

Lord Essex is gone, but I said enough to him to have learnt beyond a doubt that the step will have his full concurrence ; but I really could not trust him with a sight of the paper, as he travels to-morrow with Disbrowe (Lord Hobart's* brother-in-law).

If a spokesman and signatures fail, by all means employ the *præscript*. I am not quite sure it would not come with still greater effect, by leaving Mr. Addington's imagination to suppose signatures were more numerous and more *tremendous* than those you are sure of.

I have conformed, and shall conform strictly to what you say, in any conversation I may have with Mr. Pitt: and in the mean while I have great satisfaction in

* Lord Hobart formed part of Addington's Administration.

assuring you, that he will decidedly stay on here. It has the entire approbation of his three friends. Lord Camden said, that it was *politically* most right for him, and that he had very much at heart his being absent from Parliament on the 22nd.

The Catholic Question being mentioned, as it is in the paper I am going to send the Duke of York, makes it quite unnecessary for me to take any notice of what you wrote to me in your first letter from Dogmersfield respecting the Grenvilles ; and, if I ever communicate it, it had better be kept for a personal interview. Pray tell me what mode you determine on, and *when* the paper is to be communicated to the two parties concerned ; and pray, as much as possible, take care Pitt is not seduced by his *Ministerial* friends and correspondents to depart from his resolution. I hope they do not suspect his intentions, and that for that reason they will be kept secret till the time draws so near as to make persuasions ineffectual.

Believe me, &c.   MALMESBURY.

I wrote to the Duke of York by the same post as follows :—

Bath, 16th Nov., 1802.

SIR,—Having had nothing of importance to communicate to your Royal Highness, I have not troubled you with any letter since my arrival here; but having now received an exact copy of the paper, of which I read a rough draft to your Royal Highness in London, I consider it as my duty to transmit it to you, together with a præscript to be used eventually.

Three ways of communicating it to Mr. Addington are proposed—either by a spokesman, by sending it with signatures, or unsigned, but with the præscript.

The first is thought to be the most preferable, but also the most difficult, from the choice of a person of sufficient weight, and willing to undertake such a commission.

The second is not free from the same objections, as,

although members may be found to sign, yet a *leader* is
wanted; and it is the last mode which I apprehend will
be found to be the only feasible one.   The representation should be made immediately, or it will not be
dealing fairly with Mr. Addington.

Your Royal Highness will probably soon hear of its
effects.   I shall discover easily when it has been sent to
Mr. Pitt, to whom I, as yet, have only spoken very generally on all commonplace public points.   I exhort him,
as much as I can, not to attend the meeting.   It is very
desirable he should not commit himself politically; still
more that he should be absent, if any motion personal to
him is brought forward; and most of all, that he should
completely recover his health, in case His Majesty should
again command his services.

Your Royal Highness will be so gracious as to return
me the paper and præscript when you have read, and,
if your Royal Highness pleases, copied them.

I have, &c.   MALMESBURY.

On the 19th I received the following reply from the
Duke :—

Horse-Guards, 19th Nov., 1802.

MY DEAR LORD,—I lose no time in acknowledging
the receipt of your letter, and in returning you many
thanks for the communication of the enclosed papers,
which I return, having, according to your permission,
taken a copy of them.

You are perfectly well acquainted with my sentiments
upon the subject, and therefore will easily conceive how
anxious I shall be to hear the result.

Believe me, &c.   (Signed)   FREDERICK.

WHILE this correspondence was passing, I frequently
saw Mr. Pitt, (who was at Bath,) Lord Camden, Lord
Carrington, and Mr. G. Rose.   I rather avoided than
sought opportunities of entering into regular conversation with Mr. Pitt, as I felt it was a difficult point

where to draw the line, how to avoid saying too much, and by that means embarrassing and perplexing him, or saying too little, and appearing secret and mysterious. With Lords Camden and Carrington I had some occasional discourse; and, without entering at all deeply into the subject, or giving them room to suppose I knew anything was going forward, (of which, I fancy, they had no suspicion,) I could easily discover that they were both very anxious for Pitt's resuming office, very uneasy at the state of the country, and (Lord Carrington particularly) disliking and despising Mr. Addington and his Administration. Lord Camden was very anxious to keep Pitt on here, and promised to use every means in his power to effect it. I had a longer conversation with Mr. Rose. He expressed, in the most marked terms, his extreme concern that Pitt had supported the present Administration so long; that it was being over-scrupulous; and that, as they planned and executed measures before they communicated them to him, or advised with him concerning them, it was unfair and tricking—the calling for him to assist them afterwards, and to make him responsible for what he had no concern in.

Rose then took a general review of Mr. Addington's Administration, and dwelt on almost every measure, both foreign and domestic, with censure and reproof. He particularly reprobated the step taken with respect to Switzerland,* which, he said, was idle and dangerous; and that now they had, without Pitt's knowledge and advice, got into a scrape, they wanted him to extricate them from it. But Rose said Pitt would not hear of it, and was determined to remain on here till *after Christmas.* This Rose told me on the 16th instant, as we were walking together; and Pitt himself had, indeed,

---

* Switzerland was a prey to dissensions fomented by French intrigues. In an unfortunate moment one party appealed to the First Consul. He sent Ney with 40,000 men. The Diet was dissolved on the 28th October, and the Swiss lost their independence.

The British Government sent a Note of remonstrance October 10th, and despatched Mr. Moore to Switzerland to sound the state of parties and to offer pecuniary assistance, but he arrived too late.

said nearly as much to me the day before, and I had strongly and warmly exhorted him to abide by this resolution.

On Wednesday, the 17th, Canning, as I was going to call on him, about twelve o'clock, at the White Hart, came into my house.

Several motives had induced Canning to see Pitt. Lord Mulgrave, who had been made acquainted with the paper, and who had been solicited to sign it, (without being told, however, of any of the details, which, from Canning, I found were known, *in toto*, only to Lord Morpeth, Lord G. Leveson, Sturges, [son to the Prebendary of Winchester,] and myself,) had, perhaps, inadvertently betrayed the scheme, by writing to Pitt. This premature confidence, Canning thought, might be very hurtful; and as Lord Mulgrave himself was also coming to Bath, and to stay, Canning wished to see Mr. Pitt ·first.

In addition to this motive, as Pitt did not come up to town, it was essential to avail himself of this determination, so favourable to our views, to try to prevail on him to withhold his advice, and, in short, to say to him many things which could not be written, or which, when written, never so fully or so quickly answered the purpose.

Canning had seen Pitt before he saw me, and was highly pleased with the whole of his discourse and manner. He said it was as favourable as possible; that he (Pitt) was more confirmed than ever as to the propriety of *his* coming in, and reprobated, without reserve, several of the measures lately taken. He expressed himself so strongly, that it became a matter of deliberation with us whether it would not be better to trust him *entirely*, and to shew him the whole; and, after a good deal of debate between us, we agreed that Canning should say to Pitt that I was in possession of the whole transaction; that I was to remain at Bath, and that if Pitt wished to know either all, or any particular part of it, if he would express this wish to me, I would tell it him.

Pitt, Rose, and Canning dined with me. The conversation was general: but the next morning Canning said he had been very explicit with Pitt; had told him the part I had taken, and of my going to the Duke of York; that Pitt very much approved this, *very much;* and that he had settled it with him in the way we had agreed on, viz. that I should answer any question he pleased to put to me.

Canning returned to town on the evening of the 18th; but, before his departure, we had much conversation, the result of which was, that I had better not intrude any information or confidence on Pitt, nor refuse him any he asked; that I had better suppress everything about Lord Grenville, since Pitt had just received a most kind letter from him, and since Pitt declared and felt he could not do without his abilities in Parliament, if he again was put at the head of affairs; that Lord Mulgrave had explained away his apparent breach of confidence, by saying it was not *expressly* intrusted to him as a secret; that he was, therefore, not bound to keep it (rather Jesuitical); and that he, from acting always, and since Pitt went out, under his directions, he was particularly circumstanced, and could not dispense with consulting him now, and asking him whether he ought or ought not to attend the opening of the Session.

On talking over the names, I found those of great leading men to sign were wanting; there were hopes of getting Lord Lowther (through Ward, a friend of Sturge's), and Peel, of Liverpool, through Rose; that Pitt had seemed to hint that a *Peer's* going in to the King might do good. I expressed my disapprobation of this method; that I knew it was displeasing to the King; that it never (but once in 1783, when Lord Buckinghamshire went in on the India Bill,) was attended to, and was against its being resorted to but in the last moment: but that there existed an embarrassment on this point about Lord Carlisle, who had volunteered this service; and though he was unequal to the task, yet it would be difficult to take it from him and give it to another, could even another Peer be found.   Lord Pembroke was mentioned,—a most unexceptionable man,—but he is still at Paris.   Lord Worcester is to try to get the Duke of Beaufort.   General Egerton to act, if possible, as representative for the Duke of Bridgewater; and the Duke of Somerset to be tried through the Duchess.   All this leaves the execution of the measure, *i. e.* the presenting the paper, very loose and uncertain ; and as it met completely Pitt's wishes, that nothing should be done immediately, it was agreed with him that no Parliamentary step should be taken till after Christmas on our part, and that every means should be tried to prevent any eager or over-zealous independent member from bringing any motion forward of a similar tendency to that he had in contemplation,—to prevent even any which could produce a *division* in either House.   This I considered difficult, as it was impossible for Lord Grenville not to notice in the House of Lords what was passing ; and it was very difficult, in a debate on such a question, to hinder the House dividing.   There was some little difference of opinion between Pitt's ideas and mine, as to the *right* time of his resuming Office.   He seemed to think the moment of a *certain war* was the best.   I contended for the contrary.   That if he came in after the Swiss business was over, and it would probably be settled not very creditably for us, he would then find *enough* to do— would not be responsible for the situation in which he found the country—be relieved from the odium and disgrace of having contributed to it, and be at liberty to submit to it for a while; and, if he could, maintain the country at peace for a year or more, or, indeed, till such time as Buonaparte's insolence and oppression rendered the duration of it any longer impossible.   He (Pitt), besides the benefit the country would derive from a year's more quiet, would have it in his power to put it in a state of defence (it was now without the first means of defence); and, by manifesting his firm and steady desire to preserve peace as long as possible, deprive his enemies here and abroad from fixing on him, very improperly, the title of War Minister; from asserting, as they did, that *war* was his principle, and the leading character of his Government. This, I said, I knew by experience was the language held and *believed* on the Continent, and that it was also accredited here by the silly and disaffected; and that it was, in fact, the greatest drawback to his Administration. That, therefore, if he waited till the war was inevitable, he would confirm this opinion; whereas, if he came in after an Act of Concession, however disgraceful, he might remain at peace, being at liberty to lament the folly of his predecessors, without at once seeking redress for it by the sword.

Before Canning left Bath, we took an opportunity of stating to Mr. Pitt, how very dangerously he committed himself by allowing himself to be consulted *partially*, and by giving advice on some insulated measure, while the great system, of which this made only a part, was kept secret from him. This had its effect; and Pitt declared, that, while he remained here, he would decline giving any advice at all; and, as a proof of this, said he had received a letter, enclosing a long despatch from Lord Hawkesbury, (he did not say on what subject,) and that he intended to send the despatch back without any opinion, alleging for a reason the impossibility of judging with safety or precision on a measure or measures, with the beginning and end of which he could not be acquainted.

This was the substance of several hours' conversation with Canning, and passed on the 17th and 18th.

On the 19th, Mr. Pitt called on me; but G. Rose and Lord Mulgrave were with him, and nothing passed.

On Sunday the 21st, Pitt called on me, at half-past eight in the morning. He entered immediately on the subject by saying, " I know you are one in a plot, not quite so desperate as Col. Despard's;"* (he was just taken up for administering oaths to soldiers, and others, to disclaim their allegiance;) and then went on by expressing a wish to converse fully and confidentially with me. He said he understood I was at liberty to

---

* Colonel Despard had laid a plot to kill the King on his way to Parliament. He was hanged with six others on the 21st February.

communicate to him the measure intended to be taken;
that Canning had told him enough to leave him little
doubt of what this was; and one of his friends, (Lord
Mulgrave,) who had thought it right to consult him,
had nearly repeated to him the words in which the representation was drawn up, and he did not doubt
they were proper and well adapted to the end proposed:
he therefore would not press me to be more explicit just
now, on this particular point. He then went on by
saying, the question he wished to put was, Who were
the other persons consulted on this occasion? He feared,
if he was well informed, they were *too few*—too much
in the same predicament and way of thinking, and
considered as too much attached to him, and too inimical
to Mr. Addington. I told him their names, with which
I observed he was acquainted before, and had now
asked them with a view to be better enabled to assert
more positively what he had just said; viz. that a
measure originating with, and arranged by, persons of
this description, and those so few, would look like a plot
or cabal; and that whether *he* really did or did not
know of it, whether he knew directly, or, as was the
case, accidentally, it would be impossible for him to
escape the imputation of conniving at it, or avoid suspicions that he was a party to it; and that such a suspicion, independent of his own feelings, would defeat the
end of his coming into Office, even supposing any
good could result from it; that it was therefore his
wish, and one which he had entertained and expressed
to Canning before he left Bath, and in which since, on
reflection, he had been confirmed more and more, that
no further canvas should be made for names, supporters,
or signatures, to promote or compel Mr. Addington's
resignation. If the opinion that his coming into Office
was as generally desired and entertained as we supposed
it, it was much better for him, and for the thing itself,
to leave it to work out its own way; that this *must*
happen, if this opinion was a prevailing one in the
public mind; and that, if it was not, his coming into
Office at all was useless and improper; that, as to him-

self, he had to say, that he should consider it himself as a paramount duty, if called upon in this way; at the same time that various reasons led him to wish the business should not be hurried; and that although he felt himself much recovered, and felt well enough *to be idle*, yet that he was by no means sure that his health was sufficiently re-instated to enable him to undergo the labours and anxieties of Office; and, till he could ascertain this, his accepting it would be wrong towards himself and others; that he therefore was very desirous that the canvas *should be checked*, and that, as he before said, the business should be left to work itself.

My reply to him was, that, although the public opinion respecting his return to Office was certainly as strong and as universal as we thought and he had heard, yet, that I much feared it would never be brought to express itself in a way to produce the effect we wanted, without prompting and exhortation, unless some public calamity pressed so hard upon the country as to force it to call out. That, though his resuming Office would always be a most welcome event, yet its taking place at a well-timed moment would add most essentially to its advantages; and that it would be a much greater service to the country, could he come in to *prevent* a disaster than to extricate us from one, or help us to encounter it after it was actually come upon us. That, this being my opinion, I could not quite approve *all* canvas being put an end to, although I was very ready to acquiesce in the general principle he laid down, not to force or precipitate the step, and to leave the whole to do itself, *as far as was possible;* but that I conceived nothing of this kind ever arose of itself, *quite alone and unaided.* " Yes," said he, " often in a way not only unknown, but in a manner as if it had no concerted beginning." I said to this, that in such cases the beginning might be partially concealed or unknown, but that I could not help thinking it always did exist somewhere or somehow; and that I conceived a spontaneous act of the country at large, or a general expression of their wishes, never was produced, without some previous encouragement and preparation, except in the case I had before alluded to,—of some very pressing public danger. Pitt still maintained his opinion, and insisted earnestly on a cessation from any further *canvas*. And, besides the reasons he had already alleged, he said, it was well known that Canning was avowedly hostile to the present Government; that his being brought back through such means (for the means must ultimately be known), it would be next to impossible for him to escape the censure of being implicated in the plan, and accused, for the sake of returning to Office, of forming a cabal against a set of men for whom he continued to have a great personal regard, and from whom he *hitherto* had not withdrawn his support. But that, as he was now decided to remain at Bath, he *could* not give his support in Parliament; and, as to advising and being advised with, it was his intention to waive every thing of the kind; that he, indeed, ought *conscientiously* to decline it, since much had been done he did not approve, and his support often solicited in behalf of measures of which he knew only a very small part; that he had always prepared the way for this; and, added he, " As I neither shall attend Parliament, nor *allow* it to be said that I am consulted, and approve what is brought forward by Ministry, it will appear manifestly that there is some alteration in my opinion and sentiments; and I think that this will be as likely to bring forth the public opinion (supposing it to be as reported) as soon and as distinctly, and certainly, both for me and for general good effect, much more desirably than in consequence of the solicitations and representations of a few young men, however respectable, headed by one so very near to me in habits of political and private intimacy as Canning."

I admitted the force of this last reasoning, and assented entirely to the doing nothing decisive immediately—no action; specifying that every thing of that sort should be postponed till after the Christmas recess; not, however, concealing my alarms, lest, during the intervening period, events might take place to distress and disgrace the country; or some over-officious country gentleman get up and bring the measure, in his own awkward way, prematurely before Parliament, and thus commit votes and speakers. That, also, Windham in the House of Commons, and Lord Grenville in the House of Lords, might be forced (in order to maintain what they had said) to take a part which might pledge them *too far*, and disqualify themselves, and many others, from uniting under him, for the sole purpose for which we wish to see him again at the head of the Government; that this was to prevent war, not to make it. And this led me to observe how much better it would be if he could come into Office at the end of one difficult measure, and before a new difficult one arose; as, for example, at the pause (I feared it would be but a short one) which would succeed the termination of the Swiss remonstrance, which would be probably either a concession or a retraction ("a retreat," said Pitt); that, coming in then, he would not be responsible for what was past, as it would have been made appear by his staying here he had had no concern in it; and the past would be a reason and authority for him to put the country into that state of defence which alone could keep war at a distance, or enable us to resist it if attacked. This he admitted most fully, and considered it was a very wise thing to do. I went on by saying, that if he came in at *such* a moment, and could preserve peace, even but for a year, and till war was manifestly forced upon us, he would do away that clamor raised against him (and *no one better than myself* knew how undeservedly) of his being fond of war. This, he must know, was the Jacobin cry. It was believed on the Continent, and affected to be believed by the factious and disaffected here. "I know it," said Pitt; "the Jacobins cry louder than we can, and make themselves heard. I also feel its consequence, and agree quite with you. In short, we are agreed on every point, but in that of not checking the canvas." Not to be checked *entirely*, I said, but, perhaps, to check it moderately; for that it was impossible for me to rest any faith, or admit any

satisfactory expectation to my mind, that the public
opinion, left to itself, would operate rightly ; it was
always too rapid, or too torpid, in its progress ; too
soon, or too late; and that, although he could not reprobate and abhor cabal, intrigue, and duplicity more
than I did, yet his could not be *quite* a fair opinion on
a matter in which he was both judge and party ; that
no conduct, however correct, could hinder suspicious
minds from following the bent of their dispositions ; and
that it was enough to have an intimate conviction, as
certainly he had, that, if any such suspicion as that he
alluded to fell on him in the present instance, it was
false and unmerited—(he said, it was an imputation he
could not endure). I went on by saying, that it was
possible for him to have an individual opinion, distinct and separate from his character and name; and
that if he was called upon to reason and act upon it, as
if that name and character belonged to some one else,
I could not but believe he would act and think as
we did.

Pitt said, it might be so, but that he did not know
very well how to separate himself from himself. At the
same time, he felt himself safe in our hands, and would
claim the right of free and unreserved discussion with
me on the subject. Here our conversation ended ; the
result of which was, that it appeared to me that Lord
Mulgrave and G. Rose were against the plan Canning
proposes; that it was in consequence of their instances
that Pitt is now against a further canvas (as he calls
it); but that they agree with us as to the great object
in view entirely; and that on this, and on the *time*
(which is to be after the Christmas vacation) we are
unanimous. On the whole, they may be right; certain
it is, that the four young persons* who compose the
secret committee are not of sufficient *fathom* for so great
a purpose, and I was very sorry to hear their numbers so
confined.

* Canning, Lord G. Leveson, Lord Morpeth, and Mr. Sturges Bourne.
The last was made Secretary of State for the Home Department, and Lord
Warden of the New Forest, by Canning, when he became Premier, in 1827.

I omitted, in its right place in the conversation which I have just related, to insert that on Pitt's repeating his desire all further canvas should be stopped, I, speaking of myself, said, that my opinion on that particular point was a perfectly unprejudiced one, and that I did not give it in order to persist in a plan which 1 had been instrumental in concerting ; since the plan was concerted, and had got the length of perfect formation, before it was communicated to me; that I should be sorry to be considered in any other light than as an eager and strenuous advocate for the *end*, and to obtain the *end*.   I had a wish in common with those who concerted the means; but as to devising the means, or to any collateral consideration whatever, I felt wholly neutral.   It was the end, and the end solely, I looked to, as an event which alone could preserve the dignity and security of the country; and every thing which went hand in hand to obtain this end made me as eager and zealous as any one, and induced me readily to accept that share in the attempt to facilitate it, which it had been proposed to me to take.   (It was a very essential one indeed, said Pitt.)   That the contributing, in any degree, to lead the King's attention towards it, to prepare him for it, to dispose him to seek it by stating the removal of obstacles which he might suppose to exist, was a very *agreeable* task to undertake; that this task became even an imperious duty, when, by the subject being opened to His Majesty in a cautious way, and by a proper person, the risk would be done away of its possibly irritating his nerves or disturbing his mind, and thus endangering his health; that, if this were to happen, I should think the country but half saved, even though he (Pitt) came again into Office, surrounded by all his friends, and invested with full authority.   To this Pitt, with great warmth, replied, " You may be sure my feelings are stronger even than yours on this point ; and I not only affirm, that if the event cannot be produced without affecting in the smallest degree the King's health and tranquillity, but that if it has not his full and uncompelled concurrence, *it shall not happen at all;*

to feel and to say this, is little more than feeling and speaking like a gentleman; and neither the public voice, nor the solicitations of my friends, ever shall prevail on me to come into Office against the King's consent, much less to try to force his consent from him. What you, therefore, have done, and may do, is the first of *all* things to be done and ascertained; the one on which the others all hinge, and the one on which I have no scruple of saying my wishes and approbation, and I will even say hopes, go completely with you."

I received by this day's post the following letter from Canning :—

London, 20th Nov., 1802.

MY DEAR LORD MALMESBURY,—I can just keep my word with you by writing by this day's post, though I have nothing new to say, and no time to say it in, having lost the far greater part of the day in going down to the House of Commons to be sworn, and waiting there in vain for forty members to make a House for swearing.

The only thing that passed at Bath which I am not quite sure of having mentioned to you, is, that the allusion to *the question* was settled to be omitted. I will, on Monday, send you a copy of the paper as it stands after this omission, and one or two trifling alterations more, and will then state to you the *stateable* reasons for this last change.*

I shall be glad of a single line by Monday's post, if it be only to assure me that every thing remains as I left it. From the language that I have just heard held about *health*, I do indeed hope that no great struggle will be made by Addington to effect a change in the resolution so wisely taken. But by others I should think there would.

Ever, &c.   (Signed)   G. C.

---

* I have not thought it worth while to repeat this paper with the omission of the paragraph alluding to the Catholic Question.

P.S.—I found your letter here.

I have seen Lord Grenville and T. Grenville to-day ; nothing can be more temperate and considerate than their intentions; so you might say, if you fall in with the person* who may like to know it, as I shall not have time to write to him to-day.

Not meeting Pitt in the course of the morning, I wrote him a note to tell him what was said in Canning's letter relative to Lord Grenville and Tom Grenville; and on the 22nd I wrote the following letter to Canning:—

Bath, Monday, 22nd Nov., 1802.

MY DEAR CANNING,—I had a long and interesting conversation yesterday morning. [Here, after repeating the above written conversation with Mr. Pitt, Lord Malmesbury proceeds as follows.]

Checking the canvas seems his great object, and you will, I believe, hear from him to-day on this subject.

It embarrassed me your omitting the allusion to *the question*. If, after what I have said to the Duke of York, it should be found to be *alive and broad awake*, I have sadly misled him, and must undeceive him; but I will wait for your letter to-morrow, and answer to this, before I write.

The Duke's answer to me was very short: " You are perfectly acquainted with my sentiments, and therefore will easily conceive how anxious I shall be to hear the result." His letter is dated the 18th. Remember he is in possession of the paper, and may have made use of it.

I hope the Grenvilles will act up to their assurance of temperance and conciliation; as matters now stand, much depends on nothing being done in Parliament; no division, no committing opinions by speeches.

Ever yours,   MALMESBURY.

---

* Mr. Pitt.

I received on the 23rd of November the following
letter from Canning, and answered it on the same
day :—

Bath, Monday, 22nd Nov., 1802.

MY DEAR LORD MALMESBURY,—I enclose the corrected copy of the paper. The omission of *the question* is the
chief alteration; the others are either merely verbal, or
such as become necessary from the change of the time of
presentation.

In transmitting it, the reasons to be assigned for the
first are—That it was found upon inquiry that Pitt had
done enough three weeks after he went out to set the
King's mind completely at ease ; and that, having done
so from that motive alone, it seemed to be as *unfair* as
it was unnecessary to insert anything like a stipulation,
which would give him the appearance of making not (as
in truth it was) a voluntary renunciation for the King's
sake at a moment when restoration to Office could not
be in question, but an interested sacrifice for the sake of
Office. This, I cannot help hoping, will be felt strongly
and kindly.

Secondly, as to the alteration of *time*, it was suggested
by many persons that it would be better to wait for the
impression of the first day, now that Pitt is not to be
there, and therefore cannot, by committing himself
afresh, throw any new obstacle in the way of the plain
language (not motion, I hope—not if *we* can prevent it).
Language in Parliament may do much good in preparing Addington's mind, as well as that of the public, and
satisfying Pitt of the necessity of his return.

Besides, another practical reason is the very small
number of persons in town last week; the necessity of
waiting till they come up, to explain a measure which
cannot be explained by letter — at least, not without
such precipitate and unguarded confidence as might ruin
all; and lastly (but this point must be touched, as you
will see, with all your delicacy), Pitt's wish, *collected, got
at*, found out, or what you will, without communicating
with him in a way at all to commit him to a knowledge

of the measure; his wish clearly ascertained (known), that there should be some time given him, both with a view to his own health, in which ten days or a fortnight might make a material difference, and for the chance of the immediate scrape being got over, *tant bien que mal*, without his being implicated in it. This last would not be a sufficient reason without the other; but with it, and with his staying away, a few days' ease given to him may do no harm. He shall not, however, have more than is good for him. I am so tired and so hurried that I can write no more. This is all that is material.

Ever yours, &c. (Signed) G. C.

Bath, Tuesday, 23rd Nov., 1802.

MY DEAR CANNING,—I admit your reasons for striking out *the Question paragraph*. If the Duke of York avails himself judiciously of them in his report, its insertion in the first instance, and its being omitted on re-consideration, may both be turned to very good account.

What I wrote to you yesterday coincides so perfectly with what you say, that it is unnecessary to go over the ground again; and the practical reasons you allege in favour of delay, come all in support of the great and governing one —viz. the wish and decision of Pitt. This is now clearly ascertained ; and I have little doubt, either by imprudence, conjecture, or through some chink, may be found out and collected full enough to produce the effect, and influence the many in the way we want. I have had no material conversation with him since yesterday.

In stating to the Duke of York the difference as to the *time when*, it accounts so well for itself as to be liable to no difficulty.

Believe me, &c. MALMESBURY.

The post of the 24th brought me a short letter from Canning (as follows); and on the same day, about half-past three, P.M., Pitt called on me.

Whitehall, 23rd Nov., 1802.

My dear Lord Malmesbury, — Your letter followed me here on my way to the House. I have written in haste to Pitt, in a way that I hope will quiet him.

They have put *Church and State* into the Speech. I think I guess why.

Ever yours, &c.　　　(Signed)　　　G. C.

They have at this present writing *no mover* for the House of Lords.

———

Pitt said he felt obliged to me for what I had written to Canning, as he had received a very satisfactory letter to inform him the canvas *was* checked. He read the letter to me; it was very short; and Canning makes a merit of giving way on a point contrary to his own opinion.

I said that I had related shortly to Canning the substance of what he (Pitt) had said to me on the morning of the 21st; that I had rather inferred his opinion than stated my own, as I was persuaded that the best thing we could do to forward our great wish was this, independent of our feelings of regard and respect for him; that, on thinking it over since we had conversed, I was sure he was right; and that his remaining on here, and desisting from giving advice, would do more good than any attempts, however well planned and well executed. He said he was quite sure of it, and expressed himself so frankly and so clearly as to leave me not the smallest doubt that he looked forward to his return to Office as a near and certain event, and that no obstacle would be thrown in its way by him, unless he was *beset* too much; and that the zeal, schemes, or interests of officious and selfish people disgusted and soured him, by their too eager and too indiscreet exhortations. Pitt said, he now felt he was sure of a *pause*, and that, having *made up his mind* (a strong and satisfactory expression), he was determined not to perplex himself, nor to alter the good effects of the Bath waters by more thinking about it, but to drink them without anxiety, and live as idle and pleasant a life as he could.   I quite agreed with him, observing only that the pause must not be made *too long* — it must only be a *Christmas holiday* — and that he must not expect to be left quiet and idle after the recess.   " The longer the better," said he; " but be assured I am prepared to resume work *in its due and proper time*."

Pitt then went on by reading the King's Speech (which I had not seen).   He remarked on it, that it was very vague and loose, full of true statements that admitted *any* application; that the part of it relative to the " existing means of providing for the various branches of the Public Service, without any considerable addition to the burthens of the people," *was false;* that he knew it was impossible, unless it was intended to disarm the country entirely, and leave it in a defenceless state, *even* for the home policy of it.

I subjoin the Speech :—

" My Lords and Gentlemen, — It is highly gratifying to me to resort to your advice and assistance, after the opportunity which has been recently afforded of collecting the sense of my people.

" The internal prosperity of the country has realised our most sanguine hopes.   We have experienced the bounty of Divine Providence in the produce of an abundant harvest; the state of the manufactures, commerce, and revenue of my United Kingdom is flourishing beyond example; and the loyalty and attachment which are manifested to my person and Government afford the strongest indications of the just sense that is entertained of the numerous blessings enjoyed under the protection of our happy Constitution.

" In my intercourse with Foreign Powers I have been actuated by a sincere disposition for the maintenance of peace.   It is, nevertheless, impossible for me to lose sight of that established and wise system of policy by which the interests of other states are connected with our own; and I cannot, therefore, be indifferent to any material change in their relative condition and strength. My conduct will be invariably regulated by a due consideration of the actual situation of Europe, and by a watchful solicitude for the permanent welfare of my people. You will, I am persuaded, agree with me in thinking that it is incumbent upon us to adopt those means of security which are best calculated to afford the prospect of preserving to my subjects the blessings of peace.

" Gentlemen of the House of Commons,— I have ordered the Estimates for the ensuing year to be laid before you, and I rely on your zeal and liberality in providing for the various branches of the public service, *which, it is a great satisfaction to me to think, may be fully accomplished without any considerable addition to the burthens of my people.*

" My Lords and Gentlemen,—I contemplate with the utmost satisfaction the great and increasing benefits produced by that important measure, which has united the interests, and consolidated the resources, of Great Britain and Ireland. The improvement and extension of these advantages will be objects of your unremitting care and attention. The trade and commerce of my subjects, so essential to the support of public credit, and of our own maritime strength, will, I am persuaded, receive from you every possible encouragement; and you will readily lend your assistance in affording to mercantile transactions, in every part of my United Kingdom, all the facility and accommodation that may be consistent with the security of the public revenue.

" To uphold the honour of the country, to encourage its industry, to improve its resources, and to maintain the true principles of the Constitution in Church and State, are the great and leading duties which you are called upon to discharge. In the performance of them, you may be assured of my uniform and cordial support; it being my most earnest wish to cultivate a perfect harmony and confidence between me and my Parliament, and to promote to the utmost the welfare of my faithful subjects, whose interests and happiness I shall ever consider as inseparable from my own."

PITT seemed to rely on Lord Grenville's consideration, and said it was a good word, and he was glad Canning had used it.

On the 25th November I went with him, Lord and Lady Bathurst, Fanny,* and Lord Mulgrave, to Mr. Codrington's, Donnington; a very fine house, building by Wyatt. We dined together afterwards, and had much general conversation on the Debates, on the Address, and other subjects; on the state of the Continent, &c.; but it was quite *wine* conversation, and not worth recording.

On the same day I wrote the following letter to the Duke of York:—

Bath, Thursday, 25th Nov., 1802.

SIR,—I understand there are some hopes that your Royal Highness will soon come to Bath for a day or two. I sincerely wish it may be so on every account; and, till I hear from your Royal Highness that we are *not* to expect soon the satisfaction of seeing you, shall postpone making to your Royal Highness some further communications, which I could do much better in conversation than by the post. I am, &c.

(Signed)   MALMESBURY.

SATURDAY, Nov. 27.—The moment I came into the Pump-room, Pitt took me apart, and began talking with much warmth on Fox's conduct and language in the House, and went on with such rapidity and eloquence, that what he said to me was more like the *skeleton* of an answer to Fox, than quiet conversation. He was eager to recur to what Fox had said on the Commercial Treaty in 1787,† and we went to *Bull's* to look back into the

---

* Lord Malmesbury's second daughter, afterwards married to General the Honourable Sir Lowry Cole, G.C.B.

† On the 23rd January and 5th February, 1787, there were debates in the House of Commons on a Commercial Treaty, signed with France, September 29th, 1786. Mr. Fox condemned this Treaty, on the grounds that it was a political approximation to France. He declared it to be his opinion, that the external circumstances of the two nations rendered a rivalship, and, in some degree, an enmity, inevitable, and that it was impossible to prevent them; nay, that were it possible, it was not to be wished for by any lover of his country.

Debates. In short, he was so full of the subject as to raise apprehensions in my mind that he felt a strong hankering to go up and answer Fox; and some words, which dropped from Rose in the course of the dinner (Pitt and he dined with me,) confirmed me in my ideas. I was, therefore, very anxious to have an opportunity of resisting this idea, and expressed my disapprobation of it, without reserve, to G. Rose ; but, as several other persons dined also with me, I had no opportunity of seeing Pitt alone till the next morning, when he called on me about noon. I had received, on the 27th, a letter from Canning, of which this is a copy :—

37, Conduit Street, Friday, 26th Nov., 1802.

MY DEAR LORD MALMESBURY,—I am really so knocked up, partly by fatigue, but more perhaps by anxiety, that I feel glad to get out of town for a day or two, and am now setting off for South Hill, whence I shall return with Mrs. Canning on Sunday, or Monday at the latest.

You will probably have heard from others some account of the opening of the Session. I am particularly anxious that Pitt should have heard what is strictly true, that on the first day I was guilty of no *imprudence;* that my defence of the *old* Government went no further than was strictly called for by Fox's attack,* and by the evident pleasure with which that attack was received by the *Treasury Bench*, of which last provocation, however, I took no notice.

Anything so beaten in debate as the Ministers were, you never saw. They *cannot* uphold themselves or the country. The second day, *Fox* took their *defence*, and the statement of the line of conduct proper to be followed, *wholly upon himself;* and they acquiesced, not with complacency only, but with apparent *gratitude*, in all he uttered; amongst which were many principles utterly hostile to the whole system of the late Administration,

---

* In the debate on the Address, Nov. 23, Mr. Fox supported it, but censured the late Ministers, and imputed the aggrandizement of France to their obstinacy and misconduct. Mr. Canning defended them, citing the success of their expeditions, and of their financial policy.

and every topic that could reconcile the country to bear and forbear as long as Buonaparte pleases, and to discourage *preparation*, as well at home as by alliances abroad.

Wilberforce was baser still.* To them Addington answered not a word; but he answered Windham fiercely and venomously enough, who, agreeing with him in principle, differed certainly (and, so far, it was right to answer him,) in degree; and took occasion, in the course of his speech, to revive the abuse of the Lisle Negotiation, which you will not wonder Morpeth should feel indignantly, and will be glad to hear he defended it well. It was impossible for me to hear *it and Morpeth* (for defending it) treated as Hawkesbury treated them, without coming to their assistance; and, in truth, I did at the moment feel so warmly, from gathering indignation during the whole course of the debate, as well as from this particular outrage, that I congratulate myself now upon having put into what I said no *greater* degree of violence.

I wrote to Pitt yesterday, to much the same effect with this, I think; but under the weight of such a headache and general indisposition, that I hardly know what I wrote.

The general result of all seems to be, that Pitt *must* be Minister again, *or Fox will*. The present system cannot stand. But I do *not* think the present moment particularly favourable for Pitt's return.

The hope is that Addington, if left to himself, may feel his difficulties, and offer to give way. But I fear, on the other hand, his great vanity, and am confident that nothing but *language* in Parliament can cure it.

The paper would make no impression on him *now*. After this session and before the next, perhaps, it might. It is therefore clearly best to lay it by for the present. It is also clear, that no motion, resolution, and division, ought to be thought of. The King must be spared, the

---

* Mr. Wilberforce, who had been a uniform and zealous supporter of the war, now praised the present Ministry, and spoke against British interference on the Continent.

House must not be harassed, no division must be hazarded; but every opportunity that the course of public business affords for invigorating the tone of Government *as against Fox*, for defending, *as against Fox*, the old Administration, and producing, or rather fostering, (for it is produced without our help,) the idea of the incapacity of this man to sustain the tremendous and growing weight of the times, may fairly and advantageously be taken. And this is the only course of action to which I will be party. I do not think that any other is in the contemplation of any person whatever.

I think the suspension of *the paper* must be stated to the Duke of York, with its causes; of which the principal is, to give the public sentiment time to work. But Pitt now knows every part of this business so well, that his advice is the best you can follow in framing the communication; and as it was originally suspended, and the first chance of its success foregone, at his desire, he cannot, I should imagine, object to helping us out of the awkwardness which the delay occasions.

Let me hear from you, if you can, by Monday.

Ever, &c.   (Signed)   G. C.

You would have liked to have heard Morpeth; he did better than I ever heard him, and more promisingly for the future.

_____

I BEGAN the conversation with Pitt by endeavouring to persuade him, (rather, indeed, against my own better judgment,) that Canning had not been imprudent, or said anything uncalled for, or spoke in *his* name; but Pitt, I found, listened to what I found his friends (either Long or Ryder) had written to him, much more than to me, and expressed himself sore at least, if not angry, at the language Canning, which he had been told, had held in the first and second debate on the Address.

He said, a difference on public opinions had indeed, during eighteen months, made no alteration in their private friendship; but till it was clearly and distinctly stated this difference *no longer* existed, the duration of private regard gave no right to assert opinions and doctrines in *his* name; and that he was the more averse to it, as it went to do what of all things he most reprobated, viz. to embroil him personally with Addington and Hawkesbury. To justify his own feelings, and to combat my statement, he read me the letters I have alluded to, and they certainly did represent the language of Canning as indiscreet and unguarded. On the Lisle Negotiation, Pitt said, he was of opinion that it was not a just object of comparison with the Treaty of Amiens; that he was sorry it had ever been brought forward as one, since it led to unpleasant discussions, and furnished no one good or valid argument one way or the other. That he and I (better than anybody) knew that the *projêt* at Lisle was *not* an *ultimatum*. That I must recollect, on my leaving England for Lisle, he had, when with me at my own house in Spring Gardens, in confidence told me his ideas, (this is strictly true,) but that, besides him and me, perhaps no one knew; that, *rather than break off this treaty, we should have given way either on the Cape or Ceylon.* That Lord Grenville, who from the beginning had declared he would *never consent* to any concession on *either of these points*, was perfectly right in calling the *projêt* an *ultimatum ;* but had the negotiation gone on, and depended on this particular point, he, or Lord Grenville, *must* have gone out; and he added, *it would have been Lord Grenville.** After speaking warmly on these points, and repeating his disapprobation that any of those who termed themselves his friends should commit him beyond what he authorized, or try to produce a quarrel between him and the present Ministry, he went on by adverting to what Fox had said, and spoke with the same indignation and animation about it he had used in the Pump-room; and before I could speak, said, " I will anticipate what you, I know, have to say, by owning to you freely, that it was my intention to have gone up when the Army or Navy Estimates came before

---

* This is the key to several mysterious expressions in Pitt's letters to Lord Malmesbury at Lisle, and my authority for having stated the circumstance in a note added to that part of the Correspondence.

the House, to stay *only one day*, and to speak only *on one subject;* but what you hinted to Rose set him, and he set me, a-thinking, and on dispassionate re-consideration we agreed you were quite right. I am now," said he, " decided to stay."

Being, however, fearful, after the first symptom of giving way, that fresh provocation for going up might again occur, and with more irresistibility, I said all I had been preparing on the subject; stated the utter impracticability of his having it within his reach to confine the giving his opinion only on *one* subject, since it was clear both Government and Opposition, and even his friends, would all, from different motives, be disposed to involve him in the whole business now pending, and that it was easy for any of them to do it in a way that would compel him to commit himself. To this he acceded. I then pointed out to him the certain and manifest advantages that must attend Fox's persisting to hold the sort of language he did, and Ministers in approving it; that such sentiments must lower him in public estimation, and, what was still more important for our immediate purpose, it would raise such a jealousy in the King's mind against Addington, and indispose him so much against his Administration, that it was likely to produce from the King himself an overture for his (Pitt's) resuming office; that these were new reasons, in addition to the many powerful ones he himself had admitted for remaining on here, and that, therefore, I rejoiced most sincerely that he persisted in this resolution. Pitt said he certainly would abide by it. I then consulted him as to what I should say to the Duke of York, from whom I had just received a letter, as follows:—

Horse-Guards, 27th Nov., 1802.

MY DEAR LORD,—I lose no time in acknowledging the receipt of your very obliging letter, and am truly sorry that it is out of my power as yet to fix any time for a visit to Bath. I had hoped to have been able to have gone there for a few days both last week and the week before, but was prevented each time by particular business; and now I do not see any prospect of being able to leave London at present. I therefore trust to your friendship to let me know what is going on. I should wish to say many things to you upon the subject, but it is too wide a field for a letter.

Believe me, &c.

(Signed)   FREDERICK.

I MENTIONED to Pitt my having written to the Duke of York on the 25th. He said he did not think the words in the two last lines of the Duke's letter went to convey more than a general wish to see and converse with me, and did not imply an intimation for my coming to London; that in my answer to the Duke, it would be best to keep to general information, not to enter into details; that he knew enough of the Duke to be perfectly ready to tell him and trust him with *every particular*, both respecting himself and the measure, as far as he was concerned in its operations, if his Royal Highness came here; but that as these details were not absolutely necessary, and might, being written, be dangerous, he thought it best to keep to generals. In consequence of this conversation, I wrote the following letter to Canning on the 29th November, and that to the Duke of York on the 1st December : —

Bath, Monday, 29th Nov., 1802.

MY DEAR CANNING,—I can easily give you credit for being fatigued. You will, I trust, give me credit for sharing your anxiety.

Pitt's Parliamentary correspondents are naturally those he is disposed to attend to in preference to any reports I can make of what has passed in the House, and (very naturally also) their opinions have more weight with him than mine. His great dislike is, that anything should be said to embroil him with the present Administration *personally;* and his great wish, that this should be cautiously and carefully avoided by his friends.

On the Lisle Treaty, he said that it was not, in fact,

a point of comparison; no argument of any force could be deduced from it one way or the other; and it had better never have been brought forward, for the purpose either of justifying or condemning that of Amiens.

But if in this particular instance he differed, on all others he perfectly agreed, you may readily suppose; and felt and thought about Fox, his conduct, principles, and designs, in the same manner, and as indignantly, as we do. He was, indeed, so eager about the part Fox had taken, and the way in which it had been taken, that, when he first spoke of it to me, he did it with such warmth and animation, that I thought I perceived he had a strong inclination to go immediately to London and answer him. I was quite right in my apprehensions, since yesterday he confessed it was what occurred to him on the first impression, and that he had thought of being in the House on the day of the Army Estimates, and for that day *only;* but, on reflection, he had altered his intentions, and considered that, on the whole, it would be better to remain on here. As I had already given him my opinion on this subject, I most heartily approved his determination; and I remarked how utterly impracticable it would be for him, if in London, to stay only one or two days, and, when in the House, to confine himself to one particular subject; for, whatever command he might have over himself, it was not in his power to prevent others from introducing topics which might involve the whole question, and thus force him to commit himself prematurely, and defeat the great advantage he supposed would be obtained when he recommended delay. I also observed, that nothing would so completely alienate the King's good-will from his present Ministers, or make him so eager to replace the Government in his hands, as the idea that they were drawing towards Fox, or Fox towards them; and that as it appeared quite impossible that Fox could, in the short interval which was allotted for inaction, operate any real or permanent harm, it was better to let him proceed in the way he had begun, and by giving him more time, and fresh opportunities of being applauded and approved by the Treasury Bench, expose them probably to the public censure, and certainly to the loss of the confidence and protection of the King.

In this Pitt acquiesced, adding, " And if, in the other case, the country desires to lower itself to Fox, and to the disgraceful level to which Fox is disposed it should sink, he is the only proper man to govern it."

I dwell more on these particulars, because I am convinced Fox is the best weapon we have to use. Fox, by his very foolish and unaccountable conduct, and Addington, by his foolish and weak administration, have put into our hands the most powerful weapon against themselves that could be employed, and one which all Pitt's friends, of every colour and description, will unite in working for *this* purpose (viz. against Fox); they will clearly draw together, and I fear I am not much mistaken when I say, it is the single one in which they will be brought to act in a perfect unison, and vigorously draw together in their attacks.

In regard to the suspension of all motions, resolutions, &c., there can be but one opinion, and but one on the *no* effect the paper, if presented, would produce at this moment.

The Duke of York has written to me, to say, he is not coming here. I am, therefore, preparing a summary account for him of what has passed; and this I do after conversing with, and consulting, Pitt, who, I believe, writes to you himself.

Ever yours,   MALMESBURY.

The post of the 30th brought me the following letter from Canning:—

37, Conduit Street, 29th Nov., 1802.

MY DEAR LORD MALMESBURY,—Your very comfortable letter found me at South Hill yesterday morning, and I am unreasonable enough to regret the not finding another to meet me here to-day.

Your neighbour in Pulteney Street* does not write.

* Mr. Pitt.

Indeed, I hardly know what *he could well write*, whatever he may think; but we are all very anxious to be kept informed of the state of his mind, and particularly to learn what impression passing events and discourses seem to make upon him. He has heard from Lord Grenville, as well as from me. Does he happen to have mentioned either letter to you, and in what way? He has heard also, through Lord Mulgrave, another, and a more impartial, account of each night's debate in the House of Commons. Has he or Lord Mulgrave said anything of this to you?

They (the Government people) give out, of course, that he (Pitt) is extremely displeased with every thing that we have been doing, and that he is coming up in a great hurry to vindicate himself and them. I should like very much to receive a letter from you on Wednesday morning, to enable me to satisfy some half a dozen well-disposed persons that he is *not* stirring.

Wednesday is the day of the Navy Estimates, which will probably be a day of debate, whether any larger augmentation than they propose is moved for or not. Sheridan is to come down with a speech for large establishments, and against Buonaparte, but against Pitt and all of *us* also. If Fox had not kept him away on the first day of the Session, he would have been wholly in our sense.

My former letter will have answered your questions about Fox, as far as I can answer them. Sheridan assures me, that he (Fox) will never be Minister, but he will do all that he can to keep Pitt out. This is confessedly his present game.

You do quite right in keeping your communication with the Duke for a personal interview—only let not the young man think himself neglected; and the less pressing and frequent your communication with him just now upon the subject the better, for certainly things are not yet ripe. Your remark upon the temper of the House of Commons is perfectly well founded. Flat— flat. But, then, part of the apparent indifference is to be put to the account of undecided speculation. People

are astray, and know not what to trust to.   Keep Pitt
where he is, and things will gradually work themselves
clear.   Ever, &c.   G. C.

P.S.—Lest you should *not* have heard otherwise of
Cochin and of Tuscany, it may be as well to tell you
that there is intelligence from Vienna of the intended
annexation of Tuscany to the Grand Republic, and that
Cochin is ceded by the Dutch to France.

Both these accounts are believed here.

On the 29th and 30th I had no regular conversation
with Pitt; on mentioning the reports about Tuscany
and Cochin, he said, the last was to him a much more
serious event.

On the 1st December, George Rose was with me.   He
talked very well, and much to the purpose.   We agreed
on all points most completely.   He said, he was *now*
as anxious for Pitt not to go up, as he was that he
should go up when he dined with me, and first spoke
to me about it, and attributed (very courtier-like) his
change of opinion to what I had then thrown out.
He told me, we were to have 50,000 seamen, and
that this high establishment was a sudden thought of
Addington's—a thought of yesterday; that it was impossible to go on without borrowing *six millions yearly*;
that it was nonsense to have put words holding out a
contrary hope in the King's Speech; that Addington
was a pitiful financier: his idea of repealing the Salt
Tax absurd.   He was full of compliments; and I said,
in answer to them, that I had renounced all thoughts
of Office, and should only be of use as a *Chamber
Counsel*.

LETTER FROM LORD MALMESBURY TO THE DUKE OF YORK.

Bath, Wednesday, 1st Dec., 1802.

SIR,—I delayed a day or two before I obeyed your
Royal Highness's commands, in order to be able to do it
with more precision and certainty.

I think I can now venture to affirm, that the best disposition towards doing what is so much to be wished prevails in the mind of the person the most interested in it. The determination he took, in consequence of a considerable degree of deliberation, to remain on here, arose principally from this reason,—although there can be no doubt that his health also requires a longer use of the waters to be completely re-established.

His absenting himself from attendance in Parliament will be a fact that will speak for itself to the public; and (as I can in confidence assure your Royal Highness) his declining to interfere, either by advice or consultation, with any of the measures when or about to be taken by Ministers, will be a pretty strong indication to them that they must not reckon much on his support and countenance when he does resume his parliamentary duty. This it is settled he is not to do till after the Christmas recess. As soon as this decision was finally come to, (and I was not convinced it was till I saw he let to-day, when the Navy Estimates came on, pass over,) it became much more advisable to suspend all operations, and to make no use whatever of *the paper* for the present. It was not only wiser, as far as the success of the point in view was concerned, but because it concurred fully and entirely with his wishes and opinions; and, as I have now daily opportunities of hearing those, I am happy to be able to say they are in every point such as your Royal Highness would approve. Could I have the happiness to converse with you, I could say a good deal more; but I trust what I can *venture to write* will be sufficient to keep your Royal Highness up to the order of the day, and that the more minute details will lose nothing of their value or utility by being kept back till I have the happiness of paying my personal duties to you.

I have, &c. (Signed) MALMESBURY.

On the 2nd of December I wrote to Canning.

Bath, Thursday, 2nd Dec., 1802.

My dear Canning,—I have received yours of yesterday, and am glad to find all mine are safely come to
hand.

You will have inferred, from what I wrote on Monday,
that I was not quite satisfied with the impressions my
neighbour's* parliamentary correspondents had given
him; and I was the less so, as I had little expectation
anything I said could counteract them, as he was well
aware that it was either from you, or from persons
thinking with you and as you, my information must
come. I have, however, since had several occasional
conversations with him; and he is so perfectly steady
and right, so *thrivingly right,* on all great and essential
points, so animated against Fox, consequently so displeased with the Treasury Bench for applauding him,
and, above all, so very determined to stay on here till
the term we agreed on is expired, that I do not think
his being a little more at variance with us in the language proper to be held in the House is of very great
consequence, since, let it be ever so much *above* his feelings *at this moment,* it will, I am sure, be *below* them
when he himself decides for action. It is indifferent
what language is now held.

This I cannot say *to him;* but I endeavour to reconcile him to the conduct his friends are observing, by
trying to lead his mind to the recollection of this plain
distinction—that he is *fettered,* or at least at liberty *on
parole; they* are *free;* and the undoubted right they
have to exercise this free agency (even on his behalf, if
they please) cannot commit him, and should not displease him.

He read me your letter to him, but not Lord Grenville's. He mentioned it, but without any remarks or
communication.

I have had no conversation with Lord Mulgrave. I
am not disposed to court it, and he does not seek it.
We had better each pursue our own course. He is very

* Mr. Pitt's.

right in his principles, and we have both the same end in view.

I shall be anxious to hear of to-day's debate. Rose for a moment wanted Pitt to go up, but I soon made him perceive the danger of it.

I do not dislike the rapacious seizure of Tuscany; but Cochin comes nearer home, and may lead to very serious consequences, whether its cession is admitted or protested against. I should prefer the last mode.

I was too late for the post yesterday; nothing new has occurred since. Pitt dines with me to-day; and, if anything passes, I will write to you from Lord Bath's, where I go to-morrow for two days, and where I hope Pitt will come. If you write to-morrow, direct to Longleat.

Ever yours,　　　(Signed)　　MALMESBURY.

DEC. 2.—Nothing occurred to-day. Pitt, Rose, and Lord Mulgrave dined, and spent the evening with us; but it was all general conversation, both at wine and at cards. Cochin not considered so valuable by Pitt as at first.

On Friday the 3rd, I went to Longleat, and remained there till Tuesday the 7th. Lord and Lady Bathurst, Fitzharris, Lord Torrington, and General Grenville, our society, Fanny and myself—our time passed very pleasantly.

On Monday, I received the annexed letter from Canning:

Conduit Street, 4th Dec., 1802.

MY DEAR LORD MALMESBURY,—Your letter of Wednesday and Thursday was a great comfort to me. I had no doubt of attempts being made by some of his Parliamentary correspondents to represent things as going too fast, and too far; but, in my most sober and deliberate judgment, I assure you that I think them quite wrong. I think so, not because it is necessary to uphold what has been done and said, and what is therefore to be defended as well as one can, but because nothing has been done, and scarcely a word said except deliberately; and those who tremble and condemn, do so only from thinking (in which thought we cannot undeceive them), that it is all against Pitt's wish and will, and against the King's also; and that, therefore, if we were to succeed in what we are evidently and avowedly attempting, the discrediting Addington in Parliament, and forcing him to offer Pitt his situation, only the least part of our work would be done, as there would still be insuperable obstacles in both the questions in which Addington's proposition would be to be entertained.   Thinking thus, it is not unnatural that even Pitt's friends, *out of any confidence*, should be frightened at what they imagine a *fruitless* violence to Addington.   But Pitt, who *is* in confidence, ought to recollect, that they do judge under this false impression, and ought to make allowance for apprehensions and suggestions which have their foundation in mistakes.   To argue so much as we do for the sake of producing *one-third* of our object, namely, impression on Addington, would be rash perhaps; but we know that *one-third* includes *another*, and, probably, *the other two*.   After all, the risk is purely our own.   If we fail, we shall be accused (unjustly as we know—but we must keep our justification to ourselves,) of having spoilt everything by rashness.   If we succeed in this one point, (and what other chance of success in these than Parliamentary caution?) we have carried *all*.   Surely it is worth the trial; and, as yet, our progress is such as to satisfy our most sanguine expectations.

There is a general doubt and hesitation, and a looking about for some event *in* the House of Commons, and a questioning of everybody who takes part in the debates *out* of it, which shew the public mind to be afloat, and the imbecility of this Government to be felt very generally.   Add to this, the difference which the last debate produced between Addington's and Hawkesbury's language respecting establishments,* and the situation

---

* In a debate on Dec. 2nd, on a vote for 50,000 Seamen, Mr. Addington did not think it necessary to enter into any explanation, whilst Lord Hawkesbury did so at some length.

in which this (properly remarked upon) will put them into with respect to Fox on Wednesday;* and you will see that we have gained some ground, and have still some to gain before the debates are over.   Only let Pitt remain away, and let him remain silent (by letter) to everybody — to me, among others, if he will ; but to others as well as to me.   Others pretend to hear from him—I do not.

Let me know when you return to Bath.   A letter from Rose to-day informs me that Pitt is going to Longleat early next week.   Is this so?   And, if so, cannot you stay to meet him, and keep him?

Where is Fitzharris?   I have made some attempts to get him to dine here, with " good men and true;" but have had for answer that he is not in town.

Ever, &c.   (Signed)   G. C.

To this I replied the same day by a few lines, and more fully on Wednesday, the 8th December, from Bath.

On Tuesday morning, before we left Longleat, I had some conversation with General Grenville.   He said he was very anxious about public affairs; so was his brother, Lord Glastonbury; that their anxiety was increased from their ignorance of what was actually going on; and that they had heard with much concern that Pitt, whom they alone considered equal to direct the King's councils, *still continued to advise* the present Ministers, and that Addington had been with him at Bath.   I had no difficulty in setting him right on this last point, by telling him it was Heley Addington, not the Minister, who had been there; and I at the same time said, I could venture to assure him, Pitt did not advise now, and that his staying at Bath made it impossible, even supposing he was willing to give advice.   General Grenville expressed great satisfaction at this, but returned to his wish to see the Government in strong hands; his own friends and

---

* When the Navy Estimates were to come on,

relations (the Grenvilles) were not strong enough alone
to form a Government, and he feared they and Pitt did
not quite draw together.   As I thought this language
might be a trap, I said he naturally must know more
than I did on the real sentiments of his own family,
but that I conceived there was only a shade of difference
in their political opinions from those of Pitt; and as I
had heard Lord Grenville had been at Walmer, and Pitt
intended going to Dropmore, it was very certain no cool-
ness had taken place in their private regard for each
other.   " So much the better," said the General; " but
still I see great obstacles; at Windsor we are strongly
attached to Addington, and it will be very difficult ever
to prevail on the King to dismiss him.   The Catholic
Question, which angered him with Pitt, has rooted Addington in favour.   The King never will consent to form
a Ministry that may incline to that; it is a point of conscience, and you know enough of His Majesty's religious
mind to be sure it will supersede every other consideration."   I replied, " It ought;" that I honoured and revered him the more for it, and that not because my
opinion went the same way, but from the principle on
which His Majesty acted; however, I had hopes, and
could have no scruple of stating them to him, that this
objection of the Catholic Question would be found not to
be an insurmountable obstacle, if ever a change of Administration, or rather a re-inforcement of Administration depended on that, since I was nearly certain that all
the principal persons who had favoured it, and left Office
in consequence, considered they had done their duty sufficiently; and *now*, knowing how His Majesty felt on
the subject, would, were they to resume Office, not bring
it forward themselves, but let it rest, and look upon it as
dead.   " This is very pleasant to hear," said the General; " but can they prevent others from bringing it forward?   They will not join them, but propose the previous question, and waive the discussion.   I *hope* this
may satisfy the King; but I repeat it to you, he is so
very tenacious of his principles on this point, so conscientiously bent to support them, that I apprehend great

difficulties. It is *Addington's* stronghold on him; and as he (Addington) evidently will not quit Office voluntarily, be assured he will avail himself of it to secure the duration of his power. But you have told me what gives me comfort, may I tell it to my brother?" I said, " Certainly." At the time, and since, when ruminating over this conversation, I was doubtful whether it was meant to pump me, to instruct me, or simply one of curiosity. General Grenville's character would induce me to suppose the last; but when I look to his connexions on one side, and to the state of intimacy and favour he is in at Windsor, I am staggered. And I framed the answers I made to his questions in a way that could not commit or displease any one, and such as I thought, without departing from the real truth, the best calculated to meet our great end.

On the 7th, Tuesday, I returned to Bath. On Wednesday I called on Pitt, and communicated to him the Duke of York's answer of the 4th December, which was as follows :—

Horse Guards, 4th Dec., 1802.

MY DEAR LORD,—If I had not been under the necessity of paying my duty at Windsor, I should not have failed to have acknowledged the receipt of your very obliging letter yesterday, or to have returned you many thanks for your attention in informing me of the present state of things.

It is impossible, as you very well remark, to enter fully into such a subject in a letter; but you are t roughly acquainted with my opinion, and therefore will easily conceive how much I applaud the resolution which you mention to have been taken.

I hope still to be able to make an excursion to Bath, for a few days at least, between this and Christmas, when we shall be able to talk the whole over. Should any thing fresh occur before we meet, I trust to your friendship to inform me of it.

Believe me, &c. (Signed) FREDERICK.

I wished to know whether he (Pitt) thought it meant
to convey more than was expressed. Pitt hesitated;
said it certainly *might* be construed to mean more; but
as the Duke was not a very accurate writer, he doubted
about it; that on the whole it was very good. He went
on by saying, " I hope you continue to approve our
measure of delay. Nothing but good can come from it;
it has already produced *high establishments, as high as
any one could wish;* and, as the ways and means for
providing them are extremely fallacious and ill judged,
will not add to the merits of the present Government as
financiers."

Exchequer Bills were only a loan in another shape;
and as it was to provide for probably a *permanent* public
measure, and was in itself only a temporary supply, it
was doubly vicious. It had been deemed wise, even in
war, to try to pay the annual expenses out of the annual
revenues; and to depart from this maxim, even in the
first year of peace, and to let the public find that new
loans, and, of course, fresh taxes, must be laid on every
year, even in peace, could not tend to the advantage of
public credit, or to inspire the public mind with confidence and security; that he was, however, desirous *this*
should not be too much dwelt upon just now in debate.
That it was impossible it could escape notice, how directly it contradicted the words in the speech. He then
went on by saying, Canning was so zealous, when following his own leanings, as to be imprudent without knowing it. I mentioned Canning's argument, and the difference that *ought* to be in the opinions of those in confidence, and those out of all confidence. " I see none,"
said Pitt; " where does it exist? it militates against the
plan, or the plot, if you please, they are all forwarding;
and the committing me with Addington," said he *very
gravely*, " will, I assure you, endanger the whole." He
was getting into his chaise to go to Longleat, and, as I
was to follow him the next day, I contented myself with
saying, I hoped it was a *plan*, not a *plot*, and that, after
all, it would end well. He stated to me his intended
motions for the next month, and said he would, if possi-

ble, pass a day or two at Park Place in the first week in January; that he should meet me at Lord Bathurst's on the 18th or 19th of December.

After I had seen Mr. Pitt I wrote the following letter to Canning:—

Bath, 8th December, 1802.

MY DEAR CANNING,—I have seen Pitt only for a few moments; he was setting out for Longleat. I propose returning there to-morrow; and, as I probably may have more conversation than I could have this morning, I postpone writing to you till Friday. Pitt goes on that day to Burton; returns here on Monday; comes to Cirencester (where I shall be) on the 18th or 19th, and from thence back here for a week. After that to Cuffnalls (G. Rose's), Dropmore, and, I hope, Park Place. He intends to avoid London. We all leave Bath on the 21st; I and my daughters on the 16th or 17th: and we shall all re-unite at Park Place about Christmas. Pitt will, I fear, have left Longleat before we can receive our letters on Friday; but, as that is doubtful, pray, if you have time, write me your feelings on the debate of to-day, in order that I may bring them forward (if necessary) in opposition to those of his correspondents.

I enclose you a letter* on which I wish for your opinion; does it mean more than is simply expressed? Pitt, to whom I have shewn it, thinks not: be good enough to send it me back, directed to Longleat, if you write to-morrow or next day, as I intend writing again to the Duke on Monday, to acquaint him with my motions, and to persuade him to make Park Place his sleeping stage on his way to, or from Bath. This, if he has any thing to say, I am sure he will readily do. I received yours of the 4th.

Ever yours,   (Signed)   MALMESBURY.

---

* That from the Duke of York of the 4th December.

On Thursday, the 9th December, I returned (taking my daughter Catherine with me) to Longleat, where I remained till the Sunday following, December 12. Pitt, whom I found there, left it on the 10th. I had no opportunity of conversing with him; neither, indeed, did I seek it, having nothing to say or hear; and my object was to contribute, in conjunction with Lord and Lady Bathurst, to make him feel at his ease, and to appreciate justly the very real and solid sentiments of Lord Bath, and the extreme good-humour and civility of Lady Bath. I hope to have a little succeeded in this, as Pitt grew at last to be more conversable (he was, as I heard from Lord Bathurst, very silent and reserved the first day); but at our evening round game (*speculation*) he was quite himself. Lord Bath's horses carried him to Shepton Mallet; it was market-day, and the people took them off, and drew him to his inn. This was the more flattering as nothing had been, or could have been, prepared, and as it was clearly the honest and undisguised sentiments of the farmers and inhabitants. On the day of Pitt's leaving Longleat, viz., Friday, the 10th December, I received the following letter from Canning, with the substance of his speech on Wednesday:

Conduit Street, Thursday, 9th Dec., 1802.

MY DEAR LORD MALMESBURY,—The enclosures* which I am obliged to divide between this and the accompanying cover, will account to you for my not being able to write a very long answer to your letter, which I have just received, especially when you hear at the same time that the debate† lasted till near four o'clock in the morning, that I am consequently not long out of bed,

---

* Containing a copy of his speech upon the Army Estimates of the previous evening, which was one of the most eloquent he ever made. Speaking of Pitt's retreat, he says, " Retreat and withdraw as much as he will, he must not hope to efface the memory of his past services from the gratitude of his country : he *cannot* withdraw himself from the following of a Nation : he *must endure* the attachment of a people whom he has saved."

† On the Army Estimates, which passed without a division, Sheridan lashed Ministers with his wit, whilst he pretended to sympathise with and defend them. He also threw out insinuations about Mr. Pitt's retirement, which Canning refuted.

that there is expected to be another debate to-day, and that, before the House, I think it right to go to the drawing-room.

I thought it indispensable to write down, while my recollection was fresh, the precise words (or very nearly so) of that part of my speech yesterday which related to Pitt, as there is no knowing how newspapers, still less how correspondents, will represent them. I intended to send them to Pitt himself; but as it seems possible that he may have left Longleat before the post arrives, I enclose them to you. If he is not gone, you will have the goodness to communicate them; if he is, I hope you will be able to forward them, so that they may reach him as soon as his other intelligence of this day.

I have written so hastily, that in many parts I am afraid I may be hardly intelligible. I am confident, however, that I have written nearly the truth; for, as I was aware beforehand that Sheridan would make precisely the attack which he did make, and I was aware also how much delicacy and discretion was required in answering it, I had *measured* my phrases beforehand; and unless the heat of speaking quite confounded my memory at the time, and continues to impair my recollection still, I am persuaded that I spoke nearly what I had meditated, and have put down nearly what I spoke.

Leveson and Sturges (who are discretion and prudence personified) assured me, that I had said nothing amiss; and other people about me (Hawkins Browne, for instance), not at all *in one sense*, took what I said, as a just and called-for defence of Pitt, and were not even aware of the *sting in the tail;* that is, the *disclaimer* challenged from Addington, of *any connexion* between Pitt and the Government. This disclaimer Addington did utter, but not in many words, and so late in the debate, that (the House being much thinned) I am not sure that it made all its proper impression.

I have seen no paper, and no person to-day to enable me to judge of this circumstance. The debate, upon the whole, was a very useful one. Sheridan's speech was admirable in all ways; Ryder's was excellent in many, and, in point of tone particularly, I think it was just such as Pitt himself might have made.

Fox was completely routed and broken by Sheridan and Ryder.

Wilberforce half *recanted* his errors ; Addington *canted*, and that was all.

I return your letter, about which, I confess, I am of Pitt's opinion.

If you can shew him my enclosure, *and get it back*, I should be glad to have it again, as it is precisely the statement that one is anxious to have correctly recorded.

One point, and one only, of those which I had thought of beforehand (knowing Sheridan's intention to touch upon it), unluckily escaped me while I was speaking. That was the *forcing the King by Parliamentary measures*, to change his ministers. I think this so important that if the debate of to-day should afford an opporunity (and if Tierney speaks, as he seems to intend, it probably may), I will endeavour to supply the omission. What I mean to say upon this subject is, " that no real friend of Pitt could bear to entertain the idea; that *I*, for one, would be a party to no motion, resolution, &c., and that (in *your* words to the Duke of York) I should think the salvation of the country but half achieved, if any violence were offered to the feelings of the Sovereign in achieving it."

I will write again to-morrow if I can; but if the debate lasts again, I shall be quite knocked up.

Ever, &c.   (Signed)   G. C.

As Pitt had left Longleat, and was in a remote corner of Somersetshire, I had no means of complying with Canning's wishes sooner than the Sunday following, when I knew Pitt would return to Bath, and I therefore sent over my groom early *that* morning to meet him on his arrival.

On Monday morning, 13th December, Pitt called upon me; said he was perfectly satisfied with all Canning had said respecting him; that he had also heard from several of his friends (and, amongst others, he quoted Lord Camden), that his speech was a very good and proper one, and much to the purpose. He desired me to say as much in my answer to Canning. Pitt kept the *précis* of the speech. After having said this, Pitt spoke on the general turn of the debate on the 9th; said he readily forgave the *pretended* abuse Sheridan bestowed on him, in consequence of the real abuse he dealt out to Fox. He admired the wit and humour of the speech, and joined heartily in the laugh against Doctor Fell.[*] Pitt then fell into a sort of panegyric on the state of the country, and, in his statement of our resources and revenue, rather contradicted his former language on that subject. He said, however great France may be, we had a revenue equal to all Europe, (he made it amount to thirty-two millions sterling,) a navy superior to all Europe, and a commerce as great as that of all Europe,—and, he added, laughingly, to make us *quite gentlemen*, a *debt* as large as that of all Europe; that if with these means we acted wisely, with a just mixture of spirit and forbearance, and could protract the evil of war for a few years, *war* would be an evil much less felt. He then got back to himself, and was disposed to think that now he might be allowed (at least for a little while longer) to enjoy quiet. This led to a conversation similar to several others already related, and not necessary to be recorded. Pitt, Lord Mulgrave, and Colonel Stanley dined with me; nobody could be more cheerful or more companionable than he was after dinner; and upstairs, with Lady Malmesbury and my daughters, as usual, we played at Speculation. I wrote this day (the 13th) to Canning, and answered his letter of the 11th, which was as follows:—

[*] Sheridan said, the noble Lord's (Temple) dislike to Ministers put him in mind of the parody of two lines in Martial—

> " I do not like thee, Doctor Fell,
> The reason why, I cannot tell ;
> But this I 'm sure I know full well,
> I do not like thee, Doctor Fell."

Addington went by the nickname of the *Doctor*.

Conduit Street, Saturday, 11th Dec., 1802.

MY DEAR LORD MALMESBURY,—I am rather disappointed at not receiving your promised letter from Longleat to-day, especially as I must now fast for it till Monday—and as your last letter, though very particular about Pitt's motions, does not give me any account of your own, and shall therefore write very shortly. Bath, I suppose, is the safest direction; but I have nothing that will not keep very well till Monday.

Thursday's debate was by no means satisfactory:* indeed, the whole state of things is far otherwise in *one* point of view, or rather, perhaps, in every point of view *but* one—which exception is, that we certainly have succeeded in raising the *tone* of Government by the debate, but I think their *tone* only. The shabby *animus* still remains; and what they say is just enough to make objection seem captious, to satisfy moderate people, and to prevent the want of Pitt from being felt as it ought to be.

But all this would require a very long chapter, and I think I shall write it as soon as I can quite make up my own opinions, by reflection and comparison with that of others, to Pitt himself.

Ever yours, &c. (Signed) G. C.

P. S. Mrs. C. is not yet confined, but, I imagine, has not many days to come. I hope she will be well enough, through all her trouble, to allow of my joining your Christmas party for a day at Park Place.

I wrote to the Duke of York on the 14th, on which day I dined, by my own invitation, in consequence of Her Royal Highness's permission, with the Duchess of York. No one there but her own family; she, as she always is, was most pleasant and kind.

* On the Army Estimates.

LETTER FROM LORD MALMESBURY TO MR. CANNING.

Bath, 13th Dec., 1802.

My dear Canning,—What I wrote yesterday from Longleat will explain (if not justify) my breach of promise on Friday.

I found yours of the 11th on my return yesterday. I shall remain here till Wednesday; then go to Lord Bathurst's for a week, and afterwards become stationary at Park Place.

Pitt has this moment been with me; he is not only most perfectly satisfied *himself,* and *pleased* with what you spoke on Wednesday, but says that his correspondents (amonst whom he named Lord Camden) stated it to him as very excellent, and much to the purpose, and it went completely to do away any misconstructions or misrepresentations which people had thought proper to put on your expressions in a former debate. This will, I am sure, please you; but it will please you still more to hear, that Pitt's mind and spirits, or rather *spirit,* is exactly what we could wish, full of energy and vigour, determined to shrink from nothing *on his part* which can keep up the tone and dignity of the country. He at the same time feels a sort of comfort in the idea that he is not yet likely to be wanted, and that he may be allowed to enjoy leisure and quiet at least till the middle of February.

I did not greatly encourage this cause for comfort, as I feel as little as you do on the effects of the debates. High establishments are good things; but if we get only the *sword* of Scanderbeg, and not his *arm* to wield it, it will be of little avail.

I am very glad you think of writing to Pitt himself; he will attend much more to what you write than to what I say. He joins us at Cirencester on Wednesday.

I am very sorry you had no opportunity of saying what you had in contemplation respecting the King; it is very necessary it should be repeatedly and strongly asserted, as you may be assured no attempt will be spared to give a contrary impression.

Ever yours, &c.   (Signed)   MALMESBURY.

TO HIS ROYAL HIGHNESS THE DUKE OF YORK.

Bath, 14th Dec., 1802.

SIR,—I should not have delayed a post to acknowledge your Royal Highness's letter of the 4th instant, if I had had anything material to communicate; that not being the case, I was unwilling to give your Royal Highness unnecessary trouble. Everything is right *here* —the best mind, spirit, and disposition possible. I hope it is also equally right everywhere, but I am not quite without my fears.

I leave Bath to-morrow for Lord Bathurst's at Cirencester, where I stay a week. I shall be at Park Place on the 23d, and remain there till the birthday. I take the liberty of stating this under some faint hopes that your Royal Highness, either in your way to or from Bath, may condescend to make it your resting-place.

I am, &c.   (Signed)   MALMESBURY.

On Wednesday, the 15th of December, 1802, I went with my daughters to Lord Bathurst's, and remained there till the Wednesday following, the 22nd inst.

I received the following letter from Canning:—

Conduit Street, 14th Dec., 1802.

MY DEAR LORD MALMESBURY,—Many thanks for your letter of yesterday, which has set my mind much at ease. I had heard through Lord Spencer, of Lord Camden's satisfaction. I confess the only fear that I have remaining is, that I *un*committed Pitt too much; and I know they have taken that advantage of what I said—Ryder especially, for though (as I told you) he spoke as Pitt himself might have done, he has out of the House done

more harm to our game for Pitt than any other individual, and that too with knowledge enough of the state
of Pitt's mind to have entitled us to expect another conduct from him.   *This is my private opinion.*

I like your general account of Pitt, but not the particular expression of his wish for a long period of inaction.
Sooner or later he *must* act, or the country is gone.   All
the appearances of the present moment I am persuaded
are false and hollow.   The tone is assumed but to answer
the pressure of the moment; and nothing is really at
bottom, but concession—concession—concession.   Will
Pitt be thus satisfied?   God forbid!

What is your address at Lord Bathurst's?   Does Pitt
return to Bath, after having been at Cirencester?   I
hope not.   He will be waylaid there.   Prevent it if you
can.   Ever yours, &c.   (Signed)   G. C.

On Saturday, the 18th of December, Pitt came to
Cirencester, and also Fitzharris.   Pitt stayed till Monday, the 20th.   I purposely avoided all political conversation, wishing to let him enjoy himself; we were nobody but Lord Bathurst's family and mine.   Pitt was
very inquisitive about Malta—its old Government, the
mode of election of a Grand Master, &c., &c.   Lord
Bathurst quite right and sensible on public affairs—
moderate and candid in the true sense of the word; he
looks up to Pitt; rates Addington very low—laughs at
him for being taken in by Sheridan, who is constantly
quizzing him; and is hurt at his being the dupe of Fox,
whose intentions are more serious and more dangerous
than Sheridan's.

On Wednesday, the 22nd of December, I left Cirencester for Park Place, and received there the two following letters from Canning:—

Conduit Street, 23rd Dec., 1802.

MY DEAR LORD MALMESBURY,—I have this moment
received your letter of the 21st, which ought to have
reached me yesterday.   I should have written to you
yesterday, or the day before, had I not expected to have

heard from you, or had I been sure of your direction; but you had told me nothing of the length of your stay at Cirencester.

I trust nothing can prevent my being with you at Park Place on Tuesday.

Mrs. Canning is now going on so well again (though after a pause in her recovery yesterday, which rather alarmed me), that I do not fear any impediment to my leaving town from her situation.

The only thing that I apprehend to be possible is, that the House of Commons may not adjourn till Tuesday, or that the Bill now in the House of Lords may not come back to us till that day; and after the advantage which the Chancellor's opposition gives us, I should be sorry not to be in the way to have a parting blow at it.

It is (as you may have gathered from the spirit of the proceedings upon it) a flagrant Admiralty job—job not in the sense of *interest*, but of trumpery spite, originating in Lord St. Vincent's violence, and forced upon Addington's imbecility, in defiance of the declared opinions of the Chancellor, and all the friends of the last Administration that belong to the present, as well as of Pelham and others.*

When we opposed it in the House of Commons, we knew the Chancellor's opinion, but had no expectation that he would declare it so openly in Parliament. By what I can learn out of doors, it has done Addington a mischief, and one should be sorry not to *help* it all one can ; but I still hope that there will be an opportunity of saying what one wants to say upon it to-morrow, or at latest on Monday.

Ever yours, &c.   (Signed)   G. C.

Conduit Street, Christmas-day, 1802.

My dear Lord Malmesbury, — I will certainly be with you on Tuesday to dinner, and Morpeth will come

---

* For the appointment of Commissioners to inquire into the abuses of the Navy. It originated with Lord St. Vincent, and, notwithstanding what Mr.

with me, unless he should hear from you by Monday's
post, that you have no room for him, or had rather not
have him.   Ever yours, &c.
                              (Signed)   G. C.

My answers were of no consequence, only desiring
him to come, and bring Morpeth, &c.

On Monday, the 17th of December, Pitt came to Park
Place, about seven in the evening, to a late dinner.   I
had sent my horses to meet him at Basingstoke; he
came from Cuffnalls, G. Rose's.

Mr. Elliot was the only person in the house besides
my daughters and Fitzharris.   Pitt was the pleasantest
companion possible, at and after dinner, whether conversing with us or with them; and we sat up, without
any reference to public concerns, till near one o'clock.

On Tuesday, the 28th of December, Elliot left us, and
I received the following letter from Canning :—

                    Conduit Street, Monday, 27th Dec., 1802.

MY DEAR LORD MALMESBURY,—Since I wrote to you
on Saturday, Mrs. Canning has been going on so much
less satisfactorily than she had been during the greater
part of the preceding week, that I am almost afraid I
may be prevented from keeping my engagement with
you to-morrow.   I need not say how exceedingly desirous I am, on every account, to keep it; and though I
write to make my excuse to you beforehand, if I should
not come, I will still, if I can (with any comfort), leave
town, and be with you by dinner time.   I had intended
leaving town to-day (as the Bill that I mentioned to
you is come down much less objectionable than it went
up to the Lords), but that is now out of the question.

Mrs. Canning has been thrown back, I think, by her
extreme anxiety to be a nurse; and the question, whether she can be so or not, is yet to be decided; and Mr.
Croft and Sir Walter Farquhar seem either not to have
made up their opinions, or not to be quite agreed in

Canning says, conferred great benefits on the service, though it met with
violent opposition set on foot by those interested in the abuses.

them. The decision *either* way would, I hope, put things in a right course again; but while the decision is not yet taken, I should feel very uncomfortable indeed in being out of the way for eight and forty hours, especially as the probability is, that it may be unfavourable to the object upon which her mind is set.

This is a very long, and to you, probably, very tiresome prose upon my nursery.

I will add no more to it, but only say that if I should not be able to get to you to-morrow, and should be able to leave town the middle of the week, I must first of course endeavour not to miss Pitt entirely, and go after him to Dropmore. But I will afterwards come to you for your own sakes, if you will let me, and talk over with you all that has passed and is in prospect.

Ever yours, &c. (Signed) G. C.

Pitt, Fitzharris, and myself, rode round the grounds in the finest weather possible. On our return, which was early in the morning, we searched amongst books for the Statutes of Malta, in order to discover whether, in case of lapse, or any want of form, in the election, the nomination of the Great Master went to the Pope. Nothing like it could be found either in " Vertot" or " Histoire des Ordres Monastiques." The motive for this information was, that it was said by France that Ruspoli had been named Great Master by the Pope, and, therefore, that the conditions of the Treaty of Amiens respecting Malta were fulfilled, and we should evacuate it.* About four o'clock Lord Morpeth and Canning arrived (Mrs. Canning being better). I wished, however, that the conversation should still be general, and I

---

* In the Treaty of Amiens, signed March 25th, 1802, Art. 10 provides that Malta shall be given up to the Knights of St. John, who shall *amongst themselves* select a Grand Master. The British garrison to evacuate the island three months after the ratifications. In case of the Knights of St. John not being able to provide a garrison (and the order was nearly obsolete, and its property alienated), Malta was to be occupied by Neapolitan troops for a twelvemonth, or longer if necessary. All the Great Powers of Europe were invited to accede to this stipulation. The whole tenor of this Article was calculated to embroil the contracting parties.

warded off all politics by playing very joyously at *specu-lation* till bed-time.

The next morning (Wednesday, Dec. 29) I took an occasion of saying to Pitt, that I had endeavoured to make Park Place *really* a place of rest and repose to him, under the hopes that he would, whenever he want-ed rest and repose, return to it, and be sure of finding it. I added, that, in return for his having very often procured me *business*, I wished to procure him *quiet*, provided it did not last *too long*. This at once brought on the whole subject, which had in a manner lain dor-mant since the 13th instant. I knew that, on his re-turn to Bath on the 24th, he had found Lord Castle-reagh, and was prepared for the impressions *he* might have given. Pitt said, that he had revolved the great question of his *coming forward* again and again in his mind, and that the result of his most serious delibera-tion was, that it was not yet time. That the Govern-ment of the country had shewn a degree of energy and vigour not apparent in it when first this subject was under debate; that this made a very material difference; for, although he, *perhaps*, did not consider this spirit and energy as *genuine*, or in the character of the present Government, yet it was impossible for him to act on his own *misgivings;* neither could his conduct be grounded, much less justified, by stating that it arose, not from what appeared, but from what he supposed to be the character and intentions of Ministers; that such a con-duct might belong to unconnected or *uncommitted* per-sons, but in him it would be highly blamable, look like a dereliction of character, and thirst of Office, and, what he felt still more, a breach of faith to those he had for some time advised, and hitherto always supported. That, for this reason, which he trusted *I* should admit as a valid one, though younger and *more ardent* persons might not (he alluded evidently to Canning), he had made up his mind to remain *for some time* in the same *passive* state he had assumed for these last two months. In short, *till* he saw that either the audacity of Buona-parte, or a relapse to *concession* and yielding in Ministers, called for his stepping forward; that *then* he *would* come forward as a most bounden duty, and then he could do it with much greater effect than now, when things apparently were tolerably right.

I replied, that having acquiesced in his reasons for being *inactive* till now, I could not combat him, so long as *he* thought the same reasons existed; but I could not help observing, that *I* did not think the present aspect of firmness and vigour at all real or genuine; that I considered it as the effect of the fear of the House of Commons, not as a wise and called for State Measure— as the fear of opposition at home, not of insolence and attack from France. " It may be so," said Pitt, " but for my argument it comes to the same. *I* must not construe men's thoughts; if it is only a sham vigour, it cannot last; its consequences soon will be manifest, and then *my* time is come."

" But," said I, " may not such very great and serious evils ensue in the mean while, from this being a falla- cious, and not a *real*, courage, that you will, by your delay, have to reproach yourself with having (indirectly at least) occasioned them; and will you not most cer- tainly find the task of setting things right infinitely more difficult?"

" If I were absolutely to wait," answered Pitt, " for the sort of extreme case to which you allude, I certainly should; but I only mean to wait till there is any de- parture, on the side of Mr. Addington's Government, from the system they now affect to have assumed, or any *further* encroachment on the side of Buonaparte, which *may* materially affect the security or strength of this country. By this, I mean any grasping at *maritime* power; any attempt to add, by seizure, to his own, or to decrease our, naval strength. For I must distinguish, I fear," said he, " between maritime and Continental power, and consider the Continent and its concerns, at least for the moment, beyond the reach of our inter- ference. But, again, all and every act which tends to his maritime aggrandizement, in whatever shape it ap- pears, or however accompanied, we *must* protest against,

and, if that will not do, *act*. By this," said he, " I
mean any attempt to take possession of Holland and its
Colonies, or of Portugal; and, above all, any attempt to
break in upon our establishments and power in India.
To all these we *must* oppose the most decided resistance.
If Ministers shrink from it, *I* shall feel bound to speak
my mind, and will come forward with every means in
my power. To these cases (all, you will allow, probable
ones,) I will add, that, if *they* insist on Malta being
evacuated before the strict letter of the 10th Article in
the Treaty of Amiens is complied with, and Ministers
give way, I then, and in that case, shall also feel bound
to oppose them avowedly. It is enough, and more than
enough, that they have suffered to pass by unnoticed the
various unwarrantable encroachments which France has
made since the Preliminaries; but to allow them or the
Treaty (bad as it is) to be violated, is *a disgrace the
nation must not hear of*. To all these cases I will add,"
continued he, " any insult to our national honour, such
as an attempt to force French Consuls into our ports;*
such as (if true, which I doubt,) the Interrogatory Captain d'Auvergne is supposed to have undergone; in
short, any violation of what is the clear and specific
Law of Nations, and rights arising out of that law."

Pitt went on in this strain, with a degree of warmth
and eloquence, for nearly half an hour, that would have
well become him in the House; and when he had done, I
said, that if I did not think *his principle* a right one,
which was by no means the case, and if I still maintained, after what he had said, as eager and ardent a
desire for his immediate resuming Office as the youngest
of his friends, yet still I should be satisfied, since I was
clearly convinced that some one of the several points he
had stated as calling for *his* interposition, *must* soon
arise; and that if he had *not*, and did not so solemnly,
pledge himself to interpose, I should look forward to
them with trembling. To this he made a civil answer,
observing, that the great and most important question

* On enlarging on this afterwards he said, " Let them be either sent back,
or ordered to reside twenty miles from the Coast."—Original Note.

under deliberation was, how *to bear and to forbear*. That, *if* it were possible to go on without risking our power or safety four or five years in peace, our revenues then would be in such an improved state, that we might, without fear, look in the face of such a war as we had just ended. That this, therefore, (and he spoke, he was sure, from the safest calculation,) was a most important and high consideration, and which nothing should supersede, excepting that which ought to supersede every thing, a gross *national insult;* an open act of hostility; and an attempt at aggrandizement in such a way, on the part of France, as would comprise, in the result, both.

I omitted to say that Pitt stated, that amongst the causes which would immediately make him ready to resume Office, would be any wish expressed directly to that effect by the King, or even so expressed as to leave him in no doubt of its actual existence.

At one o'clock, Pitt and Canning went to Lord Grenville's at Dropmore, Lord Morpeth to London, Fitzharris to Shottisbrook.

Nothing could be pleasanter than the whole of Pitt's manners during his stay. Catherine and Fanny were both pleased with him, from his great good-humour and civility.

I thought from his conversation that Lord Castlereagh had made some impression upon him, though I incline, on the whole, to think Lord Castlereagh much more disposed to follow Pitt than abide by the fortune of Addington.

Pitt disapproved the protest* in the Lords, signed by Lords Grenville, Spencer, Minto, and two others. He also doubted the statement of Auvergne's case as in Cobbett.†

---

* Against the Malt Tax Bill, Dec. 15th, on the grounds that Government had not stated sufficient reasons for raising this supply, and for keeping up such large military establishments.

† Le Comte d'Auvergne, a Captain in the British Navy, succeeded to the title and estates of the Duc de Bouillon, and after the Peace went to Paris, to prosecute his claims on the property. He was imprisoned in the Temple for six days, treated with every indignity by Fouché's police, and sent out of the country.

On the 4th and 5th January, I received the two following letters from Canning:—

Conduit Street, 3rd Jan., 1803.

MY DEAR LORD MALMESBURY,—You will have given
me credit for having found it impossible to come to you
before my return to town, without knowing exactly how
I was prevented; but more so still when I tell you
exactly what prevented me. I found Pitt intended
staying at Dropmore till Saturday, and I therefore
thought it worth while to return there on Friday from
South Hill for the sake of seeing him and Lord Grenville together again after a day's *tête-à-tête*, and for the
sake also of accompanying Pitt the next day as far as
our roads should be together. I would have taken you
in my way to South Hill on Thursday, or back again on
Friday, but that I learned, upon inquiry, that all the
cross-roads by Maidenhead and Henley were impassa-
ble at this time of year, and, in fact, I was obliged to
go round by Windsor; not to mention that they proposed
riding with me as far as Windsor on my way to South
Hill, and met me the next day on my return.

Everything that passed at Dropmore was highly
satisfactory, with the exception of one single point of
difference in opinion, or rather in *statement* of opinion;
for what Lord Grenville speaks, in that particular, are
not his own sentiments, but those which are inculcated
by others. I am as confident as I was two months ago,
and Pitt is satisfied of the same thing. The point of
difference is (as you may suppose) *the question*, upon the
manner of getting rid of which Pitt has no scruples at
all, and Lord Grenville, I hope, none that are insuperable, though they must be overcome, not by argument,
but by circumstances. The circumstances arising, I
have no fear of any lasting practical difficulty.

I mention this as the only point on which there was
not, substantially, a perfect agreement. On other points
there were naturally shades of difference, both as to the
degree of opinion felt, and as to the liberty of acting up
to the full extent of their feelings.

But upon the two most important subjects, most important both in themselves, and from the greater probability of their coming soon into discussion, Malta and Holland, I think we are on sure and firm ground. Add to this, that he (Pitt) has a separate indignation of his own about the Budget, in which he says Addington has deceived the House of Commons (and he hopes *himself*, for otherwise it is a rascally deception) to the amount of about 2,800,000*l.* a-year, besides misrepresenting him (Pitt) in the most unfair manner: and add, too, that Pitt says he must set the House of Commons right, if Addington himself does not do so; and you will see that one has reason to hope that the next session may open not unfavourably.

On Saturday Pitt and I separated at Cranford Bridge, he for Long's and I for town; but he came to town yesterday, and dined with me *tête-à-tête*; and I should be most perfectly satisfied with the result of our own conversation, if I could have succeeded in persuading him to decline Addington's pressing invitations to Richmond. His going there is for appearance *very bad ;* in reality, I feel pretty well assured it is of no danger, but I wish he would not go. Addington has been writing day after day, entreating to see him. Perhaps he could not well pass through or near town without complying with his entreaty; but I wish he could have been satisfied to do so. The mischief is to be apprehended from the publicity which they will give to this visit, and the use which they will make of it to persuade people that all is well, and as usual, between them. Pitt has promised me, indeed, that he will intimate to Addington his hope and expectation that his name shall *not* be so brought forward, nor his sentiments of approbation stated so boldly, as in many former instances; and that he will, in order more effectually to secure himself against such misrepresentations, tell Addington plainly, that *we* of his friends who differ from the Government, are completely apprized of his (Pitt's) real sentiments upon the state of public affairs, and shall continue to be so from time to time as long as we choose to consult him, and as often as he has any sentiment worth communicating. This, I think, may serve as a check upon garrulity and falsehood, and may also lead Addington to reason a little inwardly on possible future consequences.

But, with all this, I do not deny that I had rather he did not go to Richmond.

I shall try again to-day what I can do to persuade him rather to wait for Addington's coming to town. I am going now to call upon him, and to walk with him to the Chancellor's, whom he certainly ought to see. He dines with me again to-day, but not alone. To-morrow is the day that he destines for Addington; on Wednesday he returns to Long's, for what time he does not seem to have determined; I think he will go nowhere else till he goes to Walmer. I shall not leave town till he is safe out of reach of it, as it is very important to know his last parting impressions.

You shall hear from me again, and shall see me when I am liberty.

Mrs. C. is going on well, but slowly.

Ever, &c.   (Signed)   G. C.

———

Conduit Street, 4th Jan., 1803.

My dear Lord Malmesbury,—I write merely to tell you, that when I called in York Place yesterday, I found that Pitt had, *upon reflection*, given up his intention of going to Richmond Park to-day, and had written his excuse, and appointed to see Addington when he comes to town to-morrow.

To-day we dine together at Nepean's (a well-disposed person), which is much better.

I am trying to persuade him to go to the Levée to-morrow, which on all accounts he ought to do, and which if he does, it will make his subsequent interview in Downing Street less observed. One thing per day is enough for the newspapers to report of him.

Ever, &c.   (Signed)   G. C.

———

To these two letters I replied :—

Park Place, Thursday, 6th Jan., 1803.

MY DEAR CANNING,—I write a day later than I intended, but a series of interruptions yesterday morning made it impossible for me to keep my promise.

Every thing you relate is satisfactory, every thing you have done excellent: the preventing the visit to Richmond Park, the substitution of the Levée in its place (*if* you carried that point), was an important measure. I cannot help wishing Pitt did not so much incline to delay and procrastination. I combated this disposition in him as far as I could, and rested my arguments on one side on the dangerous and unnatural connexions Ministry in the mean while, in order to strengthen themselves, *might* form, to secure (as they might suppose) their duration in Office, and the necessary ill consequences of such connexions; and, on the other, that Buonaparte would grow so daring in his insults from being unmolested, or from a conviction that they must be submitted to, that the country might be placed in such a predicament, that his (Pitt's) return to office *must* also be an immediate return to war, and that this we had over and over again argued was the worst possible thing that could accompany it. The details of what passed in my last conversation with Pitt will keep, but I want to know whether you and I feel alike on this particular point. Pitt mentioned to me Addington's misstatement in the budget, and I am pleased it dwells on his mind: at the same time, I have little doubt Addington will prevail on him not to expose his ignorance or deceit in the House of Commons, since either, if known, must lower him to the very dust on the floor.

That which gives me the most uneasiness is *the Question*. *I* know *to a certainty* (you must not ask me my authority), that it is perpetually dinned into the King's ears that his late servants are as strongly bent on it as ever; and that whatever he may hear of their being inclined to give way on it, is thrown out solely for the purpose of inducing him to take them into place again.

This has *its* effect, and will be found to be the great stumbling-block in our way when the hour of action comes on.

I could say a good deal more to you on this subject, but every thing material for you to know *and act upon* is comprised in the few lines I have just written.

I was not well enough to venture yesterday to Frogmore, which I much regret. I am not comfortable to-day, though I impute it more to the remedy than the complaint.

Let this be an excuse for the shortness of my letter, short at least in comparison to the subject to which it relates. We rejoice in Mrs. Canning's being so well. Shall I see you soon, or not?

Ever, &c.   (Signed)   MALMESBURY.

On the 9th and 11th I received the following letters from Canning:—

Conduit Street, 8th Jan., 1803.

MY DEAR LORD MALMESBURY,—The expectation of your letter, and the little desire that I felt to undo the satisfaction which I presumed mine had given you, prevented me from writing again on Wednesday, as I might have done, to tell you that my "capital measure" had failed, and that Pitt *did go, not* to the Levée, but to *Richmond* on that day.

For the Levée he really had no excuse but laziness; the other, which is very bad in *appearance* at least, if not in reality, he could not help. He had refused *twice*, and had actually appointed an interview in town on Wednesday; but the Premier warily answered, that he intended to be in town only for the Levée, and should return to Richmond to dinner, and would it not be the same thing to Pitt to return there with him as to dine with him in town? I do not know what he could have replied; and so he went, lamented rather than blamed.

But if he staid there *all Thursday* (as I hear)—if, instead of taking Richmond *in his way* to Long's, he made that a real substantive visit, I know not what is to be said for him.

What he has to say for himself I shall perhaps know to-day, when he returns to town (from Long's, I hope and believe), and dines where I do, at Sir Walter Farquhar's.

If he acted up to his intentions at Richmond, (which, however, knowing him as well as we do, we are both warranted to doubt,) his visit may have done good rather than harm. If not, he has manacled himself with fresh difficulties for the moment of action, when it comes; but I will not anticipate evil, and therefore will wait till I have seen him, to write to you more at large.

Did I tell you that he had seen the Chancellor?—not when he called on Monday, but the Chancellor found him at home next day. The particulars of their conversation he of course did not disclose to me: but to my question, " Was the result such as necessarily to leave upon the Chancellor's mind the impression that, in what I said to him in November, I was not wrong in principle, even if in degree?" he answered readily in the affirmative; which being so, the conference cannot but have been useful, and must have prepared the Chancellor to look forward to the time to come.

He had seen no other minister when he left town on Wednesday.

I live in hopes of being able to get to you in the course of this month. I am most anxious to do so.

Ever, &c.   (Signed)   G. C.

P.S. Remember me to Lady M. most kindly. I am sorry I missed Fitzharris. I do not like your account of yourself. Do you write, and confess the truth, to Farquhar.

Conduit Street, 10th Jan., 1803.

MY DEAR LORD MALMESBURY,—I was unjust to harbour any suspicions. Pitt did stay but the one day, and then went on, as he had intended, to Long's, from whence he came to town to dinner on Saturday; re-

turned yesterday to Long's, and from thence is to go
this day to Wilderness, there to stay the greater part
of this week, but to be in town again this day se'n-
night, in order to go to St. James's on the following
day.

This will atone for the Levée; and I am particularly
glad that he has determined upon it, as your friend at
the Horse-Guards* has, I understand, expressed himself
particularly anxious that he should do so. He had
determined upon it before he knew of this circumstance.

His visit of Wednesday turned out a *tête-à-tête*; and,
if I may trust implicitly to his own report, he made the
best use of it, by stating his general sentiments and intentions in a manner that *could not be mistaken.* This
is well; my principal fear now is, that they will endeavour to conform their conduct, or rather their language
and the *appearance* of their conduct, to his ideas, (meaning nothing less, in fact, than to act up to them in any
degree,) just enough to prevent his feeling it absolutely
necessary to declare publicly what he has declared privately, till it is too late, and till all that would remain
for him to do would be to blame instead of retrieving.
I trust, however, that he is sufficiently on his guard not
to allow himself to be so deceived.

He has seen no *other* person *of the whole set* since his
arrival, except the person whom I mentioned to you in
my last letter.

I must not omit to tell you that nothing passed on
Wednesday that had the slightest reference to any notion
of an offer—not a hint. This is all that I have to say
to you; and this can do no harm, even if the same
curiosity should be on the watch that broke my seal on
Saturday. I will endeavour to trace this roguery; at
present it is quite unaccountable to me.

                    Ever, &c.   (Signed)   G. C.

_____

To these two letters I replied as follows:—

* The Duke of York.

Park Place, Thursday, 13th Jan., 1803.

My dear Canning,—Your letter of the 10th was in
all senses acceptable ; but I really cannot understand, *if*
Pitt said to Addington all he professes to have said, how
it is possible Addington should not *immediately* propose
to make way for Pitt.   The not doing it appears to me,
not only a breach of promise (strongly *implied* at least),
but denotes such a degree of vanity and presumption as
is rare to meet with.   I do not apprehend Pitt will be
the dupe of anything Addington has said or may do.
He (Pitt) has expressed himself *too* clearly to us, and
has experienced too often the *mockery* of vigour and
energy in Addington, for this to happen ; but *I do* fear
that the waiting for events and circumstances is waiting
till the river runs by.

Farquhar writes me a satisfactory account, &c.

The breaking of the seal on your last letter but one
is, I much fear, the effect of a very knavish curiosity,
and it does not surprise me.

Believe me, &c.   (Signed)   Malmesbury.

Canning's reply to this letter was:—

Conduit Street, Friday, 14th Jan., 1803.

My dear Lord Malmesbury,—You have hit upon the
true causes of Addington's *impudent silence*—a degree of
vanity and presumption almost incredible, aided, however, by a sneaking hope that whatever Pitt may feel,
or say to *him*, he will find himself too much fettered by
difficulties (of his, Pitt's, own creating) to declare against
him in Parliament.

If in this hope Addington does not ultimately find himself mistaken, not only you and I have been wrongfully
deceived (that is a small mischief), but the country is
irretrievably undone.   *Spero meliora.*

One circumstance in the review of the state of things,
since we first began to communicate upon these subjects,
is truly provoking.   It is this, that I have now reason to
be persuaded, from many things which reach me through

a channel of the correctness of which I cannot doubt, that if the measure had been taken as originally proposed, had not Mulgrave's headlong zeal hurried him to a disclosure of it to Pitt, it would *at the time* have completely succeeded ; *now* measures ten times as strong have less chance of success. But Buonaparte will help us. The difficulty however is, as you say, to take the stream at its flood. If we wait too long, Buonaparte, like most too powerful allies, will have overwhelmed us, instead of carrying us on just as far as we want to go.

Malta and Holland !* These are the two points in *esse* and in *posse*, upon which *the stand must* (and I think will) *be made.* Honduras is something.

I have not heard, nor expected to hear, from Pitt since he left town. He returns and dines with me on Monday. I wish you were with your family party in town, if, being so, you would have been well enough to meet him.

Ever, &c.   (Signed)   G. C.

On Monday, January 24, Canning came to Park Place, and remained one day. He said, that what had passed at Dropmore (he went there on leaving me on the 29th December) amounted to nothing; that Pitt had staid there three days, one of them *tête-à-tête* with Lord Grenville. That Canning had seen both of them since; that they were perfectly satisfied with each other; mutually agreed that there was but a shade of difference in their politics, but, far from having come to a fixed system or plan for acting, it should seem that it had not been talked of, and that both purposely avoided it. " This is a bad sign," said Canning. I observed, it looked as if Lord Grenville meant to make a separate cause of it, " *bande apart*," and followed the ideas of his brother, Lord Buckingham. Canning did not *assent* to this, and I thought seemed rather too apological and candid about Lord Grenville; and, as this is stepping out of his natural way, it a little struck me. Talking

* The evacuation of Malta by the British, and the occupation of Holland by French troops.

of affairs in general, Canning said they were going on worse and worse, and would involve us all in destruction; he is piqued that the business moves so slowly, and makes no allowance for hitches.

I left Park Place on Monday, the 7th of February, and came to Spring Gardens. A few days after Canning called on me. He said that, in the visit he made to Lord Grenville, at Dropmore, on leaving me, nothing very material had passed. Lord Grenville said Pitt had not spoken decidedly to him, though cordially, and with the strongest expressions of friendship. That he and his friends, therefore, would have it to determine whether, as long as Pitt held thus back, they should keep aloof and abstain from attendance in Parliament for the purpose of opposing, or attend and oppose; that the first would perhaps, all things considered, be the most advisable, although the other mode was much more conformable to their feelings; Canning was for remaining quiet, so he said Tom Grenville seemed inclined to be; but not so Windham, Lawrence, and the sectators of Burke. Pitt, while in town, had been rather reserved, and he had not heard from him since he had left it, from which Canning inferred that he was going on, as he termed, "wrong," and this had induced him to write him a letter, which he gave me to read; too long—eight pages; not sufficiently guarded, and, although perhaps strictly true and right, *fortiter in re*, but not *suaviter in modo*; too admonitory and too fault-finding for even Pitt's very good-humoured mind to bear. I observed to Canning, that it appeared *too free*; but I found him fond of his performance, and disappointed by Pitt's silence. And it evidently was written in the tone it was from his being vexed at Pitt's not having conformed in any degree to what he wished him to do, or explained to him what he meant to do. Canning imputed Pitt's hanging back to listening to Ryder, Long, Steele, and Lord Camden, all of whom he supposed (I cannot tell why) to be adverse to Pitt's coming into Office. "All his old friends are Addington's," said he, "but G. Rose, and Rose is very sanguine." He attributed still more to

Pitt's being disappointed at not being more called for
by the public voice in the House of Commons, and possibly felt that he himself had a little deceived Pitt by
stating so very peremptorily that this would happen.

After having heard him quite *out*, I said, he seemed
to me to be over-despondent. That, after all, the present inaction of Pitt was precisely what Pitt himself had
told us all along to be his plan, which he distinctly repeated to me at Park Place on the 29th December; that
the term he allotted himself for inactivity was not yet
quite elapsed, and that, till then, it was prejudging the
case. " Yes," said Canning, " but Pitt argues as much
on the wisdom and propriety of inaction *now* as he did
before Christmas, and reasons as if it were as right it
should continue *now* as six weeks ago." To this I observed, that the moment he (Pitt) came to town, it
must cease, whatever might be his expectation or intention: supposing he attended Parliament, he would be
forced to speak, and the first sentence he uttered on his
legs would inevitably produce *all* the effects we looked
for, or at least *I* looked for; since it would either embroil him with Addington, and turn him out hostilely
by an avowed and unqualified disapprobation of the
measures of his Government; or displace him amicably,
if he did it in a qualified degree and protecting tone,
and as a principal speaking to a *locum tenens*. That, in
either case, Fox would attack Pitt; and Fox would do
more for us in a single debate than we could in twenty
conversations with Pitt. That, therefore, all we waited
for was, that Pitt should leave Walmer, (where, by the
bye, he is detained by the gout, or rather by a bilious
attack,) and it was not very material to me whether
now or a fortnight hence; that, once in London, circumstances would do the rest; and that I was sure
pressing and besetting Pitt was defeating our own
ends. That I deprecated myself all *partial* and *huz-
zar-like* opposition; it could only do harm; it would
palsy those who committed themselves by it; prevent them from acting afterwards with Pitt; and, as
their number was small and violence great, it would

strengthen Addington and weaken Pitt, inasmuch as it
would come from his former colleagues in Office, and
those who profess publicly to wish to see him in Office
again; that, besides, it would injure the general principle of Government, and, at this moment more than
ever, this should be most cautiously avoided.

Canning acquiesced, or *seemed* to acquiesce, in all
this; said he would *try* to keep the Grenvilles to their
intended neutral plan; and, after all, he believed the
best way would be for Pitt to come in *quite alone*, and
leave the rest to time and chance.

He had, indeed, written these very words in his letter
to Pitt, but they were wound up with so much impatience, that it did not look like the sincere declaration
it was.   On the 12th I saw Canning.   He had then no
answer from Pitt, and this unhinged and mortified him.
Canning has been *forced*, like a thriving plant in a well-
managed hot-house; he has prospered too luxuriantly—
has felt no check or frost.   Too early in life, he has had
many, and too easy, advantages.   This, added to very
acute parts, makes him impatient of controul.   Astonished to find obstacles and difficulties in his way; angry
with those who conceive less quickly and eagerly than
himself, or who will not keep pace with him in his rapid
plans and views ; and indulging an innate principle of
vanity, he underrates others, and *appears* arrogant and
contemptuous, although really not so.   This checks the
right and gradual growth of his abilities; lessens their
effects, and vitiates the very many excellent, honourable,
and amiable qualities he possesses.   The world, who
judge him from this, judge him harshly and unfairly ;
his success accounts for his manners.   Rapid prosperity
never creates popularity; and it requires a most careful
and conciliating conduct to make the two compatible.

On Tuesday, the 15th instant, I dined with Canning;
he had just got a very short letter from Pitt—short and
unpromising.   He (Pitt) said in it, that he saw no reason for altering his conduct, or any motive for hastening
to town, where, however, he means to be *soon ;* it looked
as if Pitt had made a dry answer, and was not pleased

with Canning's letter. Lord Titchfield and Mrs. Canning being at dinner, nothing more passed.

On Friday morning, 18th February, Canning was with me twice,—at half-past one, when we were interrupted by the Duke of York, and again after the Duke had left me: he said, Pitt was *not* coming; that every thing was marred; that Pitt had lost himself, and was losing himself more and more by his present conduct: he could not account for it. I told him what passed between me and the Duke of York, who came to hear what had passed respecting Pitt since I last wrote to him, of which I gave His Royal Highness a concise account. The Duke was either less eager, or less sanguine, than at that time. He talked with less disapprobation of the present Ministers; said we might *vivoter* with them; and that, if they had a head and energy, the different members of it were strong enough for all good purposes; praised Lord Pelham very much for the way in which he managed his department, and particularly in Despard's business; it was done well; great firmness and great judgment. Lord Chatham, he said, did also well; Lord Hobart not so. He wished *Pitt* would head them. Pitt *alone*. He dreaded the Grenvilles; and it was very evident, from his language, that the King was disinclined to admit them again to Office. He hoped any violent measures to produce a change of administration would be avoided; it would vex and worry His Majesty. That he still thought the best and only way was the same he had mentioned in October, viz., that some common friend of Pitt's and Addington's, either in or out of Office, should mediate between them. Pitt could not, however well-inclined, act for himself, and Addington would not. Addington's vanity predominates over every other consideration. He had rather fall by a majority against him in the House, than give way to persuasion. He considered himself *now* as having taken Office to save the Crown and the country; and that it became him not to resign, or be *negotiated* out of his place, but turned out by the public voice. How different this from when he affected to say, he was only "*locum tenens*" for Pitt ! " But so it is," said the Duke, " and this makes any attempt, save that I propose, ineffectual. If the Chancellor, or Ryder, or Steele, or Charles Long, would state the matter distinctly and fairly to him, he then might be, perhaps, prevailed on to go to the King, and lay before him the acquisition his Government would derive from the abilities of Pitt;" and he (the Duke) was satisfied that the business *thus* brought before His Majesty would not only take the turn we all so much desired, but also be very agreeable to the King. This gave me an opportunity of telling the Duke what Pitt had said respecting his attachment to the King.

The Duke of York spoke with some soreness of what was going to be done for the Prince;* said it was a measure that would not attach the Prince to Government, and was evidently a forced, not a gratuitous, act of theirs ; that it *must* lead to unpleasant questions and discussions in Parliament.

The Duke ended a two hours' visit by repeating his instances that he never might be mentioned in this business; that he always spoke to me as his private and confidential friend, and requested me to keep him regularly informed of every thing that passed.

He said he believed Dundas and Pitt were in regular correspondence, but whether it was one of quite private intimacy, or on public concerns, he could not pretend to say. That the Grenvilles were the great impediment, and the Catholic Question the great weapon employed by those who wish to keep up the King's adverse feelings towards Pitt.

Canning agreed, that it would be good for some one to speak to Addington; but who was to be found? Steele, the worst man possible. He again reverted to the unfortunate circumstance of Pitt's holding back; said J. Villiers had been with him at Walmer for two or

---

* On the 16th February, the King sent a message to Parliament recommending to their consideration the present situation of the Prince of Wales : 60,000*l.* a year was added to his income until July 1806, when his debts (it was supposed) would be liquidated.

three days, on his return from abroad, and was just come up; that it appeared as if Pitt had spoken very openly to him (J. Villiers), and the inference to be drawn was, that every thing was to remain just as it was when he left Bath.

I see less evil in all this than Canning; he is hurt at being thwarted; Pitt may have good reasons for what he does. I remonstrated with Canning; preached *patience*, and that, instead of repining at what we could not alter, try to pursue, with perseverance and temper, the plan we had begun; that, I freely confessed, if the country *was* well governed, I did not much care whether Pitt governed it, or any one else; but, at the same time, as I was convinced *no one could govern it so well as he*, I would use every means in my power to persuade him to resume the conduct of it.

On Saturday, the 19th, Canning went back to Welbeck.

On Tuesday, the 22nd of February, I received the following letter from Pitt:—

Walmer Castle, 21st Feb., 1803.

MY DEAR LORD,—I was on every account very sorry to lose the party you were so good as to propose to me, but it was doubly out of my power, as your letter found me still here, and I had also an invitation from the Speaker for the same day, which, if I had been in town, parliamentary etiquette would not have allowed me to decline. After braving the east wind for some weeks, I am now repaid for my perseverance by the most delightful spring weather, which, I think, unless necessity calls me to town, I shall be tempted to enjoy for some time longer. There seems to be nothing passing in the political world that can be viewed without increased regret and uneasiness.*

Believe me, &c.　　　(Signed)　　　W. PITT.

---

* The restless ambition and arrogant tone of the First Consul on one hand, and the want of firmness and frankness in the British Cabinet on the other, caused mutual distrust and constant recriminations between the two Governments. Buonaparte had annexed Parma and Piedmont to France,

I wrote the following answer:—

Spring Gardens, 23rd Feb., 1803.

MY DEAR SIR, — However anxious many of your friends may be for your return, yet, if you are enjoying yourself in the country, and *still* think that your presence here is not called for, or *as yet* necessary, I, from the entire conviction I am under that you know better than any of us what is best to be done, and when it is best to do it, have no other reason to lament your intention to remain at Walmer for some time longer, except that it deprives me of the pleasure of seeing you so soon as I had hoped for.

I do partake very strongly of the " regret and uneasiness" you express of what is passing in the political world; but these feelings would be increased if I did not entertain a hope that strong and spirited measures were in contemplation, and from the full conviction if they are determined on, and carried into effect, we shall greatly add to our consequence and security; since from all I hear, and from the little I have the opportunity to observe, Buonaparte presumes only in proportion as we yield, and that when we think it expedient to rise to our proper tone, he will sink to that which becomes him.

In the account I sent you of Holland, I should correct what I said about the attention of the Dutch at this moment to restore and increase their navy. It is not so: their fleet is left as it was at the Peace: no new ships building, or old ones fitting out; and the only exertions going on in this branch are enlarging their docks at Helvoet, and cleaning out the mouths of the Maese.

invaded Switzerland, and quartered his troops in Holland. He insolently demanded the expulsion of the Bourbons, and the prosecution of the English Press that was hostile to him. Repeated injuries were inflicted on British personal property, for which no redress could be obtained. The English Government remonstrated on the invasion of Switzerland, and at the same time, October 17th, 1802, sent orders to delay the restitution of the French and Dutch colonies. Their interference in Switzerland being of no avail, they countermanded these orders, November 15th. They delayed the evacuation of Malta rather on the grounds of policy than good faith. Great military establishments were kept up in both countries, and war daily seemed imminent.

I much fear from Woronzow's manner, and I have seen him often, that all is not right at Petersburg. France, I suspect, is tempting both Russia and Austria with plans of partition on Turkey, to which both listen, and of which, one at least, must necessarily be the dupe.

I am, &c. (Signed) MALMESBURY.

I heard from G. Rose, who is with Pitt at Walmer, that he is well, sleeps sound, and eats heartily, and intends going to Bath in the spring; but not a word of attendance in Parliament, or of coming to London.

From this date (23rd Feb., 1803) till towards the end of March, Pitt remained at Walmer Castle, where he had a slight return of his gout and bilious complaint. He saw only a few friends, and abstained even with these from talking on public subjects, further than as topics of general conversation; and carefully avoided any expression which could indicate his views and intentions respecting a return to Office.

Canning informed of this (for he did not go to Walmer); was vexed and hurt; sometimes thinking it best to leave Pitt to himself, and then, from impatient zeal, writing to him strong and pressing letters. To these he was some time without any reply, and then a very short one; but on the 28th February he received a letter from Pitt, to acknowledge one in which he sent him the *Moniteur* of 23rd February, containing Buonaparte's strange address to the Legislative Body * on the 22nd. Pitt said—The translation spoke tolerably plain *English*, but the original still plainer *French*, the result

---

* The following are extracts from this tumid manifesto :—

" En Angleterre deux partis se disputent le pouvoir. L'un a conclu la paix et parait décidé à la maintenir, l'autre a juré à la France une haine implacable," &c.

" Tant que durera cette lutte des partis, il est des mesures que la prudence commande au Gouvernement de la République. Cinq cent mille hommes doivent être, et seront prêts," &c.

" Le Gouvernement le dit avec un juste orgueil—Seule l'Angleterre ne sauroit aujourd'hui lutter contre la France," &c.

The address concludes with the expression of a wish for the continuance of peace.

of which must soon be known; that he had a clear and distinct individual opinion as to. the line of conduct which it became us to pursue; yet that *he had reasons,* which he could not disclose, which prevented him at the present from entering into explanations, and which determined him to remain on at Walmer.

Rose, about the same time, said, " Pitt *will* remain where he is," but that his opinions of the measures now pursued by Government, and of the Ministers themselves, were exactly such as his best friends could wish him to entertain.

Canning wrote to Pitt on the 9th March, and offered to come to Walmer if Pitt was (" *now*") at liberty to enter into an explanation of the secret he withheld from him in his last letter. This being *done* before it was communicated to me, *I said* nothing about it, but looked upon it as a useless and inconsiderate step. I was not wrong; for, on the 11th, Canning got a short answer, telling him frankly not to come to Walmer, as Pitt could not explain to him the reason of his silence. Still Canning persevered; and in his reply, on hearing rumours that Pitt was about to attend Parliament, entered into a long detail of reasons to dissuade him from coming up and taking *any share* in the present discussions relative to France.

On the 13th March, Ryder and Lord Camden went to Walmer, where Rose and Lord Carrington had been before; but these appeared to be like their former visits, simply of private regard, and, from all I could learn, nothing at all material passed.

It was evident that at this moment Pitt was meditating some plan, either entirely his own, or in concert with persons not his *usual* confidants, in which he wished not to commit or implicate prematurely that description of friends whom he considered as the more immediate followers of his political fortune; but still this almost self-evident conjecture did not satisfy the eager part of them. They considered it as an unfair mystery, which *must* be cleared up; and Canning, on the 14th, wrote with a view to this to Pitt, to say, that he knew from certain authority, that Addington asserted positively that he kept Pitt regularly informed of all which was passing and had passed from the beginning, and had even produced a letter from Pitt to prove his full assent and approbation of it. This *provoked* Pitt, and drew from him the following answer:—

" I am the more surprised at what you say, since I have not, during these last few months, received any letter from Addington, neither has he communicated anything to me respecting Malta, or any other depending measure ; neither have I on my part communicated, directly or indirectly, to him my political opinion on any public subject whatever during that period. I have, indeed, been in correspondence with Steele, but it was on finance, and what I said was not of a nature for Addington to *boast* of having received."

About the middle of March, Lord Melville arrived in London from Scotland. He saw Ministers, and Addington in particular, frequently. He went to Walmer on Thursday, March 19th; stayed that night at Commissioner Hope's, at Rochester; and from this moment, the mystery, as it was called, began to develop itself.

To give as impartial a statement as I can, and leave to the judgment to act for itself, I shall state what I heard of this transaction in the way each party told it; that in which *Pitt desired should be reported to me*, and that in which a Member of the Cabinet, who heard it from Addington himself, related it.*

I shall begin by Pitt's. Lord Melville came, charged with a proposal from Addington to Pitt to resume Office. Pitt and Addington to be the two Secretaries of State. Pitt to have the nomination to *one* Cabinet, and *one* Privy Councillor's office. An indifferent person to be First Lord of the Treasury, (it is thought Addington had Lord Chatham in view for this, and had fixed particularly on him to embarrass Pitt), Lord Melville himself (probably) First Lord of the Admiralty.

* Pelham.

Pitt rejected this proposal the moment it was made him; said, so far from ever listening to any plan in which the person who was to be the real and effective First Minister was to be disguised or concealed, he thought it indispensable that it should at all times, and in every Administration, be evident and manifest who this person was; and that he never would take a part in any arrangement where this did not clearly appear. That this alone would have induced him to set aside the proposal he heard, but that it was inadmissible in every part, and not worth discussion; and this Pitt said so decidedly and peremptorily, that Lord Melville did not think proper to urge or contest the point strongly; and although he stayed several days at Walmer, he did not return to the charge. He went back to London on the 25th March, but Long remained on at Walmer, and received letters from Addington to make fresh proposals to Pitt; the most material one was, that Pitt should take his former situation, and bring in more of his friends. Pitt gave no positive answer whatever.

On the 29th, Lord Grenville went there, but nothing (this Lord Grenville himself afterwards affirmed) passed between him and Pitt *on Ministerial changes*, only general conversation on political questions and public measures, in all of which they perfectly concurred. Pitt observed the same silence towards Lord Grenville on this point as towards his other friends, though Lord Grenville on his side made a sort of parade of his visit to Walmer, by leaving London very conspicuously at four in the afternoon of the 29th. Parliament adjourned for a fortnight on 31st March.

On 5th April, Long went again to Walmer, again resumed the subject, and carried an urgent request from Mr. Addington, for an interview with Pitt, and signified that he had reconsidered what had passed, and had now proposals to make on a still wider basis than those communicated to him, either through Lord Melville or Long.

Pitt in reply, declared his fixed intention of not listening to any proposals which were not made by " the

King's authority," and with His Majesty's previous knowledge; but said, if Addington, after hearing this declaration, still wished to see him, he certainly could not
refuse to meet him at Bromley, (Long's house,) on the
9th or 10th of April. Addington considered this as an
appointment, and met Pitt there on the 10th April.

Pitt began by premising what he had before intimated,
that he could consider no proposal as regular or official,
none that could lead to authenticated report, unless
coming from the King; that when this was ascertained,
he then should be ready, with all proper duty and deference, to obey His Majesty's commands; that till then,
though he could not impose silence on Addington, or refuse to hear him as an old and intimate friend, yet *he*
would abstain from entering into any details of arrangement, either of persons or measures, which at any after
time were to be treated as conditions or stipulations for
the formation of a Ministry; and that if, in the course
of their conversation, anything tending to this should
escape him, it should be considered merely as *common
conversation,* necessarily arising out of the subject itself,
and by no means set down as assent or dissent, or
as opinions given or received on a possible ministerial
arrangement, on the nature of which arrangement, he
(Pitt) must be fully acquainted with His Majesty's
pleasure before he could say a word, or pronounce a
name which should be considered as binding.

Addington apparently acquiesced in this mode of proceeding; but during the two days he passed at Bromley,
tried every means in his power to induce Pitt to deviate
from it, to commit his opinions, and compromise his
friends. *He* himself courted details of every sort, named
persons fit to be put in Office or to leave Office, and disposed of places, &c., without reserve. To all which Pitt
listened as he had promised, but never concurred in
them, but under the special reserve before stipulated,
that it should be all put down to the score of common
table-talk between two intimate acquaintance. Addington seemed so much to approve what Pitt said, and to
coincide so nearly with his ideas, that Pitt declared, *if*

the King should signify his wishes to be similar to those
Mr. Addington appeared to entertain, he (Pitt) would
lose no time in carrying into effect what he had suggested, and employ his best endeavours to form such an Administration as he should think would be the best calculated for carrying on the affairs of the country at this
anxious moment; and that he should comprise in it
every description of persons, without insisting on any
one, or proscribing any one, submitting the whole to the
King's comment and objections, to which he, as in duty,
and in grateful affection bound, should defer, as far as
the so doing did not, in his mind, completely defeat and
destroy the whole of his services to His Majesty and to
the country.

Addington appeared alarmed at the broad ground on
which Pitt declared his intention to act, and with a good
deal of anxiety and apprehension expressed a hope he
would not insist on restoring Lord Grenville, and Lord
Spencer, and Windham, to Office. Pitt said he must
on this, as on every other specific point to be complied
with or rejected, avoid in the present stage of the transaction, a positive answer; but that he did not scruple to
say, that the abilities of the persons Addington wished
to exclude would always appear to him infinitely necessary, and even indispensable, in the formation of a strong
and efficient Government. He at the same time assured
Addington, *he* did not know *their* sentiments, or what
would be their conduct, neither did *they* know *his* intentions, or what he had in contemplation; since, during
these last two months, he had most carefully, and on
purpose, avoided communicating with any of them on the
subjects of this nature. (This explains his silence towards Canning.) Addington repeated his hope, that a
Ministry might be formed without the Grenvilles, at least
in the first instance, and returned on Tuesday, the 12th
April, to London, from Bromley, apparently satisfied
with what had passed; and observed, on leaving Long's,
that the only delay which could take place before Pitt
heard from him again, would be a short one, that would
arise from a natural wish he had before he went further

in the business to speak to some of his friends. Pitt
and Long were both convinced that the whole was settled,
and expected to hear from Addington to this effect.

On the 14th April, Pitt received by a messenger at
Bromley, a letter, dated the evening of the 13th, to this
effect: That he (Addington) on his return to Downing
Street, had thought it expedient to assemble his colleagues, and communicate to them the substance of the
proposal made by Pitt, and that His Majesty's confidential servants had *all* expressed the greatest satisfaction
at the idea of an accession of his transcendant abilities
to their councils, and a readiness to promote so desirable
an end, by an arrangement which could be made. But
when they were given to understand that it was to be
coupled with a condition, *sine quâ non*, to restore to a
place in their councils all those persons whose opinions
they considered to be hostile to the interests and peace of
their country, they could not advise the laying this proposal thus accompanied before His Majesty. This, Addington said, was their unanimous opinion, which he lost
no time in communicating, according to the assurances
he had made on leaving Bromley.

To this Pitt immediately returned the following answer:—

" I have received your letter of the 13th. It requires
nothing more than a simple acknowledgment."

On reflecting, however, that if the business was to
break off here, and this letter of Addington's, which was
both in its form, and in fact, a Minute of Cabinet, be
the only voucher to produce, that the whole would be
liable to misrepresentation and misconception, he, on
Friday morning the 15th, sent a letter to Addington in
substance as follows:—

" On the receipt of your letter of Wednesday, April
13, yesterday, it appeared to me to require no other answer than a simple acknowledgment; but on reflecting
on its contents, I feel it is become necessary for me to

explain some very material points on which you appear to have mistaken my meaning, and received an impression different from that I wished to give. It is to correct this impression, and not on any grounds for renewing discussions which I consider as terminated, that I am now induced to answer it more fully.

" It should appear from what you have written, that you looked upon yourself as authorized, in consequence of what passed between us, to lay before your colleagues a regular and formal proposal, as coming from me, to return to Office under certain conditions, and an intention on my part of drawing up a detailed and specific plan for forming an Administration: no such authority was given, nor intended to be given you by me.

" The subject originally began by your having intimated to me a wish that I should resume the post I before held in His Majesty's Councils (I could not become a member of them in any other), and that the critical situation of the country required a most strong and most efficient Administration.

" To this I replied, that if called upon by His Majesty, and in that case only, I was ready to resume the office I had held, and to submit to His Majesty for his consideration the outline of such an Administration as should appear to me best suited for carrying on His Majesty's Government. I distinctly said, that till I was made acquainted with the King's pleasure, I could say nothing binding, nothing *officially* communicable; this I repeated, and that what I might say to you was as from friend to friend. *But* that when I knew His Majesty's pleasure, I would then exert my whole mind on the subject; and in laying the names of such persons as I conceived the best and most equal to discharge the duties of an efficient Government at this arduous moment, I certainly added, that in selecting these, I should not confine myself to any one description of persons; that my choice would not be regulated by those who were now in Office with you, or who had been formerly in Office with me; that I should neither stipulate for, nor proscribe any one, nor act upon any other motive or principle than the general one that I had just mentioned; that the determination and conclusion on this arrangement would be matter for His Majesty's comment and decision, liable to His Majesty's objections and animadversions; and that from every sense of duty, gratitude, and right feeling, I should pay to these the most respectful deference, and be disposed to acquiesce in them entirely, reserving only to myself the right of humbly declining a return to Office, if His Majesty should think it in his wisdom right to insist on such exclusions or such alterations as should appear to my conviction to be vital and destructive, and to render my services useless both to His Majesty and to the public.

" That with respect to those who had left Office with me, and some of whom I did not hesitate to say I looked upon as being essentially necessary to complete a strong and efficient Government, I distinctly said I had not uttered a single word to them on the subject: they did not know what I had in contemplation, neither did I know what were their wishes, or would be their conduct. That I had not sounded them, nor would not, until I was acquainted with the King's pleasure. I should act contrary to the principles of duty and respect I have invariably professed for His Majesty, were I to take a step of this nature till this was clearly and precisely ascertained. My motive for writing this is, therefore, I repeat, not to provoke the renewal of a discussion which I consider as finally and decisively closed, but in order to have an *exact record* of what has passed; and if at any future period this transaction should ever get before the public incorrectly, or be misrepresented, that there should exist an authentic document which could leave no doubt of the truth."

Addington's and his friends' account of this transaction up to the 15th is this:—

That Pitt, as long back as January, when at Richmond Park, intimated not only a readiness, but a disposition to return to Office. That Addington, most desirous of encouraging what he looked upon as so de-

sirable an acquisition to his Ministry, had endeavoured
to promote it then, and smooth the way to it since; and
that it was in consequence of knowing them to be Pitt's
sentiments, that Lord Melville, on his coming from Scotland, had undertaken to enter. into a conversation with
him on the subject. That Addington entertained an
opinion Pitt wanted only to bring Ryder as Treasurer
of the Navy, and Long into the Treasury with him;
therefore he confined his offer to this. Pitt himself to
be Secretary of State for the Home Department; Lord
Melville at the head of the Admiralty. This Pitt rejected; but that, on Lord Melville's return, Long went
to Walmer, charged with a more extensive plan, in
which Pitt was to resume his former post, and more of
his friends brought both into the Cabinet and Office.
To this Pitt listened with so much attention, that Long
felt himself authorized to give it as his opinion to Addington, that Pitt would ultimately accede to it with a
few modifications; " and," says Addington, " he would,
if Lord Grenville had not gone to Walmer on the 31st
of March, and influenced his conduct, and persuaded
him to alter his plan." That it was with a view to
counteract this, and in hopes that Pitt would on seeing
him return to his first opinion, that he had proposed,
through Long, an interview with Pitt, and in that interview he had offered to go still farther, and expressed a
readiness to go into nearly a total change. That he
had entered with Pitt into the most minute details, both
with regard to the characters of persons, and the disposal of offices. That Pitt heard and partook of these
details, but opinionatively insisted on the proposal originating directly from the King; and that Lords Grenville
and Spencer, and Windham, by name should be restored
to their former situations.* That to this, *he* should
have perhaps subscribed, but that. he deemed it previously right and proper to submit the attempting a
measure which so deeply involved the interests of the

---

* It appears from *both* accounts that Pitt stood fast by Lord Grenville, as
indeed he had always fostered him. In a year after Lord Grenville left him
in the hour of difficulty and danger !

country to his colleagues; and that they, though unanimous in their wishes to acquire the accession of Pitt's
abilities amongst them, were as unanimous in their opinion, that, with the conditions he annexed to it, it was
not such a measure as they could advise to lay before
the King. That this determination of the Cabinet he
lost no time in communicating to Pitt, who replied to it
at once by a dry letter of a single line.

This letter was afterwards followed by a longer one,
in which Pitt recapitulates the substance of what had
passed at Bromley, but which not being considered by
Addington as correct, Addington wrote an answer.
Pitt in reply (or verbally, I am not sure which) desired
Addington to lay the whole transaction, with the correspondence belonging to it, before the King, intimating
that if he did not, he should, in justice to himself, be
obliged to do it.

Addington undertook it, but added, that if Pitt had
any other channel, he would do well to make use of it
also.

————

Such are the two statements communicated to me; I
have endeavoured to give them as I heard them. It is
impossible but that in both of them there should be a
partial bearing.

One great point on which they differ is, from which
of the two, Pitt or Addington, the overture first *originated*. Each attributes it to the other.

Another is, that Addington asserts that Pitt went
into a detail of men and disposal of Offices *officially;*
Pitt says the contrary.

A third is, that by inference, Addington accuses Pitt
of making unseemly conditions with the King, attempting to force the Cabinet; Pitt says the direct contrary,
and rests his whole conduct on the most profound respect towards His Majesty.

It is, perhaps, but reasonable to admit, that there was
some real misconception on the part of Addington; but it
is impossible not to receive an impression that there was
also a wilful error, and a great appearance of cunning.

As is natural, the friends and followers of each of them take their different lines; and each, by defending their *principal*, as is usual, exaggerate and go beyond not only what is the truth, but what is right and useful. Pitt, the most forgiving and easy-minded of men, entertained very little anger against Addington in the first instance, and none which remained with him. Addington was, or appeared to be, more affected — complained with a great semblance of sensibility to his friends, and even common acquaintance, of his misfortune in having been forced to differ with Pitt, and how much he was hurt lest this should have lessened their long and intimate friendship.

It was not till the 20th of April that Addington mentioned the transaction *at all* to the King. He then did it in a common audience after the Levée ; and, to judge from what his Majesty said to those of the Cabinet Ministers who followed Addington into the closet, he told his story in his own way, as the King expressed resentment against Pitt, talked of his " putting the Crown in commission," and that " he carried his plan of *removals* so extremely far and so high, that it might reach *him*."

After this audience, Addington answered Pitt's letter of the 13th instant. Pitt received it at Lord Carrington's, at Wycombe (I never saw any one to whom Pitt shewed it); but it was a long and laboured attempt to prove Pitt had misunderstood him, or not explained himself correctly. To this Pitt sent no reply.

His friends — and I confess myself one of the most eager for it — press him to see the King, or to write to him, in order that no unfair impression of his behaviour or expressions on this occasion might remain on his mind; but this he pertinaciously objected to, and contented himself with sending the whole correspondence to the Duke of York (through Colonel Alexander Hope, I believe), under the idea that his Royal Highness would communicate it. It is not clear the Duke *did* communicate it to His Majesty; but it is very clear that if he did, he was ordered not to notice it, since, on a very long conversation with him, when he called on me on the

1st of May, and which passed entirely on this subject, he expressed perfect ignorance of the King's feelings— said that, in his own view of the transaction, both parties were in the wrong; and that it had been so managed as to put Pitt's return to Office (though more necessary than ever) at a greater distance than ever. It was evident *he* thought Pitt had held too high and imperious a language.

I, therefore, did every thing in my power to undeceive him on this point, by not only *commenting* on the evident *facts* which appeared in the course of this business, and spoke for themselves, and on Pitt's letter to Addington, but also by repeating to him what Pitt had himself said to me at Bath on 19th November, 1802. His words were these:—

" You may be sure your feelings are not stronger than mine on this point; and I not only affirm that if the event cannot be produced without affecting, in the smallest degree, the King's health, comfort, and tranquillity, but that if it has not his full and uncompelled concurrence, it shall not happen at all. To feel and to say this is little more than feeling and speaking as a gentleman; and neither the peculiar voice, nor the solicitations of my friends, shall ever prevail on me to come into office against His Majesty's consent, much less to try to force his consent from him."

I found, however, the Duke more than commonly wedded to his first notion, and was sorry to observe that the persons Pitt had employed to convey the papers to him, certainly (let them be who they may) had not commented on them, or explained them, in a way friendly to him.

At the repeated desire of his friends, Pitt, on the 25th, again pressed Addington to lay his letter before the King. Addington did not do it till the 27th, at the Queen's House; and then, probably, without any remarks, or with his *own* notes, as the King said immediately after to Lord Pelham, " I have now got the written documents, but *I will not read them, or even take any notice of them*." And afterwards (on the 29th), " It is a foolish business from one end to the other, which was begun ill, conducted ill, and terminated ill."

Pitt went from Wycombe to Frogmore and Bromley, and returned by Lord Camden's to Walmer on the 30th April.

This closed the transaction for the present, and as the Duke of York very properly said, placed Pitt further from Office than ever. I have little doubt Pitt was perfectly true and sincere when he professed, that in the whole of this business he has communicated with no one, concerted with no one, but has acted solely on his own jùdgment and opinion, and this from the most generous and best of all principles, from a wish to fetter no one, commit no one, or engage any one through private friendship to act in what he considered as a public concern.

It is, however, but too probable, and too like (not only Pitt's, but) every human mind, that though he did not ask advice, or make any *confidant*, yet, as he avowedly heard opinions on this very subject from able (though interested) persons, and such of whose judgment he thought highly, that this biassed, and perhaps governed his conduct; and I have little doubt that Lord Grenville's visit at the end of March did produce all the *exceptionable* part of Pitt's conduct in this negotiation; exceptionable inasmuch as it is nearly proved that he had expressed himself less opiniatively to Long and Lord Melville, and inasmuch as if he had come into Office on the terms to which Addington would have willingly assented, there is not a shadow of doubt but that in a very short time he would have assumed the whole power of the Government, and named to every office in the Cabinet.

[The foregoing account of the attempts made by Mr. Pitt's friends to bring him again into Office, from the 20th of October, 1802, up to this date, 20th April, 1803, was drawn up and arranged by Lord Malmesbury himself in a separate book. What follows is from his private Diary, and is resumed three months further back.]

———

SATURDAY, JANUARY 29th, 1803.—Lord Pelham came to Park Place—remained till the following Monday. His conversation was, as usual, confidential, and the expression of his political sentiments and opinions precisely what they were when we last conversed. I did not consider it either fair or honourable to conceal from him the great outlines of what had passed between Pitt and me; and, without stating to him any of those particulars which would on my part have been a breach of trust with respect to Pitt and those in the secret of that transaction, I felt it a full and complete discharge of what was due to our intimacy and my regard for him, to say that I continued to disapprove most of the measures of Government, and to apprehend severe and fatal consequences from them; and that, with these feelings in my mind, and well acquainted with Pitt's abilities and character, I could not but wish to see him in Mr. Addington's place, and that I had expressed this my wish distinctly to Pitt. Lord Pelham said he most sincerely wished Pitt was in that office again, and coincided perfectly with me both in my wishes and opinions.

We went over together all the foreign concerns, and particularly Russia; and I was sorry to find from what was passing, that this Court was not, as I had heard from H. Elliot a few days before, drawing towards us, and *convalescent*, as he termed it, but still in a close and apparent cordial feeling with France. Lord Pelham said, Addington had spoken of Fitzharris with great regard, and as if he wished to give him Office. I said, both myself and Fitzharris esteemed Mr. Addington as a respectable individual, who had always been kind and friendly; that these feelings of private regard would always remain, but it could not be supposed that they should direct or regulate our political opinions and conduct; that both of us had much rather support than oppose Government.—much rather our minds should be

satisfied with reasons for approving than be compelled
by irresistible causes to disapprove; that we really
sought for the best end — never tried by false constructions or cavil to create the latter, but that facts spoke
for themselves; it was evident a system of concession
and giving way to France was the prevailing one. This
we considered as the worst, the most disgraceful, and
most dangerous for the country. That *as long*, therefore, as this prevailed and was acted on, it was out of
the question accepting such a pledge for support as the
taking Office would be; and, as Fitzharris and myself
felt very seriously Mr. Addington's good-will, he on his
side would, I was sure, consider the motives on which we
acted to be such as became us, and the frank avowal of
which ought not to alter to us his sentiments of personal
regard. I begged, therefore, Lord Pelham, in case Mr.
Addington again mentioned Fitzharris's name coupled
with Office, to tell him fairly what I had just said, and
to prevent him making a useless tender, and to Fitzharris the disagreeable necessity of declining an act of
intended kindness coming from a person who had ever
treated him kindly.

Friday, Feb. 4.—Lord Pembroke at Park Place. He
had passed three months at Paris; seen people of all descriptions; heard everybody; and, as he is an excellent
observer and patient listener, great faith is due to his
report. He said he could not have believed any person
to be so universally disliked as Buonaparte if he had
not had such daily proofs of it; this occasioned by his
rapid rise, by his intemperate character, by his tyranny,
and the evident use he makes of his power: that this
hatred, however, leads to nothing; his power remains
the same, and he is obeyed implicitly. England is
manifestly the great object of *his* hatred and jealousy;
and all his plans, all his thoughts, go to attain the
means of lowering, if not also of subduing it. But, although there is a sufficient degree of national ill-will towards us prevailing generally, yet so vexed and tor-

mented were the French by the war, that it must be some much stronger motive than simply national dislike that can again make them relish war. This feeling also makes them endure Buonaparte's oppression and arrogance, which, bad as it is, is more tolerable than the system of terror in Robespierre's time, or the capricious and wanton violence of the Directory. The army *in part* partake of these feelings; and although they might be tempted by the prospect of plunder, yet the great majority of them would fight with reluctance. The Generals, too, who were formerly his companions, are jealous of Buonaparte. He cannot trust them with a command, and he dares not trust himself from Paris for any length of time.

MONDAY, FEB. 7. — Returned to London after an absence of near eight months. On Tuesday, 8th, Lord Pelham and Wm. Elliot called but for a moment. Nagell* dissatisfied personally; angry with Prince of Orange; not right in his politics; condemns our conduct; we have lowered and exposed ourselves to the evils we fear by the very means we take to avoid them. Rumoured in Holland that Buonaparte intends to annex it to France; doubts it, as then the Dutch must be treated *as well* as the other annexed countries. Now he can squeeze and oppress them as he pleases. No spirit or means left in the country for regeneration. Nagell hinted to me he had heard it was in contemplation to stop the allowance we made to the corps and officers who, in 1795, left Holland, and were about to form a corps under Prince Frederick of Orange in the Païs d'Oldenberg. Nagell complains of being slighted by Lord Hawkesbury; has not received the suitable present; while Schimmelpenninck has got a most rich box, with the King's portrait. This Schimmelpenninck, he says, may be turned to account; but that he is artful and fawning—originally a low attorney—still a young man.

---

* Nagell was the Stadtholder's Minister.

WEDNESDAY, FEB. 9.—Lord Pelham.—With me in the morning, and I with him in Stratton Street from eight to ten in the evening. Much confidential conversation *on Russia.* We had proposed to Russia to guarantee Malta. Russia at first declined — afterwards consented, providing the Sovereignty of the King of Naples be admitted, and the Maltese Langue* obliged to make their proofs of birth, and be provided for by France and us. France accedes to this; but we say Spain has violated the Treaty of Amiens by taking away from the Knights of Malta their commanderies, &c. in Spain, while the arrangement is pending, and that Spain should restore these, or contribute a proportionate share. Russia replies, she has nothing to do with them, and this should be settled at Madrid.

That, after all, the Emperor of Russia thought Malta would be better in our hands than any others. This, and other reasons to be found in Lord Whitworth's despatch, induced the Cabinet to come to a conclusion to send instructions to Lord Whitworth † to enter into a discussion with Talleyrand on the subject both of Malta and Alexandria; to explain the motives why we still kept them; and, in civil and guarded but clear terms, to state that it was not from any intention to violate the conditions of the Treaty of Amiens, or from a wish to misconstrue its meaning, but because the state of France was so very materially altered, that the motives which made these retrocessions safe and reasonable were done away; and that, if we still retained them, such retaining was to be attributed not to any ambitious views of ours, but simply to what struck us to be those of the First Consul. These instructions were sent on the 9th. — It was evident Buonaparte was luring both Vienna and Russia with a partition of the Turkish dominions, and that neither of these were disinclined to listen to him. *He* is to have the Morea. Whether in the upshot he

---

* Langue—Se prend quelquefois pour Nation ; ainsi on dit en parlant des différentes Nations de l'Ordre de Malte, " La Langue de Provence, La Langue d'Auvergne," &c. &c. Dict. de l'Académie.

† English Ambassador at Paris.

will stick by Russia or Austria remains to be seen; probably the latter ; and that the distant event, supposing his power to last, may be France and Austria against Russia and Prussia—in other words, the south of Europe against the north.

Woronzow, he said, in talking to him, professed the strongest attachment to an English alliance, declaring himself as friendly to no other; but added, that the way in which the Foreign Department here was conducted *spoilt all*, and went on precisely as he did with me in the last spring. He, indeed, told Pelham precisely, and in nearly the same words, what he told me in the month of May, 1802, previous to his going to Russia. From some words Woronzow dropped, it struck Pelham as if he *knew* Buonaparte's views on the Morea.

Pelham's general principles and opinions remain invariably the same; he seems to have little influence with his colleagues, or not to consult with them, or be consulted by them; he gave me the famous report of Sebastiani * in French, and we commented on it.

FRIDAY, FEB. 11.—Fagel (the Greffier) with me.—He stated Holland, where he had lately been, to be an altered country — the Hague particularly so; yet still much wealth; the Government in the hands of a trio of individuals, who are leading members of what they term a *States Government*. Spoor and Besier are names unknown to me. The union of the Provinces is dissolved, but their names and divisions remain as before. The *States Government* fix the taxes, and then order a com-

---

* Sebastiani afterwards became distinguished as one of Napoleon's best diplomatists and generals. At the French Revolution of 1830, he took a leading part in placing Louis Phillipe on the throne. He was sent by him as Ambassador to London in 1834, and afterwards made Maréchal de France. The report here alluded to was drawn up after an official tour made by him through the Levant, during which he had with much boldness attempted to rouse these nations to support French interests and oppose England. He entered into military details of our force at Alexandria, and of the powers of attack and resistance we possessed. The tone of the Report, appearing, as it did, in the Moniteur, after the insulting demands made by the First Consul respecting our controul of the Press, and the expulsion of the Emigrés, produced great indignation in England.

mittee, sitting in each Province, to raise the money as they can. Le Païs de la Généralité is become a sort of eighth province; or, to speak more correctly, the other seven are become what Le Païs de la Généralité was.

Trade begins to revive, but the French insist on the strictest prohibition of English manufactures, and the whole army of the Republic is employed on the eastern frontiers as a custom-house guard.

This army in a miserable state; four or five thousand men only. Their navy little better; building no new ships; putting none in commission, or repairing old ones.

Fagel doubted about Buonaparte's views of annexing Holland to France; said, unless from designs on the colonies, the measure would not be advantageous to him, and for the same reasons Nagell had mentioned, viz., that he could *squeeze them less.**

After saying this, the Greffier, with some short preface, produced a letter from the Princess of Orange, in which she states her apprehensions that we are going to withdraw the half-pay allowance to the officers who left the Republic, and followed their fortunes, in 1795. Her fears are grounded on a letter written to Colonel Darrell who is paymaster, by Lord Hobart, to give in an exact account of the amount of these expenses, *with a view to revise them.* The Princess says, the annual sum, but decreasing annually, amounts to about 24,000*l.*, and it provides for four hundred and eighty-five officers of different ranks, who will be left penniless if that is taken from them. That the sum, small to England, is much beyond the means of the House of Orange to supply; and she therefore urges the Greffier to use his best endeavours to prevent its being stopped or diminished.

I agreed most entirely with the reasonableness of this request, and with the folly of such shabby retrenchments. This led us to converse on what had been a subject of conversation and correspondence with us in July,

---

* Napoleon felt this afterwards, when his brother Louis refused so conscientiously to have his Dutch subjects squeezed, and preferred abdication to injustice.

1802, (vide that date, and before,) on the sum to be given by this country to the House of Orange as indemnity for their losses, &c. It was then, I thought, determined on, that the Princess should have 60,000*l.* once paid, and the Stadtholder an annuity of 20,000*l.* Now he, after consulting the Hereditary Prince, desires to have it all at once, that is to say, 160,000*l.* once paid, instead of the annuity, and to this Government has acceded; and, in my mind, very unwisely, since it is losing *all* hold on the House of Orange, and particularly leaving the Hereditary Prince to give scope to the Prussian bent of his politics — for he is not only friendly to them, but really hostile to us, and can only be kept tolerably right by such a power of control held over him. I had no scruple of declaring this my opinion to the Greffier, and he agreed with me most entirely in it. Nagell came in while we were together, and his sentiments accorded with ours. My decided opinion is, that the House of Orange is a *great card* in our hands, one we should not part with, or suffer to dwindle into a Prince of Nassau, with all the insignificance and shabbiness of a petty German Potentate, under the rule of either Prussia or Austria.

SATURDAY, FEB. 12. — William Elliot. — Egypt, he says, is evacuated; supposes Buonaparte to have known it when he published Sebastiani's report.

Inclines against Pitt; thinks he is not dealing openly, nor acting manfully; but he speaks without information, and merely from appearances.

Lord Pelham. — Went to him at two o'clock — found him alone. We went over all the Russian politics again, about which he is, and very wisely, much interested; from thence he passed to Sebastiani's report. Said the Cabinet had determined to notice it, and to draw from it an occasion to get at (if possible) Buonaparte's views, and explain their own, concerning Malta. Several councils were held on this subject, and greater pains (as it should appear) were taken to word Lord Whitworth's instructions in a way not to give offence, than to accomplish the great object of them. I did not see the despatch, but it was sent away on the 9th.

While we were conversing, the box came in with the Paris letters in circulation, and Pelham shewed them to me. They were dated the 7th, were written in the best tone and style possible. Lord Whitworth talks with spirit and dignity; not the dupe of the artifices of France, or frightened by their threats and arrogance; his despatches are advice as well as information, and manly advice arising out of self-evident truths.

He states (and it comes very opportunely) a conversation of Talleyrand's seeking, respecting Malta and our intentions. Talleyrand, he says, speaks civilly, and within bounds, but rather positively. Lord Whitworth replies, that, as long as the First Consul continues to add every day to his power and strength, it cannot be supposed we can be ready to decrease ours, particularly in the Mediterranean; and Lord Whitworth, with less management and more explicitly, appears to have anticipated the instructions sent him on the 9th; he remarks, that, paradoxical as it may appear, our fulfilling the Treaty of Amiens with respect to the retrocession of Alexandria and Malta will certainly, instead of maintaining peace, produce war, as Buonaparte's views are *all* in Egypt; and I should have said in its place, that Talleyrand began the conference by animadverting on Sebastiani's report, saying, that whatever might appear, the object of his Mission *was purely commercial* — all the First Consul's views were commercial—he would assure Lord Whitworth so " *upon his honour;*" and if in this report other objects seem to have employed Sebastiani's attention, it must be considered he was a " *young, ardent, military* man," and thought he was doing his duty by stating the force of our army, and situation of the different strong places he had visited in Egypt and Syria.

To this language of thin-spun deceit Lord Whitworth replies nothing, but remarks, that " Talleyrand's assertion, *on his honour*, did not make what he said, however binding the assurance, at all the more credible to him."

Lord Whitworth mentions that Livingston, the American Minister, is drawing towards him, and evidently is alarmed about the French becoming masters of Louisiana and the Floridas. Livingston doubts whether Buonaparte will take these last immediately; but Lord Whitworth says, the men going to St. Domingo, if that object fails, as he believes it will, probably will be sent there, in order that something may appear to have been done.

I was sorry to find from Lord Pelham orders had actually been sent to evacuate Alexandria, but that *we hoped* to keep Malta. I said the word *hope* should be changed to the word *intend*, for if we give it up we should have war, and a most unequal one, almost immediately, in the Mediterranean. To that *he* agreed; but to this *his colleagues* will not.

After talking over these subjects, and expressing our comfort that Lord Whitworth felt and acted so rightly—(N.B. His private letters to Lord Liverpool were in the same tone) — we got on the House of Orange, and I mentioned to Lord Pelham what the Greffier had said to me respecting the stopping the half-pay of the Dutch troops. Lord Pelham agreed with me on the folly and cruelty of it.

I also argued strongly against the giving 160,000*l.* in a lump to the Prince of Orange; and, for the reasons already mentioned, I proposed that the two sums—viz., the 20,000*l.* originally intended to be given as an annuity to the Stadtholder, and the 24,000*l.* for the maintenance of these half-pay officers — should be united under one head, and given *all* to the House of Orange, as a sort of subsidy, on condition they should pay these 485 officers. This would give them still a great influence over a large body of military men attached to the old interests of this House, be better understood by Parliament, and give us, what I always most anxiously wanted to preserve, a tie upon the Hereditary Prince, whose crooked politics and slippery character were but too well known to me.

Lord Pelham acceded to all I said, promised to mention it to Addington; but added, that whenever any one talked to him on subjects he did not understand, or was not used to, he always got rid of the subject by telling some *bon-mot* or dull joke of Halsell's when he was Speaker.

SUNDAY, FEB. 13.—Sloane in the morning. Reports that Lord Melville (Dundas) was to be put at the head of the Admiralty, in the room of Lord St. Vincent.

Canning.—Dined with Lord Pelham—only myself, he, and Lady Pelham.

I insisted strongly on the necessity of a clear and distinct language being held to France; that, besides its being that which becomes us as a great nation, it was the safest. A duration of obsequiousness and submission would only encourage new and greater insolence; and Buonaparte, reckoning on our giving way, would go lengths we must resent, and which, if he thought we would resent, he never would go; that his courage was not sterling, nor generous, and that it was greater in him in proportion to the want of spirit in his adverse party; that this was not only the common process in human character, but was confirmed and believed by everybody, the young and old, the well-informed and the not informed at all, the careless and the busy, who came from Paris — *all* their reports coincided in this point, viz., that he advanced as we retreated, and would retreat as we advanced; and the generality of the remark left no doubt of its truth, and Lord Whitworth's advice and opinion came most powerfully in confirmation of it. I entreated, therefore, Lord Pelham to speak to such members of the Cabinet whom he might suppose to think like him, and I named the Duke of Portland, the Chancellor, and Lord Castlereagh; not to allow the insufficiency and self-sufficiency of Mr. Addington, joined to the timidity and weakness of Lord Hawkesbury, to prevail over everything that was wise and right, and which prudence as well as national character called for.

Lord Pelham felt all I said; its effects I place little

hopes in. He agreed with me, if Pitt *would* take Addington's place, and give Addington another in the Cabinet if he wished for it, all would do well; and we reverted to what had passed in March, 1801, and what we then said on this particular point. Addington had now made provision for his friends, and therefore *ought* to be satisfied with such a quietus as might be offered him. We had much more discourse on this subject, and on Foreign Affairs, but it was little more than a repetition of what was said before.

Pelham shewed me an excellent letter from Lord Ellenborough, in which he gives him official information of the result of the trial of Despard and others, and says, after stating that Despard was found guilty, that he was recommended by the jury to mercy; but why, and from what motive, he could not conceive, since the very plea of former good character, on which alone it could rest, far from extenuating, could only aggravate the crime, which was nothing less than an intention to assassinate the King. Despard and the others are to be hanged on Monday, the 21st instant.

Lord Pelham said that Calonne, previous to his going to Paris (where he died in October), had prevailed on the Prince of Wales to try to get his name struck off the list of emigrants. The Prince had actually spoken to Lord Whitworth or Merry; but, as this had no effect, Calonne attempted to persuade the Prince to write to Buonaparte, stating foolishly (had he been speaking to any other than the Prince) as a reason, that all the Sovereigns in Europe had written to him but the King, and that a letter written by the Prince would gratify his vanity, and induce him to comply with any request he might make. Calonne went the lengths of drawing up the letter the Prince was to sign; and if by great luck the Prince had not desired Calonne to shew it first to Lord Pelham, he probably would have signed it. Lord Pelham, on whom Calonne waited with it, said he would give his opinion on it to the Prince, whom he met the same day at dinner at the Duke of Queensberry's, with Crauford (the Fish), and Calonne; he immediately took him aside, and represented to him the danger of such a step; that the letter would be instantly printed in the *Moniteur*, and the Prince held out to all Europe as a correspondent with the First Consul. Luckily this passed *before* dinner.

The Prince felt it as he ought, and refused to write the letter; but, in consequence of Lord Pelham's advice, said he would in a letter express his surprise to Lord Whitworth that Buonaparte had paid so little attention to his request. Fortunately, Calonne died, and this foolish affair with him. It was one of fifty others of a similar nature into which the Prince has got or will get.

Pelham told me that on Calonne's death he had taken possession of his papers. They filled several large coffers, and were artfully concealed in closets, on the panels of which were hung the most obscene prints possible, and left in the care of a common woman (who behaved very well), with whom Calonne had lived for a long time. These papers contain all the secret history of Coblentz, and Calonne's Negotiations there and since; and from the anxiety expressed by the Prince of Condé and Duke of Bourbon to get their letters back, it should seem that the last plan was bringing *them*, and *not* the King of France or Monsieur, forward. Lord Pelham spoke well of Andreossi;* said he was quiet and unassuming; well-informed in his line—that of engineering; wanted to be at the head of the artillery, but Buonaparte refused him, appointing him here. This rather displeased Andreossi, as he had been one of his confidential associates in Egypt.

The King's composure on hearing of Despard's horrid designs was remarkable, and evinces a strength of mind and tranquillity of conscience that prove him to be the best of men. It gave him great pleasure to hear no report was to be made to him on this occasion. The trials being out of Middlesex, it was not the practice, even though they took place under a special commission.

Lord Pelham said it was, or rather had been, in contemplation, to send Sir S. Smith to the Barbaresque

* French Ambassador at London.

Powers and Egypt; that Addington had gone so far as to desire Sir Sidney to hold himself in readiness, and to ride at single anchor. Lord Pelham approved it; thinks we should do well to pay great attention to these Powers, and that it would please the Porte, who looks on them *still as* its vassals. He quoted as an instance the Turkish Chargé des Affaires at Paris having very lately applied to Lord Whitworth for support and advice, as Minister of an ally to the Porte, on some intention expressed by Buonaparte to attack *the Dey of Algiers;* and added, the Porte is determined to support *its vassal.* It would be perhaps right to make all our Consuls and agents on the Barbary coast dependent on our Embassy at Constantinople. It is to that side we ought to turn all our attention, as Buonaparte's great object is Egypt, Eastern dominion, and the destroying our Empire in India.

MONDAY, FEB. 14TH. — Woronzow (Russian Ambassador). — I called on him; found him as much irritated against the Ministers as before he went, but much less ready to talk of the *friendly* sentiments of Russia towards us, and his own animosity against France. He was rather reserved, and, contrary to his usual practice, uncommunicative ; but he was busy, and engaged in preparing letters for a messenger he was about to despatch. I therefore think, that the first impression his manner gave me of that Court being become decidedly hostile was, perhaps, an untrue one, and I shall wait a second interview before I allow myself to admit this very unpleasant belief.

William Elliot — at dinner; he said he had been to the House to give notice, that Dr. Lawrence would bring on his motion relative to Captain d'Auvergne on the 21st; it was, he assured me, a strong case; that d'Auvergne had undergone an examination under the direction of Chaptal, Ministre de l'Intérieur, in which he was not interrogated as to present facts, but to what passed during the time he was employed in Jersey; and on d'Auvergne saying, he considered the peace as having put an end to everything which passed there, and that he could only answer as to any subsequent facts which might occasion his present detention, he was told there were none, " Mais il y a une prévention contre vous par rapport à vos liaisons avec Pitt et Windham." Chaptal went so far as to say, he really saw no justifiable cause for detaining him; but he was sent to prison, and remained there two days. *If* this is a true statement, the case is a strong one; but by no means, in my opinion, tantamount to carry it before so indefinite a tribunal as that of the Law of Nations, and from which (if you persevere) there is no appeal but the sword.

Lord Minto puts off his motion respecting Switzerland till after the Swiss Constitution is formed.

I should add, when speaking of Captain d'Auvergne, that it is said that, when he went for his passport after he was set at liberty, Desmaret observed, that he understood that he was come to Paris to claim as heir to the Duc de Bouillon; and hinted to him, that if he would communicate any thing he knew which had passed during the war, and particularly relative to Pitt and Windham, it might tend very much to the success of his pretensions.

The Greffier Fagel. — Told him my idea respecting the money to be given to the Prince of Orange, and my wish it was all lumped together as a yearly payment. He quite agreed with me, but doubted its being agreeable to the Prince of Orange, or rather the Hereditary Prince. This I admitted; but said, it was precisely the reason why it should be done; that joining the 24,000*l*. now allowed the Dutch officers who left Holland in 1795 to the 20,000*l*. intended for the Prince, and also about 12,000*l*. to which, I fancied, amounted the half-pay of the late Dutch corps, belonging to the Hereditary Prince, commanded by Constant, would make a sum of 56,000*l*.; and this sum I would propose to pay as a sort of subsidy to the House of Orange. It would, in the first place, preserve the link between England and them; and, in the next, keep up the dependence of their followers from Holland.

FEB. 15. — Dined with Canning alone. He had an answer from Pitt; very short, very dry, and, as he said, "*unpromising.*"

In the morning with Lord Granville Leveson, who was acquainted with the whole transaction; he thinks Pitt will not come forward yet. Says Fox (he heard from his friends) is vexed and disappointed at Opposition doing nothing, and wants an opportunity of affecting to support Addington. I reminded Leveson of what Addington had said to him when he resigned; Leveson said he *certainly said it*, and that he looked upon him only " as a *locum tenens* for Pitt."

WEDNESDAY, FEB. 16. — At the Levée; carried Lord Titchfield; too late to go in: crowded and long; did not get away till half-past three.

Lord Hawkesbury came, and sat down by me in the outer room; talked of Russia as an irresolute though friendly power; Kotschoubeg the only person of real merit, and he now in the Home Department. The Court not French, and that is all that can be said; the Emperor milk and water; Prussia worse and worse. Andreossi and Portalis crossing the room, I observed on them, that they looked like persons unused to such a place; not fashioned either in dress or address. Lord Hawkesbury agreed, but observed Andreossi was a very good man to have here; that his disposition was to accommodate, and be quiet; and that *he* (Lord H.) knew he did not obey his very strange instructions farther than he was obliged to do.

Lord Hawkesbury said he thought the First Consul very like Paul, really mad,— that his temper grew quite outrageous, and that his unpopularity amounted to perfect hatred,—" It must be *madness,*" Lord Hawkesbury said. I quoted to him a letter from Dresden, by the first Lord Lyttleton to his father, in 1741, or thereabouts, which said just the *same* of the *great* Frederick soon after his accession; yet he lived and reigned more than forty years afterwards, and betrayed no symptoms of insanity.   Sir C. Williams, then our Minister in Saxony, said on this occasion, " C'est parceque Frédéric a plus d'esprit qu'eux, que les Allemands le croyent fou."

The Americans, he said, were much alarmed, and drawing towards us.   He did not know but that they had actually *forestalled* the French expedition, and taken possession of New Orleans; and, that if so, this would enable us to come forward with great advantage.   I said, I very much approve the idea of coming forward on any and every occasion; but that I retained my *old* feelings about the American war; could not forget they were revolted subjects; and that, though I could not object to their being assisted by us in a point of mutual and common interest, yet we, I think, ought to be principals, and they accessories.   Lord Hawkesbury *half* acquiesced in this.   He said Livingston, at Paris, was of the democratic party, but no rooted democrat; would obey orders, and nothing more.   As Lord Hawkesbury seemed disposed to be communicative, I took this opportunity of mentioning to him my notions respecting the Prince of Orange's annuity, and the annexing to it the two sums allowed for the support of the Dutch officers, and stating my reasons on the grounds alleged by me to Pelham and the Greffier.   Lord Hawkesbury listened with great attention, and seemed to approve the idea, on the first impression it gave him; he seemed unacquainted with the detail of parts of the transaction, and it is manifest to me that the whole is done slovenly and carelessly through Lord Hobart.   Lord Hawkesbury spoke favourably of Liston,* but said there was nothing to be done in Holland.

Merry, (late Minister at Amiens, under Lord Cornwallis, and at Paris, now going to America,) a sensible, plain man, said it was difficult to conceive the strange situation Foreign Ministers were in at Paris,—that Buonaparte's temper was most suspicious and vindictive, and violent beyond measure,—that it was this which induced him to order the arrest of Captain d'Auvergne;

---

* English Minister at the Hague.

that he wished to punish him for having supported the war in La Vendée, and that La Vendée was still what he most dreaded. Fouché was at the head of the Police when d'Auvergne was arrested, but dismissed before he was released. Desmaret was a clever fellow. Merry doubts much that anything passed at the examination about Pitt or Windham,—*he* never heard of it. Talleyrand, on his (Merry's) first representing against d'Auvergne's arrest, said it was quite unknown in his department, it was *une affaire de police*; and, on his doing the same on his being sent away in twenty-four hours, Talleyrand said, " You cannot call in question our right to send any one out of the country we please, since you do the same in virtue of your Alien Bill." Merry said there were, at one time, five thousand English at Paris, but many who did not avow their Minister; he left seventeen hundred English on Whitworth's arrival.

Duke of Portland.—I took him aside and acquainted him with the manner in which I wished the money to be given to the House of Orange: he approved of it entirely, and strongly encouraged my speaking to Addington. I said I had not spoken to him since he had been Minister, but was to see him, at his own request, on Saturday.

The Duke, as usual, repeated his old profession of political faith; and that his principles, both respecting what we should do at home and abroad, never could change.

Addington.—Came up to me with great eagerness the moment he came into the room to apologize for not having answered a letter I had written to him respecting Mr. Penn's intended encroachments in Spring Gardens: he was more than necessarily civil, and expressed his earnest wish to see and converse with me; and, after numberless common-place things said on both sides, it was settled I should call on him at Twelve on Saturday next.

FRIDAY, FEB. 18.—Lord Pelham with me before Twelve. Nothing new to communicate.—Prince of

Wales's debts (that is to say, the sum remaining unpaid since the arrangement made with him in 1795) to be paid. Many new debts, illegally contracted by him, and at the risk of those who trusted him, still will exist. *It is understood* the Prince is to restore his establishment. I asked Pelham whether this was an article agreed on in writing. He said "no;" but implied by the Prince's promise. In short, it is clear the whole transaction is a compromise between the Prince and Addington, to induce the Prince to waive his claim on the arrears of the Duchy of Cornwall during his minority, and which the Crown Lawyers consider to be a fair one, and so withdraw his petition of right which the King had granted.

No terms are made with the Prince but this. None of his income (which will now be net what is paid him by the public) is appropriated to any specific purposes, as the Civil List is; and the whole will evidently be squandered away in the same way he has hitherto lived in, without his assuming any one single *exterior* mark of royalty or splendour—to prove that he and his hangers-on do not consider it a farce.

FEBRUARY 18.—Lord Moira yesterday took up what he called his ground in the House of Lords, and opposes Government on the Bill to Extend the Rights of the Bank not to pay in Specie. Lord Moira likewise is at issue on what passed between him and Mr. Addington in a *tête-à-tête* conversation, and which they represent very differently. Lord Pelham, on my telling him I expected to see the Duke of York, desired me to soften him down, if possible, about the Duke of Kent and Gibraltar; said that the Duke of York was displeased with his brother, and imputed the mutiny to him: but that it was very desirable no *éclat* should take place.

SATURDAY, FEB. 19.—With Mr. Addington by appointment at noon. His ostensible reason for wishing to see me, was to discourse about a memorial in which the inhabitants of New Street, Spring Gardens, had remonstrated against some intended building Mr. Penn was about to erect, under permission from the Surveyor of the Crown lands (Fordyce). This point he promised me should be settled in a way favourable to the memorialists.

He then passed to the Prince of Orange's concerns; stated to me on them what I knew before, with this exception, that the 160,000*l.* to be granted the Prince was *also* to be invested in trustees' hands, and the interest only applied to his use. He talked of converting this into a perpetual annuity of 10,000*l.*, to be settled on the House of Orange; but he wished to hear my opinion. This I stated to him precisely as I had before done to Lords Hawkesbury, Pelham, and the Duke of Portland, and urged my reasons.

I dwelt more particularly to him than to them on the doubtful politics of the Hereditary Prince; and that it would be letting him slip through their fingers, and gratify his own Prussian leanings and policy, if we were to entail irrevocably an annuity, or the interest of a sum of money, on him and his family.

After a good deal of conversation, all tending on the part of Addington to agree with me, he said it should be done in the way I proposed; he was confident it was the best. I then adverted to the two Dutch corps, or rather Officers of them, still in our pay; and, after giving the same reasons for what I had to propose as I had already to the other Ministers, I mentioned these sums, whatever they were, as proper to be given to the House of Orange, for enabling them to pay these officers.

Addington seemed also to approve this, but to wish to make himself more master of the subject before he engaged himself; admitting, however, the apparent wisdom of such a step, and the great use it might be in future. He also himself argued in favour of an annuity to be granted under the sort of condition, " quam diu se bene gesserit." Since these two sums, 160,000*l.* to the Prince, and 60,000*l.* to the Princess, would correspond exactly with that raised from the Dutch ships, viz. 220,000*l.*, for which the ships sold, and this would not escape the notice of either some awkward friend or artful enemy.

In speaking of the two corps on half-pay, Addington said it had been in contemplation to wait to see whether the indemnities given the House of Orange would be sufficient for them to take this charge on themselves; but that there was a dislike to be at all mixed up in this predatory system, and the idea had been dropped. I observed, it was indeed a very strange and unseemly one, not only because it *did* appertain to this predatory system, but because the *whole* revenues of Fulda and Gorea were insufficient for the purpose.

I here thought Addington had done, and was going, when he stopped me, and, after many good-humoured expressions of regard and friendship, said he had had it frequently in his wishes for some time past to consult and ask my opinion on points on which, with him, my sentiments would have great weight. That he hoped our intimate acquaintance authorized him to do it now, freely and without reserve; the more so as it was particularly on one point on which he believed the intended conduct of Government was such as (from everything he heard) would entirely concur with my principles and opinions.

After this preface, he went on by stating, in a very clear and distinct manner, the system he had laid down and acted on since His Majesty had first called him to take a share in his councils; ' that he at that period considered peace as an advisable and even necessary measure, from the state in which the Continent was at the time of his taking Office, and from that of the Exchequer, not quite exhausted indeed, but fatigued and so circumstanced as not to be able anywhere to hurt or make any impression on France. That therefore, as soon as the expeditions to the Baltic and Egypt were over, peace became his immediate object. That peace certainly was then his favourite wish, and never could be but in his mind most desirable; but *he never expected he would have lived to have seen the day* when he should stand accused of preferring peace when inglorious to the character, or injurious to the interests of the country, and particularly that, to maintain and preserve peace, he should consent tamely to the insolence and arrogance of any Power, and more especially of France. Yet of this he did stand accused, and he had borne the accusation in silence and patiently, because he was conscious it was undeserved, and because he felt within his own breast a complete vindication of his conduct, and the falsehood of the assertion. That the time was now near at hand when this justification would become manifest, and he hoped it would be such as would satisfy all reasonable, moderate, impartial, and unprejudiced men. Others, nothing he could do would satisfy, neither did he care about them. His maxim, he declared, from the moment he took Office was, first to make peace, and then to preserve it, under certain reservations in his own mind, if France chose, and as long as France chose; but to resist or bear all clamour and invective at home, till such time as France (and he ever foresaw it must happen) had filled the measure of her folly, and had put herself completely in the wrong, not only by repeated and intolerable acts of unprovoked insolence and presumption, but till these acts were, from their expressions and inference, declaratory of sundry intentions the most hostile and adverse to our own particular interest, a violation of treaty, and dangerous to the interests of Europe.

' That simple acts of insolence and impertinence, however grating, he had passed over, because he never would put on a par the sober and antient dignity of Great Britain with the infatuated mushroom arrogance of Buonaparte. That acts of this kind lost their impression when we considered by what sort of a character they were committed; an apology or explanation from such a character was equally unimportant. It was as if a sober man was to resent the impertinence of one drunk, —for a gentleman to commit himself with a carman; from neither of these could the rate of insult be reciprocal, or reparation or excuse come with equal value. That it was for this, although he had treasured them up, he had advised no notice to be taken of various little foolish tricks, insults of omission and commission, which Buonaparte had practised towards this country; and *he had waited till insolence was coupled with hostility*, or (which was the same) hostile declarations, before he moved.'

This was done in the most unquestionable way by Sebastiani's report; and, if Buonaparte had studied how to fulfil his (Addington's) prediction, he could not have accomplished it better. He then went over hastily the report, on every point of which I entirely agreed with him. "This," said he, "has from the moment it was known, occupied *our whole attention*, and the opinions of the Cabinet have been unanimous on the occasion." 'In consequence of their determination, instructions were sent ten days ago to Lord Whitworth, in which he was directed to represent to Talleyrand, that, although the general tone of this report was very offensive to this country, and such as never was before practised from one great nation to another; although the indecent aspersions flung out against His Majesty's Officer commanding in Egypt* were in themselves sufficient ground for remonstrance and complaint; yet (from a desire to avoid disagreeable discussions, and from an inclination to believe that the Officer who wrote this report might perhaps be a raw and inconsiderate soldier, who thought that he was writing only for private information, and not for publication) we should have either let them pass by under the same silence with which we have treated many others of a similar nature, or only noticed them slightly, had they not been mixed up with a clear and evident declaration of facts and intentions that called for our most serious attention. That the First Consul's views on Egypt were now made manifest; that his intentions of annulling the Republic of the Seven Islands were demonstrated; and that every part of this report, which bore reference to facts, betrayed views of hostile aggrandisement towards us, and an infraction of those principles of peace and amity which were supposed to subsist between the two countries.

* General Stuart.

' That, in conformity to these sentiments, and with a
wish they should remain, and continue unshaken, Lord
Whitworth was ordered to ask dispassionately, but
steadily, a full and unequivocal explanation of these
points; and that, till this explanation was given in the
most distinct and satisfactory way, His Majesty could
not be expected to fulfil the Tenth Article of the Treaty
of Amiens (that respecting Malta), nor enter into any
discussion with the French Government on such points
as remained to be settled arising out of the Treaty of
Amiens.'

Mr. Addington ended by observing, that ' he hoped I
approved what they had done; that *I* would at least
admit he was not of that species of Minister, who, to
preserve peace, would tamely submit to any ignominy
or disgrace, and to let the country be trampled on with
impunity! that he certainly, in common with all men
in their senses, preferred a state of peace to one of war;
but when he was *in the right*, and felt himself so completely in *the right* as on the present occasion, he was,
not as an *event*, but as a *measure* of responsibility,
perfectly indifferent whether it was to be peace or
war; that he knew from the beginning this moment
would come; that he waited till France had heaped
wrong upon wrong, and made her arrogant designs so
notorious, and her views of unceasing aggrandizement
so demonstrable, as to leave no doubt on the public mind,
nor a possibility of mistake on the part of the most uninformed pacific men; that he wished to *bear and forbear* till this hour came, but not a second beyond it: to
suffer more would justly (but this was a paltry concern)
turn him out of Office; but it would do much more, it
would expose the country to certain ruin and disgrace.
Here he finished, saying, that besides myself he had acquainted no person with what he had told me but Mr.
Bragge and Mr. Ch. Yorke; that it was now eleven
days since the despatch was sent, and no answer yet
arrived; that indeed Lord Whitworth had very fortunately and judiciously availed himself of an opportunity to prepare the way; and that, in the meanwhile,

we had sent several ships out to the Mediterranean, raised our bounty, and pushed the recruiting service.'

I asked him whether *Pitt knew* what he had told me. He said "No;" because he thought he was coming to town, and that he wished not to trust it to a letter, but that he certainly should tell him every word of it. I said *I* was particularly glad of it, as, though I very much approved everything he had done, and felt as I ought the great confidence he had placed in me, yet I had so high an opinion of Mr. Pitt's abilities, and so strong a personal attachment towards him, that it was very important to my comfort to know my opinions were not adverse to his. Addington here said very good-humouredly, and much like a gentleman, "What I have been saying to you arose solely out of my private and personal regard for you, with no view to get at your political intentions, to captivate them, or to induce you to commit yourself. Whatever they may be, I am sure they are those of an honourable man, with whom every secret is safe."

I replied, this was but doing me justice; and I added, that it was always my wish to be of service to the public under every Administration, and whoever was at the head of Government; that this was in my mind a paramount duty. Addington said, "You will allow me, then, to see and converse with you again, sometimes, in the way I have just done?" I said, "Most assuredly;" that he could not doubt my sentiments of personal regard and good-will towards him, and that these certainly could not fluctuate by any political incidents.

We then, after near two hours' conversation, and standing before the chimney in the act of going, talked a little of Russia, which Court Addington said he did not reckon upon a line farther than negatively: Sweden, he said, was most anti-French, and *coming* towards us; that this was difficult to manage on account of the jealousy of Russia; that he hoped Buonaparte's avowal about the Seven Islands would exasperate Russia; and that if, in consequence of our not evacuating Malta, the

French broke in on Naples, this might rouse Russia, who was guarantee to the integrity of Naples, and be considered as an infraction of the Treaty on the part of France, though it was evident France would try to attribute this infraction to us; Austria, he said, was detestable, talked of not being fit for war these seven years, and were reforming their cavalry.

He said the Continent *must be watched.* I said, " Certainly;" but that he must not suppose, that, by *watching,* a very easy or passive task was imposed upon us; it required even more dexterity, more management, to *watch well,* and appear inactive, than to move on a negotiation open and avowed; that the most explicit and *literal* instructions should be sent to such Ministers as required them; and that to the very few abroad in whom full confidence could be placed, the *ends* must be clearly defined, and the *means* left to them; that laboured and long despatches, intended only to justify the Secretary of State who wrote them in case of impeachment, were the bane of all Foreign Missions; they perplexed and frightened the new and uninformed Minister, while they hampered and disgusted the more experienced one; that such would be peculiarly bad when our system was *watching,* which, I repeated again and again, was one that required more abilities, more temper, more experience, and more patience, than the most intricate negotiation.

I hinted my suspicions that France was luring the two Imperial Courts with a share in the spoils of Turkey. Addington said it was so, but that Russia decidedly disclaimed any thoughts of it.

FEB. 20, SUNDAY.—Dined at Burlington House—at Lord Pelham's in the evening; he said Addington had been well pleased with what I said about the Orange Annuities, particularly the lumping all the sums paid the Dutch in one, to be distributed by the Prince of Orange.   On talking over what had been done respecting France, we both agreed it was very good *as far as it went;* but if, after all, nothing was to be required but verbal satisfaction, and all the manifest intentions expressed in Sebastiani's report to be done away by explanation similar to that Talleyrand had already made to Lord Whitworth, and we were to be assured " the First Consul's views were solely commercial," and to rest satisfied with this, it would be better nothing at all should be done; that, unless the instructions given to Lord Whitworth were to be acted up to, and the First Consul given to understand that it was not Sebastiani's report (as an insulated and abstract circumstance) which induced us to speak as we did, but because it was a clear and undoubted avowal of the system and designs of France, a broad *fact*, which arose out of, and explained other *facts*, and one which confirmed us in what we had before but too many reasons to apprehend, though hitherto we had observed perhaps an over-forbearance, —that if this was not what Addington meant, we should, in the result, be lower and worse off than we were now. *I* said, that *I* conceived that this was not his meaning; that he thought as we did, and had resolved to suspend entirely any further fulfilling of the Treaty of Amiens, and particularly the Tenth Article—that, if such was not his intention, his whole language was neither more nor less than vapouring " verbiage."

Pelham was not so confident as I was; he feared strong assurances and amicable explanations would be considered as sufficient; and lamented that Addington had some one (he knew not who) who encouraged him in this system of credulity and retreat,—he wished me to see him again, and *inspirit* him. I replied, when wanted or a wish expressed, I was very ready to go to him, but I would not volunteer a visit. " If he is in earnest," said Pelham, " or if he is puzzled, he will send for you. Letters are received from Lord Whitworth, informing us of the despatches of the 7th being arrived; the next messenger will inform us what they have produced."

Before I left Lord Pelham, a note came from Ford, who was near the gaol where Despard was confined, to say all was quiet; that there had been a great concourse of people, but assembled from curiosity, and who were now (half-past nine) dispersed.

Buonaparte sent for the Chevalier de Souza (the Portuguese Ambassador), at nine o'clock in the evening, to come to St. Cloud; he received him alone, and in the most violent language, and with the most violent gesticulation, insisted on Portugal altering her tone and conduct, shewing him *more* respect, dismissing Almeida, and said, " Sans cela je l'écraserai; vous savez que j'ai les moyens, et je vous ferai voir que j'en ai l'inclination;" but, on Souza being steady and temperate, Buonaparte grew more calm, and a conference begun in such violence ended in nothing.   This serves to prove that the First Consul *may* be resisted, and *can* give way.

MONDAY, FEB. 21.—Despard and his associate traitors hanged at half-past eight; hardened villains; Despard manifested neither fear, religion, nor remorse; died haranguing the mob, with a lie in his mouth, but it produced no effect.

Lady Hamilton, whom Lady Malmesbury met in the evening of this day at Lady Abercorn's, after singing, &c., said she had gone to see poor Mrs. Despard in the morning—she did not know her, but she went to comfort her, and that she found her much better since the body had been brought back to her.   This is the consequence of Lord Nelson having spoken to his character. Lady Hamilton was a woman * * * * whom Sir William Hamilton fell in with here when he began to doat, and married when his dotage was confirmed; she is clever and artful, but a sad * * *.

TUESDAY, FEB. 22.—With Duke of Portland in the morning; met Dean of Christchurch there; very long conversation after he went.   The Duke *invariably* the same in the opinions he gives in private, and ever observing the same invariable silence in council; his language and profession of political faith to me—and he

gave it most fully, and without reserve—was the wisest
and the most judicious possible, but it squares so little
with what Government do, that it is manifest he has no
weight.   He told me letters of the 19th were come from
Paris; that Lord Whitworth had seen Talleyrand, who
received what he had to say very calmly and civilly;
no appearance of a disposition to bluster, or take it up
on a high tone—rather complacently; but, till he had
laid it before Buonaparte, he undertook to say nothing
decisively.

SATURDAY, FEB. 26.—Lord Pelham with me in the
morning; an account of all that had passed at Paris and
here since the receipt of Lord Whitworth's instructions
of the 7th instant.

He confirmed what the Duke of Portland had told me
of Talleyrand's having, on the first communication, received them with great temper and complacency.   This
he also observed in a second interview, on the 16th and
17th instant; repeated what he had before said, that
" Sebastiani's letter was the *act of an individual*," ought
not to be treated seriously nor literally by us.   He most
solemnly disavowed all views on Egypt; reiterated his
assurances that peace was their best wish; that, even
if it was not, neither the temper of the country nor its
finances were favourable to war; that our fears of the
First Consul's aggrandizement, &c. were groundless;
and, in short, Talleyrand (without producing any proofs
or positive facts) tried to get rid of the subject by general assurances, and to let it go off without any decided
measure one way or the other being taken.   But this
seems to be rather *his* own private feeling than that of
Buonaparte.   This will appear from what follows.

On Wednesday last, 23rd, Andreossi (the French
Ambassador) desired to see Lord Hawkesbury, and
was with him the same day; he began by referring to
an interview Lord Whitworth had had with Buonaparte, but with which Lord Hawkesbury, not having
heard from Lord Whitworth, was unacquainted.   An-

dreossi expressed a concern and surprise that he should
be so uneasy about what was passing in France, (particularly at Sebastiani's report, the publishing of which,
he said, was a " *coup de téte*," since, he was sure, repented of,) and should attribute such very extensive and
dangerous designs to the First Consul, and attach so much
importance to Malta: stated the present situation of
France to be unfit for war; the people to be adverse to
it; the army to be half Jacobins; that nothing was to
be dreaded; Buonaparte *could* not go to war; his objects
were trade, &c.—Lord Hawkesbury declined entering
into discussion on these points till he had received Lord
Whitworth's letters: these arrived on Thursday, 24th,
and were dated the 21st, at night.

He states, that on Friday morning (the 18th inst.)
at nine o'clock, which appears to be Buonaparte's hour
for receiving the Foreign Ministers, he was requested to
come to the Tuileries. Buonaparte received him civilly
and walking about, but soon made him sit down by a
table, and placed himself opposite to him, and with his
elbow on it began two hours' conversation very animated and violent: " That he had done everything to
preserve the peace and good harmony between France
and England, but his efforts were useless; that we refused all his advances, misconstrued all his intentions,
imputed to him every kind of extravagant and unjust
project, suspected all his views, and that every breath
of air which blew from Dover came fraught with new
and additional instances of our dislike, *personal dislike*,
to him, and distrust of his whole conduct. That there
were two French newspapers paid by us to abuse him;
that it was unjust and indecent; that, had we thought
proper to have treated him with confidence and attention, it was *his* wish and intention that England should
have participated in all that arrangement of Europe,
had her voice in the distribution of the Indemnities, and
that *he* was ready to have joined with us in governing
the world, which, with his army and our fleet, might
certainly be done; that the unfriendly and mistrusting
(*méfiante*) manner of England made this impossible;

and that he now saw plainly the two countries must ever be at enmity, if not at war."

He would not let Lord Whitworth interrupt him, but with increased impetuosity of manner, approaching to menace, went on by saying, " That the manner in which we thought proper to take up the report of his Officer from Egypt * was injurious and unwarrantable ; that, as for Egypt, he could have taken it last year if he would, and we had just left men enough at Alexandria to justify him in so doing, but he would not do it, from the love of peace; and, after all, that Egypt (though he could take it when he pleased) must be his sooner or later, it would necessarily fall into the hands of France by negotiation, and that this we could not hinder; that, as for *Malta*, he had rather see us in possession of the *Faubourg St. Antoine* (the Jacobin suburb of Paris) than in possession of it; that he would not provoke war, but that he had an army of 400,000 men, or should have very shortly; that he was conscious many years (ten he said) must elapse before he could have a fleet equal to ours ; that we were masters of the seas, but that we had no allies, no chance of having any; and that with these 400,000 men he would attack us at home, *invade England*, command the expedition himself; and although he was aware that the chances were a hundred to one against him, yet he would run all the risks, sacrifice army after army till he succeeded, and became as terrible an enemy as he was disposed to be useful as a friend; that as for Malta (his sore place), we had never been explicit about it; we had rejected the offers of Russia, with which he had closed; that, therefore, we could expect *no* support from that quarter respecting it; that he, therefore, did expect we should without delay fulfil all the articles of the Treaty of Amiens."

Lord Whitworth had in vain tried to put in a word; Buonaparte was so eager, so intemperate, and so impetuous, that it was impossible, till he had run out his whole course; he then represented to Buonaparte how great an error he was under in imputing to us any of these

* Colonel Sebastiani.

illiberal and personal dislikes with which he had begun
the conversation; that we wished for peace sincerely
and earnestly; but that when we observed the different
situation of Europe between the signing of the Preliminaries and the present day, the acquisitions France had
made, and those it was evident she had in contemplation, it was impossible we should remain quiet, or not
leave them unnoticed, for the very object of peace requires that we should be proportionately strengthened
with France; that this was the short and explicit clue
to all we had done, and all we had or should have
to say.

"What!" said Buonaparte, "you mean France has
got Piedmont, and part of Switzerland, ' deux *misérables*
bagatelles,' " (he made use of a coarser word,) "which
you yourselves thought so at the time, as you said
nothing about them."

Lord Whitworth said it was on the *general* conduct of
France, not on any one particular instance, that we
rested our opinion; and that our endeavouring to obtain
satisfactory explanations on these points could not appear to him unreasonable, much less be deemed hostile
and adverse.

Buonaparte did not attend to this, but persevered in
all he had said, and did it with increased acrimony and
virulence. It is quite clear, *first*, that Buonaparte has
little discretion, and no command of temper; that, unused to controul or command himself, he can brook no
resistance or remonstrance; that this marks every part
of his conduct, and belongs to every word and action
during this very singular conference; secondly, that the
great end of this conference was *to terrify*, to frighten
us into submission, to blind us by fear,—the trick of an
Italian Bully; and, in justice to Lord Whitworth, he
seems to have felt it as such, taken it up very becomingly, and reported it very properly.

As a farther proof of this, Talleyrand, who sent for
Lord Whitworth on the 21st, and thus delayed his messenger (probably on purpose that Andreossi's might get
first to England), softened down extremely what Buona-

parte had said, but without referring to it directly; said, if it would answer any of our views or arrangements to keep Malta for two or three or even six months, the First Consul would consent to it very readily. All he wanted to know was, when we gave it up, as he was soon to lay before the Legislative Assembly a general statement of the situation of Europe; and that, to do this with any effect, he must have it in his power to represent the exact situation in which the Treaty of Amiens stood.

Lord Whitworth took all this for reference; and it was on this, and the whole of this very important transaction, and the singular way in which it was conducted, that a Cabinet was going to sit; and Lord Pelham took me on his way to it, partly to tell me what had passed, and also to consult me on the subject. I advised firmness and spirit; that it was *now* more evident to me than before, that Buonaparte was a bully, would recede as we advanced, and that if we retreated he would advance; that if we acted wisely and cautiously, and in time, he had put the game into our hands, since his indiscretion and hastiness of temper had led him to betray his plans.

" Certainly," said Pelham; " but Lord Hawkesbury has doubts as to the propriety and custom of considering what passes in an audience between a foreign Minister and the head of a country, whether King or Consul, as fit for the public, as a document to be produced in Parliament."

I said most assuredly it was; that many Kings had been their own Ministers; and that if what they said was to be considered as *sacred*, no minister who negotiated with them *in person* could produce any proofs of his justification if called on. I quoted the Great Frederick of Prussia, the Empress Catherine, Frederick Guillaume of Prussia, with whom I negotiated two treaties, and sometimes the Emperor Joseph. Pelham was glad to have *all* these precedents, but added, Lord Hawkesbury carried his doubts so far as to think the publication of my conferences at Paris and Lisle was irregular. On this point I said he was still more wrong, for in 1761 *all* Lord Bristol's correspondence on the Spanish war was laid before Parliament and printed: *all mine* in 1771, on the Falkland Islands; and that, in fact, the contents of *all* despatches to and from Ministers abroad, were considered as official acts, and as such must be laid before Parliament if Parliament called for them; and every Minister, whether at home or abroad, *ought* to write under the possibility of his instructions and despatches becoming public.

I advised Pelham that he should see *Andreossi*, rather than Lord Hawkesbury, and before he came to any resolution of Cabinet, to endeavour to hear from him *how* Buonaparte had related his conference with Lord Whitworth; whether he had done it in as strong terms as he had actually used, and whether it was through Talleyrand or from himself, or his Private Secretary. That it was very material to know this, as it would lead to a discovery whether Buonaparte spoke from passion and temper, or whether he cooled on reflection, and when he was putting what he had done on paper. It was more important from what had passed between Lord Whitworth and Talleyrand on the 21st, who, by the bye, in addition to what he said of our keeping Malta five or six months, added, that there was an idea of making a declaration on the integrity of the Ottoman Empire, which would make us easy about Egypt. I observed on this, to Pelham, that the *integrity* of the Ottoman Empire was guaranteed by the Treaty of Amiens; and the talking of a fresh declaration bespoke an evident intention in Buonaparte to violate that article.

I should have said in its right place, that Andreossi said to Lord Hawkesbury, about allowing time to give up Malta, the same as Talleyrand did to Lord Whitworth. He did it even more complacently, by admitting that it was a just and equitable idea, that if France increased in power and strength, we should keep pace with it. Andreossi affects to be very candid and moderate; says he does not care for his office, and that he shall always do what he thinks right and becoming without any fear of the consequences of Buonaparte's displeasure. This may or may not be: I doubt it.

SUNDAY, FEBRUARY 27.—Buonaparte's address to the Legislative body appeared this day in the *Observer* (it was presented on the 22nd, the day after Lord Whitworth despatched his messenger). After a pompous and tedious account of the prosperity of the interior situation of France, it speaks of its situation with regard to foreign powers, and uses many of the same expressions (less violent), and as in substance the same as what Buonaparte said to Lord Whitworth; and it appears to me to be quite clear he said it with a view to prepare him and us for this very strange address, which is vapouring and insolent to all Europe, and really hostile as far as relates to us; while its statement of the internal flourishing situation and resources of France is fabulous.*

Canning vexed about Pitt, whose conduct he deplores and reprobates; knows not what to do; thinks he must be left to himself; talked of the address of Buonaparte to the Legislative body as I have just stated it. Said Lord Grenville thought the same. Abused Addington for his awkward management of the Prince of Wales's business, and not without just reason.

FEB. 28th.—Canning. He had called on G. Rose; found him not quite despondent about Pitt; Lord Camden gone to him. Lord Camden had seen Lord Gren-

---

* This curious " View of the State of the Republic" begins in what we should now call the " Conservative style," by congratulating France on its return to the principles of obedience to the Law and to Religion. It proceeds to give a flourishing account of the Republic's resources, to "guarantee peace" with continental Europe, and to " hope" for its maintenance with England ; but adds, that its Government alone is disposed to keep it, and that Opposition has " taken an oath of eternal hatred to France." It concludes by declaring as an axiom, that England alone cannot maintain a struggle against that country. When Buonaparte presented this paper to the Assembly he had been made Consul for life. Maret was his Secretary of State, and it is countersigned by him.

ville before he set out, and said he was going to request
of Pitt to say what line he wished his friends to take,
and to press him to declare his sentiments. *I* apprehend Pitt to feel himself unwell, and not equal to exertion. Canning imputes his absence to *insouciance,* while
others say the King makes a point of keeping him out.
Canning said, that in consequence of what was passing
in Parliament, about increasing the Prince of Wales's
income, he had thought it right to go to Blackheath,
and to see the Princess of Wales; that he had seen her
yesterday, and had offered to take any step, respecting
her increase of appointment, she might direct. Her
Royal Highness very wisely and judiciously said, she
relied entirely on *the King's* goodness; that it did not
become her to doubt it; that she thought *no woman*
should put herself forward, or interfere in Parliamentary
concerns, in this country; and though she thanked him
for his attention, requested him not to use her name,
either in or out of the House; that she was *perfectly*
satisfied with her situation, and did not wish to make
it less tranquil and undisturbed by bringing her name,
&c. under the public eye. This very wise; and, if she
maintains this conduct, will do her infinite credit and
good.

WEDNESDAY, MARCH 2nd.—With Lord Pelham; said
Woronzow had communicated, by order, the Emperor's
instructions sent to Markoff (his Minister at Paris), in
which he is ordered to say, that notwithstanding His
Imperial Majesty's earnest desire to live on terms
of friendship, &c. with France, and to preserve peace,
yet, if the First Consul should make any attempt to
break in upon the integrity of the Turkish empire, the
Emperor will be under the necessity of opposing it *by
force* if called for.

These instructions got to Paris about the time of Lord
Whitworth's interview with Buonaparte; and it is a
matter of some doubt whether he, having just heard of
them, followed the natural impulse of his temper, and
vented without delay his spleen and anger on Lord

Whitworth, or whether they were unknown to him at that time, but told him afterwards, and that in consequence Talleyrand, in his subsequent conference with Lord Whitworth, endeavoured to soften down what Buonaparte had said.

The event is a very fortunate one; and if Lord Hawkesbury and our Ministers knew how to avail themselves of it, may turn to very great use; but this I doubt, and I find from Lord Pelham that they are but half cordial with Woronzow, while they ought, at least in appearance, to show him marks of unbounded confidence.

The Cabinet, after much deliberation, sent orders to Lord Whitworth (on the 27th) to say that, from all that had been said by Buonaparte himself, and by Talleyrand, no satisfactory explanation had been given respecting their views in the East: on the contrary, it was become more and more manifest that they had very extensive ones in contemplation. Of course that it became us to attend to our security and interests, and that it would not be expected that we should relinquish the *military* possession of Malta, till such time as France could give some equally strong means of preventing any designs she might have on Egypt. (This was the substance of what was written; worded perhaps less strongly, but strong enough, as Lord Pelham thinks, to bring the matter to a point.) Russia certainly just now *appears* friendly, but whether this be sincere, or if sincere, permanent, remains to be proved.

Lord Pelham's little boy very ill. This shortened our conversation.

Lord Bathurst at dinner; long talk about Prince of Wales's debts and the measure now going to be adopted; censures it; weak and useless; hurtful to the Prince.

The Chancellor, Lord Eldon, had mentioned to the Prince the Princess of Wales, and the hopes her dignity and comfort would be attended to. The Prince's reply was, " He was not the sort of person who let his hair grow *under his wig* to please his wife." On which the Chancellor respectfully but firmly said, " *Your Royal*

*Highness condescends to become personal—I beg leave to
withdraw;* and accordingly bowed very low, and retired.
The Prince, alarmed at this, could find no other way of
extricating himself than by causing a note to be written
the next day to Lord Eldon to say that the phrase he
made use of was nothing personal, but *simply a proverb*,
—a *proverbial* way of saying a man was governed by his
wife. Very absurd of Lord Eldon, but explained by his
having *literally* done what the Prince said.

MARCH 4.—Debate and division in the House of Commons, in going into a committee on the Prince's affairs
(pro, 139; con., 184); the minority very large; composed of those who called themselves *his* friends, and
who meant to pay their court, though the bringing the
name of the Prince and his debts before the public was
not a friendly act. N.B. The first division since Addington's Administration, and being so near run, impressed the public that his Ministry was a weak one.

Woronzow said to me, " Je suis garant que Buonaparte n'ose pas se brouiller avec vous." This confirms
what I had heard of Markoff's instructions from Lord
Pelham.

MARCH 5.—Duke of Somerset with me; talked well,
and very judiciously; said he had attended yesterday's
debate; deprecated the whole of it, as tending to lower
the Prince of Wales in the public esteem. The Duke
had been at Paris, but simply to *see it;* mixed up with
no public remarks or political curiosity.

Canning.—Rose told Canning Pitt would not come to
town, but remain at Walmer; that, however, he could
assure him, (and he did it with all the unction peculiar
to him,) " I can assure you, my dear Canning, that both
in sentiments and inclination, his (Pitt's) opinions relative to Mr. Addington are precisely those you would
wish him to have."

Canning puzzled and perplexed at this behaviour of
Pitt's; and it is indeed difficult to account for it, unless

he feels his health impaired, or unless he has an idea the King is personally indisposed towards him. This last I think possible, and that it is the effect of Court intrigue.

General disapprobation of the way in which Addington has managed the Prince's business; it has given satisfaction neither to the King, the Prince, nor the public, and done no credit to Ministers.

MONDAY, MARCH 7.—Strong language held by France; Lord Whitworth's last Despatches speak doubtfully of the issue of his instructions; he cannot be responsible for the extravagance of Buonaparte; he may invade us; certainly thinks the threat will have weight with us. Russia becoming very right; has given in a Memorial at Paris, setting forth her own invulnerable situation, her strength, &c.; that she cannot be indifferent to what is passing in Europe, and will not hear of any partition of the Turkish dominions or its dependencies; hints that she is not satisfied with the conduct of France regarding Malta, and seems as if disposed to support our views in keeping it. This, when communicated to Buonaparte by Markoff, angered him very much; and his subsequent language breathes so much hostility, that Ministers have it in contemplation to send a Message to the House, on the state of public affairs, to-morrow—on the preparations making on the French coast, as well as on the relative situation of this country to France, and the discussions depending between them ; and to hold strong and decided language on all these points.*

These facts I collected from the Duke of Portland and Lord Pelham, whom I saw the 6th and 7th.

TUESDAY, MARCH 8.—Met Addington in St. James's Park; said he wished to see me; told me of the in-

---

* The King's Message to Parliament stated, that in consequence of considerable military preparations being carried on in the ports of France and Holland, he had thought it proper to adopt additional measures of precaution for the security of his dominions. This Message of course prepared Parliament and the country for the war which broke out in May.

tended Message; appointed to call on me to-morrow; in high spirits, and apparently quite at his ease; he said, in French, " *tout va bien, vous serez content de nous.*"

Lord Pelham and the Duke of Portland, whom I saw, discoursed over the Message; Lord Pelham said it was well drawn up, cautiously yet clearly worded; so did the Duke of Portland; both laid great stress on the apparent favourable conduct of Russia. I asked both whether *Pitt* knew anything of this step; Pelham confessed ignorance, but the Duke said Addington took *no step* without previously informing Pitt; he was *sure* Pitt knew of it, and believed he would come up. I expressed my doubts. Funds a little depressed. Andreossi affects to say all will end as we desire. Lord Whitworth (his letter dated the 3rd instant) mentions Buonaparte as more angry at the " *laines de Londres* " than at our claims on Malta; thinks that the whole will blow over; yet nothing so uncertain as Buonaparte's character and temper.

Andreossi's language moderate; he professes to say that Malta is no object to France, and to blame Buonaparte for laying such stress on it.

WEDNESDAY, MARCH 9.—Mr. Addington with me at half-past twelve.—Informed me of all that had passed; nearly as I had heard it from the Duke of Portland and Lord Pelham, with this difference, that he said Russia had, amongst other things, declared, after speaking of her own temper and forbearance, that she wished it was imitated by other Powers; that *his* sole object was to secure her present security, and that she could not ever consent to change the quiet and safe neighbourhood of the Turks for a more dangerous one; and that he should consider any attempt to divide that empire as an act of hostility. This was communicated in writing by Woronzow *here* to Lord Hawkesbury, and by Markoff to Talleyrand at the same time; and it accounts for this latter having said to Lord Whitworth, that they had in contemplation a project to guarantee the integrity of the Turkish dominions.

Addington said *all* this intelligence from France justified the idea that Buonaparte really meant to invade us, or to try the effect of threatening an invasion; that he called round him those officers (Massena and others) generally kept in the back-ground, and only brought forward when he had some great enterprise in view; that besides this, the preparations on the coast were not like those destined for the colonies. He said he intended himself to move the Address to-day, which he repeated to me; it was short, and calculated to produce unanimity; confined to thanks and general assurances of support.

Sheridan, he said, he thought would go cordially with him; Fox not—as he judged from what he had said at the Whig Club, that he considered *nothing* a just cause of war but an attack on the *national honour*.

Canning, he said, was disposed to smile and sneer when the Message was read. His idea was to propose an increase of seamen, and some steps for the internal defence of the country.

The whole had been communicated to Woronzow, and sent to Admiral Sir J. Warren last night.

I asked him whether Pitt knew it—whether he approved, and if he was coming up. He said, *Pitt did know it, did approve of it*, but was not coming up yet. This I lamented, as I conceived *a speech* from him would be of the greatest effect. I lamented it also on my own account, as I should always look up to Pitt as the person to whose political conduct I paid the highest deference, and by whose judgment my opinions on all public points would be decided, when my opinion was at all doubtful, or in suspense. " Not more than I do," said Addington; " and I wish he would come up; but he is *beset;* strange stories are told him—false ones by deceived or artful men; his mind, strong as it is, is not proof against this. We cannot, nor ought not for his sake, to keep him minutely and regularly informed when he is at a distance; it would be loading him with responsibility for measures not his own ; but when near, I neither ought, nor *can*, conceal anything from him."

I urged this as a strong reason for his pressing Pitt to come up ; but Addington seems to evade a direct answer, and there is evidently some strange mystery at the bottom not to be got at.

Mr. Addington put many questions to me in the course of the conversation, as to what had been done on similar occasions, and what was the best suited to this. I said, the great and best impression to give both the public here and the Continent, was, that all Buonaparte's views were of an *offensive* nature, all our ends purely *defensive*. That this being strictly true, would be the strongest and most honourable ground to stand on ; it would satisfy and animate us at home, and it would hold out a truth and an example to the nations of Europe, which, *perhaps, might raise their tone.* That, in addition to this, he might give *now* a just value to (what I had not always approved) his forbearance and longanimity ; and from these measures of temper, and almost concession, *now* derive support, and inspirit the country. That all long and unnecessary details should be shunned ; no answers given to gratify opposition curiosity, no ill-advised candour ; but assuming on principle that what he did was right, *act on that*, and that alone, without seeking for collateral support, or sacrificing secrets to cavil. Addington approved much all this, and said, "the strongest proof I can give of our forbearance is, our having suffered passively and patiently Portugal (our ally) to be ill-treated, and her dominions endangered ; and of this," said he, "we shall avail ourselves in our language at Paris ; and certainly will adopt the precise plan you recommend."

Addington said that there was no alteration intended in the Prince of Orange's affairs. That while this discussion with France was pending, they had thought it advisable to delay them, till this business was blown over or decided. It was my opinion that it was better ; and Addington desired me to say as much to the Greffier. He said he leaned very much to my plan, and thought he should adopt it.*

Addington talked of himself and his Government; said he did not care what was said of it, provided it was not something base and degrading; he thought all common abuse not only fair, but flattering; that he however could not bear that persons absent should be committed, (and he alluded to Pitt,) and this was a species of malignant opposition not to be endured. All this was aimed at Canning, and said to me *purposely*.

When Addington left me, I called on Lord Pelham— conversed on the subject with him. On my return through St. James's Park, met Lord Chatham, walked with him; he said, after talking over the Message and Address, and in answer to my inquiry, that his brother (Mr. Pitt) was very well; that he was informed of *all* that was passing; would come up when it was time; that had he come to-day, besides the singularity of being in the House so very soon after he had asked for a month's absence, it would give to the measure too great an air of concert, weaken the support he might afford, and appear as if *he* was governing at a distance, and that the measure was his, not that of Government; besides, it would look *too* warlike, whereas the object was that it should be considered both here, and in Europe, as a step taken to prevent war. It was impossible to talk more wisely and clearly than Lord Chatham did. I asked him, how the present conduct of Russia struck him; whether it was to be looked upon as conveying a disposition to act in concert with us. No, he said, not that, but favourable; it seemed to hold out a menace to go to war with France, if France invaded the Morea, but not if hostilities broke out in consequence of any dispute between France and us.

I said I was fearful, then, that too great a reliance was placed on Russia, and we reckoned *too much* upon her support. To this Lord Chatham assented.

The debates this day on the Address, in both Houses, scarce deserve that name; they were very short—unan-

---

* For giving the Prince of Orange an annuity instead of a sum of money.

imity in both. Ministers, as Addington had said to me, confined what they had to say to a very narrow compass; and Opposition, though approving the Address, complained of being in the dark, and endeavoured to load Ministers with great responsibility in case of war.

Canning in the evening.—Spoke of the Message and Address with temper, and even praise—said it had been debated amongst *them* what line to take, and that they (viz., the Grenville party) had determined it to be best to let *Fox* take the lead. This they did; and Fox said so little, and that little of such insignificance, that there was no room for debate, even if they had wished for it, which they did not.

He had been dining with George Rose. Pitt well— not coming. It appears to me that Pitt has all along been made informed of this measure respecting France, and that his waiting at Walmer, and his mystery as to explanation, arise from his intention of not coming forward till absolutely called for; and this, though perhaps a good reason, was one he could not allege to Canning, and gave rise to the dark hint in his letter. This conjecture to my mind becomes more probable from what Lord Chatham said, who added, he was in regular correspondence with him, and would write to him when he thought he was wanted.—N. B. Lord Chatham only wrote *once* to him while he (Pitt) was at Bath, in November and December.

THURSDAY, MARCH 10.—Fagel (the Greffier) with me; told him what Addington had said; desired him to communicate it to the Princess. He thought the delay wise, and concurred with me in opinion. Lord Hawkesbury entered into a full conversation with me on the conduct of France—to the same effect as the other Ministers. I asked him if Andreossi's language to him tallied with that held to Lord Whitworth by Talleyrand. He said, Nearly; and I observed that it was material, as probably Andreossi was in direct communication with Buonaparte, and it would be important if there was any difference. Lord Hawkesbury said Andreossi's language was temperate and reserved; that his object seemed to be to soften down what came to him, if anything did come to him, *directly* from Buonaparte, which Lord Hawkesbury doubted; that another object of his was to say, that the Jacobins expected Buonaparte's downfall if he should fail in an invasion, and to impress us with the idea that we were so placed as either to be exposed to the consequences of a successful invasion, or to those which would attend the restoration of Jacobinical power. Lord Hawkesbury paid more attention to this than it deserved. Buonaparte was himself a rank Jacobin, with a Jacobin mind, Jacobin principles, and Jacobin projects; but he is a Jacobin who has attained his point, got supreme power in his hands, and is exercising this as *all* Jacobins would in the same situation. Jacobin means and Jacobin ends do not always coincide. On my questioning Lord Hawkesbury as to dates, &c., he said his first instructions got to Paris on this day se'nnight, the 3rd; and on the 7th, Monday, other instructions, signifying the message, &c., together with a *private letter*, on which he laid great stress, as it gave Lord Whitworth a latitude to treat, not expressed in his official despatches; that he knew through Andreossi that the messenger who carried these letters got to Paris on Monday, but had heard nothing from Lord Whitworth. This, however, he expected to do on Saturday the 12th, at the latest.

Lord Hawkesbury would not give a decided opinion as to what he thought the *likely* end of the business, but said he must abide by the event, let it be what it would. Government neither cared nor would *recede*. He talked with satisfaction of the reception both Houses gave to the Message, and agreed with all those I had seen, that *Fox* put an end to all debate in the outset. With respect to the preparations of France, Lord Hawkesbury said they had no craft or small vessels on their own coast, but numbers in Holland, and that it was from thence a landing would be attempted; that it was on our vulnerable side. I alleged the length of the passage, the probability of high winds, of our intercepting them, &c.; but I found he was *very uneasy* on this subject.

FRIDAY, MARCH 11,—Lord Hobart told me, at twelve this morning, that a messenger came last night from Paris; mentioned it to Lord Pelham, who went immediately to Addington.

SATURDAY, MARCH 12.—Duke of Portland—fearful that Lord Whitworth (by the last accounts) had gone too much into explanations; he wanted us to avoid all explanation, and to stick to our first point—that we could not give up Malta till we had received an equal security against any attempts on Egypt.

Canning—in the evening. Pitt declined his visit; said he could not *yet* tell him the reasons of his silence; wished him frankly not to come to Walmer. Canning vexed and hurt; tries to conjecture why Pitt is mysterious; loses himself in suppositions. Canning seems positive Addington does not communicate with Pitt, while the other Ministers are sure he does. Canning said he had received two letters from Pitt, and had written to him to-day to *dissuade* him from coming up till this business was settled. His reasons—good perhaps, as far as personal considerations, either respecting Pitt's personal interest, or those of his followers go, but wrong if we consider the good he might and must do to the cause, were he to appear in his place, and support the country. Fox, too, is gaining ground very fast, and Pitt's staying away helps this. I said as much to Canning, but he is " *têtu* " on this point.

SUNDAY, 13.—Lord Pelham confirmed what the Duke of Portland apprehended—said he feared we should get into long and tedious discussions; that Andreossi had on Tuesday presented a Note, requiring, in civil and managed terms, our reasons for not giving up Malta.

He shewed the rough copy first to Lord Hawkesbury, and offered to alter any word or words he chose ; but said now that the Message was sent to Parliament, *he* could not avoid giving in this Note.   Lord Hawkesbury demurs about how it should be answered—rather leans to a long and laboured answer, entering into details, explanations, &c.   This against the opinion of some of his colleagues, who advise a short but civil answer, referring to Lord Whitworth's instructions for the rest : this I preferred, and said to Pelham, that it appeared as if the French wished to make *a negotiation* of it, and to transfer the business from Paris, here.   This must be prevented at all risks, and the conduct of it left to the person who began it; that a short *written* answer to Andreossi would be proper; and that it should not be forgot to manage this transaction so as to have papers to produce, not conversations (which could be disavowed or misrepresented) to refer to, by way of *pièces justifica-tives.*

Buonaparte's brothers and dependants are greatly against war—are sure it will lead to his assassination or destruction.   Jacobins all look for it for the same reason—and this Andreossi admits, and urges it as a reason why *we* should not wish the downfall of Buonaparte.   This is artful enough, and at first sight specious; but in fact Buonaparte is only a Jacobin chief who has attained his end, and exercises the unbounded power he has acquired *like a successful Jacobin ;* and it is a gross attempt to intrude so absurd a fallacy on our common sense as to say we ought to dread *the return of Jacobinism,* while, in fact, it is pressing upon us in its full force.   Infant Jacobinism is better than full-grown Jacobinism.   Its peculiar characteristic is to affect to abhor and deprecate its own means when the end is obtained, and to abhor and deprecate the end it aims at while practising the means; and, from this sad nonsense having confused the understandings of some, and imposed on the imbecility of others, it is too much the general belief that Jacobinism is abated, subdued, or its sectators converted.   The thief, while he is breaking into your house, employs very different means, and is a very different person from the thief who has once got possession of it. Buonaparte pillages Italy, Flanders, Florence, and all the palaces at Rome, but he adorns and decorates St. Cloud and the Tuileries with a luxury and expense surpassing those of Louis the Fourteenth, or Sardanapalus.

Lord Whitworth, in one of his last interviews with Talleyrand, reminded him that he had told him that there was a project in contemplation respecting the integrity of the Turkish empire, and inquired whether it was finished, or going on. Talleyrand answered, that it was implied in what the First Consul had inserted about Turkey in his statement to the Legislative body. This gross attempt to do away what he had promised, did not impose on Lord Whitworth.

Ryder gone to Walmer—also Lord Camden, and some say Dundas (now Lord Melville).

Monday, March 14. — Messenger through France from Malta. Letters from Paris, dated the 9th; appears to have brought nothing new, as Lord Pelham did not call on me, as he said he would had this been the case.

Great preparations going on at the War Office, and at the Adjutant-General's Office. This from Lord Pembroke, who had been there; he and I were going to Bath next week, but think it advisable to determine on nothing till we see the event of the present discussion.—Strong and well written leading article in the *Morning Chronicle* against Addington. Morpeth and G. Leveson with me—both rather inclined to think Pitt ought to remain at Walmer; not come up to mix in the *odium* of war, should war be the result, but to wait for the result, and then leave Walmer. This also Canning's doctrine, a doctrine which, in my mind, is founded on their wishes how best to bring him in and turn Addington out; and that, listening to this wish, they rather overlook the public service ; but even as far as this is

their object, I am not sure they are right, for it will be
an *odious task* to be brought in manifestly and solely as
a war Minister, and will rivet on Pitt the character his
ill-wishers here, and those who fear him on the Continent, are eager to give him, that of being fond of war.
Again, if this Administration succeed in terminating
the present differences without a rupture, and without
receiving any aid or assistance from Pitt, they will
evidently become more confident of their own abilities,
obtain more reputation in the public, and fling Pitt
farther in the back-ground than before. But these are
paltry political considerations, to be guided or influenced by at such a conjuncture, and which I am sure my
young friends would not admit, if left to the unbiassed
exercise of their own judgment. In the mean while,
I myself feel almost certain Pitt is meditating some
step he conceals from us all; and satisfied, as I am, that
he knows best what to do, and the when and how to do
it, I wait confidently the result of his silence and *mystery*, for his conduct is mysterious.

Reports that Lord Chatham is to go to Ireland in the
room of Lord Hardwicke, and Lord Moira to replace
Lord Chatham at the Ordnance.

Report also that the Duke of Bridgewater, who was
supposed to have died on the 7th inst., was not *really*
dead; no change, they say, had taken place in his appearance yesterday; and his funeral, which was to have
taken place to-day, is postponed, under the idea he *may
be* in a long trance; he has left 70,000*l.* a-year to Lord
Gower, and 30,000*l.* to General Egerton.

Lord Morpeth's account of Paris agrees with that
of Lord Pembroke. He said he had heard to-day that
Joseph Buonaparte had declared, " Que la famille étoit
perdue si la guerre se faisoit, et qu'il craignoit tout du
caractère violent de son frère."

Maret very civil to Lord Morpeth. Maret has great
influence; has placed all his old friends and colleagues at
Lisle in lucrative offices; his wife a pretty and pleasing
woman.

TUESDAY, MARCH 15.—Sir W. Fawcett.*—Complains of the impossibility of raising men for the regulars; militia substitutes paid much higher; army very incomplete; does not like the idea of Lord Moira's coming to the Ordnance.

Note from Duke of Portland, to say no answer yet given to Andreossi's Note, and that the Negotiation does not go forward rapidly, but that Lord Pelham intends to call on me in his way from the Cabinet, and will tell me all that has passed, &c.; Duke himself confined by the gout.

I perceive from ordinary visitors that Ministers have talked of the Conference between Lord Whitworth and Buonaparte on the 17th, probably with a view to make a strong impression on the public mind of his insolence and madness.

WEDNESDAY, MARCH 16.—The messenger came yesterday—brought rather warlike news; that Buonaparte was very violent; had given, through Talleyrand, *une Note verbale*, full of anger, and talking of sending 20,000 men to Holland, as many to Switzerland, &c., &c. Also that Sir A. Ball† had written a very excellent letter from Malta by the last messenger, urging the necessity of keeping it, and that nothing could come more *à propos*.

The Duke of Portland told me afterwards that on the 10th, before dinner, Lord Whitworth saw Talleyrand, to communicate to him the intended message, which he (Lord W.) knew Andreossi had communicated the preceding night. Lord Whitworth accompanied *his* communication with the observations ordered by his instructions; and, on Talleyrand calling it a *warlike measure*, stated to him that it was simply one of prudence and

---

* Sir W. Fawcett enjoyed a high reputation as a scientific soldier. He served in Flanders and in the Seven Years' war, and died in 1804, Governor of Chelsea Hospital.

† Sir Alexander Ball was one of Nelson's favourite Captains in his band of heroes. He commanded the Alexander line-of-battle ship at the Nile, conducted the blockade of the French garrison at Malta in 1800, and on its surrender was made Governor of the island, where he died.

precaution, and that the forms of our constitution made
the notification to Parliament necessary, without any inference whatever to be drawn from its publicity.   Talleyrand answered nothing, but said he was going to the
First Consul, and would see him again at the Prussian
Minister's, where they were both to dine.

Talleyrand, after dinner, said the best way of letting
Lord Whitworth see the exact impression the message
had made on Buonaparte, was to read to him, and let
him copy, if he pleased, a paper he (Buonaparte) had
written immediately on hearing it, and given Talleyrand for his instructions how to act.   This paper stated
a long preface about his earnest desire to cultivate the
friendship of England, and to preserve peace ; a strange
misstatement of his own conduct since the beginning
of the war, to prove the sincerity of this intention ; that
this was now *all* over, and it was clear to him *we* intended the two countries should be always enemies ;
that after the King's Message, the end of which was
war, it became him to take every possible measure
becoming the situation in which France was placed
by it ; and, particularly as we had mentioned *Holland*
in it, to increase his force there, which he should do
by marching 20,000 men directly into that country,
and forming a camp on the frontiers of the King's
Electoral dominions ; that he should also form camps
all along the coast of Normandy and Brittany ; should
send an increase of troops into Switzerland, and immediately take possession of Tarentum, which he insinuated
was much more advantageously situated for the views
we so falsely attributed to him in Egypt and the Morea
than Malta ; that, in short, he would put France in such
a state, that we should see he was not to be insulted ;
and ended this strange paper by these words, " On peut
déchirer la France, mais pas l'intimider."

It is manifestly the production of a proud, angry,
hasty man—a mixture of resentment, menace, and apprehension, which are so unguardedly expressed as to
leave no doubt that our steady and decided conduct took
him unexpectedly, and that, whatever *distant* systematic

views he may have on England, they were not yet ripe, neither were his preparations and plans ready. On the whole, from *this* report, I do not think that war is inevitable, as some of the Ministers believe, or affect to believe. It is precisely the effect such a measure must produce on such a man—nothing more; and till we hear how he feels after two or three days' reflection, and till the news of what passed in the two Houses, I shall suspend my judgment.

I understand a very good and right answer is given to Andreossi's Note of the 8th instant, which required an explicit declaration from us about Malta; but, not having seen it, I cannot say what it was.

Vague report of a French ship being lost off Brighthelmstone, with arms, and colours with the Irish and French arms intermixed, destined for Ireland.

French messenger (Chazel), sent with a passport signed by Buonaparte himself, and who crossed in an open boat, came to Andreossi yesterday morning. Lord Pelham saw Andreossi since, and Andreossi told him that he hoped he had something to propose which would satisfy us. Lord Pelham had not heard from Lord Hawkesbury, but suspects it to be an island called Lampedosa, near Malta, belonging to a Neapolitan subject, where there is a good port, &c., to be given us, and Malta to be put under the protection of Naples.

Lord Pelham says, the first impression of Buonaparte was great anger, but it soon subsided.

――――――

MARCH 18.—Canning.—He told me of the strange behaviour of Buonaparte to Lord Whitworth at his Levée—passionate and absurd; saying, " Vous voulez la guerre, vous l'avez eu pendant quinze ans, et nous allons l'avoir encore. Vous autres vous violez les Traités. Il faut les faire observer; je le veux;" and he walked about quite in a passion, and thus made himself ridiculous both to the Foreign Ministers who were present, and to his own countrymen.

Nagel told me the Dutch have opened the Indian

trade. The Charter of the Dutch East India Company is at an end. This must affect us.

Schimmelpenninck (Dutch Minister) has given in a Note to say, that, if we had addressed ourselves to him, the Batavian republic would have given us a very satisfactory explanation of the armaments fitting out in their ports. This evidently done at the instigation of France.

Lord Pelham told me, he supposed the French courier had brought nothing to Andreossi material, as he had said nothing to Lord Hawkesbury, and that it was some stock-jobbing trick. Yet how does this correspond with what Andreossi told Lord Pelham at the Levée, Wednesday?

MARCH 19.—Tom Grenville said, Lord Carlisle's projected motion for an inquiry into the state of the Navy since 1st Jan. 1802, was to be withdrawn as soon as made, and only brought on to furnish a pretence for a debate.

Cape of Good Hope retained still by us, but it is said fresh orders are gone out to restore it.

Sir William Scott at dinner at Spencer House—very sensible, well-informed man—unprejudiced and temperate—strong advocate for firmness. Canning low. Lord Melville went to Walmer Castle, Tuesday.

SUNDAY, 20TH MARCH.—Sir G. Shee.—Alarms about Ireland; its defenceless state; recommends the getting over to our side, not the bishops and higher order of the Catholic clergy, but the priests; that it is these who guide the spirit of the people; they who were the most active in the late Rebellion, and many of them to fanaticism, and were killed at the mouth of the cannon.

I afterwards saw a very able paper of Sir George's drawing up, in which he advises, and supports his opinion with good argument, the erecting, in different positions, fortresses in Ireland, and citadels in Dublin and other towns.

I dined at Salt Hill with Lord Pelham in my way to Park Place. A messenger from Paris came this morning from Lord Whitworth, who states that Buonaparte is ready to give us every possible security that he will not get or take possession of Egypt, but will hear of no compromise with respect to Malta. This, it was said in the communication from the Foreign Office to Lord Pelham, Ministers *most anxiously wish* to be kept secret. Why? Lord Pelham left with me a sort of memorial he had drawn up with regard to our situation towards the Continent; advises applying to Russia, and, jointly with her and France, to go to the bottom of things—come to a complete understanding on every point in dispute, or likely to arise. The paper was well drawn up; Lord Pelham recommended that Louisiana, and also the Floridas, should be given to America. At this I demur, as it is the only point where the Americans are assailable ; and, if they had this, they would fling themselves *à corps perdu* into the hands of France.

He proposes to give Parma and Placentia to the King of Sardinia, and several other outlines of a project that might be well filled up.

I returned it to him from Park Place, with a letter containing some few observations.

21st, 22nd, 23rd, at Park Place; neither heard nor received any news.

MARCH 24TH.—Lord Whitworth writes word that Talleyrand had again repeated Buonaparte's readiness to give us every possible assurance as to the views on Egypt, but would not listen to any modification of the article about Malta; and that an answer, with full instructions, had been sent to Andreossi (this probably reached him on Monday, 21st), but he had as yet said nothing.

Lord Pelham had shewn me at Salt Hill a long rigmarole from Sir John M'Pherson, which meant, in substance, to say, that Andreossi disliked Lord Hawkesbury, and wished to confer with Lord Pelham. Sir John says, he was hurt at Lord Hawkesbury's not having shewn him the message previous to its being sent to Parliament, and that, besides this, he had been betrayed by one of his confidential people, and wished to open himself fully to Lord Pelham, to whom he, and persons still higher, (meaning, probably, Buonaparte,) were disposed to look, in preference to any other of the Ministers.

I told Pelham what I thought of Sir John; that he was an intruding man; *perhaps* well meaning; more duped than duping; that he was always for conciliatory and conceding steps, and that it was not to be forgotten *he* had been a strong advocate for Napper Tandy's* being given up.

I found to-day that Andreossi *had* called on Lord Pelham on Monday, as if eager to see him. That on Tuesday he came to his office, but though he seemed *full* of something, and staid a considerable time, said nothing of any importance, and alleged a very trivial reason (about some persons who had forged assignats) for coming; he would not avail himself of several openings Lord Pelham gave him to speak, but went away without saying anything, though he appeared like one who wanted to say something and laboured to bring it out.

No appearance of preparations on the French coasts; but great activity in the naval and army departments at Paris.

Lord Moira came to Lord Pelham with a long string of intelligence from Bourdeaux. It went to prove, that Buonaparte was decided to invade us, and that he had saved forty or sixty millions of livres for this purpose. That, when he was told of the difficulties, he said, " Oui, je les avoue; mais il y a tant de cabales et d'intrigues contre moi, qu'il n'y a que la conquête de l'Angleterre qui puisse reconcilier tous les esprits." Lord Moira behaved very handsomely, and like a man of honour, in communicating this information, which, though not new, is well worth attention.

Addington, to whom Lord Pelham had given the

* Napper Tandy in 1791 published a revolutionary Declaration in the name of the United Irishmen. He took refuge from the pursuit of the law in France, and in 1798 landed in Donegal with the French expedition, which failed. He was taken and condemned to death, but eventually given up to the French Government, as he had been captured at Hamburgh.

paper above mentioned, seemed to approve it, but
not likely to press it with Lord Hawkesbury. Lord
Hawkesbury, dispirited and low; afraid of Woronzow;
dares not speak to him, but sends Lord * * * * (his
Under Secretary of State), whom, Woronzow says,
"tout le monde sait être fou." He also is not *up* to
speak and confer with Andreossi, notwithstanding he
seems to be more easy and practicable than most Frenchmen.

———

MARCH 25.—Nothing new from France. Andreossi
is still silent, although it is now four days since Lord
Whitworth's letter, saying a reply to our answer to
his demanding the evacuation of Malta was sent. This
looks very suspicious. Ministers perplexed, but not
inclined to press Andreossi for it; though it is the only
natural step to take, and which they ought and are
authorized to do from Lord Whitworth's reports.

With the Greffier Fagel. He has seen Addington;
well satisfied about the Prince of Orange's affairs; approves the delay, and talks reasonably.

———

SATURDAY, MARCH 26.—It appears, from the intercep-
tion of Schimmelpenninck's letters, that Andreossi has
not received anything positive from Buonaparte; has
orders to temporize, and that they are taking into consideration at the Tuileries what is to be done. Schimmelpenninck (Dutch Minister), after this (which is written to Vandergoes), goes on by stating his own opinions
—rates our Administration low—asserts roundly that
the First Consul means to bamboozle us by false assurances, and to *gain time;* that *he* knows his inveteracy
to England is beyond all bounds; but that he is afraid
to *act* up to his hatred, as well from the strength of
England, as from a want of confidence in his own army,
and his consciousness of his unpopularity in France.
The Dutchman (who writes very sensibly) proceeds by
saying, he trusts a great Power (and he means Russia)

will assume the part so clearly marked out for her, and come forward to settle Europe, and insure, at least for a while, the permanency of Peace.

From secret intelligence, Buonaparte's hostile views on this country are made manifest. When told of the risks, he says, " Oui, je les reconnois bien; mais que faut il faire? il y a tant de factieux, tant de dangers qui m'environnent; la conquête de l'Angleterre réunira bien les esprits; il faut l'entreprendre."

His plan, they say, is to attack Portugal *by sea* from Toulon, put Murat at the head of this expedition, and Joseph Buonaparte to command in Italy and to invade Naples, or at least to break in upon the Neapolitan territory and take possession of Tarentum; and, what appears to be very doubtful, to send Moreau to the Morea and Egypt.

Massena to command l'armée d'Angleterre, Fouché to be the War Minister for this *special* purpose; but both are adverse to it, and enter into his views reluctantly. Berthier declares he will resign if Buonaparte goes to war, and foretels him his downfall if he undertakes one.

King sent for Addington early in the morning, to complain of the delay and slowness of his proceedings, and particularly of Lord Hawkesbury's inattention in not keeping him informed.

Canning.—Said Lord Melville was returned from Walmer; he had not seen him; Lord Grenville going there. Canning very much perplexed about Pitt's conduct, but had nothing new to say. His acrimony at its height against Addington.

Lord Bathurst approves Pitt's staying away; wants him to go to Bath, and pressed me to induce Sir Walter Farquhar* to write to him to advise his immediate going there. This I did not do—wishing to leave Pitt entirely to himself.

———

SUNDAY, MARCH 27.—Called on Pelham on my way

———

* Sir Walter Farquhar was the most distinguished physician, and one of the most accomplished men of his day.

to Wilton. Nothing new at half-past ten. He desired me to put on paper my thoughts on the general state of affairs, and send it him to give Mr. Addington.

I left London at half-past ten, and got to Andover by seven; 28th and 29th at Wilton.

Fitzharris writes on the 29th, that Lord Pelham had seen (and told him the substance) the answer Andreossi was to give in on that evening, 29th March; that it was evasive and undecisive. On the 30th, Fitzharris says, the answer was not only evasive and undecisive, but insolent; it compared Wilson's book with Sebastiani's report, and says that of this book they had not complained; that several councils had been held, and were sitting; and that I should hear the event of them from Lord Pelham as soon as they came to a determination.

APRIL 1.—Lord Pembroke said all his orders from Lord Hobart (as Lord-Lieutenant) look like war. So look the funds. Lord Grenville makes a great parade of his visit to Walmer, where he went in the evening, at four o'clock, on the 29th; talked of it to everybody with an air of mystery and importance, yet it was settled a week ago; and why Lord Grenville departs so much from his usual character as to affect importance, I cannot guess. No Minister in the House of Commons the 29th and 30th; this looks like a change; and people infer Addington's early audience on the 25th March bore reference to some alteration in the Ministry.

On Sunday, 3rd April, a strong answer was sent to that given in by Andreossi on 29th March; this considered by Ministers as no answer, and an explicit and categorical one required. *So* say Lords Pelham and Fitzharris; but it is possible private instructions to do away its effect are sent to Lord Whitworth by Lord Hawkesbury.

APRIL 6TH, 7TH, and 8TH.—Great rumours of

changes; I hear nothing from Canning; Lord Pelham went on the 6th to Brighton.

At Bath and Park Place till 20th April.

On my return to town I heard all which had passed between Addington and Pitt during the end of April.* The negotiations with France scarce can be said to proceed; messages meaning nothing pass. On the 23rd or 24th an intimation is sent from hence, which if not acceded to in seven days after its being delivered in, Lord Whitworth is to leave Paris. It gets there on Wednesday, the 27th. It requires that England should be left in possession of Malta for ten years; that the French troops should evacuate Holland and Switzerland; and that, on an adequate compensation being given to the King of Sardinia, England will acknowledge the King of Etruria and Italian Republic.

Lord Whitworth sees Talleyrand on the evening of the 27th. Talleyrand begins by asking him whether we give way about Malta; and, on Lord Whitworth saying No, he then says, " You may as well state all your instructions at once, as the Negotiation must break off, since the First Consul will never consent to let you have Malta." This Lord Whitworth does *verbally* on Thursday; and the letters written that day from Paris, which came Sunday, 1st May, announce war as certain. Thelluson, and those in the interests of France and with French connexions, spread it about assiduously.

On Friday, 29th, Joseph Buonaparte, who for some time past had taken a sort of *unauthorized* share—at least without any official full powers—in the transaction, comes up from his house near Chantilly on purpose to converse with Lord Whitworth. He expresses his concern and uneasiness; professes, as he always did, *his* eager desire for peace, *his* dread of war; but that his brother is a most violent, impracticable man; yet he still hopes some temperament may be found. He then enters into a long discourse with Lord Whitworth, which ends by desiring him to give in his demands and proposals in writing, in order that the First Consul may

---

* The account of this is given before in this Volume.

deliberate coolly upon them, *and in order that he may lay them before the Council of State, with a view that whatever may be the result, they may have their sanction;* and this wish of the First Consul he interprets to be pacific, from the known character and feelings of the Council, and from his not being in the custom of communicating with it, and that therefore he wants their opinion to be distinctly pronounced, with a view to do away an appearance of inconsistency in him, should the result be an acceding to our proposal, which he (Joseph) thinks possible, if we will shorten our claim on Malta from ten to seven or five years. This intelligence arrives in London on Sunday, May 1st.

On Monday, Addington, in the House of Commons, gets Colonel Patten to put off his motion, by saying that in a week he *must* expect certain and conclusive intelligence from Paris.

On Sunday evening, May 1st, a strong report prevails that Lauriston (the same person who brought over the ratification of the Preliminaries) is arrived in London. The report appeared to me idle; but on calling, late in the evening, on Lord Pelham, I found, by letters just received from Paris, dated the 29th, that Lord Whitworth actually says Lauriston is set out, and supposes him in England. That it is a *secret* and special commission from Buonaparte, unknown to him; but he is inclined to believe it one of an accommodating nature.

On Monday morning no Lauriston appears, neither is anything said by Andreossi, who, however, talks *sillily* pacific. He said to Lord Auckland, at the Royal Academy dinner on the 30th April, " Deux Ambassadeurs comme nous peuvent parler franchement, (not very good *political* logic,) pourquoi vous dirai-je un mensonge qui dans huit jours sera nécessairement décelé? Mais je vous promets que quoique vous entendiez dire de nos armements et *de l'arrivée de Lauriston,* le tout sera arrangé avant la fin da la semaine." And, in speaking to Hugh Elliot, he said, " Enfin les yeux du Premier Consul sont dessillés; il reconnoit la loyauté et la bonne foi de la

nation Anglaise." These are strange speeches, and Andreossi chooses strange confidants.

In the mean while the popular cry increases against
Ministry for these delays, and for keeping the country in
a state of suspense so very distressing. The Grenvilles,
a part of Pitt's friends, and many country gentlemen,
with nearly the whole of the old Opposition (Sheridan
excepted, and he only means to stay away), violent and
eager to divide the House on Patten's motion on an inquiry into the state of the Nation.

On the 2nd May, Canning writes a very long letter
to Pitt; too long, yet able and well written. It began
by a narrative of what he had collected with respect to
the effect produced on the King by Pitt's conduct; then
goes on to ask him *what* he wishes his friends to do, and
how to act.

Pitt's answer to it is, that he is coming to town, and
that it is a subject better to talk over than to write on.

On Wednesday the 27th April, with Woronzow for
two hours; he communicated to me several Despatches
of his own Court to him; of his to his Court; others to
Markoff at Paris. The result of them struck me that
Russia was now what she ever has been since she has
held or *assumed* a place amongst the *greater* Powers of
Europe—cajoling them *all*, and courting flattery from
them all, but certainly never meaning to take an active
part on behalf of any of them.

He read me his brother's long Despatch, written in
January to Markoff. It is, as was represented to me by
Pelham and the Duke of Portland, quite a political
sermon; full of good advice, and even admonition, to
Buonaparte; well written; strong and ingenious, and
expressing in distinct words, that, if any attempt is
made by France on the Turkish empire, " l'Empereur
se verra obligé d'intervenir *activement.*"

Woronzow's own statement of the conduct of Ministry
and measures of this country, since the Peace of Amiens,
is precisely such a one as Lord Grenville would have
written, only more full of accusations and slighting expressions of Mr. Addington and Lord Hawkesbury. I

observed on this to him, and said, *if* he was a sincere wellwisher to this country, as he professed to be, why lower it by depreciating its Ministers in an official correspondence? *Think* of them as he liked, but if they were not deficient either in personal regard and attention to him, or in confidence and free communication towards his Court, not to express his thoughts in a Despatch. My friend is too violent and untractable to understand this; and all he does, or I could get him to do, is to qualify his abuse of them by praises of the country at large, and of other individuals in it *he* thinks well of in his private letters.

I fear *we* here rely too much on Russia; she will certainly *do* nothing; she will give us advice, but not assistance, and is now playing the same game as she has played from the accession of the late Empress Catherine, except in the short period when the furious Paul took a turn in our favour, and sent his armies to our support, and against the French.

Russia and Sweden near a quarrel about a bridge on the river Vymene, on the frontiers of Finland; *may* end by Russia taking all the rest of that country from the Swedes. Russia stipulated in February for an indemnity for the King of Sardinia, viz. *le Siennois* and the district of Orbitello; but will not acknowledge the Italian Republic, or admit the abdication of Ferdinand. Compare this with our present proposals to France, and it will appear that we have acted foolishly, either from want of communication or from carelessness and inability.

MAY 3.—Greffier Fagel with me, on the Prince of Orange's affairs; shews me the different papers which have passed between the Princess and our Ministers since the Treaty of Amiens; most of them are in my possession; she takes an early opportunity of asking from Lord Hawkesbury, in a very proper and dignified letter, an explanation of the 18th Article, when accompanied by the separate one signed the same day between France and Holland; Lord Hawkesbury's reply weak and unstatesmanlike ; he says they were quite ignorant of this separate article till they saw it in the public prints, but fully intend that the spirit of the 18th Article shall be strictly observed.

Addington proposes 220,000*l.*, and, in short, what I have said before in my journal. The Princess wrote to me a very gracious letter to thank me for my attention and intention, but to inform me that the Prince of Orange persisted in preferring a capital so secured as to afford a permanent and perpetual interest to what she termed " *une rente viagère.*" I answered her letter on the 4th May.

I find from the Greffier that she is so distressed as to be in real want; and I undertook to press Addington, either directly or through the Duke of Portland, to remit her one year's interest on the whole sum, viz. 12,000*l.* The Hereditary Prince of Orange evidently directs all this, and *his* politics are unbecoming his name, and adverse to us. He will reduce the family into that of a petty German Prince.

Messenger from Paris at 5 P.M.—brings nothing—no farther answer. He left Paris on Saturday, the 30th of April, late—three days before the expiration of the term.

Lord Pelham thinks Buonaparte will let Lord Whitworth go, in order to see what effect his departure will produce at Paris; and then either declare war, or transfer the Negotiation to London, according as this may turn out. This seems likely.

MAY 4.—Nothing new; reports without end. Addington made a very feeble speech on the Admiralty Bill, and brought on by it (quite unnecessarily) a debate, in which he was rather laughed at. Canning spoke well on it.

THURSDAY, MAY 5.—At nine o'clock in the morning a paper was stuck up on the Stock Exchange, as a notice from Lord Hawkesbury to the Lord Mayor, stating that

every thing was arranged—that France had acceded to
all our proposals. This raised the Stocks to 70.

Canning came in a great hurry to tell me this, just at
the moment (11 o'clock) that I had received a note from
Lord Pelham, to say that a messenger arrived an hour
before, dated Paris, Tuesday morning, May 3—that
nothing *then* was done ; and Lord Pelham infers, that
Lord Whitworth must have left Paris that evening;
he had desired a packet-boat to be sent from Dover for
him.

This abominable City lie, which influenced the Stocks,
accounts either for what Andreossi thought, and said to
Lord Auckland and W. Elliot, or is the effect of it. I
left London at 12 on this day for Brighton.

MAY 6.—Addington entrusts the House, at 5 o'clock
this day, with information that Andreossi has received
orders from the First Consul to leave London on Lord
Whitworth's arrival; but no messenger from Lord Whitworth to Lord Hawkesbury was yet arrived. Till,
therefore, this happens, no regular official communication can be made to Parliament.

Great sensation in the City, on account of the forged
letter on Thursday. To cheat *them* is the most audacious, abominable of all proceedings. If any event
could be devised or forged to sink *at once* the value of
land from thirty to twenty years' purchase, not half the
noise would be made, nor the " *villains* " be deemed half
so atrocious.

MAY 7 and 8.—Brighton. The reports on the evening of this day (7th) contradicted the news of the
morning—this was war. The evening rumours were
pacific—that Lord Whitworth had not left Paris on
Wednesday the 4th.

It appeared from my letters on the 8th that this was
true, but I had no authentic details. It should appear,
from connecting the different information I received, and
that from tolerably good quarters, that, a short time

before Lord Whitworth was setting out, he received a proposal from the French Government, which he referred home for consideration, and waited at Paris till the return of the messenger (this from Canning). Another letter (from Wm. Elliot) says, the Ministers are much displeased with Lord Whitworth for having received this proposal, since it differs so widely from his instructions—that he ought to have rejected it as inadmissible at once, and that (and Elliot says he speaks from respectable authority) they have despatched a messenger to him with orders *to reject* it, and leave Paris.

Andreossi still (though this week is nearly expired) perseveres in saying that things will be arranged. He has very odd *confidants—Dr. Glass*, the schoolmaster at Hanwell, and Sir Charles Blagden.

Strong division in House of Commons on the 7th on the question of Adjournment—for it, 185; against it, 95. It was moved by Addington to be from Friday till Monday. Opposition wished to sit on Saturday; all the good speaking on their side.

MAY 9 and 10.—Ministers blame and reprimand Lord Whitworth; and it should appear as if he *really* had not acted up to his instructions, and that he had *no* private ones. As I suspected, the whole was a trick of Talleyrand's, to gain time.

CONFIDENTIAL NOTE FROM LORD PELHAM.

" We have now directed Lord Whitworth to deliver in a Note, to which he must have a satisfactory answer in 36 hours after the arrival of the messenger, or leave on Friday."

I cannot collect what modifications Buonaparte proposed to Lord Whitworth which he thought sufficient to detain him, nor yet those we now return.

May 11, 12.—On the 12th, a messenger (one of his secretaries) arrived in London, from Sir J. Warren, at Petersburg, in seventeen days, to say, that a Colonel Colbert, despatched by Buonaparte to solicit the Mediation of Russia between us and France, is arrived, and has succeeded in his Mission; and that orders had in consequence been sent to Markoff, at Paris.

This news seems to take Ministers (very oddly) by surprise; and they apprehend it will arrive just as the point is settling between us, and fling all into confusion again.

Colbert, a clever fellow, bribes Czartorinski, (the Empress's favourite,) and through him gets at the Emperor.

———

Saturday, May 14.—I return to town from Brighton.

Lord Whitworth left Paris on Thursday, 12th. Our last proposal to keep Malta for ten years—to fit out in the mean while as a naval station Lampedosa, fit for large ships, and then (at the end of ten years) Lampedosa (now belonging to the King of Naples) to be ours.

French consent, provided no definite term is stated, and some compensation given to France. This rejected by us, and Whitworth censured for listening to it.

———

Sunday, May 15.—Lord Whitworth writes from Breteuil. A French messenger arrives to Lord Hawkesbury about noon, to say that the Emperor of Russia ("un Prince magnanime") is ready to do everything we can desire respecting Malta; that therefore it will be *our* fault *now* if there is war, &c.

Rather a manifesto than anything else. No notice taken of it here, but orders to the fleet to sail under Admiral Cornwallis, and to go off Brest, and Letters of Marque to be issued. Andreossi to go on the 16th.

On this evening I read over the correspondence which is to be laid before Parliament.

It is very voluminous; a good case made out for those who wish well for the cause, and *think right*, but not a good one to those who are disposed to be captious, and cavil.

In August and September, 1802, the insolence and arrogance of Buonaparte was at its height, and increased evidently as we conceded—which we did *virtually* by entering into arguments with him on points that ought at once to have been scouted; particularly on his presumption in requiring of us to send away the Princes, the French Bishops, Georges, and the emigrants wearing orders, and to control the press. Soon after this began the discussion on Malta; but neither this discussion, nor the existence of armaments, are made out sufficiently clear to get rid of debate and dispute, and there is little doubt that Fox and his followers will hit this vulnerable part. Yet the whole is a *right* measure, *evidently* right, but not managed with address and skill—a *wise step*, but not cleverly conducted, nor well told.

MONDAY, MAY 16.—A French messenger arrives at ten o'clock, A.M., with a proposal to acquiesce in our ultimatum, and leave us Malta *for ten years*, provided we allow France to occupy *Otranto* for the same period. (Otranto is a port in the bay of Tarentum, very favourable for any views on the East, or Egypt.)

This immediately produced a Cabinet, and they as immediately decide on not accepting the proposal; and very becomingly say, neither England nor France has a right to dispose of a town or port belonging to an independent Sovereign, and that His Majesty never will participate in the smallest degree in any system of spoliation and dilapidation.

A Message is delivered in both Houses, to say the discussions are over, and the two Ambassadors recalled; that on the 18th the papers will be laid before the Houses, and on Monday, the 23rd, they are to be taken into consideration.

It appears, on reflecting on what has passed, that Russia has been gained over—won by France by corruption and flattery—lost by us by indolence, incapacity, and ignorance; that it is the manner in which Russia has declared herself (favourable to France) that terminated the discussion on war. That, had Russia been either neutral or passive, Buonaparte would have given way; and hence it follows, that Lord Whitworth is to blame in not leaving Paris on Tuesday the 11th May, as he positively was instructed to do, and, by being prevailed on to remain and listen to an inadmissible *contre-projêt*, given time for the messenger sent from Petersburg, in consequence of Colbert's Mission, to arrive at Paris, to furnish Buonaparte with the good news from Russia, and to put us in a very embarrassed situation by depriving us of the power of saying the whole was over *before* we were acquainted with the sentiments and offers from Petersburg. Yet unfavourable to us as all the conduct of Russia has been, and partial to France, (and it was easy to foresee, had our Ministers been gifted with foresight,) it is manifest Buonaparte still is very anxious for peace, rather dreads war,* and at this very hour (May 17th, 9 P.M., Tuesday,) I have a misgiving he will end by agreeing to *all* our proposals; and that *for the present* war will be evaded—*" remise, mais pas perdue."*

On the 17th May, the Duke of Portland called on me on the Princess of Orange's affairs, and there is every reason to suppose that the Princess *will* soon receive 9000*l.* on account. I wrote a very strong letter to the Duke of Portland from Brighton on the 8th instant, and this he read to Addington.

Duke of Portland, on talking of public affairs, laments the conduct of Russia; and blames, with great reason, the choice of persons employed, both there and elsewhere, by us, as Ministers. The Duke thinks both Sir J. Warren and Lord Whitworth have done ill.

---

* This was certainly the case at the time. Bourrienne says, " Le Premier Consul, qui avoit compté sur une plus longue durée de la paix d'Amiens, se trouvait à la rupture de ce Traité dans une *fâcheuse position.* Le grand nombre de congés accordés, l'état déplorable dans lequel étoit la cavalerie, la nullité momentanée de l'artillerie —résultat d'un projêt qui exigeait la refonte de toutes les pièces de campagne, appellaient toute la solicitude de Buonaparte."—Vol. v. page 197.

A Declaration and papers to be laid before the two Houses, and a Message from the Crown to-morrow. Monday, the 23rd, appointed for taking them into consideration.

MAY 18.—Canning early; little to say. Pitt (who, *he* says, thinks as *he* does) will attend on the 24th, and give his opinion; means to *fire over the heads* of the Government—*i. e.* not to blame or praise them, but to support the war measures; to confine himself *to this*, and to do or say nothing more, and then to return to Walmer.

Is this possible? (his returning to the country.)

Woronzow at two. His language hostile to Ministers, his professions friendly to the country. It was evident to me, from what he said, and the manner in which he said it, that *his* Court is perfectly unfavourable to us, and gained over by France, through Czartorinski and the Empress. Woronzow considered the sale of Louisiana to the Americans (by France) as a measure against *us*, and reasoned on it *like a Frenchman*, not like *himself*.

THURSDAY, MAY 19.—Installation of the Bath in the morning. Ball at Queen's House in the evening. The Queen uncommonly gracious; King always good. Factious motion of Grey's to disprove any armaments going on in France, and that the assertion to that effect in the Message was unfounded. He divided 59 on it.

MAY 20 and 21.—Nothing occurred. Lord Pelham was with me on the morning of 21st; dissatisfied with the way in which Lord Hawkesbury had consented to give up the intelligence of the last *unofficial* proposal from France respecting *Otranto*. They had previously agreed *not to do it*. Idle rumours of Joseph Buonaparte's being come to London; peace still talked of in the City.

MAY 22.—Dined with Pitt at Lord G. Leveson's; company, Lords Gower, Morpeth, Boringdon,* G. Rose, Ch. Long, Canning, Pitt, Villiers, and myself. General conversation about the Correspondence; Pitt approving the measure, but negatively censuring Ministers. I was sorry to perceive he *still* thinks *Russia* favours *us*, not France. This is Woronzow's influence over Lord Grenville.

MAY 23.—Dean of Christchurch (Jackson) with me for an hour and a half; said he would talk to me under the *seal of confession;* that his mind was overloaded, his anxiety excessive. After a long preface to this effect, lamenting the weakness of Administration, and particularly the weakness and partial feelings of Addington's advisers, (and he, to my surprise, fixed this imputation particularly on *Abbott*, the Speaker,) he went on by saying there must be a change; *Pitt* must come in; and, after giving me to understand he knew what had passed between Pitt and Addington, (and he appeared to state and see it fairly,) he said, after revolving in his mind, the only *quiet and safe* means of bringing in Pitt was through the medium of the Dukes of York and Portland; that the Duke of Portland *had*, he knew, no idea the Ministry could last; he had said as much to the King— *nearly* as much to Addington; that, therefore, he was ripe, and prepared to hold the sort of language necessary to produce a change; that he also stood well with Pitt, who had a very high and just opinion of the Duke's worth and integrity; that *he* might represent to *Addington* the necessity of a change; while, on the other side, the Duke of York might take an opportunity of preparing the King for it. Not a *total* change, but such a one as would give the *whole* power to Pitt, but leave Addington in Cabinet Office, with additional honours, &c., &c.; that the idea of Pitt coming in, in a second rank, *to assist and support*, was nonsense; he *must* guide and direct.

The Dean went on by saying he had already brought

* Afterwards Earl of Morley.

about an interview between the Dukes of York and Portland at Burlington House (on the 20th), and that it
passed off vastly well; but that, as they might (from
being both shy and not much acquainted) want a middle
man, he wished me to undertake that office whenever it
was necessary. I told him I thought his plan a good
one, but attended with many difficulties as to its execution; that it would be an awkward thing for a member
of the Cabinet (as the Duke of Portland was) to propose an overthrow of the Cabinet itself, and that the
Duke of York he knew never could *begin* with the King
on business; that, as for myself, I thought and felt so
much the necessity of a new Ministry, and at the same
time had such a confidence in both the Dukes, that I was
ready to do whatever I could to forward the measure he
had suggested.

MAY 24.—Pitt's speech on the 23rd the finest he
ever made—never was any speech so cheered, or such
incessant and loud applause; it was strong in support of
war, but he was silent as to Ministers; and his silence,
either as to blame or praise, was naturally construed
into negative censure. No one was heard after him,
and the debate was adjourned at ten o'clock till to-
day.

By a new arrangement of the Speaker's, strangers were
excluded till so late an hour that the newspaper printers
could not get in, and, of course, no part of Pitt's speech
can be printed.

WEDNESDAY, MAY 25.—With Lord Pelham early. A
Frenchman brought over a packet for the Dutch Minister on the 24th, and a large *portmanteau or sack*.
In this sack was the French declaration, or manifesto:
it was stopped by Stone, the agent, and sent up to
London; but a *Moniteur* (I since find) is come over
in which it is inserted. No news from Admiral Cornwallis Orders to stop any Spanish men-of-war going
into *French* ports; but not to take Spanish merchantmen. A great wish here to preserve neutrality with

Spain ; so there is in Spain. We get an immense quantity of bullion from Spain. Nothing *directly* to or from Russia. Prussia inclined to be uneasy—offers to join in the Mediation with Russia—more civil and friendly *in appearance* than for some time.

Great distress in Holland. Horror of the French universal.

Division on the adjourned debate of the 23rd, 400 to 69 — tellers included. Fox spoke three hours—very ingenious, but very mischievous. Windham answered him. Addington spoke very poorly. . (This on the 24th, Tuesday.)

***

MAY 25.—Fagel with me at one; desire him to see Duke of Portland and Addington ; tell him what I have done about the Princess of Orange.

With Lord Whitworth at two; states France quite unprepared for war; *would have* given in, and left us Malta, if we had not insisted on a specific stipulation for it. Lord Whitworth not pleased with Lord Hawkesbury and Addington; defends himself for disobeying instructions, which he confesses he did.

He said, that when Buonaparte fell out of his carriage (on the 10th May), and it was said he was in danger, his brother Lucien, before he went or sent to St. Cloud, assembled forty or fifty of his friends in order to settle the *succession,* and proposed *himself.* About twenty or twenty-five were of this opinion; about ten or twelve for sending for some foreign Sovereign, and the rest for *Cambaceres.* Before this meeting broke up, news came the First Consul was not hurt. Lucien goes immediately to St. Cloud — relates what he has done. " Vous avez été bien pressé, mon frère," says Buonaparte.

Lord Whitworth tells me, that, when Buonaparte is out of his ceremonious habits, his language is coarse and vulgar. He has an Italian accent, and writes French ill. When speaking of Piedmont and Switzerland to Lord Whitworth, he called them "des misérables f——s," a very blackguard word.

Buonaparte loves talking — has quite " un flux de

bouche," but not eloquent; does not listen.   Lord Whitworth saw *Le Tourneur* often; he was very civil in his recollection of what passed at Lisle.   Maret so closely connected with Buonaparte as not to dare to speak, but well-bred and gentlemanlike.   Lord Whitworth thinks the effects of war will soon be so severely felt in France as to produce great disgust and disaffection; that it will shake Buonaparte's power; that the army is not so much attached to him as it was.   If he trusts an army to Moreau, he will risk its acting against him.

No armaments in France — nothing but fishing-boats in Holland, yet Ministers persist that there is shipping to bring over 50,000 French.

Lord Whitworth told me that when Buonaparte was thrown out of his chariot, when he was driving himself to St. Cloud, it happened in consequence of his having set out in a phaeton and six; that he quarrelled with the postilion, and made him take off the leaders, and would drive the other four himself.   The horses immediately ran away, and the carriage struck against a pillar at the gates of St. Cloud, and flung Buonaparte to a distance; he was so much hurt, in appearance, that the report of his being in danger reached Paris.

Duke of York came to me at 5. — Uneasy lest the Duchess should be forced to sup at the same table with Mrs. Fitzherbert at the ball to be given by the Knights of the Bath on the 1st of June — talks it over with me — says the King and Queen will not hear of it; on the other side, he wishes to keep on terms with the Prince. I say I will see Lord Henley, who manages this fête, and try to manage it so that there shall be two distinct tables, one for the Prince, to which *he* is to invite, another for the Duke and Duchess, to which *she* is to invite, her company.

Rode, at four, to see Pitt—not up—he was not in bed till near six; returned with Lord Camden—much conversation with him; we agreed on all and every point. He is *sure* Pitt has no connexion with the present Administration.

Some merchant-ships sent in by our cruisers.   Cornwallis has been off Brest near a week; also ships off Rochfort.

MAY 26.—Dean of Christchurch at eleven—full of *his* plan, yet can report no progress—cannot contrive to get at the King; speaks with slight of Abbott, and says Vansittart seems to rely on Pitt, to whom they intend to submit their plan of finance when it is ready. Addington he calls a poor financier—the City has no confidence in him.

At twelve, Lord Henley—settled with him in the way stated above, at least so far that he should write to Mr. Thomas (who is about the Prince) to desire him to say which box he would choose, and in the way I mentioned.

Duke of York at one — pleased with what I had done about the supper, then entered fully into the necessity of Pitt's return to Office — wished *he* would write to the King—he was sure one half hour's audience would settle the whole.

At the Drawing-room at half-past two. — Saw the Queen immediately, not the King. No news. Lord Pelham apparently very absent.

MAY 27.— Fox, in a very able and masterly, but artful speech, proposes in the House that we ask the Mediation of Russia: Pitt and Lord Hawkesbury acquiesce, and Addington (who did not speak) apparently delighted. This measure perhaps a right one, though much may be said against it; but it is a Cabinet, not a Parliamentary measure, and Ministers, by suffering it to originate in Parliament, and from the Opposition bench, betray weakness, and authorize a new and most dangerous precedent.

MAY 28—30.—At Park Place. Buonaparte issues an order on the 27th to arrest and stop all English subjects in France, also in Holland, under the idea of making them hostages for the prizes we take, as he says, before war is declared.

MAY 30.—Tierney to be Treasurer of the Navy in room of Bragge. This seems to be an indication of Pitt's never taking Office any more.

JUNE 1.—Canning at eleven. Reads me the resolutions to be proposed on the 3rd: strong, and well drawn up. Censure Ministry for delay and silence, and deduce the proofs from their own communications. Pitt, it is said, intends on this motion (to be made by Patten) to move to adjourn, and, if Ministers afterwards propose counter resolutions, then to go away; Lord Mulgrave to take the same line to-morrow (the 2nd) in the Lords. All this sad work when the war is raging at our gates.

JUNE 2 and 3.—First day. Lord Mulgrave's motion as above—eighteen peers only for it; all the Grenvilles, &c., against it. Second day.—Pitt's motion in the Commons (the same), only 56 for it—333 against it.

Certainly not a judicious measure, though *kindly* intended towards Government by Pitt. Its effect is to furnish a plea for *the many* to desert Pitt, and blame him.

Tierney appointed to be Treasurer of the Navy in room of Bragge. This settled on Whit Tuesday at Greenwich, where these two and Addington dined in a room *within* one, where Lord and Lady Worcester, Lord Bathurst, &c. also dined, and discovered them on the dinners being carried in.

JUNE 4.—King's birthday.—Immense full drawing-room—assembly in the evening at the Queen's House.— King looking well, and in spirits.

JUNE 5.—I read over (though very cursorily) all the long French publications in a supplement of six folio sheets in the *Moniteur.**

* See *Moniteur*, 241, l'An 11.

It takes up every pacific overture from the 18th Brumaire, 1799, when Buonaparte overturned the Directory, to the rupture in May 1803.

The curious part of it is that which contains the *protocols* of the Conferences at Amiens. In these Lord Cornwallis seems to have *negotiated* very little, and always (except when forced on by his instructions) to have had nothing in view but *signing*.

This is more particularly marked in a Note of his on the 11th March, 1802, to J. Buonaparte; and in Joseph's account subsequent to it, of Lord Cornwallis's feelings, he says in his report to his Government, " Lord Cornwallis se montre *personnellement* affecté des retards qu'éprouvent *encore* la Négociation, et il exprima *l'espérance* que son Gouvernement désisteroit de quelques-uns des nouveaux changemens qu'il avoit proposé."

Lord Hawkesbury appears to have negotiated better with Otto, but still always betraying too strong a desire to conclude.

The first thing done after his coming into Office was to propose a pacific Negotiation, as appears from an Official Note sent by Lord Hawkesbury to Otto on 21st March, 1801, in which he proposes, " d'entamer immediatement des Négociations et d'envoyer à Paris ou *à tout autre endroit* un Ministre pleinement autorisé," &c.

At this date the King was but just recovered, and the new Ministry barely seated in their places; and from this day to the end of the Treaty, France assumes a tone of superiority, and, I am sorry to say, acquires it in negotiation, that is intolerable. This appears even from her own publications, which, though so very voluminous, are a garbled and incomplete account of the transaction, and full of the most audacious lies respecting Buonaparte's moderation, justice, and forbearance, that ever were yet told to the public.

Talbot (Secretary of the Embassy at Paris) called on me; said the papers alluded to had produced more effect in France than they ought to have done. They had somewhat *electrified* the nation, and made them less averse to war; that this war was unpopular with every

one but the army and its dependants; that he was
stopped at Calais, but allowed to proceed on the return
of a messenger from Paris; that he had remonstrated on
the detention and arrestation of the English, but that
Talleyrand would not allow him to be a person in a
public character, and gave him no answer.   There was,
he said, no means of invasion, yet a determined intention on the part of Buonaparte to invade England or
Ireland if he possibly could.   Talbot was in a hurry;
had not seen Lord Hawkesbury; said he would call
again.

Lord Pelham.—He stated to me what had been told
him (as manager of the Lords) by Lord Fitzwilliam, and
afterwards by Lord Camden, as to the resolutions of censure moved by the last, and Lord Mulgrave's motion of
adjournment.   He thought the whole a strange inconsistent jumble.   Pitt and Addington were quite at variance; getting every day farther from each other; yet he
still thought they might be united if Addington would
deal fairly and wisely.   He lamented the inactivity of
Government—their taking no means of *offence.*

Said the Prince of Wales wanted to go abroad and
form a Northern Confederacy.   He pretended that he
could manage the Duke of Brunswick, and, through him,
Russia and Prussia.   That he was to be assisted by
Baron Hompesch (a rank adventurer); in short, one of
the ten thousand chimeras His Royal Highness has conceived.

This idea the Prince opened to Lord Pelham at the
Knights' Ball (June 1st), and sent Hompesch to him
the next day to talk it over.   Lord Pelham declined
talking to Hompesch.

He had received a very good memorial from a Frenchman of the name of *La Touche*, with a plan of attacking
and molesting France, but that Addington had paid *no*
attention to it; not more than he did to the idea of
getting Russia over to our interests in March.

Duke of Portland dangerously ill since the morning
of the 2nd, but better on the 3rd and 4th.

Lord Bathurst at two o'clock.   Much talk about Pitt;

said he (Pitt) intended to take no steps in Parliament respecting what had passed; to absent himself on all days and debates relative to *retrospective* measures; but that, on all new ones being proposed, he would attend and watch over them. The King at first much displeased with him for his motion on the 3rd, but less so on reflection.

Duke of Portland very ill again to-day.

JUNE 6.—Duke of Portland much better, and Sir Walter Farquhar tells me he hopes he will not have a return of his complaint.

JUNE 7.—Met Talbot; he doubted the report of Buonaparte's having insulted Markoff; it was not likely Markoff should have interfered respecting the detention of the English. In general false and fawning; never *thoroughly* friendly with Lord Whitworth, or to be depended on.

Dined this day with Pitt, Lord and Lady Melville, Lord M'Cartney, and G. Rose, at Sir W. Farquhar's. Very pleasant and cheerful, and an excellent dinner.

WEDNESDAY, JUNE 8.—I was with Pitt at his breakfast. I told him that I had much satisfaction in assuring him that I should follow his line in politics; that I understood his motives and respected them, in acting as he had done.

He said it was perhaps not good *generalship*, and that he was aware of this, and of the sort of talk and blame to which it would give rise. Yet he had considered it over and over again before he had determined what to do; that his first wish was to evince to the public that he had *no* connexion *whatever* with the present Ministers; that he had no share in any of their late transactions, and that he was at liberty to remove them if he pleased, and to take any part he chose either for or

against their future conduct; that, while he was desirous
to substantiate this, he also was equally desirous not to
do anything harsh or violent which looked like *personal*
feelings; and that indeed, though he did disapprove a
great deal of what had been done and *not* done, yet it
by no means went in his mind to justify the support
of such a motion as Patten's.   That, however, *he* (and
here he called upon my recollection to vouch for him)
did consider that one of the very first points for him
and for everybody was, to be most attentive, to do nothing which could displease, irritate, or discompose the
King; and that, placed as he was, either between direct
violent opposition to the King's Government, or the sort
of *mezzo termine* line he had now taken, he did not
hesitate, although he agreed with his younger friends,
as he before said, that it was not a good piece of *generalship;* but that generalship was not in his mind the leading consideration, or that on which his conduct should
solely be regulated.

That his plan was not to take any *retrospective* view—
to be silent as to all that was past: he had wished to
prove he had nothing to do with it.   This he hoped he
had now done, and it was all he wished to do; but not
so as to *prospective* measures: the situation of the country was too serious for it not to be a governing duty
with him to watch over these most carefully; not to
oppose idly and vexatiously: on the contrary, to take as
a general principle the line of support, but to oppose
most decidedly, and with all his powers, any *weak or
pernicious half-measures*, any unequal or inferior to the
pressure of the moment, whether of finance or preparation.   Pitt then went into a kind of recital of the relative situation of this country and France, our means of
defence, their means of attacking us, ours of molesting
them; and talked on them all with his usual sagacity
and perspicuity.

He lamented much that no move had been made towards Russia, and was grieved when I told him with
how little attention Lord Pelham's proposal of the 20th
of March had been treated.

From Pitt's I came home, and went to the Levée. King very short in what he said; talked a great deal to the Dutch Minister, whom, to my surprise, I found still here.

JUNE 10.—Lord Pelham with me at eleven.—Communicated to me private intelligence from France, that the Republicans (Jacobins probably) and Royalists are very numerous; and if they could be brought to trust each other, and be convinced that if either party gained possession of the power, it would not persecute the other, a revolution might be operated.

This was the case, I said, all along, and particularly in August, 1797.

Lord Pelham said, they had put all the Dutch *craft* in requisition; that each junk would hold one hundred men; that they had 10,000 men at Cherbourg, and had sent all the English detained at Calais to Valenciennes; that the army (all but the Consular guard) were wretchedly paid, and, for the sake of plunder, eager for an invasion.

With respect to what was passing here, he said he was going to a Council in which it was to be deliberated what to do with Russia. I expressed surprise at the tardiness of this step. Lord Pelham said, however, nothing had been yet done, but that a messenger would be immediately sent. That the idea was, to propose to Russia to come forward as the general moderator of Europe; to say that Malta was out of the question as a place to be restored, unless France would renounce all it had beyond the Alps, and reinstate the King of Sardinia, or give up the Austrian Netherlands, and put them under the dominion of some powerful Sovereign. That, on either of these conditions being acceded to, we would give up Malta; but if anything short of this (though we should consent to it as a general measure) was determined on, we must keep Malta — the best and only pledge for our security and quiet in future.

Talking of home politics, he said, Addington was very sore with Pitt, but very well assured of his own power;

thought he had the ball at his foot, and would weaken himself and his Administration by his presumption.

SATURDAY, JUNE 11.—With Woronzow; he put into my hands a letter he had received on the 9th from Markoff, by a messenger despatched to Prince Esterhazy.

It begins by saying, " What I am going to write will first of all make you indignant, and afterwards make you laugh." Markoff then refers him to an enclosure, which is a Note verbale given by him to Talleyrand on the 7th. This says that, on Sunday the 5th, at the Levée, the First Consul came up to him, and said, " Je sais que le Comte de Woronzow n'est pas favorable aux Français, qu'il aime les Anglois, et qu'il n'a pas fait tout ce qui dépend de lui pour empêcher la guerre. 2do. Que *si* les intentions de l'Empereur sont bonnes, il est très mal servi par ses Ministres. 3^{tio}. Qu'il y a du double dans ceci, et que si le Comte de Woronzow l'avoit voulu, il auroit pu contenir l'Angleterre. 4to. Que si l'Empereur comptait observer une conduite si vague vis-à-vis de la France, pourquoi lui a-t-elle jamais demandé des services ?"

On this attack, similar to that made on Lord Whitworth, Markoff, in his Note verbale, makes very proper and becoming observations. He says, as to the first point, he knew from personal connexion, as well as from official reports, that Woronzow has acted always impartially; and that M. Andreossi must admit this if he is questioned. That, as to the second, it is a most ungrounded reflection to suppose that His Imperial Majesty's Ministers ever could, would, or did act contrary to his intentions and instructions; that these were such as became him to give, and were based on a principle of justice and equity, such as became a great Sovereign, who had nothing to hope or to fear. That, as to the third, it was an accusation not to be suffered to pass *sans un éclaircissement;* that to insinuate that His Imperial Majesty's conduct was one of duplicity, was a charge every action of his reign disproved ; that it had been invariably the same from the first moment, and that it would remain so. That as to the fourth, the calling his *conduite vague* towards France, he said it was equally groundless; that the Emperor was certainly desirous to cultivate and maintain friendship with the First Consul; that, to acquire this, he had acted, and ever should act, frankly and equitably, but that he was too great a Sovereign to solicit favour. That, if he joined with France in the German politics, it was because he thought the general interests of Europe were bene- fited by what he did; and that as to any separate in- terest of his own, or any other separate interest, it never had made part of this system, or would of any other.

Markoff ends this paper by saying, he trusts he shall have some *éclaircissement*, and be told why subjects were brought into discussion in a public circle, which ought only to be treated *dans le calme et la tranquillite d'un Cabinet;* he hints, that he suspects some officious or jealous stranger has been meddling, and points out indi- rectly Lucchesini.

It appears to me, that Markoff has not taken this up with sufficient indignation, and that he has been too prolix and explanatory, though he certainly acted judi- ciously in saying nothing at the time. Woronzow treated it with great contempt and indignation; and in a letter *en clair* by the post, wrote in answer —" Que quant à lui son unique ambition étoit d'obtenir et de mériter l'approbation de son Souverain légitime; et tant qu'il possédoit celle-là, il s'inquietoit très peu des suf- frages des Puissances étrangères."

It is, I think, very probable, that it was the account of what passed in the House of Commons, when Fox moved that Russia should be solicited to interpose her good offices, that put the First Consul in a passion; and it is likely that either Lucchesini, or some other time- serving Foreign Minister, increased this passion by *their* accounts of it.

Woronzow, as usual, railed bitterly against the Minis- ters; said, " Si ce Ministère dure, la Grande Brétagne ne durera pas!"

He gave me his despatch of the 29th May to read, and with it the official Note of the 28th, he had received from Lord Hawkesbury, requesting the intervention of Russia; and saying, " His Majesty was disposed to receive it, and act upon it, in any way His Imperial Majesty might judge best." This note was very well drawn up, but Woronzow does not do it justice; and though he (in his despatch) supports the proposal, yet he says it was Fox's doing, and takes away from Ministers the credit of it. In fact, they left him a fortnight without any answer to his communication; and it is impossible for him not to feel that he owes this one now sent, to what passed in the House of Commons on the 23rd of May.

He shewed me another despatch, sent by Nicolai (his secretary), much more friendly to this country; in which he does not scruple to say, that it was impossible for England to avoid war; that Buonaparte meant war all along — only wanted to gain time; and, as a proof, adduces his restoring Louisiana to the Americans. This was sent by Nicolai about the 20th of May, and it may do great good; he, however, could not help ending it with an attack on our Ministers.

Woronzow does Pitt great justice, and has written to his Court the very best and fairest account of his conduct, and his motives and actions, possible. I found Pitt had seen him on the 3rd of June, and had *quite* won him by his manners and confidence. He was quite right about him, and most desirous he should see the King, and do away with the impressions Addington and others tried to give, that Pitt was still bent on carrying the Catholic Question.

He exclaimed sadly against Lord Hawkesbury for his treatment of Naples; that Castelcicala had told him that Naples had refused every request from France to shut her ports, &c., &c., against us, and only asked what we meant or could do for its defence; yet to this, though repeated, he got no answer, not even what Lord Nelson intended to do; that H. Elliot was most disagreeable to the Court of Naples, and that the sending him was a most impolitic measure. N. B. Woronzow hates poor H. Elliot ever since he stopped the Swedish war in 1788.*

Markoff was going to the Eaux de Barèges; and from this circumstance, and the general tenor of Woronzow's language, I doubt much any real good coming from Russia. He, however, is quite right. " Have us for mediators, but do not consent to an armistice."

At four this day, a strong report was prevalent of Buonaparte's being assassinated, but it came without any appearance of probability.

It did not appear, from anything Woronzow said, that the Ministers had communicated at all with him, either as to their intentions, or by way of consulting him respecting the idea they have at this moment in agitation, of sending some specific proposal to Russia, as mentioned to me by Lord Pelham yesterday.

SUNDAY, JUNE 12.—With Lord Pelham at 11. Nothing yet done as to Russia. Idea is to ask, 1st, its Mediation between us and France, stating as basis nearly the. terms in which our Negotiation broke off. If Russia objects to this, then to propose her intervention as to the general settlement of Europe.

That, in this, the first object must be to curtail and render safe the power of France, either by giving the Austrian Netherlands to Prussia, or making a new great power, by uniting them to Holland, by restoring Piedmont to the King of Sardinia, and dividing Lombardy between him and the Emperor; that, Europe restored to this situation, Malta would lose its value, and become

---

* At the close of September, 1788, Prince Charles of Hesse and the Prince Royal of Denmark, at the head of a Norwegian army, invaded Sweden, according to a plan concerted with Russia. After various successes they besieged Gottenburgh (the principal port of Sweden), into which the gallant King had thrown himself. At this critical period Great Britain and Prussia having no minister at Stockholm, Mr. Elliot crossed over, and used such energetic remonstrance in the name of the two Courts, that he induced the Danish commanders to sign an armistice, and ultimately to withdraw their troops. Mr. Elliot acted on his own responsibility, and it was as bold a deed as was ever performed by any Diplomatist.

nearly what it was formerly, and might in that case be given up by us.

Such was the general outline of their plan, but as yet undigested and unprepared; and, what is worse, Lord Hawkesbury talks of sending Lord Harvey with it to Russia.

Sir J. Warren wishes to come home and hoist his flag.*

I deprecated Lord Harvey being sent, to the utmost of my power; mentioned Lords Castlereagh and Chatham; stated to Lord Pelham that Russia should be treated, not as a great Power, full of wisdom and knowledge, governed by great and sage public maxims, but as a proud, high-minded, vain individual, governed by temper and passion, and to whom the talking sense or reason, even though in manifest conformity to their own interests, would never be attended to, unless mixed up with flattery and unction, and offend if at all in disagreement with their self-conceit and vanity. That, for this reason, a well-mannered, supple, adroit man was necessary.

I also mentioned, that, if the general plan of *arranging* Europe was accepted or seriously wished for, we must make up our minds to give money, *large subsidies;* but I would give them only *after the work was done,* as *task work,* not as we had done hitherto, always *beforehand.*

Lord Pelham said Addington was not *up yet to this.*

JUNE 13.—News arrives of the French having taken possession of Hanover; a council on it; the King comes to town on purpose; receives the account of the loss of Hanover with great magnanimity, and a real *kingliness* of mind.

Buonaparte sends a savage answer to our proposal of exchanging the persons he has stopped, and calls prisoners; says he will keep them to the end of the war.

Budget.—Addington does better than was expected; rated our establishment at 26 millions; his taxes heavy,

* Sir J. Warren was Envoy at Petersburg.

but not bad; no opposition to him, nor any speech but his.

———

Tuesday, June 14.—Lord Hawkesbury with me by his own appointment, at seven; stated to him my ideas relative to the House of Orange, &c.; he agreed with me, and seemed disposed to assent to all I proposed.

He talked on every point of foreign politics, and talked well, very well. I wish he may act up to it. He said, of the three Sovereigns, Austria, Russia, and Prussia, he likes the first the best, but it was rather saying he was the least bad; that, however, since he had been in Office, the Court of Vienna had always acted most fairly and honourably; Russia (the Emperor) meant well; weak and philanthropical. I observed on this Court, what I had before said to Lord Pelham, and repeated the same advice.

Lord Hawkesbury said the Emperor of Russia was going into Livonia—why, he did not know—and took with him Koutchubeg, which gave him great pleasure, as he was a very right-thinking, honest man. He praised Panin, but said he was for the Armed Neutrality; spoke highly of Tlatinski, at Constantinople; wishes Kalitcheff should succeed Woronzow here, of whom he said nothing. Czartorinski was the favourite of the Empress.

Speaking of Prussia, he said nothing could be more feeble and pusillanimous than the King and his Ministers. I said, money might give them vigour; he admitted it. I said, " Subsidize them according to the work they do;" and I asked him whether he had ever seen a plan, prepared in April, 1795, for paying Prussia, in proportion as the Prussian troops advanced, &c. He said he had, and told me an odd circumstance, which explains to me what I suspected at the time, viz. that Lord Grenville never would sign this plan; that Dundas's name was put to it; it went over by Calvert, but, as I now am sure, in consequence of *private instructions given by Lord Grenville, never was produced at Berlin.* Lord Hawkesbury talked over Markoff's " *note verbale;*"

said it was a good one; must produce some effect in Russia.

He informed me that what they termed a *Convention* between the French and Hanoverians, was a complete cession of the Electorate; that the French were masters of it, to every intent and purpose; that they would occupy Hamburgh, Stade, Bremen, and that this was inevitable; that they thought of trying to send the packet-boats to the mouth of the Eider, in Holstein, but he apprehended the French would not scruple to violate the Danish territory, and shut that also against us; that, in consequence, we had determined to declare the Elbe and Weser, and all the rivers and ports on the western coast of Germany, in a state of blockade; that this would stop at once all the trade with the Continent, and would be felt much more severely by the foreign merchants, who had not the same substance and stock as ours. *We* could live on our capital for a long while; they must starve immediately. This was afterwards confirmed to me in the City by Amyand.

Lord Hawkesbury said, from a very good channel, he thought Buonaparte had no means of invasion; but that, as invasion was unquestionably his intention, we ought to provide against it by every possible preparation. He said the Duke of Cambridge was arrived; also Liston.

WEDNESDAY, JUNE 15.—With Lord Pelham at eleven o'clock.

General conversation on public affairs; no new event. Ministers busy in framing their instructions for Petersburg. I, after dwelling on the King's equanimity on the loss of Hanover, urged how right a thing it would be, if, while the French remained usurpers of the Electorate, England were to double the King's privy purse. " Give him 60,000*l.* a-year, quite at his own disposal." Pelham approved this, but it does not seem to me to be a likely measure.

Greffier with me before dinner, to communicate a letter from the Princess of Orange of the 29th of May, which she writes just as she is leaving Brunswick. Agrees very much with me as to the large annuity instead of the capital; at the same time, as the Prince (she says) has decidedly given *his* opinion, she cannot alter hers, but that *they* shall be perfectly satisfied with whatever Government does. Very civil and gracious in her message to me—very low and disquieted about the times. All the north and west of Germany threatened with French invasion (it had not then taken place). No safety or security anywhere. Prussia torpid, though frightened—inactive, though apprehensive and convinced of the danger.

The fate of the House of Orange very hard; likely to lose the county of Spiegelberg (in Hanover, near Cullenberg) by the seizure of France; and the Batavian Republic refuse them any compensation for their *rentes* in Holland, though it was expressly stipulated they should have an equivalent in the treaty signed in behalf of the House of Orange between France and Prussia. The whole letter is admirably written, though in haste, and evinces a greatness and a sensibility of mind which very seldom unite in the same person.

The Greffier talked again over their pecuniary affairs, and I advised him to have no scruple in pressing Lord Hawkesbury for the money.

THURSDAY, JUNE 16.—Left London at eleven. I called on my way at Lord Pelham's, but he was gone to Windsor. I got by dinner to Park Place.

On the 18th of June, I received a letter from the Greffier, in which he mentions the having seen Lord Hawkesbury, and that he is well satisfied with his reception. Thinks the whole will be done in the way I proposed.

JULY 4, 5, and 6.—On Monday, July 4, George Cholmondeley* came to Park Place—*as he said*, simply on

---

* Chairman of the Board of Excise. He was a man of eminent taste, whose society was much courted.

a visit; but it soon appeared to me, in the course of a great deal of conversation I had with him, that he was either sent down or had volunteered it, to sound me with regard to taking a place in the Cabinet.

He ushered in his conversation on public concerns (on which I never was in the habit of talking to him) by many fine speeches (rather ridiculous in an old acquaintance), and then by producing a paper he said Lord Pelham wished me to see: it was on the present state of affairs, chiefly relative to continental politics, and so precisely the substance of what I had said to Lord Pelham when I saw him last, on the 12th of June, that there could exist no real reason in Lord Pelham's mind for communicating it to me; still less for giving it to Cholmondeley, unless it was intended as an introduction to a political communication between us. On my observing that the paper was a very good one *in theory*, but not easy to put into practice, C. said, " That is the very point on which you are more competent to assist than any one." On my dissenting from this, he replied, " If you mean you will not be listened to, you are under an error. I *know* that Ministers have the greatest value for your opinion and advice ; and, if you would give it them, they would receive it gratefully, and certainly act up to it." I avoided, or rather tried to avoid, entering farther on the subject, by saying my health was not equal even to much and deep thinking, still less to active and laborious exertions of the mind. " But if it were," said Cholmondeley, " would you then shrink from employment?" I replied that I really did not know what I should do in that case ; but that in all and every case, I should consider it as a paramount duty to afford any assistance and advice (supposing it required) which either did, or might be thought to belong to my long habits of foreign life. " I know," said C., " you do not like or approve the present Ministers." I answered, " I do not dislike them ; but I certainly by no means approve all they have done, or rather *not* done, though I am not so uncandid as to suppose, that, if I knew all and every circumstance, a great deal might not come up in their justification; and that in fact, unless I knew *all* and every circumstance, nothing I could suggest or advise would be of any consequence, since, though it would read well, and be perhaps very good speculation, yet it would be impossible for me to know how far any measure or plan was capable of execution, possessing only the vague and commonplace information I possessed; that, with regard to the giving the assistance and advice I before mentioned, I ever should hold it as a *duty* to give it, when called upon, *to any Government, let who will be at the head of it;* that I look upon it as a sort of knowledge acquired by serving the King and public, to which *the King and public had a right, if ever they thought it worth claiming.* " Would you," said C., " take a seat in the present Councils, if offered?" I asked him, why he put such a home question to me? " Because," replied he, " I think your having a seat there would be of the greatest advantage to the country, and you would infallibly in a short time gain a preponderance in them that would be equivalent to deciding them." I answered to this, that, if no other difficulties stood in the way, my health and deafness were strong and almost invincible objections; but that, speaking to him as to an old friend, I had no hesitation in saying that I could not decide to become a partner in responsibility with men of whose system I did not on the whole approve, and whose abilities I did not consider to be at all equal to the pressure of the times; that however (as I before said) to them, as governing the country at this moment, I was ready to communicate every opinion, idea, or suggestion, which could arise from my past experience in foreign life ; and that to any one individual of them with whom I lived in habits of intimacy and friendship (such as the Duke of Portland and Lord Pelham) I was ready to open myself without reserve, and talk as freely and as confidentially as possible; that beyond this I must demur, except in consequence of direct commands from the King, towards whom (besides that duty and allegiance I felt in common with all his good subjects) I had so profound and respectful an attachment, from having been witness to his virtues, and to a magnanimity of mind which for a period of thirty-two years never varied in its character, nor departed from the most strict principle of public probity, and anxious care for the public good,—that this, joined to the endless proofs I had received of his personal favour, would make me ever obey his commands, whatever they were, without any consideration, either of health, inconvenience, or risks of any size or sort.

Cholmondeley pressed me much to come to town, and, on my saying it was not likely I should be able, he said, Lord Pelham would certainly come to Park Place, as he wanted very much to see me.

In speaking of Addington, Cholmondeley seemed to think Pitt had not dealt quite fairly by him. This I contested, and confessed to him, that one of the strongest reasons I had for declining to unite with this Government was, that I was persuaded *Addington had used Pitt ill;* had not been sincere; and had injured him with the King. I also added, that he certainly had not been true in his answers to me, since, at the very time when he assured me Pitt knew every thing, and that he (Addington) thought and felt about Pitt precisely as *I* did, Pitt himself had assured me he knew nothing ; and this was most clearly proved by subsequent occurrences. Cholmondeley abandoned Addington by saying, this was his usual way. He had no vigour of mind, and never could combat an opinion, or maintain his own, if, by so doing, he said something he thought was disagreeable to the person he was speaking to. On the 6th of July Cholmondeley returned to town.

JULY 10.—Finding myself unwell I came to town.

On the evening of this day Sir W. Farquhar, who came to visit me as a physician, began by saying he was going to write to me, for he was sure, by the very frequent and eager inquiries (Addington, Pelham, and the Duke of Portland) made after the state of my health, that they had it in contemplation to offer me

Office. I asked him what his answer was. He said, that, deafness excepted, I was as fit as ever for service. I replied, the exception was nearly equal to a complete proof of inability; but that I, besides this, felt other deficiencies, and that, unless he could *regenerate* me, I had certainly, both for my sake and the public, better not resume an active political life. He combated this, and gave it as his opinion, that if Russia came forward in a friendly way, and a Congress was to be held, the idea was entertained of putting the conduct of it into my hands.

On the 9th, Westminster Abbey took fire near the centre of the church, by the neglect of the plumbers. A dome was burnt, not to be seen from within, and the whole roof was in danger. Windham assisted; and, on seeing a great confusion amongst those disposed to assist, and great zeal, which marred all their efforts, he observed, " So it would be in case of invasion,—order and method would be wanting, and numbers be of no use."

I met George Rose early in St. James's Street; he said Pitt employed his whole time in planning measures of defence; that *now* they were going to adopt *his* last idea, and to make a general levy. That there were at least in this country 1,200,000 males between sixteen and sixty; that this, according to a safe calculation, would afford 300,000 fighting men, without taking any hurtful number from agriculture and commerce: but that Pitt's idea went only to give arms into the hands of 250,000. That these should be sedentary, and only called from home in case of the enemy being actually landed. That this force, in addition to what we had, would make us quite safe, and leave us with great means of offence.

(I omitted to say in its place that Cholmondeley, after my reading the paper, said, Addington had consented to give as far as 2,000,000*l.* in subsidies.— 500,000*l.* was asked by Monsieur to raise an army in France, under Pichegru, who is now in London.)

Pitt, according to his declaration to me on the 8th of June, now assists and helps Government very much in their measures of defence; his conduct is most manly and becoming.

On July 9th I received a letter from the Greffier Fagel, to say he had received the 10,000*l.* for the Princess and lodged it in Sir Francis Baring's hands. On the 12th he called on me, and we had a long conversation relative to the best mode of granting the assistance proposed to the House of Orange; he wished me to write to Lord Hawkesbury, which I did.

JULY 12.—With Duke of Portland at three; he much recovered, but pulled and *abattu;* his politics, as usual, steady and sound. He intimated a strong hope I would take the management of the Continent.

I said, what was strictly true, that I should ever look upon the experience and information I had obtained in the public service *as belonging to the public*, whenever called for; that I never should ask who were the individuals that formed the Government of the country, but that towards a Government where he and Lord Pelham made a part, I never could have any real ill-will, although I would not conceal from him, that I thought Addington's ability greatly inferior to the danger of the times, and Lord Hawkesbury not up to them. That I regretted much that my health was, beyond a doubt, unequal to the discharge of any very great and important Mission.

The Duke of Portland then wished me to say who was fit for such a post. I said, Lord Chatham or Lord Castlereagh. The first, the Duke said, could not talk French, and wanted decision; the other he did not know so well, but doubted the steadiness of his mind, and whether he had yet formed any correct political system. He praised Drake and H. Elliot; was inclined to think well of them. I went over with him all the Prince of Orange's affairs, and left with him a memorandum of what I proposed should be done.

Dined with Lord Pelham.—Lord Gage and Mrs. A. Robinson there. After dinner a long conversation. He referred to what G. Cholmondeley had said at Park Place. Apprehended he had been too mysterious (which was the fact). Explained to me that he had taken great pains to impress the Cabinet with the necessity of attending to the Continent and interior of France by subsidy; and that having engaged Addington to go certain lengths, viz. to grant 2,000,000*l.* before the next meeting of Parliament, his wish was to find a fit person to execute their plans, and that he, and most of his colleagues, had thought of me.

Pelham then entered into details; said Monsieur had proposed to him, after having proposed it to Addington and Lord Hawkesbury, from whom he got no answers, to collect an army in France to restore the ancient Monarchy, if he would allow him 400,000*l.* That Addington rejected this as impossible, and talked of 50,000*l.*; but Pelham had nearly persuaded him to give the 400,000*l.* Monsieur's idea was, not to bribe or seduce an army (which, he said, would desert and run away the moment they got the money), but to be able to maintain and collect those who, in case of a counter revolution, would look to be restored to their former ranks and fortunes, and that these were innumerable, and of every class; and he added, that he supposed when such a corps was collected, composed of old officers, and several of Buonaparte's best generals (Monsieur evidently alluded to Moreau), and that he was at the head of it, he should then consider him like any other Power; till then, he trusted the sum he asked was not beyond the importance of the attempt. Pelham's ideas remain the same—to induce the three great Continental Powers to act, either by large subsidies or by large offers—the *Low Countries, and even Holland,* to Prussia; all *Lombardy* to Austria; to Russia *whatever she might ask.*

Addington, he said, had the idea of sending 10,000 men to Portugal; but it would be to sacrifice them, if he could not secure a diversion on the Continent; and that, could we do this, not only Portugal, but we, should be safe from every hostile attack.

I perfectly concurred with him in all he said. With

respect to myself, I said of my health what I had said in the morning to the Duke of Portland; that the going to Russia was quite out of the question; that it was just possible I might be equal to go and reside at some quiet German Court, if a Congress took place; but that I had no hesitation in saying to him, that, ready as I most sincerely was to devote myself to the public service, yet I felt an *invincible repugnance*, and even apprehension, of acting under the direction of Addington, who I was every day more and more convinced was unequal to his situation, while he thought himself, unfortunately, superior to it; that I bear him no ill-will or personal disregard—quite the contrary; that no party feelings belonged to me; but that, to risk my character gratuitously, to lose myself, and not benefit the public, was a very serious consideration.

" You shall be left all the means to your own choice," said Pelham; " only obtain the end." I said, " I wish for no such unlimited powers; I had much rather be directed by an able Minister than act for myself; and that all I could say was, if the King commands my services, I would implicitly obey, premising to him (Pelham), my friend, the feelings and doubts I should have on my mind. Pelham said that Pichegru was the man Monsieur confided in; that he (Pelham) thought Moreau might be had. After much conversation, the substance of which I have stated, he said he would call on me tomorrow.

I gave him my letter to Lord Hawkesbury, on the concerns of the House of Orange, to read.

JULY 13.—Lord Pelham came to me at Miller's Hotel, where I lodged, at ten o'clock. He entered more fully into his views, and what he said he considered as the wishes of Government respecting Continental politics. It was, that every nerve should be strained to stop the progress and decrease the growing power of France; that this should be the great principle on which we should rest all our plans, and which we should declare

to the European Powers to be *our sole* object; that it
ought to be theirs, because their interests and safety
were involved, even more than ours, in the consequences
of this aggrandizement, and the direction given to it;
but that experience had proved to us that a measure
being right, or even imperiously necessary, was not
always a reason for its being adopted, or even admitted;
on the contrary, we had had too many proofs, and very
recent ones, that distant, though certain dangers, were
overlooked and unheeded, provided present security was
obtained, present cupidity or interests gratified, and a
rival power for the moment injured or lowered. That
our first object, therefore, should be to ascertain the
sentiments of one of these great Courts—Russia was
the most probable, as well as the most preferable: that
if we could secure the co-operation of this Court, and its
consent to enter into a system for the above purpose, it
would then become of the last importance to place the
direction and conduct of the measures which were to
perfect this system in the hands of some experienced
and able negotiator, who should reside in some centrical
town on the Continent, and from thence give instructions to His Majesty's Ministers; and receive, deliberate, and even, in most cases, *decide*, on what ought or
ought not to be done. That without such a person, and
such a full authority vested in him, it was almost impossible, considering the difficulty of our *now* getting at
the Continent, and the facility France had of earlier
intercourse, that anything could be effectuated, which
France would not have time to counteract or overset;
that the Duke of Portland himself, and one or two more
of the Cabinet, had fixed on me as the only person fit
for so important a trust; that an apprehension of my
being unequal to it from a decline of health had induced
him to desire G. Cholmondeley to question, *not to sound
me*, not to act (as he appeared to have done) myste-
riously and circuitously, but merely and simply to collect, partly by straightforward questions, and partly by
observation, how far I was equal to such a Mission, and
whether, if equal, I would undertake it. That since I

had seen him, I had heard from the Duke of Portland
his ideas and wishes; that, as for those he himself had,
they must be known to me; that their idea was, that I
should immediately become a member of the Cabinet;
and in case of such an opening as he had stated presenting itself on the Continent (supposing the plan had my
concurrence), I should be prepared and ready to avail
myself of it.

To this I replied what I had before often said, that as
far as he and the Duke of Portland were concerned, I
could not have a hesitation about my readiness to act
and concur with them; that to them, as to my private
friends, I was ready to say every thing, to do every
thing for them, to share every praise or blame with
them; but they must recollect that they formed but
a part of the Cabinet, and that inasmuch as I was
willing to share all responsibility and risks with them,
insomuch was I apprehensive to partake and associate
my responsibility and character with that of their colleagues, who were the leading part of the Cabinet;
that I had no doubt of Addington's *integrity* and sincere wish to do well, but I had doubts, and well-founded
ones, of his powers and *ability*, and every thing I heard,
saw, and observed, unfortunately confirmed me in them;
that I therefore had to declare, that, if under his
paramount direction, I should be afraid to act; that
I should feel I was exposing myself to disgrace and
difficulty, and what was worse, not serving my country
usefully, or, perhaps, judiciously; that if *left* to myself
to plan, digest, and execute my own measures, I must
be put in such a very pre-eminent situation as no
Minister could or ought to place any one in; yet without such an uncontrouled, unappealable jurisdiction,
I (under the present Government) could not serve.
Of course I could not serve at all, because it was silly
to say, " I will take Office, you being Minister ; but
I have not sufficient confidence in you to act under
your orders, and will act on no other terms but thus
being independent of you."

" You should have that independent situation," said

Lord Pelham, " you should *never refer home for any-thing,* but be considered as the *directing Minister* for Continental politics, residing on the Continent; and, as such, guide and govern, and be responsible for every thing." I said I did not fear responsibility, but the carrying such a plan into effect was impracticable; it was an *imperium in imperio* that no Minister could or ought to bear; and as, after all, every thing must necessarily be determined on in the last report *at home,* the full authority given me would be more ideal than effective. But that this was *not all :* even supposing these nearly insurmountable difficulties could be smoothed, there remained still a more insurmountable one, viz. my health; that such an undertaking required the greatest vigour of body and mind—the stoutest and most unimpaired constitution and nerves. This was far from my case, and I felt that, even with all the assistants and aides-de-camp they would allow me to choose, I should be unequal to the charge; that *deafness* alone was an insuperable objection, since I had ever found that *listening* and *hearing* were of more conse-quence in negotiation and ministerial conferences, than talking and arguing; that, therefore, flattered as I was by their friendly and partial opinion of me, yet I should make a very unjust return to their friendship and par-tiality, if I did not express myself as I had done, and state all the strong objections which oppose my being selected for this purpose. If the King commanded me to serve, and, after hearing my reasons, persisted in his desire, *then* nothing should stand in the way—it was a duty I should fulfil at all risks; that I had but one word more now to add, which was, that I should take no step without communicating with Mr. Pitt, *not for his leave* to act, but to obtain his *opinion,* to which, whether it related to me as an individual, or as likely to become a servant of the public, I should pay the great-est deference. Lord Pelham approved much what I said, admitted it all, and ended by saying, that his wishes respecting me had become stronger from what I had told him; " and I know," added he, " the King would delight in it." I said this was the kind language of friendship, and as such very gratifying to me.

We then talked on the events of the day: he said Buonaparte was determined as to invasion, he believed, but found it very difficult to know how to set about it. There were many flat-bottomed boats built at Cherbourg, but nothing like immediate readiness; that there was a great jealousy amongst the generals, and that he saw much good might be done by judicious management in France. He had not seen Woronzow, and did not know whether any thing new was come from Russia.

The Greffier came to me before I left London (which I did at half-past three), and I settled every thing with him respecting the grant to the House of Orange.

From July till October I was out of the way of hearing any thing from authority. I was in Wilts, at Bath, and, except a day or two passed with Lord Bathurst at Cirencester, had no opportunity of obtaining information, or even conversing with those who were informed on politics. Pitt, during this period, was wholly at Walmer Castle, attending strictly to his duty as Warden of the Cinque Ports, and to training and drilling his corps; and it is said he astonished the officers of the regulars, high in rank, with the rapidity with which he acquired military knowledge, and the justness of his military remarks. Buonaparte was all this time threatening us with invasion, and carrying on his preparations with incredible activity. His principal force was encamped on the heights near Boulogne, the port and road of which place he enlarged and fortified, as also that at Ambleteuse; and formed a new basin for his gun and flat-bottomed boats at Vimereux, a small river which falls into the sea between these places, and hitherto was only fit for the reception of fishing vessels.

On the 30th of October I went to London; found

Lord Pelham was dismissed, and very ill. Addington turned him out without any *ménagement*, and alleging, rather shabbily and artfully, that as Lord Pelham had, in March, expressed his readiness to withdraw when it could be attended with any advantage to His Majesty's service, he now availed himself of his declaration (though it related evidently and specifically to the idea of facilitating Pitt's coming into power, and Pitt alone), and informed him Mr. Yorke was to be appointed Secretary of State. Addington offered Pelham the Duchy of Lancaster, and to remain in the Cabinet, at the head of the Board of Trade (places held by Lord Liverpool). Lord Pelham said little to Addington, but wrote a very proper and respectful letter to the King, through the Duke of Portland, (Lord Pelham was not well enough to go out,) expressing his perfect obedience to His Majesty's orders, for such he considered what Addington had said to be, but declining Office, and wishing only to be allowed to attend to his duty at the head of his regiment, the Sussex Militia.

The King sent him a most gracious answer, expressing his satisfaction at his conduct, and urged him to take Office. After a discussion which lasted many weeks, during which Pelham was ill, but during which he expressed his wish to have the Duchy of Lancaster for life, it ended by its being given to him, liable to all the *usual contingencies*, which was the odd expression Addington employed in a very dry and short letter to him. From this time Pelham lived entirely at Brighton, and retired from Parliamentary attendance.

Lord Grenville and his friends were occupied with planning schemes to overthrow the Administration, and, through Mr. Thomas Grenville's old habits of intimacy and friendship with Fox, they began to draw towards him, and met with little or no difficulty on his side to form a junction, for the purpose they had so much at heart, viz. the downfall of Addington. Pitt, though *sounded*, would *never listen to this;* and it was in vain that Canning went backwards and forwards between Dropmore and Walmer. Pitt remained steady to his principle; and Parliament opened on the 22nd November, 1803, without Pitt attending, but with a violent and able Opposition formed between the Grenvilles, Fox, and Windham, who began by attacking Government in a very powerful way under the name of a co-operation.

I came with my family to town on the 8th of January, 1804. I found the spirit of party very high, but *Pitt still absent.* The debates in the House of Commons grew more long, and more contested; and none of the measures of Government, for the Volunteers, or indeed for any other purpose, were allowed to pass unnoticed or unopposed.

On the 12th or 13th the King (after having taken cold by remaining in wet clothes longer than should be) had symptoms of the gout ; he could not attend on the Queen's birthday, though he appeared in the evening at an assembly at the Queen's House ; he was too lame to walk without a cane, and his manner struck me as so unusual and incoherent, that I could not help remarking it to Lord Pelham, who the next day (for I went away early) told me that he had in consequence of my remark attended to it, and that it was too plain the King was beginning to be unwell. Lord Pelham, who played that evening with the Queen, added, that her anxiety was manifest, since she never kept her eyes off the King during the whole time the party lasted.

A very few days after, the gout grew worse ; it then disappeared; and though there was a Council held about the 24th of January at the Queen's House, yet before the end of that month it was no longer to be concealed that the King had a return of his old illness. For some time only his household physician attended, but at last it became necessary to call in some one used to such cases; and, as His Majesty had expressed a great dislike to the Willises, a Doctor Symonds was chosen. The King was exceedingly ill soon after this, in immense danger for forty-eight hours on the 12th and 13th January ; but from this he recovered, and the mania, though it still remained, was by no means so strong as at former times. His constitution seemed weaker, and to have suffered more ; but his mind was never so completely alienated as in 1788, and in 1801.

During the King's illness, Opposition increased both in violence and numbers. Ministers defended themselves better by voting than speaking, and lost very much in debate, though they still appeared strong in divisions, —too strong, indeed, for Opposition often to attempt it.

The public mind was very much agitated and divided. Pamphlets, that had for object the justification either of Pitt or of Addington, produced no other effect than creating a degree of personal enmity between them they till now never had, nor ever would have entertained if these officious scribblers had not come forward. The sectators of each of them, from party spirit and selfish views, increased this sentiment (not natural to either of them), by their virulent and exaggerated reports. Tierney and Sheridan were most injudiciously admitted to a show of Addington's confidence. Canning, Lord Stafford, Lord G. Leveson, were as violent on the other side; and, not contented with attacking the measures of Government, they attacked Addington's personal character and principles.

The French, in the mean while, went on with their preparations, and the country was in as perilous a state as possible.

————

About this time, in the beginning of February, the measures concerted by Pichegru, Moreau, &c., were confided to me. They were represented as *immanquable*. The idea was the restoration of the monarchy under a Bourbon Prince. Their plans were extensive, and, as they *thought*, well and secretly arranged. Pichegru left England about the middle of January. As soon as anything like a successful step had taken place, and whenever the event became certain, and the moment arrived that a more conspicuous character was necessary, Lord Hertford was to appear in the double character of making peace, and restoring the old Dynasty. The Duc d'Angou-

lême was to have gone to France, on due notice being
given him.   The event proved it was a very wide and
deep-laid plot, but it also proved that improper persons
had been confided in, or imprudent language held.*

About the middle of February, the King grew better,
and his recovery was no longer doubtful; yet some part
of the Opposition (Lords Fitzwilliam and Carlisle) called
it in question, and held rather unfair language on it in
the House of Lords.   Arthur Paget left London for
Vienna on the 8th July; but being detained by contrary
winds at Yarmouth, and hearing that the King grew
worse, he returned to London: he found the reports
exaggerated, and that in fact the King was better.   On
the 22nd, however, he again went to Yarmouth, and
sailed on the 26th.   He carried out no new instructions,
and every thing on the Continent seemed left to chance.

SUNDAY, FEB. 19.—I called on Pitt, and met him as I
was coming from his door, and returned with him.   I
said it was my wish to see him at this moment, in consequence of the assurances I had formerly made him, to
repeat them, and to hear from him his sentiments and
intentions on the present very critical situation of
affairs.

He, without hesitation, entered into a very full and
unreserved detail of both.   He began by stating that the
two very important events now pending, viz. the probability of a very formidable invasion, and the dangerous
state of the King's health, placed the country in a state
of difficulty and danger dissimilar to any former one, and
required from all those who were called on to act in
public a very different mode of reasoning and acting than
at any past period.   To these points a third might be
added, viz. the state of parties; and although these

----

* The plot of Georges, Pichegru, Moreau, Lajollais, &c., is so well known
that it is only necessary to remind the reader, that the first was executed,
with some others; and that Pichegru was found dead in his prison.   Moreau
escaped, to die on the field of battle in the Campaigns of 1813.   The failure
of this conspiracy increased Buonaparte's power and *prestige,* together with
the spirit of hatred against England in France.

three considerations were in themselves separate and distinct, yet they bore very sensibly on each other, and, taken collectively, made the actual position of the country a very serious and alarming one. That he had given each of them due and serious attention, had weighed them in his mind maturely and leisurely, in order that he might determine safely and calmly on such a line of conduct as became him, and which he might never be sorry for; and that, after the most diligent thought and reflection, he could see none better nor more conformable to his notions of what was right than to persevere in that which he had pursued for some time past. It was the only one which he could consider as calculated (independently of every other circumstance) for the public good; and by the public good he meant a continuation of the security, quiet, and prosperity of the country, and every individual in it.

That therefore *he would never make the turning out this Administration the object of his endeavours;* that though some of his best friends had united themselves avowedly for that purpose with Fox, yet he had and would uniformly reject any overture which might be made to him to become a party to such a system. On my asking the question, he said the nature of this answer went only to opposition, and to turn out Addington; that they were not pledged to come *in together.* At the same time, Pitt admitted that such a compact was delusive; and there could be little doubt, if they carried their first point, the new Administration must be composed from amongst themselves exclusively. At the same time that he assured me of his disapprobation of opposition, he begged me to understand that he had no communication, no intercourse whatever, with the present Administration; and that he certainly never would on any account listen to proposals similar, or even more conciliatory than those he had rejected last year (in March), or even again go the length he then had gone in committing himself. That, in all simple and plain questions, it was his resolution to support Government; but when Government omitted any thing he thought the

state of the country required to be done, or did it weakly
and inefficiently (as in Mr. Yorke's flimsy Volunteer
Bill), he then should deliver his sentiments clearly and
distinctly, but not even then in a spirit of opposition;
since he would never do it till he had ascertained Government would persist in what he condemned, and not
adopt what he thought essentially necessary.   Again, on
the other side, if Opposition brought forward any measure which to him might appear calculated for the good
of the public, and not a factious or party step, such a
measure should have his concurrence; entering at the
same time his solemn protest against its pledging him
beyond this single measure, or to any farther co-operation with them.*   That to such of them as he still
must consider as his friends, he had explained this in a
way not to be mistaken; and though they (he meant
Lords Grenville and Spencer, Windham, &c.) were not
satisfied, yet they were in a good humour with him, and
he remained steady to his purpose, and was not biassed
by their able attempts to persuade or gain him over.
That such would be his great line of conduct: in it
much would depend on *opinion—opinion* unconnected
with party, of course, not so readily ascertained.   He
therefore could not expect or wish to have a great following.   That towards Office he would take no other
step than such as might arise out of this conduct, and
that he said this not from any foolish affectation of
slighting the value of power and Office, or even from a
disinclination to resume it, but because he thought it
conscientiously right, and should blame himself if he
acted differently.

But *if*, said he, from being *out-debated* (which they
will be), or *out-voted* (which they will not be), Ministers
should get frightened, and want to resign; or if, from a
much greater improbability, they should, from the pressure of the times, get conscious and convinced of their
own inadequacy to administer the government of the
country, and were led to give up their places; in either

---

* How similar to the Duke of Wellington's conduct towards the Whig
Government from 1831 to 1841 !

of these cases he should look upon it as right and a duty to contribute towards forming a new Administration by any means in his power; and, added he, (stating a third case,) *this duty would be a paramount one, and superior to every thing with him,* viz. if the King should ever, from having either of the above-mentioned feelings, call upon him for his services; that then, from every motive which could influence his mind, he should be ready to offer them, unconditionally, to take any part His Majesty commanded, or seemed desirous he should take. Till one of these causes occurred, (and none of them he thought likely,) he should not depart from the principle he had laid down; and, as far as his own private enjoyments and amusements were a question with him, his present situation was one infinitely preferable and pleasanter to him than that he had been in for so many years.

I never interrupted him during this discourse. When he had finished, I thanked him most sincerely for the confidential way in which he had spoken; that it gave me infinite pleasure, because it concurred most entirely with my own sentiments and principles; and that, in now reassuring him of my adherence to him, I had no other motives than doing what I considered as essentially right.

He expressed great satisfaction at having my concurrence. He said, " I should advertise you, it has not that of my eager and ardent young friends, whom I know to be also yours (Canning and G. Leveson); but we are on the best of terms, and it is much more easy for me to forgive their impetuosity, than it is for them to be quite in charity with me, in treating *office* with so little regard, and keeping it at such a distance from those who are disposed to act with me."

To this I assented, and asked whether they would abide by him, or join the Grenvilles; adding, I had not seen Canning for several months. He said, he did not exactly foresee how that would end; that he knew they had communication with the Grenvilles, and that he himself had been assailed in prose and verse by them;

and that Canning, finding this fail, half staggered by his friendship for him, and, half disapproving all he did, knew no longer what to say, but had gone down to Mrs. Canning, where he now was.

On the King's health, he said he knew no particulars; but that, if it was not soon restored, a Regency *must* be appointed; and he could not conceive that it would be different from the last projected Regency Bill in 1789. That if the Duke of Richmond and Lord Thurlow advised (as he had heard they did) the Prince, he could not see how it could be different. " Unless," said I, " Lord Thurlow is not afraid of God's forsaking him," —alluding to his famous expression in 1788, " When I forsake him (the King), may God forsake me!" That, however, much depended on the duration of the King's illness, and of the attempts of the enemy.*

On my observing that the Prince of Wales had asserted, that it *must* last several months, Pitt said, " Thy wish was father, Harry, to that thought."

I ended the conversation by asking him whether he wished me to take my seat, and, if he did, whether he would allow me to send him my proxy, and also whether I might repeat to the Duke of York what I had heard from him.

He wished me to do the first, and allowed me to say the whole of what had passed to the Duke of York.

I left him by repeating my satisfaction, and how particularly glad I was to know *his* sentiments and plans, before I had seen Canning or G. Leveson, since they certainly would have tried to give me impressions I now should be proof against.

On the 22nd of February I was with the Duke of York at the Horse-Guards. I related to him the sub-

---

* At this time the Prince of Wales was governed by Lords Thurlow and Hutchinson, and Mr. Francis (the latter a *soi-disant* Jacobin, and very clever). These advisers induced him to publish in the *Morning Chronicle* of December 7, 1803, his Correspondence with the King relative to the Prince holding high command in the army, which the King had always declared, on principle, he would not permit. When the Prince reiterated his demand, at a moment of danger to the nation, he probably did so from the best feelings :— not so those, who made him expose this family correspondence.— *Harris Papers*.

stance of what I had heard from Pitt. He was much pleased with it, but rather from his supposing it went to an indirect disavowal of any junction between him and the Grenvilles and Fox, than from viewing it, as I did, in the light of a conduct which, if followed up steadily and firmly, would tend to bring him back to Office, without any violent shock of parties, or uneasiness to the King. The Duke, however, expressed the same opinion on this subject he ever had, viz. the inability of the present Administration, and the urgent necessity for its being strengthened. He said they were of late become more attentive to him, though he was under a cloud. And this led the Duke to mention the Prince, who, just at this time, had refused to see him; and nothing could be more temperate than the terms in which he expressed himself, or the concern he felt, both as an individual, a brother, and a subject, at this breach of harmony between them. It was *patched up* about a week afterwards by the means of Lord Paget, who mediated between them with great good sense. The reconciliation, however, was not, I fear, very cordial, nor likely to last long.

FEBRUARY 24.—On the 23rd I dined with Duke of Portland. I acquainted him that I had given my proxy to Pitt, and with my motives. He (though in the Cabinet) strongly wishes for Pitt's accession, and heard with great pleasure all I said.

On the 24th, Pitt and Lord Camden dined with me. No politics passed; but Pitt was in high spirits and excellent conversation. He stayed till past ten.

The King remained nearly the same. The bulletins at St. James's varied very little, but it was understood he was getting gradually well.

On the 9th of March (Friday) I went to Cirencester, and remained till the 17th. Lord Bathurst's politics and opinions correspond entirely with mine.

The Grenvilles and Fox unite closer and closer every day.

Little passed during the remainder of March and beginning of April, except the Opposition gaining strength, and Pitt opposing *at times* the measures of Government, and bringing on a question to inquire into the conduct of the Admiralty, on which he divided strong.

The plan of Pichegru, &c. was detected at Paris, either by the treachery or folly of those in the secret; and, at the same time, an absurd correspondence of Drake's (our Minister at Munich) with a Frenchman named Méhée de la Touche was intercepted and published.*

The Duc d'Enghien was carried off from Ettenheim by a French detachment from Strasburg on the 16th of March, and shot at Vincennes on the 20th, by Buonaparte's order. The whole scheme was discovered and defeated; but its extent, or, as they call it, its ramifications, spread so wide as to give great alarm to Buonaparte, and to excite in him temporary fits of passion, similar to those Paul had towards the close of his reign.

April 16.—The divisions in the House were chiefly on the Volunteer Bill, and augmentation of the Irish Militia; or, in other words, on the defence of the country. On this there was the first very strong one (Pitt being in the House),

For Government	.	. 127
Against it	. .	. 106
Majority	. .	. 21

* Mr. Drake was deceived by a false agent, Méhée de la Touche, who, after entrapping him into a correspondence, betrayed him to Buonaparte. The First Consul published it, and convicted Drake of a treasonable attempt to overturn his Government, under the sacred protection of diplomatic office. The *exposé* was complete, proving the part which England took in the plots of the Royalists and other discontented persons, and shewing the incapacity of the agent our Government employed. The Court of Munich expelled our Minister, Drake; and the indignation of the French was naturally roused to the utmost pitch that Buonaparte could desire.

On the 24th, Monday, (Pitt also present,) still stronger: it was on a motion of Fox to inquire into the state of the nation:—

Ayes 204
Noes 256

Majority . . . 52

On the 26th, on Pitt's opposing the New Defence Bill: —With him 203
With Ministers 240

Majority 37

In the House of Lords Ministers were once beaten, and often very nearly run; and the great trial of strength there was to take place on the 30th April, on a motion to be made by Lord Stafford, similar to that Fox made on the 24th.

I was with Pitt several times during this time. I informed him of all I knew relative to the plot in France, and I required him to give my proxy to some personal friend of his own, that no doubt might arise why I give it, and *for whom*. It was entered on the 24th of April by Lord Camden.

In a conversation I had with Pitt at his own house in York Place, on Thursday, April 12th, which was prior to any of the strong divisions in the House of Commons, he repeated to me the same sentiments he had expressed on the 19th Feb., and declared his decided intention of making a communication to the King previous to his taking any conclusive step. I applauded extremely this, and repeated what I had so often said, that too much care and attention could not be paid to the King's ease and comfort, not only because it was what the whole of his reign and conduct most justly called for, but because the very existence of the country hung, perhaps, on his life. To all this, Pitt over and over again agreed.

APRIL 25.—With Pitt.—He observed that " the language held by dependent courtiers and creatures of the
Ministry is, that the question is, ' *a King or a Regency*,'
and that I am for the latter, and, at the same time,
acting in the strictest offensive and defensive union with
Fox.   It is," added he, " the most *likely lie* to hurt
me in the public esteem; but so palpable a lie, that
I trust even the most artless and credulous (who are
not prejudiced) will at once discover its drift· and
object."

I agreed with him, but observed that little, artful
cunning often defeated steady, open, and conscious integrity; that it was not enough that he himself and
a few friends should be acquainted with his real and
genuine sentiments and intentions, but that they should
be made notorious, and, for this end, nothing could
contribute so completely as his opening himself to the
King.

" *It is done*," he replied.   " I wrote to His Majesty
on the 23rd, prior to any of the great divisions; the
Chancellor took charge of the letter; he promised not to
communicate it to any one (it was under a flying seal),
and he was fully informed by me of the motives of my
past conduct, and of by what my future conduct would
be regulated.   To this I have neither received, nor do I
as yet expect an answer; but I have done what I know
you will approve, and what, most certainly, I was from
every feeling bound to do."*

On Thursday, April 26th, Addington informed the
King that he foresaw an impossibility of his carrying on
the public business any longer, or of the present Administration being able to remain in Office.   *He* reports
that the King received this with great marks of concern
and indignation; asked whether a new Parliament would
do better; and proposed an immediate dissolution, which
violent step Addington takes the merit of having dis-

* For this letter, *vide* " Life of Lord Eldon," vol. i. p. 440.

couraged and declined. Addington also hinted the great
satisfaction the King expressed at the whole of his conduct, and talked of very high honours and emoluments
being offered him.

It appears a matter of some doubt whether Addington
had heard from the Chancellor what had passed between
Pitt and him, or seen the letter. I incline to believe the
first, not the *latter;* and that this, and the strong divisions, induced him to take this step on the Thursday,
and to advise the Chancellor not to deliver Pitt's letter
till the Friday (the 27th April). The Chancellor's account (as he gave it to Pitt, and to the Duke of Portland, from whom I had it *quite warm*) of the way in
which the King took the business, varies very materially
from Addington's; he says, the first impression was
certainly one of displeasure and anger, but that, after
a very short pause, the King recollected himself, and
used nearly these words:—" After the severe affliction
with which I have been visited, and from which it has
pleased Providence to relieve me, it would ill become me
to give way to any unseemly hastiness or impatience;
still less could I be justified at a moment like this to
add to the difficulties of the day by listening to any
private feelings or personal prejudices. It is my duty
to prevent confusion in my kingdom, and that duty I
will perform." And from that moment, added the
Chancellor, His Majesty never betrayed the least hastiness of temper, but attended to all that was said with
the greatest attention, and in the most placid manner.
The Chancellor did not enter into details, which the
King wished for, and this led him naturally to talk
of Pitt, whom the King praised, and said, (and this
proves neither alienation of mind, nor that Addington's
great pains to conceal every thing from him had succeeded,) " Notwithstanding the reports and surmises
I hear, I am persuaded Mr. Pitt will never form any
engagements, or enter into any connexion, which will be
injurious either to the rights of my subjects or to the
Royal Prerogative. *I feel sure of this*, and," added the
King, with emphasis, "I also feel *my Coronation Oath*

safe in his hands." (Alluding to the Catholic Question.)*

From Friday, April 27th, to Monday, April 30th, Ministers deliberated on what they should do. What passed in these councils I cannot say, but early on Monday, April 30th, the Chancellor called on Pitt; related to him what had passed between the King and him; what farther the King desired to hear; added, that, under every circumstance, Mr. Addington was inclined to consider his Administration as at an end, and that as much would be intimated in both Houses, by proposing to put off *Fox's motion on the Hanoverian Transports*, and Lord Stafford's on the State of the Nation; and this was already done. Pitt had but barely time to notify it to Lord Grenville, and most of the Lords were taken by surprise.

Addington opened his budget this day (April 30th), and did it well,—16,000,000*l.* loan, and 7,000,000*l.* new taxes. After which he said, in answer to a few words of Fox, that circumstances had arisen that were of a nature to make him confident the public would approve all motions of consequence to be postponed for some time.

On Wednesday, May 2nd (I believe I am correct), Pitt put into the Chancellor's hand the heads of what he should say to the King. He did this as well in compliance with the Chancellor's wishes, that the King in his present state might not be taken by surprise, and led to commit himself either way suddenly, as because he himself considered it the surest and safest mode of proceeding.

What these heads were I cannot (at least now) exactly say, but it is presumed that they were perfectly conformable to Pitt's assurances, and went to *propose* a very great number of persons, of all colours and descriptions,

---

* The exact part which Lord Eldon took in preparing the King for Pitt's accession to power is not given in his " Life ;" but an interesting account, from Lord Eldon's " Note Book," of his fetching Pitt from his house to the King, will be found in vol. i. p. 447. In the first five minutes Pitt contrived to offend the Chancellor.

of whose abilities he had a high opinion, without insisting on any one positively and specifically.

Be it as it may, it remained unnoticed and unacknowledged all that week;* and not only the public in general, but the most confidential friends of Pitt, and I believe even of Addington, were kept in the dark. No rumours even transpired before Sunday, 6th May, except that Addington had complained of being betrayed by the Chancellor; and on Sunday noon a vague and loose report was in circulation that the King had written on Saturday a very angry letter to Pitt, rejecting every thing, and expressive of high displeasure; but this report came from Sheridan and Tierney. It was also rumoured at the Opera on Saturday evening, that Addington was determined to stand his ground, and that on Monday he would try his strength.

In this precarious and anxious state the public was kept during this whole first week in May.

The strongest proof of Buonaparte's inability to invade us is his not attempting it at such a moment.

The Prince was at first wavering in his politics, but got finally all the votes he could for the Opposition. The Duke of Clarence would have voted with it; but the other Royal Dukes, and very properly, *if they vote at all*, will vote with Government.

The only proof I could collect this week of Pitt's opinion was from his telling Fitzharris, who dined with him on the 3rd May at Lord Carrington's, that he would not be wanted in the House, and might go to take charge of his Regiment, of which he was Lieutenant-Colonel (2nd Wilts Militia), and which was to be inspected very soon. Fitzharris, therefore, left London on Saturday the 6th, for Bristol.

I omitted to insert, at the period when it ought to have been mentioned, that Pitt never had any personal interview with Fox, never made him any specific pledge

---

* George III. acknowledged the receipt of this paper by a note to Lord Eldon, which savours either of his malady, or of a strong dislike to Pitt. It was one which the Chancellor *could not shew him*, and hence arose the delay mentioned by Lord Malmesbury.—*Vide* Lord Eldon's "Life," vol. i. p. 443.

farther than saying, that, if the time ever came when he
should be called upon to frame an Administration, he
(Pitt) would name him (Fox) as a person whose great
abilities might be usefully employed in the present crisis;
but that if the King objected to the admission of him in
his councils, he should not press Fox on his Majesty,
but endeavour to form a Government according to the
King's pleasure.   This was perfectly understood by Fox
so long ago as March, and he was perfectly satisfied
with it; and it was with this conviction on his mind
that he continued to act with Pitt and the Grenvilles in
their endeavours to overset Addington's Government.

It will be, perhaps, essential not to forget this circumstance as future events arise.

Canning and Granville Leveson were the go-betweens,
and they were extremely anxious to unite Pitt and Fox,
and to have the abilities of both of them in Office.

———

MONDAY, MAY 7.—Greffier Fagel with me—early—
he had dined the day before at Lord Grenville's, with all
the family ; in good spirits, and liking a caricature representing them as the giants waging war on the *gods*
(Addington, &c.)

At half-past two, Lord Bulkeley stopped my carriage
to tell me Pitt had been all the morning with the King,
from half-past ten to that hour.   He had just seen him
come out of the Queen's House with the Chancellor.   At
half-past five the Greffier came to me from the House of
Lords, to say Lord Stafford's motion was again postponed.   He said Wickham had told him that the King
was too ill to see Pitt; this I set right.   The Greffier
returned to Wickham, and in an hour wrote me a note to
say Wickham acknowledged his error, and that he could
NOW assure him, *Pitt had been with the King three hours,*
and was amazed at the cool and collected manner in which
*His Majesty had carried on the conversation.**

* This is confirmed in the " Life of Lord Eldon," (vol. i. p. 449,) where
Mr. Pitt says he was surprised at the King's ability, and never had been so
" baffled " by him in any conversation during his life.

Lord Minto came soon after five, and confirmed what Lord Bulkeley had said; he added, from authority, that the King positively *proscribed* Fox, *and no one else.* This he (Lord Minto) seemed to regret.

At ten o'clock William Elliot came from the House of Commons: he said G. Rose had got up (on Fox's putting off his motion) to say, that " *a member of the House, not present, had received His Majesty's commands to form a new Administration.*" This very odd declaration was not noticed by any of the Ministers, who were all on the Treasury bench. Fox postponed his motion (that relative to the Transports for the Hanoverian Army) till Friday, when he declared he would bring it on, let who would be Minister.

William Elliot was called out by Windham, and on his return after dinner, when we were alone, he lamented sincerely the exclusion of Fox. Fox, he said, had contributed more than half to overthrow Addington, and his talents were such as claimed a high place in the Cabinet. There was, he confessed, no specific pledge anywhere; but, whatever the Grenvilles might do, *he* did not think they could accept Office; he himself, and those *he* was connected with, (Lord Fitzwilliam, &c.) certainly would not.

I asked, if no pledge, where was the forfeit ? Did he recollect what Fox's conduct had been ? Was he not aware of what had happened? Did he expect the King's ready assent to admit Fox to a share in his councils ? could it be expected? though he and perhaps myself knew, that a great deal of Fox's language and conduct was to be attributed to personal disappointment, and to the influence of his *followers*, and that, being on the same level with him, *we* might understand it. Yet could it be supposed that the King, placed at the distance he was from Fox, and to whom all Fox's words and actions had been aggravated by the very man (Pitt) who now named him as qualified for Office, could distinguish or admit this ? And although I agreed with him, that it was to be lamented that *all* the abilities of the country could not be united under the same government at such a critical moment, yet I really did not think what had passed a cause of surprise or anger, and that I was in confident hopes Fox would recollect all this (I was sure he would if left to himself); and instead of returning to violent opposition, I flattered myself he would follow what I was persuaded was the bent of his own temper and disposition, and, by supporting Government for a while out of Office, recover the King's good opinion, and thus qualify himself for Office. That such a conduct, assisted by Pitt (when Minister), would infallibly succeed, and in a very short time, *that broad and extensive union of abilities*, so devoutly to be wished for, might be brought about.

Elliot assented in part to this, and, almost for the first time in his life, (after he had made up an opinion, or received one from Windham, and it was evidently from him it came,) was somewhat inclined to recede, and think me not wrong.

The result in my mind of what I heard was, that the Grenvilles had, for the purposes of opposition, formed closer connexions with Fox than they were aware; and that what Pitt said, when he called their " idea of acting together for the purpose of turning Addington out, and not *for coming in together*, delusive," now proves to be strictly true.

Half-past nine in the evening.—Bouverie (son to Mr. Bouverie, of Old Burlington Street) came to me; he confirmed *from Fox* what I have just written, viz. that the King *proscribed* him. From Bouverie's language it was to be feared Fox was more hurt and disappointed than in reason he ought to be; but that he indulged very sanguine hopes that Lord Grenville and his party would not come into Office without him, and these hopes alone go to prove to demonstration the justness of Pitt's prediction.

It is not, perhaps, a very false mode of reasoning on this event, to suppose that the Grenville party, now united by means of Tom Grenville with Fox, think it a better calculation, as far as relates to permanent power and office, to wait till a new reign. That this (but I trust they are mistaken) is drawing towards its close;

and that under the next, connected as they are with Fox,
they shall be able to act with much more pre-eminence
than while this lasts, since they feel the King cannot like
them, and that at best they must be subordinate to Pitt;
and this *emancipation from Pitt*, strange as it may seem,
has, I have for many years perceived, been the ruling
wish in Lord Grenville's mind. He now throws off the
mask, and he does it more confidently, as being connected with a strong party; and any idea of past obligation, or consanguinity with Pitt, has no effect on him.
The French proverb is here verified—" Un bon ami
vaut mieux que trois mauvais parents."

TUESDAY, MAY 8.—Dean of Christchurch* at eleven;
said Addington expressed himself to him that he was
sure, if he had dissolved Parliament, he should in a
new one have had a considerable majority; that the
King was earnest for it, but that he could not bring himself to consent to a measure which would, at a moment
like this, throw the country into confusion.—*Quære*.

Airing with Lord Pembroke. He said he had heard
the King had made up his mind to consent to a new
Administration, *but that was all;* that he was *far from
pleased* with the idea.

A Council at the Queen's House to-day, at three.

Lord Minto at four; declares his intention of abiding
by Lord Grenville, and by inference signified Lord Grenville's resolution not to take Office unless Fox did, but
to abide by him.

Lord Minto called it " a point of honour." This confirmed to me at dinner by William Elliot; and it seemed
to be settled that Pitt was now so limited in his choice
as to have no other but either amongst his own individual friends, or by keeping part of the present Cabinet. I did not choose to trouble him; and, as neither

---

* Dr. Jackson, whose memory is still venerated at Christchurch, as a
man whose popular and successful rule united the discipline of scholastic
life to a great knowledge of human nature, and the habits of the class which
he governed.

Canning nor any of his party called on me, I conjecture they are not elated.

Sir W. Farquhar said (but I do not give it as truth), when the King observed to Pitt that he was rather surprised to see Fox's name amongst those *he* mentioned as fit for being a member of the Cabinet, after his name having been struck off the Privy Council during the time Pitt was Minister—

Pitt replied, " Your Majesty will perhaps not have forgotten that *I* did not at the time recommend this step. I considered it then as giving Mr. Fox too much consequence."

WEDNESDAY, MAY 9.—Greffier with me at eleven; said he had dined the day before with Lord Grenville, *who, from his tone and manner*, clearly meant to be in opposition. His family dined there; and there seems no doubt that they have *all* (Lord Spencer, Windham, &c.) left Pitt for Fox. This confirmed from what Lord Minto declared to Lady Malmesbury—it was a *point of honour*, according to him, not to accept Office if Fox was precluded from it.

Lord St. Helens.—Thought the King quite recovered, but fearful lest he should become melancholy and low; that appeared to be the present cast of his mind. Said that Pitt, previous to his seeing the King on Monday the 7th, had asked the physicians before he went into the audience, and who were in waiting, whether the King's state of health was sufficiently recovered to allow him to discourse—whether the sight of him (Pitt), whom the King now had not seen for three years,* might not disturb him, and whether the grave and serious business on which he had to speak might not be too much for him. The physicians assured him *not*, and he (Pitt) then put his queries on paper, and desired them to write their opinions under them and sign them, which they did. Pitt then declared that without such an authority, and such an assurance, he

* It is curious that Pitt should have avoided the King's presence at Court for so long, and a remarkable instance of his pride.

should have hesitated going into the closet; and, if they had at all demurred, he certainly would have returned without going in.

Arbuthnot at noon; he thinks Lord Hawkesbury, Castlereagh, and the Chancellor will remain. Nothing was settled; no business going on.

Dean of Christchurch.—Said he had been with Lord Auckland, who knew nothing, and was rather low.

Lord Pelham and Lord Grantham. I told them what I had heard had passed, as far as I knew of. Lord Grantham came to me by appointment to hear it, and Lord Pelham was just come up from the country, and it was new to him. Both favouring Pitt, and condemning the Grenvilles.

Lord Uxbridge.—He said the King had been out in his carriage, and looked well.

Woronzow at two, for an hour and a half. His old story; expressing great love for the country; his little hopes of a strong Administration, the meaning of which is, that he always wishes to have an apology for being less friendly towards us *in fact* than in *expressions*. It is the trick of his Court, and has been for these forty years. On other subjects he was most reasonable and judicious.

Greffier dined with me, and lamented Lord Grenville's conduct.

Lord Pelham in the evening; he told me Pitt was to have seen the King again to-day at two o'clock, and, he believed, did see him. Lord Camden, he said, was sorry that so much was said about Fox and the Grenvilles, since he (Lord C.) *still* entertained a hope they might become part of the new Ministry; but that the publicity of these reports flung obstacles in the way of bringing it about.

———

MAY 10.—Difficulties increase as to naming an Administration.

At four, Pitt's writ was moved for by Ch. Long. He had kissed the King's hand at the Queen's House, at three o'clock, for the places he held before.

Drove with Lord Pembroke; he very justly indignant at the conduct of the Grenvilles, and grieved at Lord Spencer's adhering to them.

Dined at Uxbridge House with Duke of York; said he would call on me on Saturday; wanted much to see me, &c. Nothing new, nor no more offices filled up. Rumour says Lord Moira is sent for. The King earnestly wishes to keep Duke of Portland, Lord Chatham, and Lord Eldon.

MAY 11 and 12.—The King, the Duke of Portland said, was getting rapidly well. He told him that *now* he and Pitt met like old friends who had never parted. It seems certain that what has passed, far from hurting the King, seems to have relieved him. Lord Melville goes to the Admiralty; Lord Harrowby, the Foreign Department; Lord Hawkesbury, the Home one. Buonaparte elected Emperor of the French (not the Gauls) on the 5th; declared to be *the first of the Line*, and the Empire hereditary. All this by acclamation. Carnot gave a dissentient voice, with his reasons.

Arbuthnot with me on the 12th; he is appointed Ambassador at Constantinople. Jenkinson goes as Secretary of Legation to Vienna. Frere has actually left Madrid, and appointed his brother Chargé des Affaires, of his own head, and without any orders from home; his despatches state a conversation in which he differed violently with the Prince of Peace, but nothing can justify such an unauthorized step.

SUNDAY, MAY 13. —Dean of Christchurch.—Lord Winchelsea Groom of the Stole. Dean said Lord Pembroke had refused to succeed Lord Salisbury as Chamberlain; he told me himself, the sort of life it would oblige him to lead would make him quite wretched. I could not blame him; yet, in my mind, wish he had accepted, for the King's sake. It is now said, either Lord Bath or the Duke of Beaufort is to have it.

Whilst at dinner with a large company at home, I received a most kind letter from Pitt, proposing a seat at the Treasury Board to Fitzharris.

It took me by surprise; and it gratified me the more, as it was done without an application. Woronzow, who was present, much more reasonable than I have seen him for a long while; he was fearful Lord Harrowby had not health ; was not used to foreign business; and that he was *trop boutonné.* He himself said he was going away in a month; blames without reserve; and is concerned at the behaviour of Lord Grenville. Imputes it all to the influence of Tom Grenville ; amazed at Lord Spencer's joining in such a system; said Buonaparte becoming Emperor was " un enfantillage—le nom ne faisoit rien."

MONDAY, MAY 14.—George Rose to congratulate on Fitzharris's nomination : said Lord Lovaine and Ch. Long were to be his colleagues at the Treasury ; Canning Treasurer of the Navy : blamed the Grenvilles ; was sanguine ; said he was perhaps too much of an optimist.

Charles Greville, Lord Warwick's brother, dismissed, and succeeded by Lord G. Thynne ; Lord Salisbury by Lord Dartmouth.

TUESDAY, MAY 15.—Lord Pelham removed; Lord Mulgrave takes his office; early with Pitt in York Place.

General Grenville with me at three ; he blamed without reserve Lord Grenville in his conduct; said it was incomprehensible ; was amused with the idea of Lord Buckingham at Carlton House (now to become the *foyer* of Opposition); he was persuaded the Catholic Emancipation would be brought on, and even perhaps an attempt at a Regency, by trying to prove the King to be incapable of governing. William Elliot (Lord Elliot's brother) to be Under Secretary of State to Lord Harrowby.

WEDNESDAY, MAY 16.—Lord Pelham confirms me in his letter that the Duke of Leeds' interest at Helstone is on the decline, but he thinks that the borough may still be carried. I told this to Charles Long, who called on me about three. He said he was in little doubt about it; but, at all events, Fitzharris's seat must be vacated, as he was *actually* gazetted as Lord of the Treasury—Pitt would have it so; that, if I could not re-elect him for Helstone, they must. This fills the measure of Pitt's kindness, who, during the whole of this transaction, has behaved towards Fitzharris and me as he would towards his nearest relations.

Lord Auckland out of the Post Office; Lord Amherst dismissed from the Bedchamber—he was with me in the evening of the 16th, to communicate Lord Winchelsea's (now Groom of the Stole) letter, and to consult what was to be done. With what I had heard from Lord Uxbridge fresh in my mind, I had no doubt but that it was a hasty measure, in consequence of the idea that had fastened on the King's mind to new-model his household, and I advised Lord Amherst to wait. I knew Lord Winchelsea would not see the King till Saturday, and I wished Lord Amherst simply to answer the letter (with deference) and to see Lord Winchelsea. Lord Rivers appointed by the King, in the room of his father; although Lord Hobart had actually announced to the Irish Lord Westmeath, many months ago, that he was actually named to be Lord of the Bedchamber.

THURSDAY, MAY 17.—Met Rose early in the Park; he very sorry about Lord Pelham. Sturges Bourne and Huskisson the two Secretaries of the Treasury.

Walked in the Park with General Harcourt—he, as always, most right and reasonable.

Lords Pembroke and Amherst at dinner. Much serious conversation with the first on the dangerous state of things, and more especially if the King should not get *quite* well, or relapse; that it was devoutly to be wished, that as one of these was probable, indeed nearly certain, an eventual Regency Bill could be passed *in time;* that without this it was impossible to calculate the mischief which might follow; that Opposition was powerful, rich, and determined; that if it became a contest between the King *ill* and the Prince *well*, about the nature of a Regency, the common and usual bounds of Opposition might be *overstepped*, and civil discord, if not civil war, was not absolutely impossible; that this step must originate with the King, and that, from the real virtues and goodness of his character, and his religious conscientious character, this might be brought about; that it was certain (this I observed and knew) no Minister could venture the proposal, since the King, being rather prone to be suspicious, would suppose it arose from a desire of power, and that only could be brought about by some sedate, wise, and deliberate person, high in rank, who was in possession of the King's confidence and good opinion. We could devise no one. The persons who see the King the most are quite *incapable*— perfectly torpid courtiers. Neither of the Archbishops is fit for it, nor any of the great officers of the household; yet it was of such immense consequence, that Pitt would be to blame if he did not provide against so evident a danger in prospect.

Lord Amherst returned from Pitt, who had appointed him to talk over Lord Winchelsea's letter of dismission. Pitt said, "It must be a mistake, or a step taken in haste. Pray suppress it, and take no notice of it. Withdraw your answer to Lord Winchelsea, and let me see the King."

Lord Amherst explained to Pitt what he thought might have occasioned it, and read him a letter he had written to Addington in the end of April, to say how he should vote. This letter was as handsome as possible, and could not displease the King, if he had seen it. In short, Pitt thought nearly as I did, and considered the step as taken in a hurry, and under the rather crude idea of new-modelling his household; but, at all events, Pitt said, it must be made up to Lord Amherst.

FRIDAY, MAY 18.—I received a note from Lord Camden relating to Lord Pelham, and I appointed to call on Lord Camden to-morrow morning.

With Lord Camden soon after ten. Much regret expressed by us both that Pitt should have removed Pelham; it was not only unfair but unwise, as Pelham had great influence (four votes) in the House of Peers, also two members in the House of Commons. Lord Camden said he had always urged Pitt to deal handsomely by Pelham; his services required it; that Pitt admitted the justice of the demand; that also Pelham had come into Office almost at Pitt's request, certainly with his approbation; that he was always ready to leave it, to make an arrangement in which Pitt was to be included, and was actually turned out because Addington chose to put a false construction on this offer. What was to be done?

I read Lord Camden two letters I had just received from Lord Pelham, by which it clearly appears that he had received no other account of his removal than by public rumour; and that this, joined to the thing itself, (which he did not doubt,) probably would sour and indispose him. That I advised that Pitt should write to him the civilest letter—to-day, if possible—and make him some handsome proposal in lieu of the Duchy. Lord Camden then reverted to an old idea of Pelham's going to Russia. I told him what I knew on that subject; that I could not be responsible for Pelham's acceptance of it; but if it came in the shape of a special Mission, and some Home Office was coupled with it, it would do.

Lord Camden thought of Captain of the Yeomen of the Guard, in the room of Lord Aylesford; said this was 3000*l.* a-year, and vacant.

This appeared to me as possible, and after an hour's conversation he said he would immediately write to Pitt, and tell him what had passed between us.

At one, George Rose and Mr. Sturges Bourne (Secretary to the Treasury). Visit of civility.

They got on foreign politics, in which Sturges joined. This arose from Livingston, the American Minister at

Paris, being come over, as it was supposed, on the idea
of Fox being in Office, and with some pacific proposals.
These, he said, should not be rebuffed, as in Lord Grenville's time, but at least listened to civilly.　Much good
might come from it.

The Greffier Fagel gave them a Leyden Gazette of the
13th, in which there is the Correspondence between the
Senate and Buonaparte, on his election to the Imperial
dignity.　More bombast, sophistry, and vapid nonsense,
with worse logic, never yet was written; but it appeared
to me to be so curious, that I sent it to Pitt; particularly as it is much fresher than any other news from
France.

Pitt has offered the Mint to Lord Bathurst, who, in
the handsomest way, begs Pitt to bestow it where it
may be more useful to the purposes of his Government;
that *he* shall ever act with him, and that he really felt
such a very high Office as one he is by no means entitled to.　Pitt will, I dare say, persevere and insist on
Lord Bathurst's taking it.

SUNDAY, MAY 20.—Mrs. Harcourt.　Uneasy about
the King.　He was apparently quite himself when talking on business, and to his Ministers.　He then collected
and *re*collected himself; but, in his family and usual
society, his manners and conversation were far from
steady—fanciful, suspicious, &c.

If he went to Weymouth, it was absolutely necessary
he should have some very wise and steady person about
him.　Symonds, she said, wanted to go with him, but
she thought him an improper man; that he had his own
interest in view.　Willis (the son and clergyman) managed him much better, and understood what was to be
done.　She wished he could be with him.　All this she
declared to be the *General's* sentiments as well as her
own.

In the first illness, when Willis, who was a clergyman,
entered the room, the King asked him, if he, who was a
clergyman, was not ashamed of himself for exercising

such a profession. " Sir," said Willis, " our Saviour himself went about healing the sick." " Yes," answered the King, " but he had not 700*l.* a-year for it."

Arbuthnot with me in the morning. He had nothing new. He was going (being still in Office) to attend a Cabinet, and said he would call on me when it was ended. This he did, but I was out. He left word Lord Harrowby would come to me in the evening.

Greffier at dinner; said his brother Jacques was arrived; had a great wish to see me, as he had much to say; that Buonaparte's title was to be *Majesté Impératoriale*, not Impériale; that his establishment was to be immense. The first idea was, to be crowned *by the Pope* at Lyons; but, on this being found difficult, the Coronation was to be at Rheims.

He said his brother came over without any impediment. He was supposed to be going to Embden; but the French Commissary at Cattwyk, where he embarked, knew he was going to England, and said, when he was on board, " You will be at *Harwich* in about thirty-six hours."

Lord Harrowby (Secretary of State for Foreign Affairs) with me this evening from nine till eleven. He said, that, with regard to himself, he was in a situation he by no means coveted, but his friendship for Pitt made him not hesitate in accepting it. Neither his health nor his habits were calculated for it, and he had for three years been totally inattentive to public business. He therefore claimed of me, as an old and intimate acquaintance, assistance and help. This I assured him was at his service, though I feared it would amount to very little.

Lord Harrowby then stated the Continent as quite in awe of France; Austria unrecovered from her panic; and, besides the natural pusillanimity of Cobenzel, the idea of seeing again a French victorious army at the gates of Vienna terrified them all. That the French had certainly a very great force in Lombardy and towards Venice, and this keeps them in a constant state of apprehension; that he therefore despaired of bringing this Court forward.

Berlin he stated rather less unfavourably than I should have expected. He said, the evil arose from the King *supposing* he was, like the great Frederick, to govern by himself, when, in fact, he was led by flatterers and traitors; that, besides, the French had filled the north-west side of Germany so full of troops, and posted them in such a way, that he doubted, *if* the Court of Berlin was supposed to act, whether before a Prussian army of sufficient force could be collected, the French would not be at Berlin, since there was nothing between them but Magdeburg. Prussia, he knew, had rejected a French alliance, and that on this account Lucchesini was under a cloud at Paris; that *Russia* was the Court the most likely to be brought into action; but still he saw little hopes, as long as France remained in her present state of high power, and the Invasion was pending.

That the murder of the Duc d'Enghien had been very much felt on the Continent, and particularly at Petersburg. That the King of Sweden was well inclined, and had recalled his Minister from Paris, but he was not *by himself* strong enough to be of great use. That the French had prevented the Landgrave of Hesse having his annual reviews, and perhaps even the Prussian ones in Westphalia, saying, that an assemblage of 15,000 men would not be a measure the First Consul would see with pleasure; and to this both the Hessians and Prussians submitted. That Spain was completely subservient to France, and that should Buonaparte think the Spanish, by going to war with us, would be more useful for his purposes than the tribute he now received, this would happen. The question with us, therefore, was, whether we had better wait for this or not. That every day furnished us with a just cause to declare war on Spain; that Frere *was* coming. He had had a personal quarrel with the Prince of Peace.

Lord Harrowby mentioned news was received of Sir Sidney Smith having attempted to interrupt some boats coming from Flushing to Ostend; that he had succeeded in part, but that the success was far from complete.

That the preparations in Holland were in great forwardness, and that Boulogne was evidently the point where all the force was to be collected.

On all these facts we conversed and reasoned, and he entreated me to speak to him freely, and to give my opinion without reserve.   I said I hoped that the picture Paget had drawn of Vienna was too darkly coloured. That I knew well that Cobenzel was in his heart French; that he had been bred up to admire and fear them, and that, whether a Buonaparte or a Bourbon, this sentiment in his mind would remain the same.   Lord Harrowby asked if there was any other person at Vienna fit to be First Minister.   I said I knew none but Thugut; and the Archduke Charles would oppose his return to power, even if the Emperor dared to restore it to him.   That I did not believe (as he supposed) that the finances of Austria were so low, and that I conceive this as a *finesse* to induce us (when the time came) to give a larger subsidy; while the report, attended with some retrenchments in the army expenses, would, as they thought, and it was thinking like cowards, satisfy the French, and keep them quiet.

That, as for Prussia, I had little hopes; but that I could not believe that the French army could get to Berlin by surprise, since that part of the Prussian army in Westphalia, near Berlin, and at Magdeburg, was, I conceived, very easily to be united, and certainly would form a force fully sufficient to repel invasion, particularly as they would be secure on their eastern frontiers, and on the side of Austria.

We agreed that, till the invasion was attempted, or laid aside, it was not likely the Continent would stir. That, if we succeeded in resisting it, it was still most material to form Continental connexions and alliances, since, without them, Europe never could be restored to a situation of security against France.   Our conversation was very long; and, on parting, Lord Harrowby said he should often renew it, and consider me as his political tutor.

I recommended him, in his conferences with the Foreign Ministers, to hear more than to speak, and that

the little he did say should be neutral, unmeaning civilities, unless some real and important business was the
object of the conference; and that then I should much
advise asking for something in writing—merely as a
memorandum.   That in this country particularly, and
indeed every day, the Ministers of inferior Courts came
to the Secretary of State in order to obtain *matter for a
despatch*, rather as *questions* than on business, and that
it was essential he should make them soon perceive he
was aware of this trick.

MONDAY, MAY 21.—Lord Camden with me at four ;
much talk about Pelham, and, as we had not heard from
him, supposed he would come up.   Lord Camden very
anxious Pitt should see him ; complains and laments
Pitt's want of *little attentions.*   To this he imputed Lord
Darnley's defection (with which I acquainted him).
Pitt had left two notes from him without any answer.
Darnley had told me, a few moments before, that he was
sorry he and I differed completely in politics ; but I
would not contend with him.

Lord Camden told me, he would take Lord Ashbur-
ton's proxy himself, and give the Duke of Buccleuch's to
some one else.   We both agreed that it was much to be
wished that this end of the Session should pass over
without any violent debate, that all acrimony might be
avoided, and that during the summer many conciliatory
measures might be taken.

The Greffier, with his brother James Fagel (just come
from Holland).   He treated the preparations for the invasion lightly ; said their men were adverse to it ; that
Verhuill was the man Buonaparte depended on in Holland ; about 25,000 French there.

Arbuthnot told me, Woronzow had been five hours
this morning with Lord Harrowby.

Lord Pelham came to town by dinner, and was with
me from eight this evening till nine.   He was in very
good temper, and reasonable.   He said, the first
authentic account he heard of his being removed was

through a letter from Lord Mulgrave to Charles Long, who acquainted him of his being appointed to the Duchy, with a seat in the Cabinet.   Lord Pelham went over all his past conduct for these last four years; and very justly deduced from it, that he in every instance acted with Pitt, in many after his advice, and in none (particularly his taking office in 1801) without his previous knowledge and approbation.*   He also adverted to what he had said to Addington, when he came from a conference with Pitt at Charles Long's, in March, 1803; and also the use Addington made of this.

After discussing the business fully, I desired him to see Lord Camden this evening, and to go early to-morrow to Pitt, and that I had confident hopes all would end well.   Lord Pelham shewed me Pitt's letter to him—it was *a little* formal, but announced good intentions.

MAY 22.—Went to Kenwood with Lord Pembroke. Lord Pelham in the evening ; said he had seen Pitt at three o'clock ; that what he said to him was very civil and explanatory, as far as the necessity of arrangements of office could account for his being removed; that Pitt expressed a wish to give him, after some foreign employment, the place of Captain of the Yeomen of the Guard. Pelham declined the first, on account of the very precarious state of his father's health; and demurred about the latter, and came to consult with me what he should do respecting it.   He said, the principal objection to it in his mind was, that he was not sure of the King's feelings on this occasion, and that he felt a repugnance in taking an office immediately about his person, unless he was *quite* sure that it was not disagreeable to His Majesty; that he himself could have no opportunity of ascertaining this till Wednesday fortnight (the 6th of June), as he could not deliver up the seals of the Duchy sooner, and that indeed it was the day appointed by Pitt for that purpose ; that, besides, he was not sure whether it

* Vide an account of it in these Memoirs at that time.

was not lowering himself ; and even that the income was
not adequate.

As it was my wish Pelham should accept Office, and
not be lost to Government, which if he did not I was
apprehensive (from his connexions with the Prince and
Devonshire House) would happen, the bent of my arguments was to persuade him to take this place. I observed, he had every reason to suppose he stood well
with the King; but, if he doubted it, this could be ascertained through Pitt. That, as to the *rank* of the office,
it had always been filled by persons of distinction—Lord
Aylesford, Lord Leicester, Duke of Dorset, &c.; and
that *I* understood it was worth near 3000*l.* a-year,
which was almost as good as the Duchy. Pelham admitted to a degree my reasonings; said he had asked
two or three days to consider of it, and wished me
to communicate any ideas which might arise, as he was
going to Brighton to-morrow, to stay till Monday.

MAY 23.—Nothing.—Russian Memorial to the Diet,
on the violation of the Territory of the Empire by
Buonaparte; strong and well written, but means nothing
more than a sort of protest Russia wishes to enter on
this occasion, which she thinks will please posterity.
We shall see how it is taken by France, and then judge
of the real intentions of Alexander.

MAY 24.—Charles Long at twelve; anxious about
Lord Pelham; wished him to take Office; thought him
ill-used.

Lord Camden at half-past one, about Pelham; doubted
his taking the office offered him. I expressed my fears,
if he did not, that he would leave us. I said I would
write to him, provided the place was not disposed of; and
I had actually begun my letter, when at half-past five I
received a note from Lord Camden, to say Lord Pelham
had written to Pitt to decline the Captaincy of the Yeomen of the Guard.

I of course destroyed my letter.

Charles Long told me that the complexion of the House of Commons yesterday clearly denoted determined opposition; but he thought well of the members.

Some doubts as to the King's health; yet there was a Council to-day, and many new officers kissed hands.

MAY 25.—Wrote to Pitt to repeat my desire of not being a charge to Government on Fitzharris's re-election. Arbuthnot said Woronzow was pleased with Lord Harrowby; that he thought Berlin would certainly follow Russia. The King of Prussia evidently angry, and afraid of Buonaparte; and, if not under the rule of Lombard, would act right. This confirmed to me in a very excellent letter I received to-day from H. Pierrepoint. When Drake passed through Dresden, the Saxon Minister, le Comte de Loss, intimated to him that he could not stay there, and must go on directly. This an additional instance of the insolence of France, and the subserviency of the German empire.

I received a letter from Lord Pelham, acquainting me with the step he had taken, and his reasons (see it); I thought it right to communicate it to Lord Camden.

Lord St. Helens and Lord Arden appointed Lords of the Bedchamber.

MAY 26.—With Duke of Portland at eleven; he very sanguine as to the duration of Pitt in power—confident of a majority in the House of Lords—equally so in the Commons—thinks Lord Grenville will not oppose this session, but violently the next.

The King calls the Grenvilles the " brotherhood "— says " they *must* always either govern despotically, or oppose Government violently." Duke of Portland has little doubts of the King's doing well—quiet will set him right, and nothing else; he has been fatigued by being too much talked to on the new arrangements. Duke of

Portland very right and decided about Fox—says he has a high opinion of his abilities, but Fox has by his conduct disqualified himself decidedly for Cabinet office, since he has maintained opinions which would (if carried into effect) militate against the received and constitutional duties of every department where he could be placed; that Lord Grenville *used* to say this, and how he could now reconcile himself to a contrary idea passed his comprehension. Windham was still more unintelligible; *all* Fox's politics were *contrary to his*, yet Windham says he cannot come into Office without Fox.

The Duke of Portland felt about Lord Pelham as Lord Camden did. We entered into conversation on the grant to the House of Orange. I left with him the two papers I had received from Lord Auckland, containing a mode, proposed by the Attorney-General Perceval, for accomplishing the object without recurring to a new act; but they did not appear to the Duke to do it completely, and we agreed to go together to Pitt on the subject.

Lady Uxbridge at half-past two—very uneasy about the King—said his family were quite unhappy—that his temper was altered. He had just dismissed his faithful and favourite page (Brown), who had served him during his illness with the greatest attention. Quiet and repose were the only chance. She said the Chancellor was to go to Windsor with him, which she was glad of. Lord Uxbridge gone, not meaning to appear, but to be with his regiment (the Staffordshire). King had stipulated, before he went to Windsor, that he would not go to chapel, nor on the Terrace, nor take long rides. Lady Uxbridge thinks Dr. Symonds an unfit man—that the Willises, and particularly the clergyman Willis, was a much properer person to be about the King when he was getting well—so thinks Mrs. Harcourt.

I dine this day at Kenwood; Lord Mansfield not with us, I fear.

SUNDAY, MAY 27.—Fitzharris came from his regiment at Bristol, to dinner. Mrs. Harcourt confirmed all Lady Uxbridge had told me—that the King was apparently quite well when speaking to his Ministers, or those who kept him in a little awe; but that towards his family and dependants his language was incoherent and harsh, quite unlike his usual character. (Mrs. Harcourt here quoted a similar case in her own mother.) She said Symonds did not possess, in any degree, the talents required to lead the mind from wandering to steadiness; that, in the King's two former illnesses, this had been most ably managed by the Willises, who had this faculty to a wonderful degree, and were men of the world, who saw Ministers, and knew what the King ought to do; that the not suffering them to be called in, was an unpardonable proof of folly (not to say worse) in Addington, and now it was impossible, since the King's aversion for them was rooted; that Pitt judged ill in leaving the sole disposal of the Household to the King—that this sort of power in his present weak and, of course, suspicious state of mind, had been exercised by him most improperly; he had dismissed and turned away, and made capricious changes everywhere, from the Lord Chamberlain to the grooms and footmen; he had turned away the Queen's favourite coachman, made footmen grooms, and *vice versâ;* and what was still worse, because more notorious, had removed Lords of the Bedchamber without a shadow of reason. That all this afflicted the Royal Family beyond measure; the Queen was ill and *cross,* the Princesses low, depressed, and quite sinking under it; and that, unless means could be found to place some very strong-minded and temperate person about the King, he would either commit some extravagance, or he would by violent exercise and carelessness injure his health, and bring on a deadly illness. I asked where such a man did exist, or had existed. She said, none she knew of : that Smart, when alive, had *some* authority over him; that John Willis (the clergyman) also had acquired it, but in a different way; the first obtained it from regard and high opinion, the other from fear. That, as was always the case, cunning and art kept pace in the King's character with his suspicion and misgivings, and that he was become so very acute that nothing escaped him.

Mrs. Harcourt ended her recital by great recommendations of secrecy, and submitting it to me whether I would or would not state it to Mr. Pitt. I asked her if the Chancellor knew it. She said *all*; he is the only person who can in any degree control the King; he is the best man possible, and, when he is near, things go on well. I said, in that case Mr. Pitt *must* know it; and if he knew it, would, if he could, apply a remedy; and that if he did not, I must suppose he was at a loss what to do: and that the hearing what he already knew from me, would be useless to him, and look like a pushing intrusion on my part. To this Mrs. Harcourt agreed.

After her, Lord Pembroke came into my room, and asked me whether I was aware of what was passing at the Queen's House; and he then repeated, but in a still stronger manner, and with additional circumstances, what I had before heard. We then both dwelt on the very serious and dangerous consequences to which it might lead, and in vain sought about for a remedy. (Our conversation was interrupted.)

MAY 28.—Fitzharris took his seat at the Treasury. —With Lord Harrowby at the Office, at three; demurs about Paget's return, which he had intended should be directly, and had actually written to that effect, but shews me a long and studied letter from Gentz to Vansittart, (Secretary to the late Treasury,) in which he enters into a long detail of the present state of affairs, and infers from it the necessity of Paget's not leaving Vienna just now; of Paget he speaks highly.

Lord Harrowby adds, that Paget had also written a letter to Lord Hawkesbury, somewhat to this effect— and he now inclines to think that he had better stay at Vienna till this *Chasse aux Ministres*, meaning the

attempt of the French to drive away Drake and Smith*
from Munich and Stutgard, is over.   This led us to a
long conversation on this subject, and he sent me Drake's
and Smith's correspondence, requesting I would give him
my opinion of it, and what ought to be done.   This I
did in a letter dated the 29th.

It is evident both Drake and Smith were terrified, the
latter still more than the former; and that both behaved
without spirit or dignity.   But the two Courts of Bavaria
and Wurtemburg were still more void of these qualities,
and never was such a complete scene of base submission
ever exhibited in diplomatic history.

MAY 29.—Arbuthnot expresses a wish to take Vienna
on his way to Constantinople, and to remain there while
Paget is here.   This a good idea.—Lord Uxbridge at
two ; very low about the King.—He was just come from
Windsor ; " Don't question me," he said, " I am quite
unhappy ; Symonds is a * * * *.—The Willises say, that
they were paid so shabbily by Addington that they would
not return to the Court; but I do not believe they had
the choice."

MAY 30.—Canning in the evening from ten to half-
past eleven; I had not seen him for a long while; his
leanings entirely with Fox and the Grenvilles, and disposed to think Pitt might have done more with the
King, and should not have closed at the first audience.
Pitt on coming from it immediately sent him (Canning)
to Lord Grenville, and Granville Leveson to Fox, to
acquaint them with what had passed.   Lord Grenville
said it was what he expected, and did not hesitate in
saying he could not now take Office.   Fox, either more

---

* The discovery of our intrigues with the Bourbon Royalists through our
Minister at Munich, and his expulsion at Napoleon's request, has been
already explained. Mr. Spencer Smith, our Minister at Stutgard, fell into the
same predicament. A man named Rosey denounced him as plotting against
France and the person of the First Consul. A report was drawn up exposing these functionaries to the abhorrence of France and all Europe.

cautious, or more moderate, expressed no surprise, anger, or disappointment; said, " I am myself too old to care now about Office, but I have many friends who for years have followed me, and whom I shall advise now to join Government, and I trust Pitt can give them places."

When the two *employés* returned to Pitt, he testified (and I think very justly) great *anger* at Lord Grenville's behaviour, and great *pleasure* at Fox's. He immediately desired Granville Leveson to say how ready he was to comply with Fox's wishes, and that he hoped to see him next morning (Tuesday, May 8th). To *this* Fox readily assented. Canning, in the mean while, went to Grey (considering him as the chief person to whom Fox alluded); but he found that, previous to his seeing him, he and Fox's other friends had had a meeting, and *unanimously decided not to take Office without Fox* ; and they contrived to place this in such a light to Fox, that he excused himself from seeing Pitt next morning; and the whole ended in Pitt's being left to form an Administration (as he has done) from amongst his own personal friends.

With respect to the Grenvilles, and Lord Grenville in particular, Canning rests their apology for declining to come into the Administration on Fox's very disinterested and magnanimous behaviour. He related a note Fox had left at Tom Grenville's on Sunday morning, May 6th, stating he wished it should appear as a record, and be known, that *he* stood in the way of no arrangement, that he *was sure the King would exclude him ;* but that this ought not on any account to prevent the Grenvilles from coming in, and that, as far as his influence went, it should not prevent his own friends from coming in.

This note Lord Grenville said was so very noble, that in his mind it obliged him to stand steady by Fox; and neither he nor any of that set hesitated *an hour* since. It was declared and known the same day (May 7th), on which Pitt saw the King, what their resolutions were. This looks as if their minds had been made up ; and the haste in which they determine betrays an eagerness to excuse their defection from Pitt, and to avail themselves, by an early and ready avowal of their intentions, of the advantages that might one day or another come from it, if either circumstances or the reign changes.*

On every other point Canning confirmed all I had heard and knew ; that Pitt had acted in perfect conformity to his assurances and intentions; that neither Fox nor the Grenvilles did or could accuse him of the contrary ; that there was *no pledge* anywhere ; that *he* (Canning) only regretted that Pitt had not left the King on the 7th, taking twenty-four hours to consider, and not at once accepted the Ministry; but this, on my referring to his recollection, he was forced to admit was all along Pitt's declared intention.

Canning defended what Lord Grenville called a *point of honour*, as a legitimate cause for his conduct. I said it was one on which there was no means of argument, as a " point of honour" was what struck the fancy of the person who professed it to be such, and, if he was in earnest, superseded every other consideration. It certainly did in this case supersede early and intimate connexions, both political and of friendship, obligations without end received; and broke up a uniformity of conduct which had begun with Lord Grenville's public existence.

Canning evidently wished to see Fox in Office, and dwelt on the importance of forming an Administration on a very extended basis. Now, he said, it was just the contrary; and he strongly reprobated the introduction of the Duke of Montrose and Lord Mulgrave into the Cabinet. He thought, on the whole, it was too much for Pitt; taxed Lord Camden with being the great cause of it, and said his views were to keep in his nephew, Lord Castlereagh, and to come himself into the Cabinet. This I by no means give credit to.

Canning then related to me the causes of his own conduct. He said, before any arrangements could be taken with respect to the forming a new Administration, he

---

* At Pitt's death in 1806, Lord Grenville came in as Premier with Fox under him.

had made a point of seeing Pitt; that he did not conceal from him his concern and dissatisfaction, and even disapprobation, of what had passed; that he considered the great and only opportunity of uniting the whole ability of the country gone by and lost; that as for himself, and left to himself, he had rather take *no office ;* that, as to a Cabinet office, he considered that his taking one would be injurious to himself and to Pitt—to himself, because the public would evidently look upon him as not *yet* qualified for it; to Pitt, because the same public would consider it as a mark of partiality and personal favour; that against this, therefore, he protested; that with respect to other offices to which he was entitled from those he had already held, as they in a manner came to him in the line of promotion and seniority, he could speak more at his ease—they were reduced to two, Treasurer of the Navy and Secretary at War; that in these he could not but feel he could no longer be so useful to Pitt as before, since, as he did not mean or wish to be in the secrets of the Cabinet (under the Administration now about to be formed), he could never talk to him confidentially and without reserve; that the single reason which could induce him to accept one of them was, that he might be of some service to Pitt in the House of Commons, and that Pitt might be glad to have a Parliamentary friend always close to him; that having thus expressed his feelings—and he said he hoped there was no false modesty in the first, as there was no false pride in the last case he stated—he could only repeat what he began by saying, that he should prefer being left out of Office, but that his obligations and attachment to Pitt would induce him to consent to whatever he (Pitt) wished.

Canning did not report to me Pitt's answer, which probably was short; but said he went out of town the next day, Wednesday the 9th of May (I believe), and returned on the Saturday following, when he received from Pitt a letter, offering to him the choice of the Treasurership of the Navy, or Secretary of War; but desired, if it was repugnant to his feelings, he would take neither. Canning chose the Navy, and in a day or two returned to South Hill, where he remained till this day, when he took possession of his office.

On talking over the different subjects, I observed that the first fault seemed to lie with *Fox's friends*, and that they had acted with great precipitation. To this he agreed.

I next expressed an idea that they might be now sorry for this; to this he also agreed, and said Grey had hinted something like it. I then said that I was willing to hope, that, if the end of this short session passed over without angry debating, and creating personal animosities, something might be effected in the course of the summer to bring about a wider base for the Government. This Canning wished, but seemed to doubt its being likely.

———

MAY 31.—Lord Pelham just come to town—had seen no one; hopes Pitt will keep his word—very reasonable. The Mint, he supposed, not filled up, and said he believed Lord Bathurst would still have it, although he had most handsomely declined the offer of it at first. Arbuthnot wishes me to see Lord Harrowby.

Lord Harrowby in the evening.—Much conversation on Foreign Affairs; he wished me to prepare a manifesto to be sent to all the powers on the Continent. I said, and said truly, that I did not feel equal to it; that, besides want of information, " non eadem est ætas, non mens." Lord Harrowby shewed me a letter from the King, most perfectly well conceived and written on the subject of the Emperor being to invest Arthur Paget.

The election of Buonaparte to be Emperor of the French, and all the ceremonies, &c., this day received here — an evident *singerie* of Charlemagne, Charles Quint, &c. Lord Harrowby objected to Arbuthnot staying at all at Vienna, from his presence being essentially necessary at Constantinople, which was likely to become a very important post.

———

FRIDAY, JUNE 1.—Arbuthnot. He acquiesced in Lord

Harrowby's reasons, and renounced any idea of going through Vienna.

General Harcourt, who came to me in the evening from the Queen's House, gave a most comfortable account of the King. He had seen him often, and for a long time; and that he was in looks, manner, conduct, and conversation quite different from what he had been since his illness—very different indeed from what he was at Windsor; and General Harcourt (who is not a sanguine man) really seemed to think most favourably of the King.

JUNE 4.—Nothing.—Birth-day immensely crowded—Queen and Princesses very civil. King not there, but continues well, and mending.

TUESDAY, JUNE 5.—Lord Camden with me—anxious about Pelham. Pitt wants to please three persons—him, Lord Ch. Somerset, and Lord Amherst, and has only two places vacant—the Pay-Office, and Captain of the Yeomen of the Guard. He agreed in my wishes to see Pelham in Office, and thought he might still be induced to accept of it, could it be so managed as to appear the King wished it, and some certain employment held out to him in expectation. Lord Camden said he would see Pitt about it, and appointed me to meet Pelham at dinner with him on Thursday.

Lord Bathurst has the Mint. Pitt persevered in making him accept it.

A messenger went to Vienna to-day, carrying the Order of the Bath to A. Paget.

WEDNESDAY, JUNE 6.—Fitzharris kissed hands for the Treasury at the Queen's House, also Lord Mulgrave for the Duchy. When Lord Pelham carried in the Seals to give them up, the King said, " Before I can allow you to empty *your* hands, you must empty mine," and gave him *the Stick* as Captain of the Yeomen of the Guard; adding, " It will be less a sinecure than formerly, as I intend living more with my great Officers;" and added several gracious things. Pelham had been apprized of it just as he was going into the closet, but he had not time to recollect himself, neither indeed could he return it.

I received, soon after this event, a note from Lord Camden to mention it; adding, that although it was attended with some *awkward* circumstances, yet .on the whole he was glad of it.

THURSDAY, JUNE 7.—With Lord Camden at his office; he explained to me the *awkward* circumstance, viz. that the King had given Pelham the Stick without giving any previous notice of it to Pitt; that this was provoking and vexatious, and Pitt *felt* it severely, yet scarce knew what was right to be done. I advised that it should be considered *by him* (whatever might be the real fact), that it was done by the King in the way it was, because the King thought it would be agreeable to Pitt; that this was better than a remonstrance, which, in the present state of the King's mind, could avail nothing.

FRIDAY, JUNE 8.—Greffier with me, on the grant to the House of Orange. At twelve with the Duke of Portland. Long conversation on the same subject. Appointed by Pitt for to-morrow to settle this business.

With Lord Pelham at five; he very much out of sorts, and dissatisfied. Said Pitt had *entrapped* him into the office of Captain of Yeomen, and took it up on *this score* very sourly. I *could* not set him right, and, by knowing the real truth, was tied up from saying any thing. I however left him in better humour than I found him. Lady Pelham much hurt at it.

JUNE 10.—Greffier with me previous to my seeing Pitt on the Orange grant. Duke of Portland called on me

at half-past twelve.   With Pitt some time.   I read him
the necessary papers to make him acquainted with the
original intention of the grant, and how it had failed in
its intended effect, from a miswording in the original
Message.   Pitt conceived it in a minute, and readily
agreed to rectify it, by a new Message and new Act.

I also left a paper with Pitt from the Greffier, requesting the release of some Dutch fishermen, taken prisoners.

JUNE 11.—I went to Park Place for the summer.   On
the 13th, I wrote a letter to the Princess of Orange,
stating what had passed, and sent it through the Greffier.

JUNE 15.—Finding little hopes of Fitzharris getting
into Parliament this Session,* and the Opposition gaining
ground, and also receiving a letter from him strongly expressive of his feelings, I wrote as follows to Pitt:—

Park Place, 14th June, 1804.

MY DEAR SIR,—Fitzharris, whilst out of Parliament,
is of no use to you, at a moment when you are entitled
to every assistance the country and your friends can
give you.   His being able to obtain a seat is, perhaps,
not a near event.   Thus circumstanced, if by removing
him from the Treasury you can in any manner add to
your Parliamentary strength, whatever value belongs to
so respectable an employment, we should renounce it
without hesitation, and even look upon its disposal for
such a purpose as a mark of your confidence and reliance
on us.

In every situation we should be equally mindful of the
very kind manner in which it was conferred, equally
bound and attached to you; and the certainty we should
feel of retaining your good-will would act in our minds

---

* Lord Fitzharris had sat during the last Parliament for Helstone, where
the Duke of Leeds, who had returned him, had now lost his interest.
Christchurch, which Lord Malmesbury and his father represented for many
years, was now in possession of Mr. Rose.

as powerfully and as satisfactorily as if we were in possession of the most conspicuous proofs of it.

I am speaking Fitzharris's sentiments as well as my own. They are indeed, if possible, still more his, since the idea originated with him, and I am doing little more than transcribing one of his last letters to me.

Fitzharris saw Pitt, and gave him this letter on the 16th. Pitt took its contents very kindly, and felt our motive. He said he saw no reason whatever for Fitzharris's resignation; that he wished much to have him at the Board; that if ever his not being at it could be attended with real and essential advantage to him, he would not be scrupulous in availing himself of the offer.

He talked with confidence of his Parliamentary strength; but on the same evening, on the Defence Bill, lost one question by 69 to 63, and carried the main question only by 28, viz. 212 to 184.

I remained in the country almost the whole of this summer. I once came up to London, and dined with Pitt and Lord Harrowby at Putney, but nothing remarkable occurred. Méhée de la Touche, the Frenchman who imposed on and betrayed Drake and S. Smith, published a very amusing, though probably very lying, account of the whole transaction. It certainly, as he states it, makes the dupery and terror of our two Ministers equal to his own rascality, and he seems to take pains to make both appear as clear and as notorious as possible. The account is well and clearly written. Hammond, John King, and Drake, very well described; and also Bertrand de Melville, on whom he also imposed most egregiously.

This book was lent me by the Greffier. Unfortunately I lent it to Pitt (when I dined with him), and Pitt never returned it to me.

On Friday, June 22, Lord Pembroke came to me at Heron Court, where I then was, to consult with me on an offer which had been made him by Lord Harrowby to go as Ambassador to Russia. I was rather inclined to advise him to accept, but under the condition it should not be for a length of time, and be considered rather as a Special Mission than as simply the appointment to an Embassy. He, when he left me on Sunday, appeared also of that opinion; but whether he altered it before he saw Lord Harrowby, or whether he did not speak clearly and explicitly to him, I learnt from him that the whole was at an end; and in the beginning of July Lord G. Leveson came to Park Place to tell me it had been offered to him, and that, unless I stated some great motive against it, he should accept it. I asked him if he knew of any other candidate; he said, no, but that it had been offered to Lord Powis, who had positively declined it. Lord G. Leveson I thought very well qualified for it. We talked much on Russian politics. He wished to take, and did take, Ross as his private secretary; and, though he was to sail the first week in August, it was not till the 8th October that they left Yarmouth.

About the end of September Frere returned from Spain, and I had a great deal of very long and interesting conversation with him during the first week in October.

He states Spain on the eve of a Revolution,—not a *French*, but Spanish Revolution; so very unpopular are the Court and Government, that is to say, the Queen and the Prince of Peace.

I asked him, supposing we had 20,000 disposable men, whether such a force would be equal to produce this *Spanish* Revolution, and to prevent Buonaparte from availing himself of it. Frere did not doubt it. He said the people were more anti-French than ever, and, if they had Ministers in whom they confided, and the King left to himself, he was persuaded, with the sort of force I mentioned, Spain might be saved, and become a close, steady, and most useful friend and ally to England. Frere was much hurt at his being recalled; said he could have effected anything in Spain, and that the ordering him away was as unwise towards the public as unfair towards him. (Allowances must always be made when a man, even an honest and good one, like Frere, argues his own cause.)

In October Fitzharris was returned for Horsham. I was glad to get him a seat without any Treasury assistance.

PARK PLACE, DEC. 6.—I received from Sir G. Rumbold* a copy of the despatch he drew up on his return from France to Lord Harrowby (on Sunday, Nov. 18), by way of narrative of what had passed from the time of his seizure on Thursday, 25th October, till that of his being liberated on Monday, 12th November. " His house was forced, and he himself seized on the 25th October by a detachment of 100 men, commanded by General Frère in person: his papers were *torn* (to use his expression) out of the drawers and cases which contained them, and tied up in one of the sheets of his bed; Sir G. himself being scarcely allowed time to put on his clothes. He was carried to *Harburg*, where he staid all Thursday, the 26th. On the 27th he was sent on to Hanover, under an escort of four officers, some hussars, and gens-d'armes. They reached Hanover at midnight, and found at the gates an order for him to proceed to Neustadt, about twenty-five miles distant, on the great Osnaburgh road. He remained there three days, during which he says he was well-treated, when a M. Hautesauville (Aide-de-Camp to Berthier, and nephew to the Minister at War,) came with orders to conduct him to Paris. Sir George was in one coach with this Aide-de-Camp, and in another his servant (who had been permitted to follow him) with a lieutenant of gens-d'armes and a brigadier. They travelled night and day, accompanied by strong detachments of hussars and gens-d'armes, passing through Overyssell by a circuitous route. When they arrived at Brabant, he was less watched. They made easy journeys, and travelled only by day. On the Friday, 10th November, about noon, they got to Paris. Sir George was set down at a house adjoining to Fouché's

---

* English Chargé des Affaires in Lower Saxony, carried off by Buonaparte's orders as a spy; his history was a corollary on Drake's and Smith's.

(Ministre de Police), inhabited by the police agents, and communicating with Fouché's house. He staid there till six, when he was conveyed to the Temple in a hackney-coach, attended by two police officers." Sir George speaks with great, and *even affected*, praise of the very civil treatment he experienced on the road from his French conductors, which, he says, was that of the *most studied attention, and contrasted singularly with the outrageous measure which occasioned his journey and the captivity in which he was.*

(*I* have on this only to remark, that it was very natural, under the circumstances Sir George was in, to consider every thing short of *ill* treatment as *good* treatment; and what he terms *studied attention* was only allowing him to sleep and eat unmolested, and neither to abuse him nor beat him.) Sir George's first idea on being confined in the Temple was, that he was to *perish by secret means*, (why, I do not discover,) and that, in order to attribute to him *suicide*, they would forge papers which would be declared to have been found amongst his, to demonstrate the *state of despondency* he was under. (*Quære*, Whether he did not betray this " *state* ? ")

This apprehension, he says, was perceived on the following morning, (Sir George does not say *how*,) by the Superintendent of the Temple; and, on Fouché sending for him, he (Fouché), having been made acquainted with these alarms, reproached him for them, and, after lamenting the " *préventions* " (prejudices as Sir George calls them) of England against the French Government, enters into a laborious eulogium of the moral virtues of Buonaparte's Government, and begs Sir George to be without any fears of sinister purposes, and encourages him to take the *food* he chose.

Sir George, after appealing to his (Fouché's) *candour!* whether, after what he had experienced, it was extraordinary in him to entertain such suspicions, and alluding, as Sir George terms it, to " recent and melancholy events,"* and assuring Fouché it was *secret means only*

---

* Duc D'Enghien, Pichegru, Mr. Wright, &c.

he feared, he admits Fouché's assurance unqualifiedly, and says, " *J'abandonne mes soupçons;* " and, as he concluded his confinement in the Temple would be long, he determined to prove his confidence in Fouché's promise, by ordering a good dinner and wine, of which " he ate and drank " (I use his own words) " *heartily.*" Fouché behaved with great civility (says Sir George) ; hoped Sir George was as well taken care of as the nature of his confinement would allow, and said " he might have books, &c." (quære, What does this &c. mean ?), and his servant to wait on him.

The next morning, Sunday, 29th October, Sir George is summoned at nine o'clock to attend Fouché; he finds him dressed and going to St. Cloud. Fouché tells him that the King of Prussia, as Director of the Circle of Lower Saxony, had written a very amicable letter to the Emperor (Buonaparte), " et l'avoit prié de ne pas mettre de suite à l'affaire du Chevalier; " that therefore Buonaparte had determined he should be carried to Cherbourg, and there embarked on board a *Parlamentaire* (a flag of truce) to be conveyed to the first English port they could make. Sir George expressed a wish to go to Berlin. Fouché said he should be happy to effect any arrangement that would be agreeable to Sir George, and, as he was going to St. Cloud, would see and mention it to Buonaparte. Fouché returned in about two hours; said Buonaparte would not consent to his going *at once* to Berlin, whatever he (Sir George) might choose to do afterwards; and that he must go to Cherbourg, and be landed on the coast of England, on Sir George signing an engagement *not to reside within fifty post leagues of the present station of the French armies during the war ;* Fouché adding, " *Cela vaut mieux que le Temple, et vous avez l'alternative.*" Sir George puts in a parenthesis, just before he mentions this proposed signature, that he had obtained, after the first order from M. Fouché, leave to be put on board the first British cruiser they should meet, and this in such a way as to leave it a little ambiguous whether this species of mitigation and favour was not coupled with his signing the paper, which (by

the bye) was written in presence of Sir George by a
scribe of the police, and presented to him by *Desmaret*,
the first secretary in that department. Sir George takes
merit in refusing to sign the words " *Empereur des
Français*," and that Fouché changed them without any
demur to *Gouvernement Français*. His papers, which
he was taught to believe were to be restored to him,
were ultimately refused him. He set off for Cherbourg
at 5 P.M. on Monday, 12th November, accompanied by
a M. Mechem of Buonaparte's Guard, (who again be-
haves with much civility,) as did General La Gorgue at
Valogne. Here he was stopped by La Roche, General
of Division, who, says Sir George, (did not approve his
seeing the works going on at Cherbourg,) but soon after
an order came for him at Valogne to proceed, and he
reached Cherbourg at midnight, on Thursday, 15th November, where he was immediately conducted by General
d'Aubigné to the cutter prepared for him; and on the
16th he fell in with H.M.S. Niobe, on board which
Captain Scott *joyfully* took him under the protection of
the British flag. Sir George arrived in London on Sunday morning, the 18th November.

Sir George begins his letter, which is not ill-written
as to style, with declaring that during the three years he
has been Chargé des Affaires in the Circle of Lower
Saxony, " he has maintained the most scrupulous obser-
vance of the principles and relative duties on which are
founded the sacred rights and privileges of Foreign
Ministers; and that, after the most accurate research into
every part of his own conduct, it is *in vain* he attempts
to penetrate the motives of an action that justice,
morality, and even policy must condemn ;" (of this I
have no doubt;) and Sir George afterwards, as a sort of
apology for speaking so strongly of the *obliging* and
polite conduct of his French keepers, says, he does it, not
only in justice to them, but because (I however cannot
follow his logic) " the knowledge of *these incidents* may
possibly guide Lord Harrowby to conclusions on the
motives of the unexampled occurrence which *he strives
in vain to interpret*."

He says, M. Fouché once hinted at an interrogatory; on which Sir George tells him he will not answer any interrogatory, and goes on by saying, that the *only* motive he could discover on conversing with M. Fouché for the extraordinary measure of his seizure was derived from a forced construction of a passage in Lord Hawkesbury's circular letter, after the affair of Mr. Drake, which, according to the French Government, placed all the English Ministers on the Continent in the situation of spies and conspirators plotting against Buonaparte's life.

Sir George replies very properly to this by adverting to the King's Christian and moral virtues, and to the approved loyalty of the English. Sir George is uneasy, very naturally, on his having signed the paper, and fears its being disapproved. He relates this circumstance awkwardly and confusedly, and wishes to impress Lord Harrowby with the notion that the King of Prussia must be offended that his representation was complied with, in so flagrant a case, only under *an allegation forced* (I use Sir George's words), and which left the public question where it was. This is far-fetched, weak reasoning, not likely to gain admittance anywhere.

The fact is, Sir George was in a very unpleasant and fearful situation ; his apology for *signing* must be found in *this,* and in his very justifiable and natural dread of the consequences of the known iniquity of the persons in whose power he was. *This* induced him to sign; no other good reason *can* be given, for his signing was a breach of duty and of trust ; but if not an *entirely* good reason, it is at least a sufficiently pardonable one to be listened to. Sir George not having proved a *Mutius Scævola* or a *Regulus* is not *his* fault, but the fault of those who placed him in a situation where such stern virtues might be called for.

The satisfaction with which he dwells on the civility of his French gaolers, and his signing the paper, are bad points. It indeed appears to me, that, had he been firm in his refusal, the signing would not have been enforced. It was a trick of Fouché, for Fouché would not have

dared to have altered the words *Empereur des Français*
into *Gouvernement Français* of his own head, and if the
paper had been really worded by or came from Buonaparte.
Had Sir George been *firm*, I feel sure he need not have
signed, and might have recovered his papers (which he
never should have had at a villa so near the French
army); yet his situation was, doubtless, one which entitles
him individually to very great indulgence, though it cannot and ought not to change opinions and *principles*.

DECEMBER 6, 7, & 8.—Mrs. Harcourt at Park Place—
full of anxiety about the issue of the sort of contest prevailing between the King and Prince, relative to Princess Charlotte.　The King wants her established at
Windsor, and educated *as a Queen* that is to be.　The
Prince, from Opposition feelings and advisers, demurs.
Mrs. Harcourt insists that the King is so bent on it, that,
if it does not take place, it will make him ill.

The two factions pulled the Prince different ways—
Ladies Moira, Hutchinson, and Mrs. Fitzherbert were
for his ceding the child to the King—the Duke of Clarence and Devonshire House most violent against it,
and the Prince ever inclines to the faction he saw
last.　In the Devonshire House cabal, Lady Mel-
bourne and Mrs. Fox act conspicuous parts, so that
the alternative for *our future Queen* seems to be
whether *Mrs. Fox* or *Mrs. Fitzherbert* shall have the
ascendancy !

Mrs. Harcourt said the Prince came down to the
King on the 20th November, and they met for the first
time for nearly a year; that, for *one day*, it went off
very well, but that it did not last.

The King sent his plan for the Princess, in writing, to
the Prince, by the Chancellor, on or about the 28th.　It
was not only a very judicious and wise one, but drawn
up most admirably, and full of fine and affectionate feelings.　Yet to this the Prince made such an answer, (also
in writing,) that the Chancellor could not present it to
the King; and, on the 2nd December, he and Mr. Pitt

(who feared the consequences either of producing this answer, or of the delay of any answer,) went down to Windsor, and, in order to avoid affecting the King, said the Prince had misconceived part of His Majesty's letter, and that, before he could answer it at all, they must set him right on these points. In the mean while, they have sent for Lord Moira, and they depend on what he may do.

The sons behave tolerably, the Princesses most perfectly.

The Queen will never receive the King without one of the Princesses being present; never says, in reply, a word ; piques herself on this discreet silence; and, when in London, locks the door of her *white room* (her *boudoir*) against him. The behaviour of the Queen alarms me more than all the others of Mrs. Harcourt's stories; for, if the Queen did not think the King likely to relapse, she would not alter in her manners towards him; and her having altered her manners, proves that she thinks he may relapse.

Mrs. Harcourt seems to think better of Lord Moira's influence, or rather of the manner in which he will employ it, than I do.

Lord Harrowby, by a fall down a staircase in his house in Park Lane, hurt himself most dangerously. He fell on the front part of his head.

As I was well aware of the difficulty Pitt would be under to find an immediate successor to Lord Harrowby, who by his accident was totally disqualified for so laborious an office as that he filled, I commissioned Fitzharris (who was going from Park Place to London) to say to Pitt, that, if he thought I could fill the situation as *locum tenens* till such time as Lord Harrowby recovered, I was quite at his orders for a short time; but that I wished only *to do the business*, and to have nothing whatever to do with the patronage of the Foreign Department.

Pitt received this offer with his accustomed good-nature ; said it was kind, and he would, if circumstances rendered it necessary, avail himself of it. Charles Long wished him to accept it; and it remained in doubt for some days in Pitt's mind. But Lord Harrowby growing worse, and declaring to Pitt, that, even if he did recover, he never should again think of undertaking such anxious employment, and as my offer (and, indeed, intention) was literally to keep this office in Lord Harrowby's hands, whom I thought peculiarly fit for it, the matter dropped, and Lord Mulgrave was named in his stead.

On my coming to town, on 18th January, 1805, I found, from Lord Bathurst, that Pitt had taken my offer just as I knew he would, and considered it as an act of friendship and good-will towards him. He called it to Lord Bathurst " a very liberal and handsome proposal, very unlike those he was used to receive."

Towards the end of 1804, and beginning of 1805, a Negotiation was opened with Addington, through Lord Hawkesbury. Addington was created Lord Sidmouth, and appointed President of the Council; Lord Buckinghamshire to the Duchy, in room of Lord Mulgrave. This party acted with Pitt during four or five months, when Addington resigned in a pet, because some of his friends, particularly Bond Hopkins, were not given Office. Pitt intended and promised to do it soon, but Addington wanted it immediately.

In April and May, Whitbread brought forward his attack on Lord Melville, founded on a part of the report from the Commissioners appointed to inquire into the Management of the Navy.

The object evidently was political; but unfortunately it came out on investigation, that Lord Melville, either through carelessness or too great confidence in the Deputy Treasurer of the Navy (*Trotter*), had manifestly violated a clause in an Act of Parliament; and this was so warmly taken up by the country gentlemen, and so eagerly and adroitly enforced by Opposition, that Whitbread's measure was carried, and followed up by an Impeachment.* Pitt lost several questions, and was deserted by the Addingtonites. This, however, would not have produced the breach; but, as Bond Hopkins was the mover of a question adverse to Pitt, Pitt could not, and would not, give him an office just at this moment; and on this Addington broke with him.

The transactions relative to Lord Melville exceeded in party spirit and savage feeling all that I ever recollect in this country. Admitting his guilt to its full extent (which I am far from doing), what can be said to the huzzas and shouts of the House of Commons upon his condemnation; Sir Thomas Mostyn giving a *view-hollo,* and a *" We have killed the Fox !"* What would these very men have said to the Judges and Jury, had they behaved thus at the sentence of the most bloodthirsty felon? Disgraceful, and un-English!

When he went to the King, Addington very foolishly offered His Majesty *the key* of the Council-box. " You must not give it to me," said the King, rather offended, " but to Lord Hawkesbury." " Sir," replied Addington, " I am not on speaking terms with Lord Hawkesbury." (They had quarrelled on his [Addington's] going out.) " This is nothing to me," said the King, and would have ended the audience; but he almost forced His Majesty to listen to him for an hour, and so fatigued and displeased him, that, when the King returned to his family, (it passed at Windsor,) he said, " That *   *   * has been plaguing me to death!"

In the course of the summer, Addington had great family misfortunes, and he himself was at death's door with a liver complaint. Pitt very kindly called on him, and forgot all animosity.

During the whole of this year, Pitt was negotiating his great Alliances with Russia and Austria, a very

* On the 6th of April Mr. Whitbread moved a set of resolutions against Lord Melville. The House divided, 216 to 216, and the Speaker gave the casting vote for Mr. Whitbread. On the 11th of June Mr. Whitbread moved that Lord Melville should be impeached. This was lost; but an amendment for " a criminal prosecution " was carried by Mr. Bond Hopkins The question for his impeachment was, however, passed on the 25th of June.

exact account of which is to be found in my correspondence.*

Never was any measure (as far as human foresight
can go) better combined, or better negotiated. Its
failure was solely in the execution; and, for this, either
the precipitancy of Austria herself, or the treachery
and imbecility of her Commanders, are *solely* responsible.

If any blame attached to us, it is either the not re-
calling or instructing Sir A. Paget, who knew nothing
till the whole was concluded. Had he been kept informed, we should probably have been acquainted with
the military plans of Austria in time to alter them,
and to prevent the disasters which followed.

Pitt, whom I saw in Downing Street on the 26th of
September, gave me a most minute and clear account of
this whole measure, and was very justly sanguine as to
its result. As his communication was precisely what
appears in my correspondence, it is useless to repeat it.

I DINED with Pitt on 30th October, at Sturges
Bourne's, and on 2nd November at his own house.
Though the rumours of Mack's surrender of his army at
Ulm had come in so many shapes as to give it but too
much the appearance of truth, Pitt discredited it.† I
sat next to him each day, and I clearly perceived he
disbelieved it more from the *dread* of its being true,
than from any well-grounded cause. He, particularly
on the 2nd, on my still expressing my fears, almost pee-
vishly said, " Don't believe a word of it, it is all a
fiction," and in so loud a voice as to be heard by all
who were near us. But on Sunday, 3rd November,
he and Lord Mulgrave came to me in Spring Gardens
about one o'clock with a Dutch newspaper, in which

* I have not space for these papers.
† Napoleon, having abandoned his project of invading England, had
marched upon Vienna, and got between that city and General Mack's army,
which surrendered at Ulm.

the capitulation of Ulm was inserted at full length. As they neither of them understood Dutch, and as all the offices were empty, they came to me to translate it, which I did as well as I could; and I observed but too clearly 'the effect it had on Pitt, though he did his utmost to conceal it. *This was the last time I saw him.* He promised me to come for a few days to Park Place on his return from Bath, where he was then going, but was too ill to keep his word. This visit has left an *indelible impression* on my mind, as his manner and look were not *his own*, and gave me, in spite of myself, a foreboding of the loss with which we were threatened.

CANNING, whom I had not seen for months, expressed a wish to see me; he came to me on the 1st November, talked of the times and events sensibly. I urged the necessity of *our* taking a more forward place in these foreign transactions, and not appearing in them simply as pay-masters, as *milord pot au feu.* He asked me how this could be. I said, by an " *exposé*," or manifesto: that, from the beginning of this war (in 1802), nothing of the kind had appeared, and we suffered not only the Powers friendly to us to say what they pleased, and take all the merit on themselves, but our enemies to get complete possession of the public ear, *even in England,* by letting all their trash and bulletins stand at the head of all our newspapers, as well ministerial ones as others. To this he assented, and it was agreed that I should put the materials together, and he draw up such a paper; and that, for this purpose, I should pass a day with him at South Hill (his house in the country); but unforeseen and disastrous events destroyed this plan, and made the writing of such a paper impossible.

ON the 7th November, the news of the great Naval Victory off Cape Trafalgar, and of the death of Nelson, arrived.* A few days after, Pitt made quite a tri-

* The following memorandum appeared to me apposite. " On the

umphal entry on Lord Mayor's Day into the City, and was in apparent high spirits at dinner.

The first impression was not joy, for Nelson fell! —the hero, who was regretted with all the tenderness of gratitude, and all the more selfish feeling that the bulwark of England was gone; and that this circumstance would be equivalent to Buonaparte for the loss of his fleet.

He added to genius, valour, and energy, the singular power of electrifying all within his atmosphere, and making them only minor constellations to this most luminous planet. The confidence he inspired in his followers, and the terror of his name to our enemies, are what make his loss an irreparable one. Others may be great in many points; nay, admit that another, like himself, might appear again amongst the disciples he has formed, there would yet be wanting *all he had done*, and all the *circumstances* of the times in which he *did* these wondrous deeds. Every victory was greater than the last. Every additional difficulty seemed only to bring out some new proof of the combination and powers of his mind, as well as the invincible force of his arms; and, had he survived this last victory, the next and the next would have still surpassed each other. *All this is sorrow for ourselves;* but still more deeply do I regret that *he* cannot see the *effect* his death produced. Not one individual who felt *joy* at this victory so well-timed and so complete, but first had an *instinctive* feeling of *sorrow*, not *selfish sorrow*, (for it came before the reflection of the *consequences* of his loss to us,) but the sorrow of affection and gratitude for what he *had*

receipt of the news of the memorable battle of Trafalgar (some day in November, 1805), I happened to dine with Pitt, and it was naturally the engrossing subject of our conversation. I shall *never forget* the eloquent manner in which he described his conflicting feelings, when roused in the night to read Collingwood's despatches. Pitt observed, that he had been called up at various hours in his eventful life by the arrival of news of various hues; but that whether good or bad he could always lay his head on his pillow and sink into sound sleep again. On *this occasion*, however, the great event announced brought with it so much to weep over, as well as to rejoice at, that he could not calm his thoughts, but at length got up, though it was three in the morning."—*Lord Fitzharris' Note Book, 1805.*

done for us; and the first regret was, that *he* who did the deed should be deprived of the enjoyment which he above all other men, from his character, would have derived from its effects.

Could he have lived but long enough to have known that *no victory*, not even *his victories*, could weigh in the hearts of Englishmen against his most precious life, it would have been some consolation. I never saw so little public joy. The illumination seemed dim, and, as it were, half clouded, by the desire of expressing the mixture of contending feelings; every common person in the streets speaking *first* of their sorrow for *him*, and *then* of the victory.

Collingwood's letter (which is admirable) proves that it was his art to make all under him love him, and own his superiority without a ray of jealousy. He never was a *party man* himself, and there never was a party in his fleets. All were governed by *one mind*, and this made them invincible. He was a true patriot, which is nearly as rare a character as to be the hero he was. He had the arm and spirit of chivalry, and he was the most loyal subject; living and dying for his country, without reference to those who held the helm under that Sovereign to whom, next to her, he considered himself bound. This completes a character which cannot, I fear, appear again in *our time*.

_____

On the 3rd December I went to Canning's at South Hill. Frere and Sturges Bourne (Secretary to the Treasury) there. Our news was *then* rather favourable. Berlin had declared *for* the Coalition—a *voluntary* declaration; pretending to be violently displeased and angry at Buonaparte having violated its territory, by marching his troops through the Margraviates in Franconia, and holding out pompous conditions of peace or war to Buonaparte as an alternative.

Lord Harrowby, who on this intelligence was sent with Hammond to accompany him to Berlin, writes however rather *discouragingly*, and his presentiments were but too true.

Canning told me in confidence, Pitt intended to put him and Charles Yorke with the Board of Controul into the Cabinet, on the opening of the Session. That all attempts to gain over the Grenvilles had failed through the influence of Tom Grenville, who would not hear of a separation from Fox; that, therefore, nothing remained but for Pitt to strengthen his Administration from his own stock; and, if anything like success *should* happen on the Continent, he would certainly withstand all the efforts of Opposition.

A sort of success *then* was not unreasonably expected; and, to give time to wait the issue, I strongly recommended the putting off the meeting of Parliament as long as possible.

Bourne argued against this the extreme want of money, and the necessity in such case of issuing bills at three months' date. He, however, admitted the wisdom of the measure; the more necessary, he said, from the state of Pitt's health, about which he was extremely uneasy.

Canning was of the same opinion.

BOURNE returned with me on the 5th December, 1805, to Park Place ; and soon after the farther prorogation of Parliament, first to the 15th, then to the 22nd January, 1806, was determined on. On the 7th or 8th December, Pitt went to Bath. The first effect of the waters was, to produce a fit of the gout—but not a salutary one; it was attended with great pain, and produced excessive weakness, and a total debility of digestion. I intended to visit him at Bath about Christmas, and wrote to him to this effect; but he was then too unwell to leave his house, or see even those he was in the habit of being with.

At the worst period of his illness, the first rumours of the Battle of Austerlitz and subsequent Armistice reached us. They came through France, and were expressive of complete victory to them, and destruction to the Russians. At the same time, (as if meant to make the truth still more painful,) there came such well-authenticated accounts from Hambro', Berlin, &c., that the Russians had rallied the day after the battle, and regained all they had lost, that notwithstanding Sir A. Paget's despatches, and the almost positive evidence from Holland, people's hopes were kept alive, particularly Pitt's; and when a few days afterwards, I believe about the end of December, Lord Castlereagh went to Bath to communicate to him the event, and to confirm all the French reports, it struck Pitt so deeply, and found him in such an enfeebled state, that he certainly *never recovered it*.

———————

PARK PLACE, JAN. 8, 1806—(the day after Lord Nelson's funeral) Lord Auckland and his family came here.

I distinctly saw his leanings, and augured from them that *he* thought Pitt's Ministry, if not his life, drawing towards its close. I therefore avoided all political discussion with him, contenting myself by flatly contradicting him when he asserted that nothing was ever so ill-managed or so ill-conducted as the Foreign Alliances. His letter, and my answer on this point, I have preserved.

On the 10th January, Sir W. Farquhar, who had been with Pitt during ten days at Bath, passed through Park Place on his way from Reading to Salt Hill; he had left Pitt, whom he was attending on the road, in bed at Reading, and was to join him at Salt Hill. Sir Walter said, Pitt was emaciated so as not to be known, and nothing could save him but *complete and entire rest*; that any exertion, mental or bodily, would infallibly kill him: and I manifestly perceived from Sir Walter's manner and feelings (for he was sincerely attached to Pitt), that he thought him in the greatest danger; and from this moment, knowing as I did Pitt's exhausted constitution, I entertained no hopes of his recovery. I entreated Sir Walter, in the most earnest way, not to conceal from Pitt what he thought and what he had just said to me; to urge him to *resign* immediately; not to go to his own house at Putney, where he necessarily *must* see official people, but to some quiet retired place,—to this (Park Place, if he liked it); if not, to the Wilderness (Lord Camden's), or to Lord Carrington's. All this Sir W. said he would do, and, I do not doubt, did.

On the 14th January I went to London, and dined that day with Lord Mulgrave. I found him alone; he gave no hopes of Pitt, and as little of the Continent. Woronzow and Count Stroganoff (whom I knew at Petersburg) dined there; also the Duke of Montrose, Lord Hawkesbury, and Ward. Their language was that of Ministers going out. Stroganoff, who is a favourite of the Emperor, and friend of Czartorinski, sent over here to cement the alliance, and to decide on what is to be done. (He comes at a most untimely moment.)

All this week unusual anxiety prevailed with respect to Pitt: sometimes faint hopes were given; and even so late as the 20th he was pronounced to be in so little immediate danger, that his usual Parliamentary dinner, his Birthday dinner, had taken place the day before the meeting of Parliament, at his house.

On Wednesday morning, the 23rd, Sturges Bourne called on me about ten o'clock to say Pitt died at a quarter past four that morning at Putney. It appeared that he himself considered his illness as mortal immediately after he got to Putney; for, on Monday the 12th, when he saw for the last time Lord Castlereagh and Lord Hawkesbury, (though each separately and but for a short time, and though both avoided every possible subject which could distress him,) he said, after they were gone, to the Bishop of Lincoln, " I feel something here," putting his hands on his stomach, " that reminds me I never shall recover; not cold, but a general giving way." On Tuesday the 13th he saw Lord Wellesley, who was just returned from India. Lord Wellesley kept clear of all business; but even common conversation with an old friend long absent overcame Pitt, and he fainted away before Lord Wellesley left the room. From all I can learn, this was the last *official* friend he saw.   The two Stanhopes, the Bishop of Lincoln, and occasionally Lady Hester Stanhope, his niece, (for he would not allow her *always* to be at Putney,) were with him; and Sir W. Farquhar told me that he preserved his faculties till within twelve or fourteen hours of his death, which came on *rapidly*, and that Pitt died of *old age* at forty-six, as much as if he had been ninety.

Lady Malmesbury, who saw Sir W. Farquhar three days after Pitt's death, and received from him an account of his last hours, says, that almost the last words he spoke intelligibly were these, to himself, and more than once repeated, " Oh, what times! Oh, my country!"

The death of no individual ever left so wide a gap in the world—none ever so materially affected the state of the general welfare—none ever was more sincerely and deeply lamented, not only by private friends, but by numberless individuals who honoured his worth, and knew the value of his character and his talents.*

* The death of Pitt, at a moment when it must have appeared to him that all his vast combinations and his gigantic efforts to oppose Napoleon had failed, is one of the saddest lessons which history offers to human ambition.   This great and true *English* Minister died in the moment of our utmost political adversity and danger, with nothing to console him but the " Mens conscia recti."

The following Notices of Mr. Pitt are from my father's Note Book :—

The battle of Austerlitz and its consequences, which he saw in their true light, greatly disappointed and depressed him, and certainly rather accelerated his end.   I well remember walking round St. James's Park with him in November, 1805.   He was naturally of a sanguine disposition.   His plans were vast and comprehensive, and held out to his powerful mind the hope of establishing a European Confederacy, that should crush French ascendancy. When *that battle* was fought, the last ray of hope was so dimmed as to leave him without the possible expectation of seeing the fulfilment of that for which he had so long, so strenuously, and so successfully exerted himself, and which he felt (if ever accomplished) must be brought about by other hands than his.   He resigned himself to the will of that Providence to whom he had always looked up, as well in the days of victory as in the hour of peril, and calmly awaited that last call to which we must all respond, with the true spirit of a Christian, and felt that his sand had too nearly run out for him to think any longer of worldly matters.   He went to Bath, and only returned to Wimbledon (where he had a villa) to *die* there.

Before I take my leave, I must mention an anecdote or two of him, as they now occur to me.   I supped with Pitt after the debate on the Catholic Question, in which *Grattan* first appeared in the British House of Commons, whose action was of so grotesque a character as a Speaker (that of a *Mower*), and his pronunciation so singular (that of an *Italian*), that his fate hung on

JANUARY 22.—On the day of Mr. Pitt's death I was with the Duke of York. He was deeply affected by the event, but *would* not consider it as a loss which necessarily must break up the Administration. I found him, contrary to his usual good-humour, peevish and angered. When I represented to him how perfectly impossible it was, when we looked to the string of adverse incidents which had occurred abroad, and which had

a straw. *Five minutes* later, and the House would have been in a roar of laughter, when he burst forth into one of his flowery but at the same time strikingly eloquent periods, and retrieved the day; leaving himself, however, with fewer admirers than he had possessed in the Legislative Assembly of his native country. Pitt was very much struck with him ; saw the danger he had incurred of failure ; with his usual kind-heartedness expressed pleasure at his narrow escape, for such he deemed it, and admiration of Grattan's great, but singular, display of talent in that peculiar style of oratory (which, however, Pitt did not approve of). He gave us some specimens of passages in Grattan's speech, in which the correctness of Pitt's powers of imitation, both as regarded the tone and action of the speaker, was very striking, but almost less so than the display that it afforded us of the capability of his retentive memory. *Whole sentences* to our ears appeared to be repeated *verbatim*, and to have been conveyed without the loss of even an *article* from St. Stephen's to Downing Street.

I have ever thought that an *aiding cause* of Pitt's death, certainly one that tended to *shorten* his existence, was the result of the proceedings against his old friend and colleague, Lord Melville. I sat wedged close to Pitt himself the night when we were 216 to 216; and the Speaker, Abbott, (after looking as white as a sheet, and pausing for ten minutes,) gave the casting vote *against* us. Pitt immediately put on the little cocked hat that he was in the habit of wearing when dressed for the evening, and jammed it deeply over his forehead, and I distinctly saw the *tears trickling down his cheeks*. We had overheard one or two, such as Colonel Wardle (of notorious memory), say, they would see " *how Billy looked after it.*" A few young ardent followers of Pitt, with myself, locked their arms together, and formed a circle, in which he moved, I believe, *unconsciously* out of the House ; and neither the Colonel nor his friends could approach him.

I met Pitt at Lord Bathurst's in Gloucestershire, where he passed some days. We went to church at Cirencester. In discoursing afterwards on the beauties of our Liturgy, he selected the *Thanksgiving Prayer* as one particularly impressive and comprehensive. The one, " In Time of War and Tumults," he thought admirably well drawn up, as well as that for the Parliament ; but added, with respect to the first of the two, that he never in hearing it could divest himself of the analogy between " Abate their pride," assuage their malice," and the line in the song of " God save the King,' " Confound their politics, frustrate their knavish tricks." I observed, that Pitt was constantly taking down and quoting from *Lucan*, of which author he appeared to be extremely fond. Nothing could be more playful, and at the same time more instructive, than Pitt's conversation, on a variety of subjects, while sitting in the Library at Cirencester. You never would have guessed that the man before you was Prime Minister of the country, and one of the greatest that ever filled that situation. His style and manner were quite those of an *accomplished idler.—Lord Fitzharris's Note Book,* 1806.

operated on the public mind in a way (however unjustly) as misfortunes owing to the King's Ministers, and that so powerfully, that I felt convinced, even *with Mr. Pitt alive* and in possession of all his powers, he could not have stood—and that without him, it was utterly out of the question for the remainder of the Cabinet to carry on the King's business—the Duke was impatient with me, and even imperious; but I persisted, and the next day sent him the substance of what I had said, which is here annexed:—

" That the present Administration cannot stand, unless it acquires an accession of abilities and consequence equal to that which it has lost.

" But no such abilities or consequence can be found in any one individual.

" That to attempt to carry on the business of the country at a moment like this, by patching up an Administration, would be putting its interests and safety in the most imminent danger.

" That to this paramount consideration, a minor one, equally true, may be added; that such a Ministry could not last, and that the framers and advisers of it would only postpone the evil they try to avoid, and, by postponing, increase it.

" That however painful it might be to His Majesty to admit into his Councils persons disagreeable to him, yet this feeling would be more sensibly felt when such persons could and *would force* themselves upon him.

" That a strong and efficient Administration ever must find its account in endeavouring to obtain the favour and good-will of the Crown; and the Crown in giving its support and confidence to such an Administration would enjoy the fullest and most unmolested exercise of its prerogatives.

" That wavering or delay in forming a new Administration would be equally fatal with an attempt to patch up this.

" It would palsy the country, and afford the most dangerous opportunity to Buonaparte for carrying into execution his designs on it.

" Every idea of *compromise* or *bargain* with a new Government is absurd; Opposition is too strong to listen to any; and such is the present hazardous state of the country that they *must*, when in office, employ all their thoughts and talents in the defence of it.

" If they force themselves in, the Prince of Wales will be a greater personage than the King, for he already considers himself as the head of the party; and, if the King rejects them, as such they *must* consider and treat him.

" If they are admitted into power willingly, it is reasonable to suppose that on every account they will prefer the countenance of the King, who is beloved by his subjects, and whose character stands high.

" That, as far as relates to the Duke of York's personal interest, there can be little doubt, if the King and his Ministers were at variance, that he could expect no favours; while, on the contrary, a Ministry desirous of pleasing the King would naturally incline to gratify his wishes, whom they knew to be the King's favourite."

FEBRUARY 1.—His Royal Highness was cold with me for several days; but when he found my opinion to be the prevalent one, and even that of the King himself, he very handsomely gave way; and, having sent for me, by a fair and honest avowal of his mistake, left me more satisfied with him than before.   The new Ministry was appointed a few days after this.

Lord Grenville and Fox were its two leaders, and their respective adherents and friends made up the Cabinet.*

The Prince of Wales went most heartily and *unbecomingly* with them, and lowered his dignity by soliciting office and places for his dependants, and by degrading himself into the size of a common party leader.

From this moment I withdrew entirely from official men, my determination being to act as if Mr. Pitt was alive, and to endeavour to regulate my political conduct,

* This Administration went by the name of " All the Talents."

and that of those I influenced, on what I supposed would be his, were he still in existence, whether in or out of office.

I told this to Lords Bathurst and Camden on the 27th January, considering these two as more *personally*, and less politically, attached to him, than any one else, not excepting Canning himself.

On the 4th February, Lord Carrington came to me in consequence of my having canvassed him for his interest at Cambridge University for Lord Palmerston. This he promised me in the handsomest manner; but I was surprised, when I lamented Mr. Pitt's death, and spoke of the wisdom and propriety of his friends' acting together, and in conformity to his doctrines and principles—to find Lord Carrington lukewarm on the subject. He said he conceived "*we* were all *now* free to act as we pleased. All bond of union was dissolved; no obligation remained with any one to abide by a party which had lost its leader, *and with its leader every thing.*" He said this in so very positive a way, that I contented myself with saying, my sentiments were directly contrary to his, but that it was not for me to dispute with him on a point rather of feeling than of party. Lord Carrington was profuse in his lamentations on the death of Pitt, and equally so in his profession of friendship and gratitude to him, and respect for his memory; and, as a proof, he instanced his wish that the part of Mr. Pitt's debts arising from a loan his friends contributed to raise for him in 1800 should not be produced when the items of them were laid before the House. (N.B. The House had voted a public funeral, and to pay Mr. Pitt's debts immediately after his death, which Windham (strange to say) opposed, giving as a motive that no public funeral had been decreed to Burke.) Lord Carrington, however, said he was overruled by the Bishop of Lincoln, Prettyman,* (who had been Pitt's private tutor at Cambridge,) who assured him it was one of Pitt's last dying requests that the six friends who had advanced him certain sums should be repaid. (They

* Formerly Mr. Pitt's tutor, and afterwards Bishop of Winchester.

were Lords Bathurst and Carrington, Steele, Bishop of Lincoln, and two others, and who at the time never would take any acknowledgment, or ever expected to be repaid.) This assertion of the Bishop of Lincoln, Lord Carrington said, shut his mouth; and the debt was laid before the House, which raised his (Pitt's) debts to 43,000*l.**

Ministers went on quietly, and with a very large majority, the whole year of 1806. In June an idea was suggested to make a push at them before the Recess; and I had several conversations with Canning, and one with Perceval on the subject, and constant ones with the Duke of Portland, who, by having undergone an operation for the stone, was wonderfully recovered.

The inclosed letter to Canning will explain what the idea was: it however came to nothing.

Spring Gardens, Saturday, 3 P.M., June 7th, 1807.

MY DEAR CANNING,—Just after you left me I met the Duke of York, who carried me with him to the Horse-Guards; and although he did not name Lord Chatham, it is evident that what he said to me, and which on meeting me he had expressed a wish to do, was the substance of what passed between them yesterday morning.

The Duke considers the duration of the present Government as very doubtful, and that if it does last it will be attended with serious misfortunes to the country. That it was greatly to be desired that Mr. Pitt's friends should unite *under a chief.* That they should recollect what *he* did in 1783 (*mark this*), and not be discouraged by appearances of numbers against them, *in the first instance.*

That the finding a leader was difficult, as there were amongst them as they now stood too many persons of the same rank, and nearly the same political considera-

---

* The present Lord Carrington informed me that his father had never received this debt of Mr. Pitt, and that the Bishop of Lincoln took the Minister's Library in lieu of the sum which he had lent to his illustrious pupil.

tion. That neither the Dukes of Rutland nor Beaufort would do. The Duke of Portland *ought* to be the man, but he was fearful his health was not equal to it.

This, as you perceive, opened the whole subject at once, and it gave me great pleasure to find that on every point we mentioned this morning the Duke of York's opinions and wishes concurred most entirely with ours. He, of his own accord, and unprovoked by me, urged the necessity of an early attempt *before the Recess*, and reasoned so exactly as you did on that particular subject, that there can be no doubt of the way in which he would use his influence in a certain quarter, if a fair opportunity offered.

On my asking him if he had seen the Duke of Portland, he said he had, either yesterday or the day before, and that he thought him wonderfully recovered; but repeated his apprehensions of his not being sufficiently so as to undertake the lead of a strong Administration.

I asked him if he had at all touched on this point to the Duke: he said " No." I replied I was sorry for it, as I was persuaded one word from him would go a great way. " I am to see him again to-day," said the Duke of York, " at *one*, and, if you think it advisable, will then mention it to him."

I answered, His Royal Highness was a much better judge whether the doing of it would (*if known*) be approved at Windsor, and that I never could wish him to take any step which might commit him there. " I will run that risk," said the Duke laughingly.

Lord Grenville was not named, and I felt no necessity for naming him. The Duke requested secrecy as far as he was concerned, and said I should hear from him when he returned to London, which would be about Thursday or Friday next.

I thought you would like to hear all this, as parts of it are very cheering.

Ever most affectionately yours, MALMESBURY.

Towards the end of October, the Duke of Portland wrote me word of the intended dissolution of Parliament.

I went immediately to Bulstrode. It was a question whether it would be advisable to make an attempt at this moment to see the King. Lord Camden consulted; but it was both his and my opinion that it would be of no avail, as the King had been, four or five days previous to the measure of dissolution, to visit the Duke at Bulstrode, and had cautiously avoided touching on any public subject whatever, and only by implication referred to what was passing in his mind, by saying twice, " It is a sad thing, Duke of Portland, to have too good a memory." The King even would not admit the Duke of Portland when he went the next day to Windsor to return thanks for this visit, neither would the Queen see Lady Mary Bentinck. There were such manifest indications that the King was inaccessible, either from not thinking the matter ripe, or from apathy and indifference, that there could be no hesitation in advising against all forward movements, and this advice was followed.

About this time happened the battle of Auerstadt, or Jena, and the total overthrow of the King of Prussia.*

A little before, and during it, Fox had opened a Negotiation for peace, which began by a private correspondence between him and Talleyrand, continued by his appointing Lord Yarmouth (then a prisoner at Verdun) as a negotiator, and ended by his sending Lord Lauderdale to Paris. Lord Lauderdale acted well, and with spirit; and proved, what I had ascertained at Paris and Lisle in 1796 and 1797, that, though revolutionary France was ever ready to listen to pacific Negotiation, it never meant, and probably never will mean, to conclude a just and equitable peace. *That of Amiens was not so : it was scarce an armed truce or cessation of hostilities.*

On the 13th September, 1806, after having been several times tapped for a dropsy, Fox died at Chiswick House. His death seemed from the time he took Office

----

* Fought on the 14th October, 1806. The Duke of Brunswick, who commanded the Prussian army, was mortally wounded, and died 10th November, aged seventy-two.

to be a near event; and the assiduity and diligence with which he attended both his Official and Parliamentary duties, for he did so till even the last days of his existence, hastened the event.   No country within the short space of six months ever lost two such able statesmen as Pitt and Fox, or ever at a more important moment;—a loss less felt at the instant than it will be some time hence.   They left no equal in their line, and after such superiority the *nation* will not be contented with moderate abilities.   Fox lived long enough to be regretted by all, as he certainly acted his part most ably and honourably from the time he took Office.

Lord Thurlow died on the 12th, also an able man, but from temper and character never a useful friend to the Government he served with.

In November, and during the elections, Lord Grenville made several attempts to disunite Pitt's friends; he offered splendidly to Canning, and to any three or four friends he would name.   Lord Wellesley was the intermediary, and negotiated ably; but Canning remained steady, and from *principle*.

Dr. Fellowes, who lately travelled round Spain to investigate the causes of the yellow fever, saw Gravina (the Spanish Admiral at Trafalgar) lying wounded at Cadiz, a few days before his death.   He had refused to have his arm amputated.   He told Dr. Fellowes, " I am a dying man, but I hope and trust that I am going to join the greatest hero the world almost ever produced."   Dr. Fellowes related this himself to Lady Malmesbury.

Buonaparte's progress in Germany and Poland caused at this moment great alarm; but Ministers took no measures to assist Russia, except sending Lord Hutchinson to the Prussian army, and the Marquis of Douglas to Petersburg.   Adair was not quite the size for Vienna, but he was clever, and used to business.   Lord Hutchinson took quite a *staff* with him; and it was easy to foresee, from the cast of his temper, and his general turn to

admire Buonaparte, that he will effect no good purpose.
Luckily a right spirit seems to prevail in Russia, and
the Russian army under Beningsen is the first that has
resisted and checked the French. Things remained in
this state, with no business in Parliament (except the
new plan of Finance), and no reference to Foreign Politics, till the middle of February, 1807, when a very rash
and unwise attempt of Lords Grenville and Howick
worked in its consequences the downfall of their Administration; and on this it is necessary for me to speak
with detail, as I was very much interested and somewhat concerned in this very important measure.

I HAVE omitted to insert a very singular transaction
relative to the Princess of Wales, the end of which was
to destroy at least her fame, if not to take away her life.
A very minute and circumstantial detail of it will be
found in a portfolio by itself. I took a very large share
in it, and what I have noted down may be considered as
most authentic.*

THE famous battle of Auerstadt, or Jena, had been
fought on 14th October. Never was any one battle so
decisive, since it went to the entire overthrow of the
Prussian monarchy. But why such a battle was lost,
and why its consequences extended so far, is enveloped
in a mystery as yet impossible to unveil.

I never could consider the Prussian army as one to be
depended on, the moment Frederic the Great was dead.
I was witness to what it was during his life, and its ex-
ploits in the Seven Years' War gave convincing proofs of
its excellence. But the six months I was with the Prussian army in 1794, when it was in the neighbourhood of

---

* I do not think it expedient to publish these papers. I shall content
myself by saying that they refer to the attempt to fix a charge of adultery
on the Princess, which could not be proved; and that the part that Lord
Malmesbury took in advising Her Royal Highness in these difficult circumstances was very useful to her cause, and displays the most generous
feelings, combined with judgment and a great knowledge of the world.
Unhappily, this narrow escape brought no lesson with it to the Princess.

Mentz and Lauter, I was also witness to its intrigues, its inactivity, its reluctance to fight, though commanded by Möllendorf, who himself also evinced the same character as his army, and fixed in my mind the opinion I had always entertained,—that the military defence of Prussia was like its geographical position, a sort of *rope of sand*, which would fall to pieces when brought into action, or vigorously opposed. The two succeeding Kings to Frederic hastened the dissolution of this baseless fabric. Frederic Guillaume, though brave, was enervated by debauchery; and though with good sense, and not a bad heart, from total negligence in his education, from the severity with which his Uncle treated him to the last, and from mixing with the lowest and most profligate society, was without any of those substantive virtues necessary to govern so helpless a kingdom as that over which he reigned. He exhausted the public treasure, and, except the first two years of his reign, every act and measure of his went to shake or weaken the monarchy.

His son, also Frederic Guillaume, began by shedding tears, *not* for the loss of his father, but from the labour and trouble a Crown brought with it; and this, not from philosophy, but from an indolent, sleepy, selfish, torpid mind. He is wilful and obstinate, yet without a system or opinion; he thinks he governs and does the business himself, because he has four private secretaries (like his great-uncle), yet he is governed and betrayed by his Ministers. He courted France servilely, and went all the length of political immorality with Buonaparte, when he might have resisted him most effectually; and he went to war with him when he had no friend, no ally, and when his chance of success was nearly out of the question.

The battle of Auerstadt, or Jena, proved this. His army, excellent on the parade, was far from it on the field; his Council of War were of as many opinions as there were Members, and the magazines were burnt in the midst of their army, when they thought the enemy far removed from their front; and Buonaparte was opposite to them, when they were *sure* he was still at Paris.

In all this there was certainly much treachery, but much more *nigauderie* and want of common military prudence and foresight. No measures had been prepared for defeat—no "*point de réunion*" determined; and, after the defeat, all that remained of the army was hunted down and captured, because each division took a different route, and the King himself escaped, or rather fled, without one hundred men assembled round him.

The Duke of Brunswick, who died in consequence of his wound, is of course (*being dead*) said to be the planner of this battle, and the cause of its loss.

This *I* do not credit; as, whatever faults he had, his military science and personal courage were most extraordinary. But he, too, was betrayed. He (very foolishly at his age) kept a French actress. Montjoy, his aide-de-camp, procured her for him. She attended him to the camp. Montjoy never left his person; he was close to him when he was shot, which was by a Jäger *on foot*, who presented his carabine so close, that the ball went in under the left eye (the Duke was on horseback), and came out above the right, quite through the upper part of the nose. Yet the Duke was not in the *French mêlée;* and how any *enemy* could be so near him, surrounded as he was by his staff, is not easy to decide, unless we suppose that Montjoy's brother, who was Grand Veneur to Prince Max, the pretended King of Bavaria, and who was with Buonaparte, knew exactly where the Duke of Brunswick was to be found, and, by a connivance with Montjoy, produced the event. This I cannot pretend to ascertain, but I cannot either avoid having my misgivings.

SOME time about the middle of February, 1807, it became very notorious that it was in the contemplation of Ministers to introduce, in some shape or other, measures leading to the Catholic Emancipation; and in the several interviews I had with Lord Eldon, and particularly in conversing with the Duke of Portland (which I did daily), it was the serious and very anxious subject of our thoughts.

We were totally in the dark as to what was going on; it had indeed transpired that the intention actually existed in the minds of Lord Grenville and Lord Howick, and that it was opposed, but as we understood feebly, by Lords Sidmouth and Ellenborough; and the former was even quoted on good authority as having said, that His Majesty was grown indifferent respecting business, and that in that quarter the measure would probably not meet the resistance every attempt of this kind had hitherto done. This intelligence, which, from the channel it came from, we were inclined to credit, was very distressing, as it went to prove that which was so much to be dreaded from what we knew to have been the King's conduct on the Princess's business, " that His Majesty was growing every day more and more apathetic and insensible to what was passing, and appearing to entertain no other wish than to pass the remainder of his days in rest and quiet."

I left town on the 2nd of March with things thus circumstanced; on my return on the 9th I found the alarms amongst our friends increased, and that a bill was actually preparing, evidently as a sort of preliminary step to other bills still more explicit to take off the restrictions now existing against the Catholics. The Bill in the first instance was stated to be one that had no other object in view than to give the Irish Catholics, serving in England, the same security against the pains and penalty of the law against Popery as they enjoyed in Ireland by the Bill of 1793; which bill enabled them to hold Commissions in the Army, as far as the rank of Colonels.

The Union made these regiments liable to serve in England and Scotland, and the Act as it now stood (they said) gave them security in Ireland only. This appeared a just measure if pursued, and one not to be opposed; although Perceval, Lord Eldon, and other eminent lawyers deemed it to be perfectly unnecessary, not only because no attempt had been made to vex or disturb the Irish Catholics, but because they considered that they (from the Spirit of the Union) actually did enjoy the security in England which had been given them in Ireland.

To this Bill the King did not object; and in this shape it first appeared in the House of Commons, as a clause tacked to the Mutiny Bill, of which it was naturally to make a part.   But Ministers, finding this go down with scarce any remark made upon it, thought they might go a step further; they withdrew the clause to the Mutiny Bill, and substituted in its room a Bill which, by one stride, gave to the Catholics in every part of His Majesty's dominions the privilege of entering into the Army or Navy, of holding *any* rank in either, and of being allowed to attend their own places of worship.   This gave rise to a very spirited debate, in which Perceval, with great force and ability, shewed to the House the radical alterations such a measure would make in our Constitution, and the dangerous innovations with which it would be attended both in Church and State.   Government was violent in support of it, and Lords Howick* and Temple talked vehemently.

Strong symptoms however soon appeared that they met with opposition in the Closet, as the second reading of the Bill was postponed from day to day.   On Wednesday, the 11th, the King came to town, and saw his Ministers as usual at the Queen's House, to whom (it was told us) he expressed himself very distinctly that to such a measure *he never could assent.*

I passed several hours on the evening of this day with the Duke of Portland, and, after considering the business in every point of view, we found we were debarred from taking any effective measure, since though we *suspected* what the King's sentiments were, yet we possessed no positive proof of it, and were perfectly ignorant of his intentions, of which we knew nothing from authority.

On Thursday morning, 12th March, I received a note

* Afterwards Earl Grey ; he became Prime Minister in 1830.

from the Duke of Portland requesting me to call on him the next day at twelve. I went to him at the hour he named, and remained with him till five. He said, on my coming into the room, that he had been thinking all night of our conversation, and that it had dwelt so painfully and anxiously on his mind, that at all risks he had come to the determination to write to the King, and it was to consult me on the drawing up this letter that he had sent for me. I greatly approved and encouraged the notion; and after a great deal of thought, various alterations, and amendments, a letter nearly to the effect of that annexed was written.

COPY of a letter from the Duke of Portland to the King, sent Thursday evening, March 12th, 1807, to the Queen's House, acknowledged by Colonel Taylor Friday morning the 13th.

Burlington House, March 12th, 1807.

SIR,—I am so sensible of my presumption in addressing your Majesty on a subject of a public nature, that nothing but the confidence I have in your Majesty's goodness, and the attachment I bear your Majesty, would induce me to do it. But it is a subject of such infinite magnitude, that, were I silent, I feel I should deserve to forfeit that I am most ambitious to be considered, of being looked upon by your Majesty as one of your Majesty's most loyal and devoted subjects and servants.

Your Majesty will probably anticipate the subject on which I cannot but express my anxiety to lay my sentiments at your Majesty's feet.

It is the Bill just proposed by Lord Howick, granting indulgences to the Catholics; a measure, that should any peculiarity of circumstances have induced your Majesty to acquiesce in, I should still think that by following the dictates of my own conscience and voting against it, I should not offend your Majesty.

But, impressed as I am with a belief of what must be your Majesty's opinions and wishes, I could not forgive myself were I to conceal from your Majesty that your

opinion is mistaken and your wishes not generally understood; and humbly permit me to represent to your Majesty that it cannot well be otherwise, since one of your
Majesty's principal Ministers in the House of Commons
brings in the Bill. Should I be wrong, and your Majesty has not given your consent to the measure in its
present shape, I have little apprehension in giving it as
my opinion that it may ultimately be defeated in its progress, though not, I fear, till it comes into the House of
Lords; but, for this purpose, I must fairly state to your
Majesty, that your wishes must be distinctly known, and
that your present Ministers should not have any pretext
for equivocating upon the subject, or any ground whatever to pretend ignorance of your Majesty's sentiments
and determination, not only to withhold your sanction
from the present measure, but to use all your influence
in resisting it.

The effect of such a proceeding is so obvious, that I
would not suggest it, did I believe that your Majesty's
business would be at a stand in such a case; and that
persons would not be ready to come forward (should your
Majesty think fit to call upon them) who are capable and
willing to undertake the management of your Majesty's
affairs. But for this purpose it would be highly necessary and advantageous that the public should know the
necessity to which your Majesty was driven of taking
the conduct of your affairs out of the hands of those who
now administer them; that for this purpose your Majesty
should send for Lord Grenville, and state to him distinctly, that either your sentiments had been misrepresented or that you never had consented to the measure
proposed by Lord Howick, and that, consistently with
the opinion your Majesty had uniformly expressed, it
never could or would have your Royal assent. It would
then remain with Lord Grenville and his colleagues to
take their part: possibly they might give way, and still
remain your Majesty's Ministers; but, should they refuse
to submit themselves to your Majesty's pleasure, the
necessity of employing other persons would be obvious to
the whole world. The designs (which my feelings may

possibly lead me unjustly to attribute to them) could no longer be mistaken, viz. that the most venerated and sacred barriers of our constitution should be undermined and sapped for the purpose of introducing a new system into Church and State, and that your Majesty was reduced to the necessity of submitting to them or quarrelling with your Parliament.

Under such circumstances I cannot but believe, and cannot fear to assure your Majesty, that the nation as well as individuals will come forward in support of the established laws of the realm; and that persons will be found able to carry on your Majesty's business with talents and abilities equal to those of your present Ministers. If your Majesty should suppose that in the forming of such an Administration I can offer your Majesty any services, I am devoted to your Majesty's commands; but, while I say this, I feel conscious that my time of life, my infirmities, and my want of abilities are not calculated for so high a trust. I, however, can say, that if, in this very momentous crisis, your Majesty calls upon me, I will serve you zealously and faithfully to the end of my existence.*

THE Duke went to the Drawing-room, and said he would copy this letter at his return. Conscious the Duke of Portland moved slowly, and of the great importance no time should be lost, I wrote to press him, very late in the evening, and got early the next morning, Friday, his answer; which, as it gave me the idea, from a dubious expression in it, that his letter to the King was not gone, induced me to write to him again. I had scarce sent this when Miss Goldsworthy called on me to say, she came ordered and authorized to say what is in the last of the annexed letters, which I immediately, at half-past 10 o'clock, sent to the Duke of Portland.

---

* This letter is so carelessly composed and worded, that it is probably from the rough copy that it is taken.

LETTER FROM THE DUKE OF PORTLAND TO LORD MALMESBURY.

Thursday, 12th March, half-past Eleven, P.M.

MY DEAR LORD,—Your letter, which I receive this moment, is a great comfort to me. I have been employed the whole evening in copying that of which I hope your kind partiality does not mislead your opinion; but I have the still greater comfort of telling you that *mine* is no longer necessary, because His Majesty has told Lord G. that he never *had* consented, and never would consent, to Lord Howick's Bill; and His Majesty has signified his orders to my Nephews Lords George and James Thynne to vote against it. Lord Grenville told His Majesty, that, if the Bill did not pass, he would not retain his official situation.

Ever most truly yours,

PORTLAND.

LETTER FROM LORD MALMESBURY TO THE DUKE OF PORTLAND.

Spring Gardens, Friday, March 13, 1807. Half-past Ten, A.M.

MY DEAR LORD,—It is a matter of great satisfaction to receive the important information you are so good as to give me, that His Majesty has at last explained himself as to his feelings and wishes on Lord Howick's Bill; and I am not less pleased, though not surprised, with the opiniativeness of Lord Grenville on the same measure. What came to my knowledge in the course of yesterday evening first gave me a certainty of the King's sentiments and distress on this occasion; but it did not appear, from anything I heard, that he had taken the resolution to declare himself, and to act in the way he has since done. It was this that induced me to urge so strongly, as I took the liberty to do, the sending your letter, on the merits of which I never in my life felt I had formed a safer judgment, or one less biassed by partiality or personal regard.

I almost regret it did not go to its destination, as it is now made evident that it would have met the full concurrence of His Majesty ; and, at the same time, it would have afforded the strongest, and, I am confident, the most agreeable proof of your affection for his person, and zeal for the dearest interests of his Crown and People.

The value of this last consideration both to the King and to the Public is so strongly impressed on my mind, that I venture to submit to you, whether it would be improper for you still to address His Majesty; to do it, in consequence of your *now* being in possession of his intentions and wishes, and stating that, being acquainted with them, you hold it a duty to tender your services, and to express yourself ready and willing to take any commands he may give you, in case he should be driven to the necessity of dismissing his present Servants. The general substance of the letter would be the same; but its conclusion, instead of resting on a step you considered as most essential for His Majesty to take, would rest on this step having been actually adopted by him.

If you admit my idea, you will also admit the eligibility of the letter's getting to the King before the event of this day's debate is known ; for, although it is only the second reading of the Bill, and that future discussions and divisions may take place on other stages of it, yet it is very material to the cause, and but fair towards yourself, that His Majesty should be acquainted with your sentiments and your patriotic offer while the result is still pending.

I am, &c.

LETTER FROM THE DUKE OF PORTLAND TO LORD MALMESBURY.

Friday, 13th March, 1807.   Fifteen minutes past Four, P.M.

Dear Lord Malmesbury,—I am *sadly afraid* that I shall not get rid of my company sooner than, if so soon as, ten o'clock.   I must have expressed myself very differently from what I intended, or forgot to say *what I* intended, to have left you as much in the dark about my letter as you appear to be; for I meant to tell you, that I had sent, or would send, my letter to His Majesty, but that I could not suppress my apprehensions that your partiality might have influenced your judgment respecting it. You will, therefore, understand that the letter went, and I *know from* Taylor that he delivered it to the King, *and that is all I know.* Lord Grenville's carriage was at the Queen's House this morning, and you will have heard that the *second* reading of the Bill was put off *yesterday* till Tuesday. I think it *just possible* that this matter may be compromised. I only hope, and I trust, that there will not be a possibility for two opinions concerning the King's conduct. I told my sister, when she came to tell me the intimation that her sons had received respecting the Bill, that I had written to His Majesty and to what purport. She begged me to send my letter, and said she would let *them* know that she had found me *in the act of writing to His Majesty.*

Everybody I see is quite right upon this business; but it must now necessarily *stop short*, and *cannot be* brought forward by the present Ministers while they remain in Office.　　　　　Most truly yours, &c.

PORTLAND.

LETTER FROM LORD MALMESBURY TO THE DUKE OF PORTLAND.

Spring Gardens, Friday, March 13, 1807.
Three-quarters past Eleven, A.M.

MY DEAR LORD,—Since I wrote to you an hour ago, a person has come to me from the Queen's House *authorized* to say, " That His Majesty's wishes, sentiments, and intentions, respecting every measure which may lead to alter the legal restrictions the Catholics are liable to, are invariably the same as they always have been, *and always will be so.* That it is very important this should be *generally* known, as the greatest pains have been taken by his Ministers to impress the public with an idea that His Majesty was become indifferent on the subject, *while the direct contrary is the fact.*   It has occupied his mind most painfully and anxiously from the time he knew the measure was in contemplation; but it was anxiety *without agitation,* and his mind, though never more determined, was never more quiet and composed."

I thought it very material you should know this *immediately,* and also that the King remains in town *to-day,* perhaps to-morrow.   If, therefore, you judge proper to write your letter, it will find him at the Queen's House.

From some words my informant dropped, I am inclined to suppose that a similar communication to the one I have received either has, or will be made to your Grace.   I am, &c.

FRIDAY, MARCH 13.—The King this same morning (for he remained in town) had sent for Lords Grenville and Howick, and declared to them fully his intentions never to consent to the Bill as it now stood.   We did not learn at the time what they replied to the King, but it appeared a few days later.   Lord Sidmouth, it was said, had also seen the King, and declared to his colleagues that he never could agree with them on this point; but the precise line Lord Sidmouth took, how far he informed the King, or how decidedly he talked to Ministers, is not known to us.

I was with the Duke of Portland in the morning; much conversation on the means of forming a new Administration.   Great difficulties, but considerably smoothed by the whole body of Pitt's friends being now united; every shade of difference of opinion done away, and all ready to range round the Duke of Portland, and desirous of his being their chief.   This led to his infirmities, and physical inability to undertake so arduous a post.   Nothing could be more noble or more magnanimous than his feelings on the occasion.   He said, he was very sure the labours and anxieties attendant on such a very important situation would be more than his constitution could bear, but he felt it his duty not to shrink from it; and, if it should shorten his life, he should by no means regret a few years, or perhaps months, more or less, when he had the inward satisfaction of thinking they were sacrificed in his endeavours to serve his King and his country, and in preventing, as far as lay in his power, the dangers which were impending over both. It was impossible after this to say a word more; no urging, indeed, was necessary; neither, had it been so, could I have brought myself to employ it. I meant to have returned to him in the evening, but was prevented by a cold.

_____

SATURDAY, 14.—Canning was with me; entered into a long account of his own conduct, principles, and intentions, his professions of political faith, &c. He said, what he had told me before, that he had received and rejected overtures from Lord Grenville; but that he had not explained himself fully and decidedly till this morning, when he told Lord Grenville that, as the King's sentiments were now fully and distinctly pronounced (which was all that he wanted to know), his part was decidedly taken to support the King, without entering into the merits or demerits of the Bill, or on the advisability or otherwise of the Catholic Emancipation.

Canning spoke as if the choice of Cabinet places was to be at his refusal, and declared with a threat that he never would sit in the same Cabinet with Addington. Canning possesses the peculiar talent of justifying ably and forcibly all he does, or wishes to be done; and that so rapidly and so eloquently, that it is very difficult not to be carried away by what he says. He is unquestionably very clever, very essential to Government; but he is *hardly yet a Statesman,* and his dangerous habit of *quizzing* (which he cannot restrain) would be most unpopular in any department which required pliancy, tact, or conciliatory behaviour. He is honourable and honest, with a dash of the Irishman; and all his plans and ideas of governing would partake of this, and might be as dangerous in practice as he makes them appear plausible by the eloquent way in which he expresses them. He is right, however, quite right about Lord Sidmouth.

Canning may be safely trusted, for, I repeat it, he is honourable and honest; and if Pitt had not forced him in his hot-house of partiality and *engouement* (for it amounted to that), but had left him to ripen gradually, and allowed him in the early part of his political life, which began only *eleven* years ago, to experience some hardships, or even contradictions, his mind would have taken a better bent ; but, spoiled as he has been— feared and wanted as he finds himself—no place is now high enough for him ; his ambition rises beyond this visible diurnal sphere, and I fear he may lose many real and cordial friends for uncertain political connexions.

SATURDAY, 14.—In the morning at Burlington House, with Lords Hawkesbury, Castlereagh, and Eldon. Much conversation on the state of things. Still uncertain what Ministers would do ; various reports contradictory to each other. I went to Lady Pembroke to hear what she knew, for she was just returned from Windsor, and before I got back to Burlington House the meeting had separated; but I learnt from the Duke of Portland that Perceval had come in just after I went away, and communicated what had passed between him and Addington. It was a sort of offer made by Addington to unite with Perceval in opposing the Catholic Bill, throwing out a general hint of coming round. Perceval drew up, in the presence of the meeting, a letter, which had their consent, and which *declined all junction*, but with great civility towards Addington, and expressions of the sentiments entertained of him, from the part he was disposed to take regarding the Catholic Bill.

I dined with Alopeus and others at the Duke of York's—general conversation—Duke of York *seemingly* right on the Catholic Question; but not so *hearty* and decided as usual. On my expressing a wish to see him alone on the subject, he appointed Four the next day. I told him I was going to Blackheath.* He then, with-

* The Princess of Wales had lived at Blackheath since her separation from her husband.

out commenting on this, (N. B. he is against the Princess,) said he would call on me at Half-past Eleven next day. Dinner very pleasant. Duchess there.

MARCH 15. SUNDAY. — Dined with a large party at the Princess of Wales's at Blackheath.

MONDAY, 16.—At Burlington House a considerable time. Lord Grenville gone to Windsor ; speculations thereon. Canning came in with Lord Lowther, who is quite right. We left him with the Duke. I returned with Canning to his rooms in Albany. Settling Administrations. Castles in the air. He for a dissolution ; I not ; Huskisson for it. Dinner with Batt; he right, and, as usual, eager. Lady Pembroke dined there; she anxious Lord Pembroke should come up to town ; I told her I had written to him every day, and would keep him informed, but she knew he was not a very persuadable man.

WEDNESDAY, 18.—I was for a few moments at Burlington House in the morning, but, as the Duke was going an airing, I did not stay long. I met Lord Titchfield upon the steps of Burlington House, when I was going to dine, and he confirmed what is stated. I went with him for a moment into his room; found him very desponding about every thing, with no opinion that a good administration could be formed, and regretting the change. He evidently was alarmed at the idea of his father taking the Treasury, and felt, as I certainly do, that it is a perilous undertaking at his age, and with his ailings.

After dinner I had an hour's conversation with the Duke. Perceval had come in to tell him what had passed at the House, and of Lord Grenville's journey, the object of which he conceived would be known the next day, when the King came to town.

[In a letter to the Duke, dated the 17th, Lord M.

assures him that he would (in the event of his being Premier) assist him by holding any office *temporarily*, but that he considers his deafness and inexperience in debate disqualify him for permanently keeping the Seals.]

The Duke said every thing that was kind respecting my letter to him. Said he knew no one but myself quite fit for the Foreign Department. He then (and I clearly perceived Lord Tichfield had been speaking to him) talked with great anxiety about his accepting the Office proposed to him; that he felt he was not equal to it; that he hoped the King would not force it on him, &c.—As he had no answer from His Majesty, I stated, that I was certain that the message sent to me on the preceding Friday from the Queen's House was intended as an intimation that the letter had been received and approved. That it was sent *to me*, and not to any of those who had in the late Administration held Cabinet places, to avoid observation; and that, if he would recollect the hour his letter reached the King, it corresponded *exactly* with that at which I received the message.—The Duke was struck with this, and rallied; and before we parted seemed to have made up his mind. He talked of how much assistance he should want, and particularly private Secretaries. I mentioned Ross.

———————

THURSDAY, 19.—With Lord Camden; learnt from him that Lords Hawkesbury and Eldon had been sent for by the King, and were gone to Windsor. They were waked in the night, and the hour of Audience fixed for ten. I have since heard that the King wrote these letters after he had despatched his messenger on Wednesday night on his return to Windsor, and sent them by a servant of his own, who did not get to London till one in the morning. Lord Camden right as to the Catholic Bill; but, like many others, not so much against the principle of Emancipation, as because the King has declared himself, and he conceived it to be a sort of *pledge he had given to Pitt that the question should*

not be mooted during the King's life. Charles Long
with him—he right. Lord Camden mentioned Lord
Chichester. I said I would write to him. From Lord
Camden's I called on the Bishop of Hereford; knew
every thing, but fishing, particularly about who was
to have the Seals for the Foreign Office.

At Five at Burlington House ; Lords Hawkesbury and
Eldon just returned from Windsor. They came to give
the Duke of Portland an exact account of their Audience; it lasted two-and-a-half hours, from Twelve till
Half-past Two. The King stated the reasons which had
induced him to order them to attend him, and then produced a bundle of papers which he told them to read.
They contained the whole of what had passed between
him and his Ministers respecting the Catholic Bill, from
the first day any intention on their part to touch
on the subject was made known to him. The documents began so far back as the 8th of February, and
went down to the Wednesday, 18th of March. They
were *Minutes* of Cabinet transmitted to the King, and
his answers to them; from these it appeared, what we
had learnt before, that in the first instance they confined their measures to the simple introduction of the
Clause of Security, to the Catholics serving in England,
into the Mutiny Bill; and, on the King not refusing his
consent to this, they soon after proposed to him the one
of more extended indulgences, to which *he never* consented, but from the *beginning* refused it. Ministers
persist, and some days pass in this mutual refusal to
give way. On Wednesday the 11th Lord Howick, as I
before said, brings the Bill to the King. The King refuses to assent to it. Lord Howick withdraws from the
closet, and either does, or affects to, misunderstand the
King, and brings in the Bill. This is the only part of
the proceeding which passed *verbally*, and on which they
are at issue : and it seemed as if Lord Sidmouth had,
in his Audience of that day, the 11th March, expressed
to the King his alarm, and put him on his guard; for, on
or about the 12th, Ministers propose to withdraw the
Bill, and talk of a compromise; but on the King's insist-

ing that he must receive assurances that the measure
never should be again mooted during his reign, they
explain what they mean by a compromise, viz. that
they will withdraw the Bill; but that the Petition coming from the Irish Catholics must be received and discussed, and that they must reserve to themselves the
faculty of bringing forward at any future period any
motions respecting the taking restrictions from the Catholics to *any extent.*

This appears from the Minutes, and was confirmed by
what passed between the King and Lord Grenville, Monday, 16th, and was still more confirmed by what passed
on the several audiences on Wednesday, the 18th.   After
the two Lords had read these very important papers, the
King said that it was now become impossible for him to
keep his present Ministers; that he wished his reasons
should be known to them for taking so decided and
perhaps so difficult a step before he explained to them
his pleasure.   That *they* (Lords Eldon and Hawkesbury) *must* see that *he* could not act otherwise; *they*
knew his sentiments on this subject.   Those sentiments could not vary, unless his whole idea of what
his religion and his oath called upon him to do, could
alter.   That it was a measure *of necessity;* and that
between dismissing his Ministers or forfeiting his crown,
he saw no medium.   He then said, that, from the
earliest moment he saw what was meant; and, fully
determined to avoid the consequences he had incurred in
1801 by communications with others, he now had communicated with no one single person, not even the Archbishop of Canterbury (for he added, he was sure the
Archbishop would act right, and as became him).   That he
also chose the whole should be put in writing, and therefore had ordered that every thing which came should be
as a Minute of Cabinet, in order that no cavil could be
made, or by any possible misconstruction a doubt remain
on which was the real fact.   That in talking to Lord
Grenville he had never talked harshly or hastily, but
contented himself with maintaining steadily and calmly
his opinion.   That Lord Grenville had behaved towards

him very properly, and never forgot himself, or manifested any unbecoming hastiness, or used any expression
at all bordering on menace to go out. He only said at
the conclusion of his audience, Monday, that, if the Bill
did not pass, he could not consistently with his principles
and duty continue to serve His Majesty in any Official
capacity; that on their parting he added—and spoke in
the name of his colleagues—that they were ready to remain in office till His Majesty could form a new Administration, and would not distress him by an abrupt resignation.

The King said, the Prince had come down on purpose
on Saturday to declare his intentions of acting *and
speaking* against the Bill; that the Chancellor (Erskine)
has also been from the beginning against it, as well as
Lord Ellenborough and Lord Sidmouth. This last he
said had behaved handsomely. After stating all this,
he said he had now to signify to them that it was his
wish they should return to London, make an immediate
report to the Duke of Portland, (it does not appear that
the King noticed the letter he had written to him,) and
say it was his desire that the Duke should immediately
set about framing a New Administration, and that he
wished Lord Chatham might be sent for (out of regard
to the memory of Mr. Pitt), to be consulted on the
occasion. The King added, " I have no restrictions, no
exceptions to lay on the Duke of Portland ; no engagements or promises ; he may dispose of *every thing*."
" Only," said the King laughingly, " Westmoreland *must*
have a place, and I am desirous Lord Charles Somerset
should be taken care of." (N.B. this last a singular
person for the King to be anxious about; but he had a
command at Weymouth, and his wife, a Miss Courteney,
who talks the western dialect like Parson Trulliber, is a
favourite with the Princesses.)

Lords Eldon and Hawkesbury said they never saw
the King more collected, more quiet, or more composed,
and more cheerful than when they saw him.

It was past six before all this could be communicated,
and I left the Duke writing to Lord Chatham, and went

to dine at Lord Whitworth's grand dinner. Woronzow, Alopeus,* and all the Foreign Ministers there. From this dinner I returned to Burlington House, and staid till twelve. We went over the whole that had passed, particularly on the audience of Lords Eldon and Hawkesbury. The Duke's fits of fear and diffidence were again upon him, and I had great difficulty in cheering him. I observed, his amended health ought to encourage him. To this he replied, " My health I admit is better than it was, but I can assure you (and remember what I say), that it will not be equal to the task I am going to undertake. Its labours, and the anxieties inseparable from it, (and he again repeated, ' remember what I say,') will be too much for me; but this I heed very little, for I cannot consume, or even sacrifice the little of life that remains in me, with more interior satisfaction to myself than doing what I consider as my first duty. My fears are not that the attempt to perform this duty will shorten my life, but that I shall neither bodily nor mentally perform it as I ought."

On Friday I abstained from seeing the Duke, and, dining at Morton Pitt's, heard nothing during all this time. I had many visitors when at home, *some* out of *curiosity*, and *some* under the impression I was a man probably to be in Office, *some* out of real regard. Sturges Bourne, amongst the *last*, came constantly, and I kept him regularly informed. I also wrote regularly to Lord Pembroke at Bath, and on Friday to Lord Chichester, recommending him strongly to come to town.

SATURDAY, MARCH 21.—Sturges Bourne said Yorke had declined all Office (from fear), but had declared his fixed intention to afford the Duke of Portland every possible support. This I was less surprised at, knowing that the Yorkes had long a sort of family dislike of the Duke of Portland, and also a spirit of irresolution and political timidity which pervades them all: but it did not surprise me at all when I heard from Lord Elliot

* Prussian Minister.

that he was in the greatest perplexity, since he heard two such different opinions, or rather constructions, put on the meaning of the papers the King had shewn to Lords Eldon and Hawkesbury ; viz. those who stated them to contain hard and inadmissible conditions proposed by Lord Grenville and his colleagues to the King as terms for giving up the question; and those of Lord Hardwicke, and, strange to say, the Bishop of Lincoln (Prettyman), who contended (and they say they have seen them) that no such hard conditions did appear in these papers, and that Ministers gave up the question without any one stipulated concession on the part of the King that could possibly offend him now, or at any other time.

To this I replied only, that it was most wonderful; that I felt sure that the Bishop and Lord Hardwicke had not seen *all* the papers. Lord Elliot said they had, and quoted numbers and dates very exactly; and repeated the embarrassment it caused him, since he entertained the highest opinion and the firmest reliance on the four Lords mentioned. I said no more: but it struck me as manifest that Lord Grenville had been tampering, and successfully, with Lord Hardwicke; and that Prettyman, who from the hour of Pitt's death behaved shabbily, now acts up to his character, and gratifies at the same time his spleen against the King, who refused to make him Archbishop of Canterbury on Moore's death; alleging for reason, " that, if a private Secretary of a first Minister was put at the head of the Church, it would make all his Bishops party-men and politicians."

SUNDAY, MARCH 22. Sir W. Scott.—Said his brother (Lord Eldon) went yesterday to Windsor to see the King and get the documents alluded to. Went to Burlington House. Lord Chatham closeted with the Duke of Beaufort; came into the room where I was. He was sent for; destined for Ireland. This he did not know, neither did I tell it him. Lord Eldon came in with Lord Redesdale.

He said the King would not give up the original papers, and no copies were to be made; and Lord Hawkesbury is gone to-day to bring them up from Windsor, which he did about 4 o'clock. He said Lord Hardwicke went there yesterday to ask an Audience, and to persuade the King not to change his Administration. It appeared that Lord Grenville prevailed on Lord Hardwicke to take this unusual step. He returned directly from Windsor to dine with Lord Grenville. The King saw him after Lord Eldon ; but told Lord Eldon that he would hear him, and then tell him his reasons for what he was about, and his determination of abiding by them. Sturges Bourne told me Lord Melville had declined Office, and Lord Wellesley waiting to determine till he could see Lord Grenville. Wellesley Pole talked of for Ireland. I do not think him a fit man. Respecting other arrangements I hear nothing with certainty. Lord Chichester with me in the evening. I had written to him to come up. He wants the Duchy of Lancaster *for life*. He will hardly obtain it, though he certainly deserves some Office, having served long and been ill-used.

MONDAY, MARCH 23.—Lord Hawkesbury told me there was a chance still of Lord Wellesley's taking Office ; all his family wished it. That the Cabinet places would be all filled by Wednesday. That he would take care I should see all the papers the King had shewn to him and to Lord Eldon. Lord Buckinghamshire (Postmaster), with whom I walked down Pall Mall, called what Lord Grenville had done " an act of suicide, with this difference only, that he believed they should come to life again. Yet it was very hard, not on him, who was used to be buffeted about, but on the Foxites, who had for *thirty years* been struggling for Office, and, now that they had obtained it, were turned out *in one year*, from the unaccountable measures of Lords Grenville and Howick."

Fawkes, Member for Yorkshire, was to make a motion

in the House of Commons, to say the present Ministers were entitled to the gratitude of this country. No such motion was made, or notice given; but Martin made one about reversionary places, and to prevent the King's giving Perceval the Duchy of Lancaster *for life.*＊

I called at Burlington House, but did not go in. I wish to be absent from thence during the arrangements.

TUESDAY, MARCH 24.—Lord Wellesley still wavering all day. At last decided not to accept the Seals. Dined with Lord Camden. Lord Bathurst came in the evening; he to be in the Cabinet. Conversation confidential, but unimportant.

MARCH 25.—Canning with me early; he came, he said, to consult me. He had been offered the Foreign Department or the Admiralty. As to the first, if *I* chose it, or Lord Wellesley accepted it, he had told the Duke of Portland he would give way; but he thought he had as good a claim as Lord Chichester, or *any other old* Official man. That the choice, therefore, as we were out of the question, was left him, and he asked me which I advised his taking. I recommended the Foreign Office. *That* I found met *his* wishes; and he went immediately from me to the Duke of Portland, who, at two o'clock, carried him to the Queen's House, and he kissed hands. Before he left me, he asked me if Fitzharris would like to be Under-Secretary of State. I demurred till I should see him.

At half-past seven Lady Fitzharris was brought to bed of a son, and I had no opportunity of speaking to Fitzharris till towards nine. He then, without hesitation, chose the Under-Secretaryship, from thinking that confinement *with* business was better than confine-

---

＊ Mr. Martin lost his motion by a majority of 93 : the numbers being, for his Address to the King, 115 ; against it, 208.

ment and *no* business, which would have been the case at the Treasury.*

WEDNESDAY and THURSDAY, 25 and 26.—Nothing material occurred. I called on Canning, and walked with him to the Office. Duke of Richmond thought of for Ireland. Sturges Bourne disposed to decline all Office. Many of the new Ministers kissed hands.

FRIDAY, MARCH 27.— Canning with me. At two with him at the office. Conversation much interrupted by visits on Foreign Affairs, Foreign Appointments, &c. &c. Ross to be his Private Secretary *ad interim*. Canning disposed to be very kind. Lord Castlereagh came in; Sir Arthur Wellesley† was to be Irish Secretary; Lord Tichfield to be in the Treasury; Lord Mulgrave, Admiralty.

Dinner at Burlington House. I carried Lord Chichester there ; he said he had declined *all* Cabinet Offices ; lamented, and so do I, that the Duke of Portland had so few, or rather *no* person in the Cabinet he could call his personal friend. I regretted his refusal; he told me the old *story*—" He had consulted his wife and his pillow, and had determined in consequence." No one at dinner but Lord Charles Spencer. George Rose came soon after coffee; he had complained bitterly in the morning that it was not notified to him *officially* that he was to be Treasurer of the Navy. He remained with the Duke till very late; after him came Lord Chatham and Dr. Reynolds, and it was past twelve o'clock before he was alone. I then saw him for five minutes. He said, that from eleven in the morning till that moment he had not been by himself a minute. " Recollect," said he, " what I told you a week ago, it will be too much for me; but it shall go on as long as it can, and I care not for the consequences." I

---

* The Duke of Portland, at the same time, offered him a seat at the Treasury.
† Afterwards Duke of Wellington.

repeated my idea of his getting help, and offered myself to assist in any capacity. He said, if I would come often and dine with him, it would be a very great comfort to him ; that it was his moment of relaxation, and that we might then get some quiet comfortable conversation. This I engaged to do the next day, and whenever he pleased.

SATURDAY, MARCH 28.—Dined and passed the day at Burlington House. No one there but Lord Tichfield, just come from Welbeck to be a Lord of the Treasury. In a conversation I had with him before dinner, he expressed great apprehensions for the health of his father ; said his servant (Salter, his valet-de-chambre) told him (though the Duke denied it himself) that he was very unwell, kept up by cordials, &c. We talked over the means, if any could be found, of lessening his fatigues and labours, and Lord Tichfield said he was sure he would allow *no one* to help him; and we both lamented that he had not the talent of getting rid of prosing, disagreeable, and useless people. Lord Tichfield himself *submits* with a good grace to what he dislikes, and takes Office from right and honourable principles.

In the evening I urged the Duke, both when alone with him, and before Lord Tichfield, to *spare* himself ; but he was not disposed to listen to it : he said his arrangements were nearly concluded, and he *then* should be more quiet. Lord Powis offered, and has refused Ireland; Lord Hertford to have the Garter; Fred. Robinson,* the Admiralty ; Wm. Elliot, the Treasury ; Sturges Bourne he wished to get there, but *he* wants to be a Privy Councillor—and would prefer that, and a nomination to the Board of Trade, to any office with a salary.

The Duke said Lord Lowther† expressly declared he would not take Office, and spoke with some heat of Canning's having taken upon himself to mention him as desirous of it; that he confessed *the Garter* in due time would gratify him. The Duke of Portland agreed to

---

* Son of Lord Grantham, and now Earl of Ripon.

† He was afterwards created Earl of Lonsdale.

this, and has mentioned it to the King, who said he should be the first promoted in the Peerage, and then the Garter might follow with propriety. Much talk on general politics, foreign and domestic. Duke of Portland quite right on both.

SUNDAY, MARCH 29.—Canning with me early; talked over arrangements and appointments in his office; settled Ross to be his Private Secretary, and also assistant to Fitzharris. Went to Canning at the office at three o'clock; Duke of Cumberland there; Lord Castlereagh and Sir Vicary Gibbs. No time for conversation.

MONDAY, 30.—Canning dined with me, in trio, with Fitzharris; long conversation. I advise subsidies rather than loans,—diversions near home, not in Germany. Mention the Isle of Walcheren: recommend that the person who is to command the expedition, be not the one sent (as in the case of Sir John Moore) to examine and reconnoître. Great abuses, I observed, in the office; no secrets kept, either from carelessness or treachery. Messengers very idle, lazy, and talking. All circulation dangerous, particularly in a Cabinet like the present.

In the morning I spoke to Fred. Robinson about his accepting the Admiralty; he doubtful, with no good reason, but influenced by the Yorkes and his own family. Spoke to Lady Grantham; she irresolute, and, though not saying so, manifestly against his taking Office under an Administration she did not think would last.

TUESDAY, MARCH 31.—Lord Bathurst with me; always acute, sensible, and upright. The King, he says, is most firm, and quite well. He (Lord Bathurst) thinks that, if Government can stand the first attack, it will last a long time. Sturges Bourne accepts the Treasury; Fred. Robinson declines the Admiralty.

WEDNESDAY, APRIL 1.—Duke of Richmond, with Sir
Arthur Wellesley as Secretary, goes to Ireland; Dukes
of Rutland, Beaufort, and Lord Powis have declined
it.

APRIL 3.—Letter from Lord Mulgrave, offering the
Admiralty to Lord Palmerston. I sent him the proposal to Broadlands; he comes up the next day, and
accepts it.

At the Office, great wish to get G. Leveson to accept
the Mission to Russia. Canning writes to him, and proposes it quite on public grounds, and wishes not to see
him unless he accepts. I called on G. Leveson; he
writes to Canning, consenting to go, provided it does
not prevent his voting with Opposition on Thursday.
I think this a right and natural condition, and was
glad to find the Duke of Portland, and also Canning,
assent to it. I dined at Burlington House with Fitzharris, Finch Hatton, and Lord Tichfield. Duke of
Portland well. Short conversation with him, but on no
material points, after dinner. Lord Chatham came at
eleven o'clock, with some commission, as the Duke of
Portland suspects, from Lord Sidmouth.

APRIL 4.—Nothing remarkable; Lords Tichfield and
Palmerston dined with me.

APRIL 7.—Canning with me to advise whether it
would not be a very useful measure if the King would
write to the Emperor of Russia,—I think it certainly
would; but very difficult to induce the King to write
as he ought, in order to obtain the object intended.
Went with Canning to the Office; he draws up a draft
to send to the King on the subject, which I advise him
to do, rather than to mention it abruptly in an audience. I hint, that writing in English might be taken
right; the Emperor Alexander understands it perfectly.
Much talk about filling up the Foreign Missions; Lord
Douglas recalled; Granville Leveson goes; Sir A. Paget
and Jackson not to return. Pierrepont wants Vienna;

not of a size for it: I mention Lords Cathcart, Amherst, Mansfield. Canning approves them all. Lord Aberdeen to go to Palermo at his own request. G. Rose, jun. with me about Cambridge (University) Address of congratulation on the change of Ministers; wants to get persons to go down and vote for it—it is to come into the senate to-morrow, no time for canvassing; Lord Palmerston cannot go, as he is to kiss hands for the Admiralty. Lord Tichfield at dinner with me. We lament the fatigue the Duke of Portland will undergo; he supports it solely by opiates and laudanum, but there is no prevailing on him to be assisted. Lord Pembroke arrives.

THURSDAY, APRIL 9.—At Court; drawing-room very full. Spoke to Perceval about his standing for Cambridge; he is doubtful about himself, but is ready to support, if he does not join, Lord Palmerston. Dine at Burlington House; Lord Stamford and Sir Robert Miles; Lord Chichester came in the evening. No opportunity for private talk; Sutton goes Chancellor to Ireland.

FRIDAY, APRIL 10.—Got an early account of the division—for Government, 258; Minority, 226.*
Lord Whitworth with me to inquire about Russia; alarmed at the reports respecting the commercial treaty. Richard Ryder praises Canning's speech; says, the temper of the House was even better than the division. Canning too imperious about the threat of dissolution. Pierrepont called; explained to him why he should not ask for Vienna in the *first instance;* it was too great a stride; declined interfering for him personally. At Burlington House for a moment. Company at home— Canning, Lord Tichfield, Grantham, Bourne, &c. After dinner Canning shewed me the draft of a letter the

* Mr. Brand, on the 9th, moved a resolution condemning the dismissal of the late Government, viz. " That it is contrary to the first duties of the confidential servants of the Crown to restrain themselves by any pledge, expressed or implied, from offering to the King any advice which the course of circumstances may render necessary for the welfare and security of the Empire."

King was to write to the Emperor Alexander in English
—very good and well turned. Spoke of sending Lord
Pembroke on an extra Mission to Vienna.

SATURDAY, APRIL 11.—At the Office; read Canning's
draft to Lord Hutchinson, sent by George Jackson on
Monday.   Prince Castelcicala with me for two hours:—
tedious but clever relation of what was done, and what
he wished should be done, respecting his Court (Naples);
he himself talking like a Neapolitan advocate or lawyer,
prolix, pedantic, and quick.   I advised him, that all
should be new-modelled.   Evident that there are sad
intrigues and tricking going on on all sides at Palermo;
a Frenchman—favourite of the Queen—probably betrays
every thing,—he is Adjutant General to the Army.

A'Court* (the son) calls on me; confirms in part, and
explains on the whole, what Castelcicala had been saying.
I write to Lord Pembroke to propose Vienna to him; he
declines *faintly*.   He and Canning dine with me, and
Lord Pembroke ends by taking the proposal for consideration.

SUNDAY, APRIL 12.—Lord Pembroke at breakfast; he,
after many doubts, inquiries, and difficulties, nearly decides to accept the extra Mission to Vienna.   Dined at
Burlington House.

MONDAY, APRIL 13.—Lord Pembroke desires me, before he sees Canning himself, to state to him that his
sole motive for accepting the Appointment is from a
feeling of propriety, nearly approaching duty; that it is
in every other respect inconvenient and disagreeable to
him.   That he *must* stipulate it should be only for a
limited time.

We went together to the Office, and I communicated
all this to Canning.   We settled that A'Court would be
the best person to go with Lord Pembroke as Secretary of
the Embassy; and Douglas, Canning's private Secretary,

* Afterwards Lord Heytesbury, and now Lord Lieutenant of Ireland.

as his.   In every thing I said Canning acquiesced.   Lord
Pembroke went to Canning, and the whole was settled.
I saw Canning afterwards, and he was greatly delighted;
he wrote immediately to the King.   Canning and Lord
Pembroke dined with me.   Debate in the House of Lords
on Lord Stafford's motion.*   Sat till half-past seven.

Division for Government .   135
Proxies   .   .   .   36—171

Against   69
Proxies   .   .   .   21— 90
                                 ———
Majority for Government   81

SATURDAY, 18. — Canning with me early; question
how Lord Pembroke should be gazetted; ill done after
all.   Sir W. A'Court came, rather disposed to complain
of not having been sooner informed of his son's appointment; but I soon pacified him and made him sensible of
its advantage.   A'Court himself, who came soon after,
felt it as it deserves to be felt, and expressed himself
much pleased.

Jackson very anxious to be employed again at Berlin.
He certainly has a fair and just claim, but there exist
strong prejudices against him in the Office.

Lord Pembroke inquires what he is to take, &c. ; I
give him the best information I can.   The King was very
kind to him; said he had acted *handsomely*.   The
expectations raised by reports of good news from Constantinople put an end to, by being informed our Fleet
had *repassed* the Dardanelles.†

SUNDAY, APRIL 19. — Lord Hutchinson writes unfa-

---

* On the change of Administration, and similar in substance to that made
by Mr. Brand on the 9th.

† Our fleet, under Sir John Duckworth, ran the gauntlet twice through
the Dardanelles, and burnt the Turkish squadron. In the second passage
the Windsor Castle line-of-battle-ship had her main-mast struck by a stone
shot weighing eight hundred pounds.

vourable accounts of the state of the Russian Army, both as to numbers and military service; but he admits its bravery. France accepts the Mediation of Austria. It does not oppose, but disapproves a General Congress.

Swedes raise the Siege of Stralsund, and drive the French, or rather Dutch, out of Swedish Pomerania.

Thursday, April 23.—Dinner at Burlington House; long prose with the Duke of Portland till one in the morning; went over all subjects, particularly on the necessity of a Dissolution of Parliament. The Duke said we had only a sure majority of *twenty-three*, and with that there was no going on. I rather dislike the measure, though I admit its being expedient. The Duke said it was indispensable, and must be immediately.

I mentioned Lord Lavington. The Duke of Portland said no pensions were ever given to Governors on quitting their government. That he had been trying, but in vain, to find a precedent, in order to give one to Sir R. Miles, his relation by marriage, and now returning to Canada. This I told to Lady Lavington.

Friday, April 24. — Lady Malmesbury, Catherine, and Fanny dine at Princess of Wales's with Princess Charlotte. No men; twelve ladies; pleasant dinner. Princess Charlotte full of play, but well-mannered. No events for several days. Sir Arthur Paget appointed to Constantinople.

Saturday, April 25.—Dissolution resolved on, and communicated in the evening to the confidential friends of Government. Lord Palmerston goes instantly to Cambridge.

All the next week taken up in Parliamentary arrangements.

Government, it is thought, will gain one hundred and fifty or two hundred votes. Late Ministers furious in their language and advertisements. They are very unpopular. I dined at Burlington House. The Dissolution to take place, and be proclaimed Wednesday, 29th inst.

In the next three weeks no events came to my knowledge at all worth recording. I saw the Duke of Portland daily, but he and his colleagues were entirely occupied with the New Parliament. There is every appearance that in the Elections they will gain a great deal more strength than the most sanguine expectations ventured to foretell.

The spirit of the whole country is with the King; and the idea of the Church being in danger (perhaps not quite untrue) makes Lord Grenville and the Foxites most unpopular. Their demonstrations of anger and disappointment, so injudiciously manifested in their Election advertisements, add to the ill-will of the people towards them.

In the course of the last three weeks, it has, from various little facts, struck me that the Duke of Portland's colleagues are swerving from him; that they take a great deal on themselves, immediately belonging to *him*, and treat him more as a nominal than as a real head of the Ministry.

I have attempted to find whether he observed and felt it, but in vain; he displayed the talent he possesses in an eminent degree, that of dead silence, and was " *Quam si dura silex.*" It is, in fact, all his own fault; he missed the game at the beginning, by suffering Lords Hawkesbury and Eldon to go between him and the King, and by associating Lord Chatham to assist him in forming a Cabinet. He has now not a single person in it on whom he can depend, and would, if ever he had a point to contend, or ever was disposed to contend one, be left in a very small minority.

I should, from this consideration, *regret* my having declined and shrunk from Office, if I did not feel that my deafness completely disqualifies me for a wrangling Cabinet, and that I should be a useless or rather a burthensome friend to the Duke did I belong to it.

On Friday, May 8th, I received an express from Lord Palmerston, to say that he had lost his election at Cambridge by two.   His poll was

Euston	.	324	Palmerston	.	311
Gibbs	.	313	Petty	.	. 269

Nothing could be more honourable than Lord Palmerston's conduct.   He would not allow his friends to give him single votes, which many wanted to do; and which, necessarily, would have put him ahead of Sir Vicary Gibbs—who, also, I must say, behaved with equal honour in influencing his votes.   *If* a vacancy happens, there can be no doubt of Palmerston's election—in the mean time he is elected for Newport.

———

FRIDAY, MAY 15.—Canning and Lord Pembroke dined with me, to talk over the instructions given to him, Lord G. Leveson, and Sir A. Paget.   They are in substance as follow:—

Sir A. Paget to propose peace to the Turks on the *status ante bellum*, and to ensure them from any dismemberment on the part of Russia.   To this Russia, it is said, consents.   Pozzo di Borgo is their negotiator, and now abroad.   Admiral Siniavin's fleet is in the Archipelago.

Lord G. Leveson's are much more minute and detailed.   He is to give the strongest assurance of the King's decided intention not to withdraw himself from the Continent; and this is said in a very pointed manner, in order to do away some very injudicious language held by our late Ambassador to Merfeldt, the Austrian Minister at St. Petersburg.   Leveson is then, without any reserve, to state to what pecuniary amount we can go this year—it is about two-and-a-half millions.   £150,000 of this is already given to the King of Prussia; 40 or 50,000*l.* to the King of Sweden; and something is due to the King of Naples,—leaving a remainder of about 2,300,000*l.*   This sum *must last* till the 5th of January; but it is left with Russia to decide how much she thinks it would be proper to ensure the active co-operation of Austria; whether, if he sets a very high value on this, a large contribution should be given. The remainder, whatever it may be, is at the disposal of Russia; but we can guarantee no loan, or exceed this original sum *this year*, of two-and-a-half millions.

Assurances of a disposition to make peace if it can be at all attained on reasonable and secure terms, which seems quite impossible. No objection to Prussia recovering *all* her dominions; but, as they were scattered, and she, as it was proved at Jena and Auerstadt (the same battle), was simply a military power, whose existence depended on one battle, it is submitted whether, if Prussia could collect her dominions more together, by "*exchange* or *arrangement*," it would not be better. This was at my suggestion. Canning had put "*conquest* and *aggrandizement by force*," and this I objected to.

Lord Pembroke's instructions are short, but very clear and wise. He is to make declarations similar to Leveson's with regard to His Majesty's invariable intention not to forsake the Continent. He is then to propose a Treaty of Concert, consisting of two or three articles; and, this signed, then to enter into pecuniary arrangements: but he is not to open himself on these to the Court of Vienna—as Leveson is authorized to do to that of St. Petersburg—but to offer first 300,000*l*., and to go as far as 500,000*l*. whenever Austria has declared war, and her army passed the frontiers; holding out that this sum, which is larger than any *first* payment possibly can be of a subsidiary treaty, is to be looked upon as leading to such treaty, and to be taken in the event as so much given in advance.

If Lord Pembroke succeeds, he is to produce his credentials as Ambassador; if not, to return. A'Court goes with him as Secretary of the Embassy. Douglas (Sir Andrew's son) as Private Secretary, and Frederick Robinson as a friend.

I could make no remark on Lord Pembroke's instructions, as they were perfectly judicious and sensible; but I much doubt whether they will satisfy the Court of

Vienna, who, besides being at this moment very jealous of Russia, on account of her Turkish war and close connexion with Prussia, is, I fancy, very craving and exorbitant indeed in her subsidiary demands.

Pierrepont returns to Sweden with the feather of Privy Councillor.

Lord Whitworth and Mr. Heathcote (Sir William's son) urged me to apply for peerages. I told them truly there were no less than *fifty-three* candidates for peerage, and to none of which the King would listen.

THE new Parliament met on 26th June, 1807. The division on that day was still more favourable to the Administration than their calculations. The supporters of the late Administration were only 155, those of the new one 350; majority, 195. This fixed them in their authority. On the 9th April, 1807, their first division before the dissolution, numbers were—

> Government . 　. 258
> Opposition 　. 　. 226
> ----
> Majority 　. 32

The whole of this short Session went to confirm this: it ended on the 14th August, when Parliament was prorogued.

On the 28th July I received a letter from G. Rose stating Lord Bolton was dying, and intimating to me that I might have the Lieutenancy of Hampshire and Government of the Isle of Wight. I went to London (G. Rose's letter having found me at Heron Court); I got there on the 31st, and Lord Bolton died on that morning. The Duke of Portland was all friendship; offered me both the situations; but, as Fitzharris was quite worn down by the fatigue and attendance at the Foreign Office, I requested the Government of the Isle of Wight might be given to *him* instead of *me*, and that, if he had it for life, he would give up the pension of 1,200*l.* he was to receive on my death. This was readily agreed to. I took the Lieutenancy, for which I was sworn in on Wednesday the 12th day of August, and Fitzharris kissed hands the same day for the Government for his life. The Prince of Wales wanted both these Offices for Lord Winchester; but did not apply for them to the Duke of Portland. Fitzharris immediately after his appointment returned his reversionary pension warrant to Perceval (Chancellor of the Exchequer), and resigned his Office of Under-Secretary of State.*

Great reverses were in the mean while experienced in Polish Prussia by the Russians and Prussians. Dantzic was taken, Kœnigsberg was taken; and on the 5th of June was fought the battle of Friedland, which, though not decisive as a battle, was a complete victory over the mind of the Emperor of Russia. From that day all his boasted courage ended; and though he had written in the strongest terms *in his own hand* to the King a very few days before in answer to the letter His Majesty had sent him, and which I have noticed before, " that there was no salvation *to himself or to Europe but by eternal resistance to Buonaparte*," yet on this day, the 5th June, all was forgotten; fear, panic, and every dastardly feeling terror and dismay could suggest, seem to have taken at once possession of him, though Beningsen did not think himself defeated, and assured him he could still make a powerful stand—this very Beningsen, whom he had abused a week before to Lord G. Leveson for want of spirit and perseverance.

On the 24th June, Alexander and Buonaparte met on a raft moored on the river Niemen, and on the 8th July, 1807, a most ignominious peace was signed at Tilsit. The helpless and unfortunate Frederick William, King of Prussia, was neither consulted nor remembered; and Alexander was base enough to receive part of the dominions, in Polish Prussia, of a Sovereign who had been fighting by his side, for whose interests he professedly drew the sword a few months before, as an indemnity for the expenses of the war he had been engaged in. General

* At the second Lord Malmesbury's death, in 1841, the Office of Governor of the Isle of Wight became extinct.

Kalkreuther,* whom I well knew, who is in his heart a
Democrat, and has all his life been devoted to the views
and principles of the late Prince Henry, was sent (as a
man of straw) to negotiate for the King of Prussia. *He*
foolishly trusted in him; though there is little doubt
Kalkreuther delivered up Dantzic by treachery. Talleyrand signed on the part of Buonaparte; that vain man,
Prince Alexander Kourakin, and Labanoff, on the part of
Alexander; and in such haste was Buonaparte, that he
had the Ratifications signed the next day, the 9th. I
shall not enter into the Articles of this Peace, as they
will undoubtedly make a part (and a very disgraceful
one, as far as relates to Russia,) of the History of
Europe.

While this was passing in the North, a plan was
forming here of surprising the Danish Fleet. Ministers
had received the most undoubted information, (and,
strange to say, the *first* information came through the
Prince of Wales to the Duke of Portland in an audience
he had at Carlton House in May,) that, by the assistance
of this Fleet Buonaparte intended to invade the North-
east Coast of England; and this came from Portugal,
whose Fleet Buonaparte also wanted. The Regent of
Portugal rejected the proposal, and communicated it to
us. The Danes accepted it, were silent at the time,
and afterwards denied it.†

No expedition was ever better planned, or better
executed; and none ever occasioned more clamour.
The Emperor of Russia (though *dates made it impossible*)
endeavoured to palliate his defection and cowardice at
Tilsit by alluding to this event ; and the Opposition at
home, particularly Lord Sidmouth's party, declaimed
against it as the most immoral, iniquitous measure ever

---

* The reader will recollect his conduct in 1794, during the events treated
of in vol. iii.

† After the battles of Jena and Friedland, Buonaparte insisted upon Denmark (a neutral Power) joining in the Continental system of blockading
England and refusing our ships a passage through the Sound. The Danes
were threatened both by him and us ; and we ended by anticipating Buonaparte's intention of quarrelling with them, and bombarded Copenhagen, and
secured the Danish fleet, on the 2nd of September.

conceived. The details and success of .this expedition are sufficiently known. Jackson was sent on the forlorn hope to induce the Prince Regent of Denmark to give up his Fleet—a cession impossible for him to make, though it was politically wise to propose it before we proceeded to hostilities. Jackson did his business well, but got no credit for it. Thornton, who was at Hamburgh, acted more like a Dane than an Englishman, yet he was praised; greatly owing to Jackson's forbearance in not shewing his letters to him.

After the signature of the peace at Tilsit, Buona-parte returned to Paris, Alexander to Petersburgh. He dismissed Czartorinski, Stroganoff, and Kouschebey, or rather they dismissed themselves; and appointed, first, a heavy man of the name of Budberg, Prime Minister; then for a moment one of the Soltikoffs (equally incapa-ble); and, last of all, my old friend Nicholas Romanzoff: from him I was in hope some good might have arisen; but he *at once* became the slave of France, and the will-ing tool to every act of disgrace and submission his master proposed to him,—*he*, who had resided at Cob-lentz with the French Princes on the part of the Empress Catherine, and who appeared (as I myself was witness, both there in 1792, and at Frankfort in 1794,) so devoted to them as to be in a manner identified with them, and considered by them almost as an Associate Emigrant!

I passed August and September chiefly at Park Place, and nothing memorable passed, except repeated instances of the unfitness both of * * * * and * * * * for the situations for which Fox had chosen them. Canning had in a very *mild* manner recalled them both; but, contrary to all precedent, they did not return home till a long time after. * * * * remained about the Allied Armies till October; and * * * * followed an old bat-tered beauty into Poland, now the widow of the head of the * * * *, and in possession of the larger share of their immense property. I remember her under the name of De Witt in 1782, then not young, but very handsome. She was originally sent to Constantinople by the late

King of Poland, Stanislaus, to learn Turkish embroidery;
and her life from the beginning has been one of intrigue,
in both senses of the word. She told * * * * " Si cela
vous amuse, suivez moi sur mes terres, mais je vous
avertis que cela ne vous menera à rien." He *did* follow,
and then returned home convinced she had told him
truth.

I passed much time at Bulstrode, and, as I was getting
into my carriage there on the 19th September, the Duke
of Portland ordered his servant to stop me till he got up;
he then told me that Sir Robert Wilson was just arrived
in sixteen days from Petersburg, and that he brought
accounts that Alexander repented, and was again coming
round to us. The Duke had not the particulars, as he
was expected in town, where indeed he was going; he
said he should return in a few days, and wished me then
to come again to Bulstrode. This I did, and met Canning there, who confirmed all that Sir Robert Wilson
had said, and brought with him copies of the Instructions with which he had sent him back, which he did
immediately. Sir Robert sailed from Yarmouth for
Petersburg on the 4th October.

On the 5th, Canning at Bulstrode; made me acquainted more minutely with what Sir R. Wilson
brought, and it struck me that Sir Robert (rather a
sanguine, credulous man) had been induced to interpret what the Emperor of Russia said to him (for Sir
Robert dined with him at Petersburg on the 31st
August) more favourably for us than was really expressed; and it was evident that this short turn was
greatly owing to the dread the Emperor of Russia had
of our armament then at Copenhagen, and which, having
done its task, was ready, in case of need, to proceed to
Cronstadt.

When first the Emperor heard of this expedition, he
ordered Budberg to address a note in strong terms, requiring to know what it meant, to Lord G. Leveson, who,
though uninstructed *then*, very properly replied, " *self-
preservation*." This concise but firm answer appears to
have satisfied, or rather put an end to all farther official

interference, but it left a fear on Alexander's mind (con-
science-struck as he probably was) that our fleet might
proceed to attack his possessions in the Gulf of Finland;
and this, added to the universal dissatisfaction which at
that moment prevailed, and was strongly marked at Petersburg, on the transactions at Tilsit, evidently accounts
for this apparent alteration in his language; for Budberg
not only changed his manners towards Lord G. Leveson,
from haughtiness and reserve, to a tone of conciliation
and affectation of frankness, but went the length of saying (though he termed it talking as an individual, not
ministerially,—a common *cant* practised by the Russian
and other Foreign Ministers), " that the Peace of Tilsit
could not last; that it was made under the pressure of
the moment, with a view to gain breathing-time; that
neither this nor any other peace, as long as the Revolutionary system prevailed in France, could be permanent;
that things *must* come round again, and Russia, England,
and Austria be united."

He said this and much more, all of which ought to
have been the genuine and true sentiments of his Master;
but he said it, not because it was right and true, but
manifestly from the proximity of our Fleet, and its
irresistible strength: for this language lasted no longer
than this Fleet remained in the Baltic; and, as the
season changed, so did the behaviour of the Court of
St. Petersburg. In fact, (though it is scarce to be
supposed it was known to Budberg,) G. Leveson had
received full powers to send for, *if necessary*, a large
detachment of this Fleet to act against Alexander;
but he very wisely did not act upon them. Such a
measure would have been productive of no good in
the first instance beyond a little mischief on the Russian coasts, and it would have given a mortal offence
to the pride of the Russian nation, *then* well-disposed
to us, and shifted all the hatred it had for France to
England.

Amongst the public Articles of the Peace of Tilsit was
one to offer the Mediation of Russia for peace between
France and us, and this Buonaparte was ready to accept.

In the last Conference G. Leveson had with Budbreg,
before he touched on this point, he adverted to what had
passed between him and Czartorinski respecting the
renewal of our Treaty of Commerce, and which had been
a measure nearly settled. Budberg neither objected nor
assented, but got rid of the question by pleading ignorance of the subject, and that he must apply, before he
could enter farther on it, to Count Romanzow, Minister
for the Commercial Department. G. Leveson did not
persist on this point, but proceeded to that, much more
important, of the proposed Mediation. On this he said
at once, that, before it could be accepted, he must be
shewn the *Secret* Articles of the Treaty of Tilsit; and
he insists on it as a *sine quâ non* preliminary, in a
very peremptory but very proper way. Budberg tries
to evade an explicit answer, by assurances that the
Emperor's friendship for England was still the same; and
that the neglect with which Russia had been treated by
the last Ministry (Lord Grenville's), joined to the misfortunes of the war, had produced this peace. G. Leveson stopped him by stating the inutility and danger of
recrimination; that what had passed had better be forgotten, and the business taken up from the present,
when an entire new question arose, viz. the acceptance
or the refusal of the proffered Mediation; and that this
could not be determined on till England was placed on
an equal footing with France, and knew as well as France
what Secret Articles had been entered into.*—Budberg,
thus pushed to the wall, said (but he spoke not the
truth), that some of them bore no reference to England
at all, and that there were none which could be injurious
to our interests ; and *in explicit terms* said, there was
nothing like an engagement to shut the Russian Ports
against us.— G. Leveson replied, he could not doubt
what he heard, yet that it was very difficult for him to
suppose *any* Secret Articles between Russia and France,
that, in *his* view of the subject, did not affect either the
present or future interests of Great Britain ; and that

---

* The Secret Articles of the Peace of Tilsit were obtained by our Government.

nothing short of unreserved official communication
could be sufficient to authorize him to speak on the proposal of Mediation.   This, G. Leveson said, was indispensable.—Budberg grew very complaisant and supple;
said he would take the Emperor's pleasure; and went so
far as to intimate, that he expected to have orders to
make the desired communication.

Although G. Leveson's despatches were very sensible,
and although he did his duty well, it was evidently not
con amore. Canning sent him incomparable instructions
in answer, very long and very clear, as will appear
shortly; he also wrote to Sir R. Wilson a private letter
to Novosilkoff, and instructions to Pierrepont and Merry
by the same messenger.

To G. Leveson, Canning writes to the following effect.
He gives him great credit for all he had done and said,
both with respect to the Danish expedition, and to the
Mediation ; that he had anticipated the King's wishes on
both these subjects.   Canning expatiates forcibly and
ably on the absolute necessity of abiding by what G.
Leveson said in his conference with Budberg, and
puts in the strongest point of view the imperious reasons why we should not only see the Secret Articles,
but know the general political views of Russia.   That,
without this previous knowledge, no *fair* mediation can
be established; for it is evident France knows them, and,
till it is disproved, we must fear had a great share in
directing them.   That it was not required, nor could
be, that, at the instant after a peace with France was
signed, Russia should take any step inimical to France;
yet it was necessary, in order to constitute a fair equality between her and England, that some measure
friendly towards England should be made manifest,
otherwise Europe (and very reasonably) would suppose Russia influenced by France, and acting partially
by her.   That nothing was better calculated to do this
than a renewal of our Commercial Treaty.   It would not
be a *new* act, but simply the revival of an old and
established peaceable connexion ; and that, if not done
for its usual term (twelve years), it had better be

done for two, or three, or for as many as the Commercial Treaty between Russia and France, made by Segur, had to run. That so many strong reasons, and all beneficial to Russia, could be adduced to induce Russia to do this, that, if it was declined, the refusal could only be imputed to unfriendly motives and unfriendly intentions. That on this, therefore, Leveson should insist with earnestness. That on Russia's acceding to this renewal, and on an unreserved exposure of the Secret Articles of the Peace of Tilsit, depended the King's acceptance of the Mediation; and that although, even supposing (which was not likely) Russia complied with what was asked, and we accepted the Mediation, there was little prospect that it would lead to peace; yet nothing should be wanted on our side to encourage and promote the *possibility* of its being effected, and nothing but advantage follow from the preliminary arrangements being protracted and spun out to any length. That a much more material object was to state to Russia our views with respect to the Powers that surround the Baltic. That the reasons G. Leveson had alleged for our seizure of the Danish fleet were the *true* ones; and they were unanswerable.* That he had behaved *most judiciously in not sending for any part of our fleet*, as well for the reasons he assigned, as because, from our being masters of the entrance of the Baltic, it was of little advantage to be also masters of the Gulf of Finland. That the great point, now we had so completely succeeded at the Sound, was to prevent the French getting possession of Zealand. That, having agreed to its evacuation, we must keep faith; but, if the Court of Denmark refuses to make peace, our troops need only retire to Scania, and from thence retake it. That it was however to be apprehended, that, although we were strong enough (our fleet being in the Sound) to effect this, it was doubtful whether we were powerful enough to maintain ourselves in it during the winter, when our fleet could not act: that, therefore, it was

---

* If England had not anticipated Napoleon, he would have done so, and used it against England.

His Majesty's intention to propose to the Danes the alternative of a neutrality or an alliance. That in either case the guarantee of Russia would be a *sine quâ non*: for Sweden, unless assured of the concurrence of Russia, could not join with England, or venture to furnish us with troops; and our idea was to leave 20,000 of our troops, and as many Swedes, for the defence of Zealand; a force deemed sufficient to maintain it. That this guarantee, therefore, must be pressed; and that it was hoped Alexander would recollect, that, if the French once got into Sweden, they could very soon be in Finland, and at the gates of Petersburg.

That with regard to the change of language, as mentioned by Sir Robert Wilson, and confirmed by G. Leveson's letters,. though very satisfactory, and such as ought to be sincere, yet it should be taken with a few scruples of disbelief; since, as it was evident Fear produced all that passed at Tilsit, fear might again have operated on this occasion, with a view to gain by this change of language the winter months, get our fleet *out of* the Baltic, and their own (now in the Mediterranean) *into* it. On this last point, Canning demurs as to the propriety of detaining them, should this fleet, on their way home, come into a British port;—it certainly would have been detained, if what was now reported by Sir R. Wilson had not come. Canning, however, supposes that Russia, or rather Buonaparte, aware of this, had sent orders to Siniavin to winter in some friendly port in the Mediterranean,—where, he cannot say, but surely not Naples, as that would be immediately giving it up to France. He thinks the best line to take is, if the Russian fleet comes late in the year (as it probably will, if it comes at all) to England, to keep it till the Baltic was open; but on this subject he can give no decided instructions, only recommends to G. Leveson to bear it in his mind. Canning, then, in the greatest confidence, communicates to G. Leveson the intelligence he had received, that, on breaking up the conference between Alexander and Buonaparte at Tilsit, Alexander had been weak enough to leave to Buonaparte the faculty of framing, and wording in his own way, the several Secret Articles they had been discussing, on his return to Paris. They were simply *sketched* out at their interview; but so much was Alexander at the feet of Buonaparte, that he consented to every thing, and left to Buonaparte this most dangerous power. It was said, that, after Buonaparte had drawn them up at Paris, he would send them by Soult† to Petersburg. This is certainly one of the most extraordinary examples of folly and cowardice existing in History; and, though beyond doubt, a fact that will scarcely be credited.

On talking this over with Canning, I admitted they were incomparable, but, if anything, too detailed. They were, in fact, infinitely more so than I have been able to note down.

What Canning wrote to Sir Robert Wilson was short, and in general terms: " That we were disposed most fully to renew our friendly habits with Russia, and to effect this by every practicable means." Canning, I believe, and with reason, considered Sir R. as too flighty, and as a partisan rather than an able Officer; and, though he applauded his eagerness, he made due allowances for it. Canning's letter to Novosilkoff was a private one, simply to recall himself to his recollection, and written in terms the most likely to please and flatter him and to obtain his support. Novosilkoff had been an officer in the * * * * ‡ Guards, and was a sort of favourite of Alexander from his infancy, and placed by him when he became Emperor in confidential Office.

Canning determined to send Merry (a very worthy but nervous man) to the Court of Denmark, to endeavour (a most arduous task) to conciliate them to what we had done, and so prevail on them, if possible, to concur with what G. Leveson was to propose to Russia. This was the more arduous, as the Prince Regent of Denmark had issued a thundering declaration against

---

† They were carried there, not by Soult, but by Caulaincourt, in as short a time as possible after Buonaparte's return to France.—*Original Note.*

‡ Illegible in manuscript.

England on the 16th of August,—in fact, a Declaration of war.

The substance of Merry's instructions were, " That he was, in the first instance, to proceed to our fleet in the Sound; to send a messenger from thence to Kiel to the Russian Minister, desiring him to forward on to Count Bernsdorff the notification of his arrival ; to demand passports, which if granted, he is to proceed to Kiel, and there to state, what Jackson had before stated, that the sole motive of our expedition to Copenhagen or seizing the Danish fleet was grounded on the *certainty* we had of Buonaparte's views on it, and of the *probability* that the Danes would concur in them." (This, as I before said, was made known to us through the Prince Regent of Portugal ; but Merry was not to say it.) Buonaparte, in July, it seems, offered the choice of giving up *voluntarily* the Portuguese fleet to act with the other fleets of Europe, indicating clearly those of Denmark and Russia, on an attack on England ; and, in case of a refusal, a threat of an immediate invasion of Portugal by a French army, which was already on the frontiers and *in* Spain.   This intelligence, confirmed by many collateral circumstances, authenticated the fact, and made the measure adopted against Denmark indispensably necessary for our own defence.   All this Merry was told ; but he was instructed not to divulge it, or to make any comparison between the conduct of Portugal and that of Denmark towards England, however glaring it had been.   He, after having endeavoured (a very difficult attempt) to prove and convince the Danes that our expedition to Copenhagen, and its consequence, war, is not of imperious State necessity, is to say that not the most remote wish to quarrel with Denmark existed on our part; that if Bernsdorff had heard from Jackson this truth, which he had accompanied with the most conciliatory terms that could be devised, and which assented to every thing save what formed the vital principle of the measure, the destruction of Copenhagen and the total loss of their marine would not have occurred : yet, to prove these terms were not fallacious, His Majesty offered them again, and still left to Den-

mark the option either for neutrality or of alliance; if
neutrality, the most binding engagements must be made
for keeping Zealand out of the hands of the French, and
a competent force stipulated to be maintained there to
ensure its security; and this under the guarantee of
England, Russia, and Sweden.

That if *alliance with England* was preferred, England
would engage to furnish a contingent of troops, which,
joined to the Danish troops, would be equal (with perhaps a few auxiliaries from Sweden) to the defence of
Zealand. England would liberate all the Danish merchant-ships taken or seized since the war (begun 16th
August); would restore *all* the Danish property taken
since that period; would revoke the orders sent to His
Majesty's Commanders in the West Indies to take those
Islands; and would, in case they should lose Holstein,
give them, by way of compensation, the colony of Suri-
nam; that even, (though this was to be kept for the
last,) if the Danes came cordially into this measure,
His Majesty *might* in the event not be averse to have a
calculation made of the mischief done by the bombard-
ment of Copenhagen, and be disposed to contribute
largely towards the repairing and rebuilding of the
town; and (but this was not to be intimated unless the
most willing and cordial alliance took place), that even
the value of the fleet should be paid for *now*, or the
fleet itself restored to them at a general peace.

That if both these proposals, viz. of Neutrality and
Alliance, were rejected, His Majesty would nevertheless
(though the state of war would then be inevitable)
keep faith with respect to the evacuation of Zealand
as stipulated by her commanders; that he would only
remove his army *to a shorter distance*, in Scania, or
some of the adjacent islands; that it might be immediately conquered, and certainly should be re-conquered
unconditionally; and that in all cases *Hielegoland* was
to remain to England. That, if the Court of Denmark
forced us to the unpleasant extremity, we probably, on
the event, should cede Zealand and *Norway* to the King
of Sweden.

The substance of Merry's instructions Canning communicated to M. Rist, the Danish Chargé des Affaires
here, saying that if the King of Denmark preferred
negotiating through him (Rist) in London, there would
be no objection; but in order that no mistake might
arise as to the *sine quâ non Basis* on which all negotiation, whether for Neutrality or for Alliance, was to rest,
Canning desired M. Rist to put in writing all he had
heard from him, Canning, and afterwards send the
paper to him to be revised. This, it is but justice to
say, Rist did in a very fair and sensible manner, and
such as required very little alteration. Rist very properly observed that *his* Ministerial functions were at an
end, in consequence of the Declaration of War, and that
all he could do was to communicate what Canning had
said to him, to his Court.

The instructions to Pierrepont (our Minister in
Sweden, with whom Canning is much satisfied) are
easily to be inferred from those given to G. Leveson
and to Merry; it was to obtain the guarantee of the
King of Sweden, and troops for Zealand (for we will
not hear of Prussians), and offering him troops in the
West Indies—Essequibo, Curaçoa, or Demerary—in
compensation for his having lost his German dominions.
He is entitled to this. He has behaved most handsomely, and offered us 20,000 men if we will secure
him against an attack from Russia; this is most reasonable, and even more than we could expect.

Nothing could be more judiciously and ably drawn up
than these instructions; unfortunately, from the distance
and from the unceasing activity of Buonaparte, they
became useless. Before G. Leveson could receive his,
Russia had declared war against us (31st of October)
in the most hasty and unaccountable manner possible.
Romanzow mixed up no amenity in his language (though
he is naturally a smooth-tongued and gentle-mannered
character); he took no pains either to explain or qualify
the hostile conduct of his Court, and he seemed to consider this as fully done in their very feeble and ill-argued
Declaration. The system of Russia was to *obey* France,

and to this Nicholas Romanzow most obsequiously subscribed.   Merry was not admitted or received by the
Regent of Denmark, and Lusakinsk refused to have
any communication with him.   Pierrepont executed
his part of the instructions with ability; but the case
was desperate, and he had to do with a Sovereign
who thought very right, but who was half mad at the
time.

We, too, as far as our naval administration in the
North was concerned, did not do well: our officers were
in too great a hurry to get home ; and, by suffering our
ships to quit the Baltic prematurely, we lost nearly as
much in naval stores captured by the Danes as we had
gained by seizing their Fleet.   The truth is, neither
Gambier* nor Lord Cathcart were up to so decided a
measure; it was above their sphere; and, though they
did what was ordered, they did not go a step *beyond*
it—like unwilling servants.   They were both made English Peers.

Buonaparte carried his threats against Portugal into
effect with such force and such rapidity, that the Regent
was *in the first instance* obliged to give way, to appear
as submitting to him; and to this he was encouraged by
Aranjo, his Minister (a modern philosopher), who was
employed at the same time I was at Paris, and though
imprisoned by the Directory, and treated most contemp-
tuously, still remained an admirer of the Revolution and
its principles.   Almeida, my colleague at the Hague,
was of a quite different cast; he retired from Office the
moment any concessions were talked of to be made to
France; and it was his spirit, and undoubtedly also the
good conduct of Lord Strangford, that prevailed on the
Regent of Portugal to go with his whole Fleet, a great
treasure, and many of his Grandees, to the Brazils, on
the 29th November, 1807, to which he was escorted
by a fleet of ours (in addition to his own) under the
command of Moore.

Little more passed that came *authentically* to my

---

* Admiral Gambier commanded the fleet, and Lord Cathcart the land-
forces (25,000 men), in the Danish expedition.

knowledge during the end of 1807.   Sir A. Paget was
sent to Turkey, but returned *re infectâ;* he came by
sea, and got to Spithead 13th November.   Lord Pembroke did the same, from Vienna; he announced to me
his intention to return, and gave a melancholy report
of the Court of Vienna.   He was, *proprio motu* of the
King, appointed Governor of Guernsey.   Lord G Leveson
got back from Russia through Sweden, and Merry (without ever landing) from Denmark.   Yet the getting possession of the Danish Fleet, and the escape of the Portuguese Fleet from the clutches of Buonaparte, made
Ministers disposed to meet Parliament boldly and cheer-
fully.

A little previous to its meeting, on January 21st,
1808, Canning came to Park Place with Ross; Fitzharris was with me, and he passed two days in reading
over the foreign correspondence, and in selecting such
parts of it (particularly relative to the Danish business)
as seemed the most advisable to lay before Parliament.
I am against this sort of *new* habit, and wished to re·
strain it to a very few documents; but I was overruled at the time, though it ended by a very few indeed
being produced—not for want of clamour about the
Danish expedition, particularly from Lord Sidmouth and
his friends.   *He* certainly thought he was paying his
court to the King, who he had heard (and with some
reason, as the Duke of Portland told me at the time,)
had consented very reluctantly to it.   But Lord Sidmouth knew little of the King's character, if, after
having consented, he ever would be pleased in having
Ministers censured and condemned.   This, amongst a
thousand instances which have come under my observation, is one, that political wisdom very often overshoots
its mark.

_____

ALTHOUGH I saw the Duke of Portland constantly
during the year 1808, yet I have scarce an incident
to record that is not to be found in the prints of the
year.   His complaint (the stone) was returning; and
the excruciating pain this occasioned, joined to the

worry and torment of his official situation, quite broke him down. I have been often with him when I thought he would have died in his chair; and his powers of attention were so weakened that he could neither read a paper, nor listen for a while, without becoming drowsy and falling asleep. Yet he never would let me go away after dinner, when the rest of the company went, but always urged me to remain on with him; which I often did for hours, when he was equal neither to talk nor to hear. About twelve or one o'clock he generally rallied, and he has made me sit up many nights after my usual hour of retiring, particularly *two*—the 18th and 19th of Jan. 1808—when he wished me to assist him in drawing up the King's speech for the opening of Parliament on the 21st.

I omitted to mention in its right date the declaration of war of Austria and Prussia, as all the papers that passed on these strange proceedings were laid before Parliament, and are now published. Prince Staremberg's behaviour was most prevaricating and offensive.

A Flag of Truce arrives on the 16th at Deal, with despatches for Prince Staremberg: he at first says they are nothing but private papers relative to his family concerns, but on Thursday, the 19th, informs Canning that he has received positive orders from his Court to declare, that the inconveniences which result to the Continental Powers from the continuation of the struggle between France and England are so great, that Austria can no longer see with indifference its duration, and that they hope some place will be fixed on the Continent to conclude a Maritime Peace. No offer of Mediation accompanied this; and though no direct threat was made, yet it was evidently to be implied, that, if England declined this offer, Austria would join France. Prince Staremberg did not conceal that it was the act of Buonaparte, to which he was *compelled to subscribe*. Canning desired him to give what he said in writing, which he did: " Qu'il avait des ordres positifs de sa Cour de déclarer que la lutte entre l'Angleterre et la France était si préjudiciable aux intérêts des puissances de l'Europe que sa Cour se croyait obligée d'appuyer sur la nécessité d'une paix maritime," &c. Canning, in his reply to this request, desired Staremberg to explain whether this official document contained all he had to say; and, before he could give him a precise answer, he begged Prince Staremberg to be more explicit, and particularly to state how much threat was meant, and how much was to be considered only as friendly advice. ·On its being sent to the King, His Majesty wrote for answer, that he heard with surprise the communication that the Emperor of Austria had made; that it was as *insulting* to England, as disgraceful to Austria; that it was the more servile and more extraordinary act of submission to Buonaparte, since Austria could do us no harm; he did not doubt but that the blood of every Englishman would boil when it became known. Canning and the Duke of Portland agree quite with the King; so probably will the whole Cabinet.

Staremberg is by far the most insincere Minister ever employed. He is trusted neither by his own Court nor the Court where he resides; yet his high rank and his manœuvring keep him afloat; he never will be set aside. A * * * *, contrary to the assurances Canning had given A'Court, remained on at Vienna after Lord Pembroke's departure, till war was declared. Canning then appointed him Ambassador to Turkey, though he could not but know he was attached to the Opposition, and communicated with them; and, though not without abilities, such a dupe of women, that no secret was safe with him. This Fox, his intimate friend and patron, knew so well, that, when he named him for Vienna, he stipulated that Mrs. A * * * * (a French woman) should not go with him, and that, if ever she followed him, his Mission should terminate. Yet *she* did go after Fox's death, and Canning suffered A * * * * to remain at Vienna, and employed him elsewhere.† He also left Erskine in

† Since the first Edition of this work appeared, Sir Robert Adair has published in the Preface to his Account of his Mission to the Porte, some remarks upon this passage, in which he states that Mrs. Adair (who was of an old Royalist family) joined him abroad unexpected by him. He also

America, and Forster (Lady Elizabeth's son) at Stockholm.

The affairs of Spain during the course of this year, 1808, are public, and I know little more than what is public. Amongst all his attempts at usurpation, Buonaparte never exhibited any equal to this, and never did any one exist in which every principle of truth, good faith, and honour was so unblushingly violated. The Spaniards shewed a just and noble indignation, and resisted it stoutly and with spirit. We were, as became us, liberal and zealous in support of them; but I think we acted too precipitately, and, by betraying the excessive interest we took in their affairs and over-eagerness to aid them, enfeebled the efforts they would have made themselves, had they met with less ardent encouragement. The character of the Spaniard is to let every thing be done for him, if he finds any one disposed to do it, and never to act till obliged to do so. This has appeared, and will appear, in every event of the contest with France. Not knowing this, and placing an implicit confidence in the first two Deputies who arrived from Gijon (in Asturias) in May, we have, by wishing to do too much, injured the cause. These two deputies, Materasa and Don Diego de Vega, left Gijon in an open boat, and were taken up at sea by one of our frigates. I dined with them immediately after their arrival at Burlington House, for they were received with open arms. I at once saw what they were—Materasa (a Viscount), a young, raw Asturian Hidalgo; and Don Diego de Vega, an Asturian attorney: both, I dare say, well-meaning and well-thinking, but of no consequence. In fact, Asturias is a province that is of as little consequence with reference to the Kingdom of Spain, as Glamorganshire is to England; and it was injudicious, and a want of consideration, and I will add also of experience and information, to look upon these two persons *as types* of the sentiments of the whole nation.

The treating them as such, deprived us of having

states, that he was employed by many succeeding governments, and justly infers that he deserved public confidence.

more important and abler men sent, while it drew down
upon us crowds of Galicians, and Biscayans, Deputies
who, in their own country, would not have ventured
to have had an opinion. *To all these* we listened; we
gave them money (which I fear they never accounted
for), arms, and every thing they asked; and when Admiral Apoduca came from the southern provinces, and
after that Don Pedro Cevallos, who had been Minister
for foreign affairs, and published the famous *exposé*
of Buonaparte's perfidy and cruelty towards King Ferdinand, we had so little choice left as to what we were
to do, that we did all they desired. *I* did represent
this both to the Duke of Portland and to Canning;
but the Duke, as I before have observed, was really
exhausted, and Canning would not listen.

It was through the Duke of Portland that, in October
1808, I learnt the first intimation of Austria's disposition to go to war with France; it came to him through
Charles Bentinck, who had it from his brother, Monsieur de Rhoon; and both the source from whence it
came, and the way in which it was told, were so strange
and so improbable, that we gave no credit to it:—
it was, however, soon after confirmed on better authority; and, as far as I could influence the Duke of Portland, I earnestly recommended affording every possible
support to Austria. I wrote him several letters on the
subject, and had frequent and long conversations with
him at Bulstrode, where he always is in a better state
to hear and discuss than in London. The Austrians
want spirit—we have not enough—and Perceval is
too parsimonious. The Duke of Portland right, as he
always is, when he follows the impressions of his own
excellent judgment and sound principles; but never a
good wrangler, and especially now too infirm to maintain
them.

I did not learn Canning's sentiments, as he never
spoke to me on the subject of Austria; but I should
suppose them to be perfectly right. Early in March,
Count Walmoden (son to the natural son of George
the Second by Lady Y * * *) was sent from Austria

to England; and, as I was intimately acquainted with him, he constantly consulted with me previous to his conferences with Canning. Walmoden, though a soldier, has a very sound and clear head, and executed his commission ably, faithfully, and honourably. He communicated, and, I really believe, without exaggeration, what, at the time he left Vienna, were the spirit and feelings of the nation: that, *till now*, the great families and mass of the country were adverse to all the wars waged with France; that their eyes had not been opened to the extent and danger of the increasing power and overweening ambition of Buonaparte; that *now*, his ill-judged conduct towards the Pope had set all the legates (numerous in the Austrian empire) against him; and that the insincerity of his promises, and insolence of his explanation, left no doubt that his object was to crush Austria entirely, and to obtain universal monarchy in Europe. He was impressed with this idea, that the Austrian *people* now were eager for war, and that the army (hitherto backward) were actuated by the same principle; in which two of the most powerful agents on human conduct united to make them act vigorously, viz. *Self-defence* and *Resentment*. That their army consisted of four hundred thousand regular troops, two hundred thousand militia, and the finest train of artillery that was ever known. That their plan was for the main army to take possession of Bavaria, another to enter Saxony, and a large detachment reserved for operations in the North of Germany, where they were to be joined by the Duke of Brunswick and Landgrave of Hesse; that on the side of Dresden they expected also great assistance. What they wanted, and it was their only want, *money*—bullion, &c.; that they had enough to go on for a few months, but not longer; therefore, if we would supply them with this, they would enter into every connexion of alliance and amity we pleased.

Walmoden gave in a very detailed and fair Memorial to Canning; but he forgot, and so did the Ministry, that we were still at war with Austria. Walmoden, therefore, at my suggestion, sent in, as a supplement to his Memorial, a proposal for *peace*. *This* was accepted; but to all the other points the language of our Government was unexplicit, and in good truth cold. We engaged for no fixed sum; (that of fifty thousand per month had been asked;) and we declined all idea of sending men to the North of Germany. It should seem, from what the Duke of Portland said to me, that this was not *his* opinion, but the prevailing one of the Cabinet, which he did not think it right to oppose. *I* (as I have before said), both in conversation and by letter, continued to remonstrate against this milk-and-water conduct; I did it solely because I wished to explain my sentiments, and not under the smallest hope that it would be attended to, or produce any change of measures; and, although the Duke of Portland confessed that it met his ideas, I feel assured it never was mentioned again by him to the Cabinet; and that, against his better judgment, either from increasing apathy, or increasing infirmity, he never gave, *distinctly* and *decidedly*, his opinion there.

In Parliament the whole time was wasted in the infamous attack on the Duke of York*— infamous, not because it was entirely groundless, but because the real movers of it were instigated by levelling principles, and had no other view than the sinking and degrading all rank; but they unfortunately found many persons either of their own cast, or who were weak enough to be the dupes of their pretended patriotism; and the result was the forcing the Duke of York to resign his office as Commander-in-chief, and a sad degradation of the House of Commons.

On this occasion a person of the name of Wardle (till

---

* Colonel Wardle (of Militia) began this attack in the House of Commons, Jan. 27, 1809. He charged the Duke of York with conniving at Mrs. Clarke (his mistress) receiving money from several Officers for their Commissions, and moved, that the conduct of His Royal Highness should be investigated. Perceval and Sir Arthur Wellesley denied the charge for the Duke, but courted the Inquiry.—For an account of this transaction, and the connexion between Mrs. Clarke and Wardle and others, see the *Annual Register of* 1809.

then unknown), Lord Folkestone, instigated by Cobbett, and Maddocks, governed by a strumpet, were the Rodrigos; the Iagos kept in the back-ground; Whitbread alone had not sufficient temper to conceal himself. But I cannot but consider the origin of this mischief to be in the *candour*, as it is called, of Ministers even to allow it to be the subject-matter of Parliamentary discussion. This and other equally mischievous subjects occupied the whole session, by far the worst attended and the most insignificant I ever remember.

The Convention of Cintra excited great dissatisfaction, and I think very justly.* Canning protested against an opinion of Cabinet given when he was *absent*, and which went to confirm it. This was the beginning of all the subsequent disputes between him and his colleagues, and led to the more serious one between him and Lord Castlereagh.

The war broke out between Austria and France in May. Buonaparte withdrew his army from Spain, and by very rapid marches reached Bavaria. The course of this war was like that of the preceding ones; the French had the advantage in almost all the battles, except Asperno,† which, had the advantages obtained by the Archduke been followed up, might have given a different turn to the termination of it. After this battle several weeks passed in inactivity. Buonaparte, who was in possession of Vienna, was careful not to attempt to repass the Danube till he was in full force. This he then did, and gained the battle of Wagram,‡ and soon after forced the Archduke to sign an Armistice. There appears in the whole of this short campaign the public spirit which Walmoden announced, but the

---

* The Convention of Cintra, signed August 30, 1808, was brought forward by Lord H. Petty (afterwards Lord Lansdowne) in the House of Commons. He moved resolutions condemnatory of Ministers, and was beaten by a majority of 50.

† The battle of Asperno was fought on the 21st of May, 1809. The French had, for the first time, to give way, losing five Generals killed, and a vast number of men. The Austrian loss was also immense.

‡ The battle of Wagram was fought on the 5th and 6th of July. The Austrians were totally defeated, and made peace with France on the 14th of October, 1809. The power of Napoleon was now at its zenith.

same want of military skill and resolution in the commanders as had produced all the failures of those preceding it.

[Here Lord Malmesbury appears to have closed this Diary. When resumed, it was written in the style I have described in my Introductory Memoir, where I have quoted its last sentences, penned but a few days before his death.

Of the Journal which I have published, and which composes this fourth volume, it may be said that it contains much matter already known to the reader. I have not suppressed it on that account, because I think that no corroborative evidence of History can be produced so unsuspicious as a Diary, in which events and conversations are regularly recorded within a few hours of their occurrence, and that by an intelligent observer (like Lord Malmesbury), whose personal ambition has been satisfied with high rewards, or arrested by incurable infirmity. The man who is in this position, having nothing to hope or to fear, and writing for no immediate purpose of the day, will probably relate History with as little excitement or prejudice as can possibly be found in any active mind.]

[The following letter to Lord Camden was written four years after the date to which I have restricted these Memoirs; but it may not be thought misplaced at the end of such a work.]

LETTER TO LORD CAMDEN, WRITTEN AT HIS REQUEST, ON HIS NEPHEW, MR. JAMES, BEING DESTINED FOR THE FOREIGN LINE.

Park Place, April 11th, 1813.

MY DEAR LORD,—It is not an easy matter, in times like these, to write anything on the subject of a Foreign Minister's conduct that might not be rendered quite inapplicable to the purpose by daily events. Mr.

James's best school will be the advantage he will derive from the abilities of his Principal, and from his own observations.

The first and best advice I can give a young man on entering this career, is *to listen, not to talk*—at least, not more than is necessary to induce others to talk. I have in the course of my life, by endeavouring to follow this method, drawn from my opponents much information, and concealed from them my own views, much more than by the employment of spies or money.

To be very cautious in *any* country, or at *any* court, of such as, on your first arrival, appear the most eager to make your acquaintance and communicate their ideas to you. I have ever found their professions insincere, and their intelligence false. They have been the first I have wished to shake off, whenever I have been so imprudent as to give them credit for sincerity. They are either persons who are not considered or respected in their own country, or are put about you to entrap and circumvent you as newly arrived.

Englishmen should be most particularly on their guard against such men, for we have none such on our side the water, and are ourselves so little *coming* towards foreigners, that we are astonished and gratified when we find a different treatment from that which strangers experience here ; but our reserve and *ill manners* are infinitely less dangerous to the stranger than these premature and hollow civilities.

To avoid what is termed abroad an *attachement*. If the other party concerned should happen to be sincere, it absorbs too much time, occupies too much your thoughts; if insincere, it leaves you at the mercy of a profligate and probably interested character.

Never to attempt to export English habits and manners, but to conform as far as possible to those of the country where you reside—to do this even in the most trivial things—to learn to speak their language, and never to sneer at what may strike you as singular and absurd. Nothing goes to conciliate so much, or to amalgamate you more cordially with its inhabitants, as this very easy sacrifice of *your* national prejudices to *theirs*.

To keep your cypher and all your official papers under a very secure lock and key; but not to *boast* of your precautions, as Mr. Drake did to Méhée de la Touche.

Not to allow any opponent to carry away any official document, under the pretext that he wishes " to study it more carefully ;" let him read it as often as he wishes, and, if it is necessary, allow him to take minutes of it, but *both in your presence.*

Not to be carried away by any real or supposed distinctions from the Sovereign at whose Court you reside, or to imagine, because he may say a few more commonplace sentences to you than to your colleagues, that he entertains a special personal predilection for you, or is more disposed to favour the views and interests of your Court than if he did not notice you at all. This is a species of royal stage-trick, often practised, and for which it is right to be prepared.

Whenever you receive *discretionary* instructions (that is, when authority is given you) in order to obtain any very desirable end, to decrease your demands or increase your concessions according as you find the temper and disposition of the Court where you are employed, and to be extremely careful not to let it be supposed that you have any such authority; to make a firm, resolute stand on the first offer you are instructed to make, and, if you find " *this nail will not drive,*" to bring forward your others *most gradually*, and not, either from an apprehension of not succeeding at all, or from an over-eagerness to succeed too rapidly, injure essentially the interests of your Court.

It is scarce necessary to say that no occasion, no provocation, no anxiety to rebut an unjust accusation, no idea, however tempting, of promoting the object you have in view, can *need*, much less justify, a *falsehood*. Success obtained by one, is a precarious and baseless success. Detection would ruin, not only your own reputation for ever, but deeply wound the honour of your Court. If, as frequently happens, an indiscreet question, which seems to require a distinct answer, is put to you abruptly by an artful Minister, parry it either by treating it as an indiscreet question, or get rid of it by a grave and serious look : but on no account contradict the assertion flatly if it be true, or admit it as true, if false and of a dangerous tendency.

In Ministerial conferences, to exert every effort of *memory* to carry away faithfully and correctly what *you hear* (what *you say* in them yourself you will not forget); and, in drawing your report, to be most careful it should be faithful and correct. I dwell the more on this (seemingly a useless hint), because it is a most seducing temptation, and one to which we often give way almost unconsciously, in order to give a better turn to a phrase, or to enhance our skill in negotiation; but we must remember we mislead and deceive our Government by it.   I am, &c.

Such were the terse rules which Lord Malmesbury gave to the young Diplomatist for his guide, and which it may be inferred were those that regulated his own conduct ; but, like all similar advice, it is practically fruitless if unaccompanied by that constitutional energy of purpose and action which was the real source of Lord Malmesbury's success in his profession.

It was this that gained him, at twenty-four, his first praise and promotion after the affair of the Falkland Islands, when, acting upon the knowledge he had acquired of the unprepared state of the Spanish navy, he roughly resented to Grimaldi the insult, and from the beginning urged Ministers to hold a high tone, for that the Spanish Premier must yield.* That transaction, now remote, may appear trifling at this time; but it must be remembered that in 1770 Spain was a first-rate Power, and that her Family Compact with France was the bugbear of every Statesman in Europe.

It was the same activity shewn in his efforts to carry out his impracticable instructions in Russia which in-

---

* Vide Mr. Harris' private letter to Lord Weymouth of 28th Sept. 1770, and his Despatch of Oct. 4, 1770. Vol. i. pp. 54, 55.

duced, first Mr. Fox, and afterwards Mr. Pitt, to appoint him (although then his political opponent) at the distracted Court of the Hague.*   The same energy gained him his peerage at that Mission, where he may be said to have gone a step beyond the path permitted to a Foreign Minister, and to have become almost a conspirator. Soon perceiving how much might be done for the Stadtholder, and by England, against France, he prepared his way by disclosing, as early as 1785, his plan in his private letters to Mr. Ewart at Berlin, and engaging him to predispose the Prince of Prussia and the Prussian Ministers for the blow which could not be struck until after the Great Frederick's death.† He gradually opened his views to Lord Carmarthen, and finally came over to England to explain them, and press them upon Pitt and the Cabinet, who were long lukewarm on the subject;‡ and although the author of the proposed Anglo-Prussian intervention in 1787 was known to Mirabeau, he scouted the idea as too audacious for execution, and thereby misled his own Court.   The French Revolution, which followed two years after this event, and which came like death to annihilate all past and present projects, hopes, treaties, enmities, and friendships between the nations of Europe, deprived us of the results of this transaction; but the immense importance attached to it at the time is evinced by the letters of Lord Carmarthen and Pitt, by the speeches of the latter, and by the expressions of our national opponent, the French Prince Louis.§

Lord Malmesbury's Mission to Prussia in 1794

* Vide Mr. Fox's letter to Sir J. Harris of July 27th, 1783 (vol. i. p. 520), and Sir J. Harris' account of his appointment to the Hague (vol. ii. page 11).

† Vide Sir J. Harris' letters to Lord Carmarthen, with the Inclosures of Feb. 2nd, 1785, to Mr. Ewart, of March 18, and April 19, 1785. I have been obliged from want of space to suppress most of his voluminous correspondence with Mr. Ewart on this subject, in which the latter shews great intelligence.

‡ Vide " Considerations to be employed with Ministers" (vol. ii. p. 260), and " Minutes of Cabinet " (p. 261).

§ Vide Lord Carmarthen's letter of Sept. 25, 1787 (vol. ii. p. 345); Pitt's letter of Sept. 28, 1787, and his speech of April 18, 1788 (p. 383) ; and Louis the Eighteenth's letter (vol. ii. p. 11).

evinces (I form my judgment from his papers) still greater physical and mental energy than the preceding one. His efforts were untiring, first to reclaim the Prussian King and his Ministers, and, when they broke their treaty with us, to urge the Generals to repair the evil. At this time his correspondence was immense, for it was carried on with our Ministers at every Court, and with every General commanding the armies in Austria, Holland, Hanover, and Prussia, so as to keep them informed of his progress or difficulties. I have been obliged to abridge it very considerably.

The difference of character between old and modern diplomacy fostered his disposition to assume responsibility, and seek the most laborious and hopeless Missions; for when the European Capitals were, in point of communication with England, at treble the distance at which they now stand, the resident Minister had necessarily far greater latitude and scope for action, and was constantly obliged and expected to trust to his own judgment, when instructions were beyond his reach.

Despotism, too, was then universal in Europe, and its power so absolute, yet its exercise so uncertain, and so dependent on the various vices, intrigues, and snares to which its representatives were, above all men, subject, that a peculiar tact, temper, and astuteness, (forming a feature of those times,) was necessary to watch and even to guide the causes which swayed the politics of those unprincipled and irresponsible monarchs. Now the most distant European Court can be reached in a week from London, and instructions from home can never be long wanting. Moreover, the knowledge of Public Opinion easily guides the Minister as to the probability of events; and that mighty power, unknown in the last century, has been felt and obeyed by those absolute Sovereigns who still remain. They are, perhaps, unconscious of its influence on themselves, yet, both in morals and politics, they certainly yield to its force; and we must attribute to its rude voice, as well as to the awful lessons of the past, much of the greatness and mildness of their present rule, and the comparative happiness of their people.

But should the maxims given to Lord Camden's nephew by Lord Malmesbury be partly inapplicable to present times, and should the personal position by which he was constrained to govern his own diplomatic conduct be no less changed than the nations and Courts where he resided, and appear to be now less favourable than formerly to a Foreign Minister; still diplomacy affords a fair field for obtaining distinction. It will, probably, be to most a life of dull expatriation or idle pleasure, yet will certainly prove as fruitful as ever of interest and honours to the man of energy, decision, and national pride, who, starting in this profession, feels as Lord Malmesbury wrote in 1773, from Berlin, to his friend: "I am resolved to push on in my career as long as I see a round of the ladder which it is within my compass to mount."

INDEX.

A.

C.

Calder, Sir B., his blockade of Brent, iv. 47.

Calonne, Mons., leading man among the French at Coblentz, ii. 407 ; satisfied with England, 412 ; in exile, iii. 207 ; French revolution attributed to him, 370 ; wishes to be struck off the list of emigrants, iv. 203 ; papers of, 204 ; papers of, how concealed, *ib.* ; death of, *ib.*

Camperdown, battle of, iii. 574.

Canning, George, account of, iii. 281 ; sends over to France for the dead body of Brooks, 553 ; wishes to resign, 568 ; his interview with Lord Malmesbury, iv. 77 ; eloquent speech of, upon the army estimates, 148 *n.* ; character of, 174 ; wishes to behold Fox return to office, 330 ; conduct and principles of, 375.

Carlisle, Frederick Howard, eighth Lord, persuades Lord Loughborough to accept the seals, ii. 449.

Carlton House, the scene of dancing and gaiety during the King's illness, iv. 15.

Carmarthen, Marquis of, letters of, to Sir James Harris, ii. 18 ; disapproves of the idea of separating Zealand from the Union, 133 ; illness of, 207 ; tenders his resignation, 213 ; his opinion of the French, 217 ; recommends Sir Jas. Harris to insist on lenity towards the Patriots, 366.

Cassy, Mons. de, cruel treatment of, by the French Directory, iii. 315.

Catholic emancipation, conduct of persons with respect to, iv. 16 ; measure concerning, 22 ; mention of, 365 *n.*

Catholics, Irish, their suspicions of Pitt, iv. 30.

Charleroi relieved, iii. 97.

Charles the Third, Emperor of Germany, current opinion of him false, i. 42 ; his character and disposition, 43.

Charlotte, Princess, daughter of George IV., discussions as to her residence, iv. 343.

Chateau Trompette, i. 29.

Chatham, Lord, accuses the Government of compromising the country, i. 67.

Chauvelin, M., ministerial note of, ii. 465.

Cholmondeley, George, solicits Lord Malmesbury to accept office, iv. 279.

Clarke, M., account of, iii. 317.

Cleves, Gazette of, forbidden to insert any thing injurious to France, ii. 221.

Cobenzel, Count, i. 224 ; timidity of, iv. 75.

Coblentz, party schemes of the French re-

sidents at, ii. 407 ; evacuated by the Austrians, iii. 148.

Cochin, ceded to the French by the Dutch, iv. 138.

Coin, debasement of, in Russia, in 1782, i. 481.

Colchen, M., his views on the state of affairs in France in 1797, iii. 521.

Colonies, American, reported treaty of the French with, i. 155.

Commissioners of War, power of, curtailed, i. 19 ; sent to Poland, 98.

Commons, House of, debates in, ii. 4 ; on the Alien Bill, 466 ; on the affairs of the Prince of Wales, iv. 229 ; divisions in, on the Volunteer Bill, and Augmentation of the Irish Militia, 300.

Concordat, procession of the, to Notre Dame in Paris, iv. 75.

Condé, Prince of, attempts to form a counter-revolution, ii. 402.

Congress at Vienna, expected termination of, i. 74.

Conspiracy, rumoured, at Vienna, iii. 120 ; in favour of Royalism in Paris, 513.

Conspiration Royale, the words of alarm in Paris, iii. 509.

Conventionalists, account of, iii. 277 ; attached to the Directory, 514.

Cook, Captain, killed at Owyhee, i. 230.

Copenhagen, injudicious conduct of the English ministers at, i. 82 ; climate of, 104.

Copenhagen, battle of, iv. 59.

Cornwallis, Lord, declaration of, on the resignation of ministers, iv. 30 ; letter of, 44.

Corsica, evacuation of, by the English, iii. 567, *n.*

Cracow, bishop of, declared out of his mind, i. 90.

Crimea, disturbances of, i. 466 ; troubles in, 468 ; character of the deposed Khan of, 470 ; news from, 486 ; to be annexed to the Russian empire, 511.

Cronstadt, Russian fleet sails from, i. 274.

Crown, General, of Poland, formerly held the reins with Great Treasurer, i. 10.

Custom-house guard in Holland, iv. 198.

Czarina, private correspondence of, with the King of Prussia, i. 94. See *Russia*.

Czartoriski, Prince, Chancellor of Lithuania, his liberality, i. 22 ; his magnanimity during his disgrace, 27 ; pardoned, *ib.*

D.

D'Alberg, Baron, coadjutor of Mentz, iii. 136 ; infected with the principles of the Illuminés, 137.

tion, 95 ; wilfully diminishes his treasure, 96 ; boundless ambition of, 97 ; his
claims of territory, 98 ; behaviour of, to
his nephew, 100 ; good politician, 103 ;
anecdote of, 104 ; reasons for his bad
temper, 105 ; superstitious, 106 ; considerable presents made by him, 108 ;
decline of his health, 117 ; deserted
by those around him, 118 ; his inability
to conduct affairs, 119 ; uneasy at
the intimacy between the courts of
Versailles and Vienna, 120 ; attacked
by the gout, 122 ; his income, 123 ;
conduct of, during his illness, 125 ;
foments dissensions in Poland, ib. ;
affable behaviour of, 129 ; his liberal
presents, 131 ; his letter to Mr. Harris,
133 ; causes of his hostility to England, 138 ; makes advances towards
England, 162 ; interest of, declining
at the Russian Court, 238 ; letter
of, to Prince Potemkin, 255 ; diminished influence of, in Russia,
280 ; desires to be admitted into the
Northern League, 365 ; his letter to
Count Goertz, 452 ; wishes to make an
aristocracy of Holland, ii. 22 ; raises
the German confederation, 40 ; declines taking an active part in the
affairs of Holland, 87 ; false and hollow, 91 ; deception of, 98 ; affects to be
desirous of the friendship of England,
101 ; ready to sign the Triple Alliance,
102 ; objects to England taking any
part in the affairs of Holland, 167 ;
declares his disapprobation of the memorial presented by Sir James Harris,
172 ; approaching end of, 173 ; death
of, 175.

Prussia, Frederick William, Crown Prince,
and afterwards King of, desirous of obtaining assistance from England, i. 100 ;
his embarrassed situation, 107 ; appearance and character, 109, 112 ; his behaviour to his uncle the King of Prussia, 119 ; dissipated habits, 121 ; his
reception at the court of St. Petersburg,
285 ; leaves that capital, 290 ; unwilling to interrupt the peace of his kingdom, ii. 200 ; purport of his mediation
for the assistance of the Prince of
Orange, 203 ; his mistress, 204 ; termed
a "Boy King," 216 ; his advice to the
Princess of Orange, his sister, 222 ;
demands satisfaction for the insult
offered to her by the Dutch, 291, 300,
328 ; the satisfaction refused him, 331 ;
his meanness, 359 ; renounces the idea
of levying contributions in Amsterdam,
363 ; afraid of Sir James Harris, 387 ;
his feelings towards England, 391 ; his

connection with the court of Vienna,
406 ; his ministers favourable to the
French Revolutionists, 478 ; his refusal
of the demand of succour from England,
iii. 2 ; violation of the treaty with England, ib. ; declines all interference with
the war, unless paid, 6 ; treasure of, 21 ;
displeased with the treaty between Prussia and Poland, ib. ; altered in his looks,
27 ; in want of money, 37 ; afraid of the
opening of Parliament, 47 ; doubts Vienna's subscribing to the convention,
69 ; ready to enter into engagements
with England and Holland, 76 ; force
of, 77 ; refuses to lend his troops, 81 ;
rejects the proposal of Lord Granville,
ib. ; obliged to furnish England with an
army, 88 ; deceived by his ministers,
118 ; raises money by a paper currency,
176 ; will listen to no proposals from
England until the whole subsidy is paid,
178 ; his conduct during the campaign,
180 ; determined to pursue the war,
232 ; measures of, 233 ; conditions proposed by him to France, 241.

Prussia, troops of, advance towards Poland, i. 80 ; embargo on corn in, 85 ;
designs of, on Poland, 92 ; bribery of,
374 ; desires a separate alliance with
England, 445 ; the friend of France,
493 ; influence of, in Holland, ii. 25 ;
the occasional ally of England, 166 ;
fears of a civil war in, 221 ; army of,
marches to Holland, 299 ; secret convention of, with England, 311 ; *Contre-
Projet*, or treaty of Defensive Alliance
between England and, 385 ; negotiations respecting the troops of, in Holland, iii. 82, 86 ; troops defeated in the
Low Countries, 114 ; party spirit in,
139 ; remarks on the state of, in 1794,
146 ; treaty of, with France, 241 ; great
reverses experienced in, iv. 398.

R.

Radzivil, Prince, his power and influence
in Poland, i. 21.
Rayneval, M. de, his mission to Holland,
ii. 205 ; his abilities, 212 ; attempts to
induce the Prince of Orange to negotiate with the States, 225 ; rich presents
made to him, 227 ; views of his court in
sending him to Holland, 241.
Reede, M., Dutch minister in Prussia,
iii. 47.
Reichenbach, account of negotiation at,
ii. 399.
Remfner, M., secretary to the Prussian

THE END.